LIE ON YOUR **WOUNDS**

LIE ON YOUR WOUNDS

The Prison Correspondence of Robert Mangaliso Sobukwe

Selected and edited by Derek Hook

WITS UNIVERSITY PRESS

In association with

AFRICAN LIVES

Published in South Africa by:
Wits University Press
1 Jan Smuts Avenue
Johannesburg 2001

www.witspress.co.za

First published 2019

http://dx.doi.org.10.18772/22019012408

978-1-77614-240-8 (Paperback)
978-1-77614-241-5 (Web PDF)
978-1-77614-242-2 (EPUB)
978-1-77614-272-9 (Mobi)

This book is number 14 in the African Lives series, an independent writing and publishing initiative that aims to contribute to a post-colonial intellectual history of South Africa. The series editor is Professor Andre Odendaal, Honorary Professor in History and Heritage Studies, University of the Western Cape.

The letter on page 524 reprinted with kind permission of Frances Suzman Jowell and the Helen Suzman Foundation.
Images on pages 53, 127, 333, 415 and 491 taken by Derek Hook.
Images on pages xv and 3 courtesy of Peter Magubane.
Images on xvii and xx courtesy of the SA Jewish Museum and the Jewish Digital Archive Project.
Images on back cover and on page 221 reproduced with permission from the Sobukwe family.
Image on page 15 courtesy of Wits Historical Papers, photographer unknown.

Project manager: Julie Miller
Editor: Russell Martin
Proofreader: Janine Loedolff
Indexer: Sanet le Roux
Cover design: Hybrid Creative
Typesetter: Newgen
Typeset in 11 point Crimson

Table of Contents

Preface
By Otua Sobukwe

My Robben Island Awakening

During the apartheid regime, Robben Island was the most notorious prison in South Africa. Enclosed in its prison walls were struggle icons whose names we continue to celebrate today – Sisulu, Mandela and many other unsung heroes. Amongst them but purposely separated was Robert Sobukwe, a freedom fighter who was banned to solitary confinement for leading an anti-pass march campaign that galvanised people on the path to the country's democracy. About thirty years later, the same island became the home of a young, adventurous little girl – me; his granddaughter. I lived on the island with my uncle who worked there for 8 months.

Paradoxically, Robben Island is one of the most beautiful places in the world. But when you put yourself in the shoes of a prisoner, there comes a shift of perspective.

Suddenly, things begin to lose their beauty.

The blueness of the sky loses its colour, as candyfloss clouds morph into grey patches, the singing tune of seagulls begins to mimic a pained cry, the once tranquil ebb and flow of the sea is now melancholic, yearning, and, more so, the mainland, its shimmering lights, their faintness, is no longer picturesque, no longer romantic, but just a cold reminder of the separating distance and the harsh reality, the harsh juxtaposition, that you are indeed alone.

The seven-year-old me was oblivious to this atmosphere of solitude. The place where my grandfather stood for his battle, longed for his family, and wept in his loneliness was the same place that framed my warm, explorative childhood. I didn't realize the weight of the island nor the significance of its history.

But ten years later, I understood. Intimately complex and profound – I realised that somehow my surroundings had brought me closer to a man that I had never met and opened my eyes to an identity I had never fully grasped.

That my roots are of an African soil has never been an incongruity to me. I have always wholly embraced my African identity; I am of its branches, its rivers, its auburn sunsets. However, when I returned to Robben Island, now seventeen, it occurred to me, this sudden epiphany, that I am not only a reflection of Africa, but a continuation of AfriKa. And these two Afric(k)as are not the same; one is the vessel and the other the spirit.

I stood there, in its beauty. My Afrikan seed beginning to germinate, I let my grandfather's words "Love your Afrika" water my roots, and as I felt the connection of our souls, it dawned on me, quite frighteningly, but beautifully too, that I am not only of his blood, but of his battle.

You see, Africa is not free, I whispered. She is a frightened bird in a rusting cage, with bent bars painted in crusting promises. She limps on a beaten leg too exhausted to bleed and bows her head when she speaks. She needs to be freed. But only Afrika can free Africa.

Like most young people, I didn't get this at first. My life was my own and my goals were fixed. I didn't understand that there was a continental vision or an ancestral goal that I was intertwined with. Yet the clues were there, my grandfather being one.

What Sobukwe started in South Africa, the unconditional passion he devoted to his movement, I realized, was the same fire that would ignite mine, whatever it be, in my life. Energy can never be created or destroyed, but only transferred or changed from one form to another.

And so there I was. A growing, energised Afrikan plant. One that would grow tall and blossom and, as if self-pollinating, return to its home, my Afrika, and give back to what it previously could not help fix. For education was three things: One, to break the shackles of my circumstance and end the cycle of my poverty. Two, to achieve a monumental freedom which my grandfather was never granted. And three, to be part of the key that would one day release the frightened bird.

How ironic life is, that Robben Island prison was to me not only a home, but one of the most liberating experiences of my life. And so, it is in this spirit that I encourage you to read the letters that my grandfather Sobukwe wrote, because captured in his words is not only his pain, but the beauty of his pain as a sacrifice for freedom.

Acknowledgements

The Sobukwe family – Dini, Miliswa and Otua in particular – were supportive and encouraging at each step of the book's production. I am particularly grateful to have been invited by the family in December 2014 to Graaff-Reinet to celebrate the 90th anniversary of Robert Mangaliso Sobukwe's birth. Benjamin Pogrund deserves thanks not only for having the foresight to save all his correspondence with (and related to) Sobukwe – the historical value of these documents speaks for itself – but for being so willing to review and provide expert commentary on my attempts at transcription and editing. I visited him in Jerusalem in late 2014, and the time I spent with him was invaluable. Although I have worked with many people whom I have respected in my career, rarely have I had the privilege of such generous support by a person with the moral integrity and courage – as the letters collected here will certainly demonstrate – of Benjamin Pogrund. It goes without saying that people interested in the life of Sobukwe would benefit from reading this volume alongside Benjamin Pogrund's book *How Can Man Die Better: The Life of Robert Sobukwe* (2015).

Transcribing and editing Sobukwe's letters was a difficult task, although I had excellent help. Lucas Goodwin and Alida Bonnet were tireless transcribers, each painstakingly converting in excess of a hundred (often poorly copied) handwritten and typed letters into text documents. They were assisted by Merryn Hook, Otua Sobukwe-Whyte (to whom I am also much indebted for her preface to this book), Julie Miller and Russell Martin. David Tomaselli helped with further editorial additions and checking dates, and Sanet le Roux compiled the index. My thanks to both.

I visited the Department of Psychology at Wits University during the time I was preparing this manuscript. I am hugely appreciative both of my colleagues in the department – Sumaya Laher and Michael Pitman particularly – but also of the research funding from both the Department of Psychology and the Faculty of Humanities at Wits. It seems fitting that the university where Sobukwe taught should have played such an important role in publishing his letters.

Gabriele Mohale at the Historical Papers Research Archive at Wits University was gracious both in helping me access the original handwritten letters and in guiding me to documents I would have overlooked. The Wits University Library deserves commendation for their upkeep of the Sobukwe letters (archived among the Robert Sobukwe Papers, Historical Papers Research Archive, University of the Witwatersrand, Johannesburg, South Africa), and for making much of this material available online: see http://www.historicalpapers.wits.ac.za/index.php?inventory/U/collections&c=A2618/R/6325. I would also like to thank the SA Jewish Museum and the Jewish Digital Archive Project for permission to reproduce a photograph of Robert Sobukwe with Benjamin Pogrund, as well as a photograph of Robert Sobukwe's children with Benjamin Pogrund's daughter.

Thanks are due also to Norman Duncan, and David and Marinda Maree, at the University of Pretoria, the South African university to which I am affiliated. Terblanche Delport and Ndumiso Dladla at Unisa were great colleagues to work with (especially in setting up a research seminar on the topic of "Sobukwe Today" at the University of Pretoria), as was Grahame Hayes, who, as editor of the journal *Psychology in Society*, made possible – and along with me co-edited – a special issue on Sobukwe (see: http://www.pins.org.za/issue.php?num=50).

I also wish to thank several colleagues at Duquesne University: Dean Jim Swindal (for his encouragement and support of the research costs), the Chair of the Psychology Department, Leswin Laubscher (for assisting in Afrikaans–English translation), Gerald Boodoo at the Duquesne Center for African Studies (where I benefited from being awarded the Loogman Faculty Research Grant) and Marilyn Henline. Colleagues at Birkbeck College, most notably Dan Alexander and Stephen Frosh, were also extremely supportive of the project. The Department of Psychosocial Studies at Birkbeck made it possible for me to travel to Jerusalem to visit Benjamin Pogrund. Julie Miller, my production editor at Wits University Press, went frequently beyond the call of duty in finding photographs, in having texts converted, and in many other ways. Thanks also to Russell Martin for his editorial input, and to Veronica Klipp, Corina van der Spoel, Sue Ogterop, Jeremy Phillips and Sipho Mbuqe. Finally, my thanks to the people I met with or interviewed as part of the preliminary research on the life of Robert Mangaliso Sobukwe, including Saths Cooper, Gail Gerhart, the Rev. Dumisani Methula, Johnson Mlambo, Thami ka Plaatjie, Mogobe Bernard Ramose, Dini Sobukwe, Mangaliso Sobukwe and Malaika wa Azania.

The week before this book was to be submitted for publication, Robert Sobukwe's wife, Zondeni Veronica Sobukwe, died at the age of 91. It is to her memory that this book is dedicated.

Introduction

In a letter of condolence written on 5 August 1974 to Nell Marquard, a friend with whom he had been corresponding since his time on Robben Island, Robert Mangaliso Sobukwe made a telling observation:

> I learnt some time ago that one cannot put oneself in another's position. We may express sympathy, feel it and even imagine the pain. But we cannot feel it as the one who suffers it. They have a saying in Xhosa that the toothache is felt by the one whose tooth is aching.

Sobukwe, who clearly knew about suffering, loneliness and the impossibility of ever fully communicating one's pain to another, was writing just after the death of Nell's husband, the noted Cape liberal, author and historian, Leo Marquard. Given that Leo was a prominent liberal, and that white liberals had not always been friendly to the aims and agendas of the Pan Africanist Congress (PAC) – the organisation that Sobukwe led from 1959 until his arrest in 1960 – one might have expected coolness from Sobukwe. Not at all. Sobukwe, as always, was gracious:

> I am thankful that I was able to talk to you two years before Leo's death and more thankful that he died knowing how much his contribution had been appreciated.

Touching as this acknowledgement of his contribution would have been for Marquard, the real poignancy of Sobukwe's letter comes a little further on, when he starts speaking of the myriad difficulties he has faced since leaving Robben Island.

> It has not been a good year for me. I had planned to leave [from Kimberley] ... by car on the 31st May and make straight for Cape Town. But these boys beat me to it. They came on the 30th May, 1974 to serve the fresh lot of bureaucratic output. Well it's good to know that our security is entrusted to such alert people.

Despite the fact that he makes light of it, one senses in Sobukwe's letter that the constant surveillance and harassment of the Security Police was taking its toll. Behind the ironic salute to the astuteness of the police, there is also a disturbing foreshadowing. Steve Biko, in many respects Sobukwe's most direct political heir, would be stopped and arrested on a not dissimilar road trip from Cape Town four years later, an event which would lead directly to his death at the hands of the Security Police. Sobukwe continues:

> Veronica has had a major operation as you probably read in the papers. She should have had this operation last year, but did not and the condition got worse.
>
> She has made a remarkable recovery, thanks to my very efficient and tender nursing, and has now gone back to Joh'burg for a check up. From there she will be in Durban to spend a week or so with her sister before proceeding to Swaziland to see the children.

These understated lines could only have masked Sobukwe's sadness and frustration at not being able to accompany his wife in this time of need, at being apart from his children, and at being alone again after his ordeal of six years of near-complete solitary confinement (May 1963 – May 1969) on Robben Island.

These circumstances had their origins in a momentous historical event organised by Sobukwe himself. On 21 March 1960, Sobukwe had led the PAC in what he called a "positive action" campaign, protesting against the oppressive pass laws that governed the movements – and indeed the lives – of black South Africans. This mass action resulted in the Sharpeville massacre, later that same day, in which at least 69 people were killed when the South African police opened fire on a crowd of protesters. This event, which drew international attention to the injustices and brutality of apartheid, was a watershed moment in the history of South Africa, and it led to a three-year jail sentence for Sobukwe for inciting people to protest against the laws of the country.

Sobukwe, inside the grounds of Orlando Police Station, awaiting arrest, on the morning of 21 March 1960.

Not content that by 3 May 1963 Sobukwe would have served the three years of his sentence, the South African government intervened by passing an amendment to the General Law Amendment Act, the notorious "Sobukwe Clause", which enabled Parliament to prolong the detention of any political prisoner year after year. Sobukwe was then relocated to Robben Island, and kept apart from other prisoners – technically, he was no longer a prisoner as he had served his sentence – where he remained for six years. The clause – never used to detain anyone else – was renewed annually by the Minister of Justice.

Sobukwe, in a very significant sense, was never a free man again after his 1960 arrest and imprisonment. The apartheid government unleashed a series of bureaucratic cruelties upon Sobukwe after his May 1969 release from Robben Island. They forced him to live in the geographically remote town of Kimberley – far removed from any friends, family or associates; they insisted he take on a low-ranking job that would have made him complicit in the apartheid policies that he went to jail protesting (Sobukwe, needless to say, refused); they repeatedly refused to allow him to leave the country to take up offers of employment he had received from the United States; and they obstructed his attempts to access the medical treatments that he needed, and that could have extended his life (he died on 27 February 1978).

This then is the background to the consolations that Sobukwe sought to offer Nell Marquard in his 1974 letter. It is only on the last page of that letter that Sobukwe seemed finally to find the words that suited both his emotions and the note of commiseration that he wished to convey to Nell:

> The Xhosa have standard words of condolence. They say
>
> Akuhlanga lungehlanga hala ngenxeba
> (There has not occurred what has not occurred before ... LIE ON YOUR WOUND).
>
> God bless you.
> Affectionately
> Robert.

Whether he realised it or not, Sobukwe had used the same phrase in a letter to Nell written six years earlier (on 26 June 1968) on Robben Island:

> We have a saying in Xhosa, used for purposes of condolence. It is a little stoic: akuhlanga lungehlanga – lala ngenxeba: (Daar het nie gebeur wat nie al gebeur het nie: slaap op jou wond).

This resonant phrase – which also appears in Sobukwe's letters to his friend Benjamin Pogrund – applies equally, if not more so, to Sobukwe himself. "Lie on your wound(s)" is a call to bide one's time, to heal, and to reconstitute one's self despite evident suffering. It is a call to have courage, to bear the moral burden of pain, and it provides an apt title for what was the most difficult period of Sobukwe's life, namely his time on Robben Island, which the selection of letters collected in this book represents.

* * *

In a personal note, written in 1986, eight years after his death, Nell Marquard (1986: 8) provided an insightful characterisation of Sobukwe's letters:

> A letter from Robert was always an event. His "mundane" included talk of books and articles, happenings in the outside world,

Robert Sobukwe and Benjamin Pogrund, Kimberley.

> education, gardening in the arid soil of Kimberley, and much more. His comments were always interesting and thought-provoking. But what gave his letters their chief interest was the quality of the man himself. The tacit assumption of standards was not infrequently underlined by gentle irony. Humane, compassionate, humorous, his letters were a constant pleasure.

This is true. Despite the conditions of censorship – all of Sobukwe's correspondence was carefully monitored by the Security Police and the island's warders – his erudition, his unwavering interest in global events, and his love of literature are all clearly evident in the letters. As is his sense of humour. Responding, on 26 June 1968, to a card that Marquard had incorrectly dated before sending to him, Sobukwe remarked:

> Thank you for both your card of the 1st June *1868* and your letter of 8th June, a century later. I have been long on this island, haven't I?

Sobukwe possessed not only a political, but also a wonderfully literary mind. He taught African languages at the University of the Witwatersrand (hence the nickname of "Prof"); he dreamed of translating Shakespeare into Zulu; he planned to study Arabic while on Robben Island; and he could cite Afrikaans poetry – particularly that of Jan Celliers – by heart. The letters are as engaging as they are eclectic. It is not unusual in a Sobukwe letter for a biblical reference to follow after a recalled snippet of Russian poetry, for a citation from Tennyson or Wordsworth to accompany a memory of his formative years in Graaff-Reinet, or for a Xhosa proverb to be interlaced with thoughts on the characters of Lyndon Johnson or Robert Kennedy. Sobukwe the letter-writer moves seamlessly from discussion of the history of the Xhosa people to the new boxing world heavyweight champion, from the relative merits of Christianity and Judaism to Kwame Nkrumah's notion of the African Personality.

Thanks to the efforts of the *Rand Daily Mail* journalist, Benjamin Pogrund, – by far Sobukwe's most regular correspondent in the collected letters that follow – Sobukwe received a great many books, as well as newspapers and journals (when permitted, that is) during his time on Robben Island. Sobukwe clearly had great flair in analysing global political events – such as the 1968 protest movements sweeping across Europe, the state of China–US relations, the 1966 coup d'etat in Nigeria – events which, as he tells Pogrund, formed the historical context necessary for understanding the South African situation ("There is a *verligte-verkrampte* [progressive-conservative] battle royal raging all over the world," he laments to Marquard in his letter of 27 March 1968). Many of the letters are surprisingly topical, even today – see, for example, Sobukwe's comments on mass immigration into Britain in his 5 June 1968 letter to Marquard – just as his political views are not always easy to predict – he was not, as one might expect, a supporter of Robert Kennedy, and he admired Lyndon Johnson despite his role in prolonging the Vietnam War.

None of this is to imply that either Sobukwe or his correspondents could speak freely in the letters. Nor is it to suggest that communication between parties was uninterrupted or without restriction. Sobukwe was allowed to receive and write only a limited number of letters. Length of letter was also controlled. As Benjamin Pogrund explained to me, all letters were subject to capricious censorship: if some faceless security warder did not like a sentence or perhaps a word, the entire letter was withheld, without telling Sobukwe or the author of the letter. It could take months to realise that a letter had been seized. As Pogrund (2015: 194) recalls:

> the official hold-up of letters was maddening. It was made even worse by the arbitrariness of the censorship. I never once received a letter from him with any part blacked out; what the authorities did was to seize letters and not tell either of us that they had done so. It might have been that a single sentence – or a single word? – offended some faceless security official. Whatever it might be, the entire letter disappeared ... it could take several months before it dawned on me that I was not getting Sobukwe's reply on an issue I had raised because the letter hadn't got through to him, or a letter from him had been blocked.

Even more seriously, the contents of the letters were scrutinised for any signals as to whether Sobukwe might have changed his political views. The implications of a stray phrase or unintended implication could have very serious consequences. As Pogrund (2015: 207) recalls:

> I was ... more conscious than ever that some or other comment or bit of information ... might actually help prolong his imprisonment. I

Robert Sobukwe's four children, Dini and Miliswa (back row) and the twins Dali and Dedani (in matching jerseys) with Pogrund's daughter Jenny and another friend (looking into the camera).

> spent hours writing and re-writing letters, trying to convey as much as possible but frightened of saying the wrong thing, without a clear idea as to what the wrong thing might be. Blandness and banality was the safe way out, as was discussion about his needs and reports about my young daughter.

These are important comments to bear in mind when reading the letters that follow. This selection of letters is, importantly, incomplete. Perhaps this is obvious, for only a portion of the letters received or sent by Sobukwe during his years of imprisonment survive. Some of the surviving letters, furthermore, are not particularly clear or even legible. Where I have been unable to decipher words or passages, these have been indicated in the text by [illegible]. Where I have omitted passages that have personal references to people still alive, I have indicated this by […]. I have supplied, with each letter, the reference number corresponding to the cataloguing system used by the Historical Papers Research Archive at the University of the Witwatersrand for ordering the Robert Sobukwe Papers. (See: http://www.historicalpapers.wits.ac.za/index.php?inventory/U/collections&c=A2618/R/6325). Providing this reference number – just after the date of each letter (for example: Ba3.41) - allows readers to refer back to the original (often handwritten) letters, many of which are available online.

We have, then, a collection of letters that is both necessarily incomplete (we do not have access to Nell Marquard's letters to Sobukwe, for instance) and that includes many instances of correspondence not directly written to or by Sobukwe (such as the letters by Veronica Sobukwe and Benjamin Pogrund). The latter are included because they play an invaluable part in grounding the personal and historical context of Sobukwe's letters. Particularly noteworthy here are the letters that Veronica Sobukwe and Benjamin Pogrund wrote to B.J. Vorster, then Minister of Justice (on 4 March and 3 February 1966, respectively), and Pogrund's exchange of letters with Helen Suzman in April and May 1969.

I have tried to let the letters speak for themselves in the sense of adding only minimal annotations. Unnecessary commentary on my part would only have distracted from the content of the letters themselves. I have, however, added footnotes on significant historical figures or events that help contextualise what is being spoken about. This too remains an incomplete process. Despite many online searches and the generous help of both Benjamin Pogrund and Miliswa Sobukwe, I have not been able to identify everyone – or every event – mentioned in the letters. At first this struck me as a limitation. It then occurred to me that my task as editor was less to explain the letters than to arrange and present them. As such, my hope is that the letters can be read not only as a historical document, but as an epistolary novel which calls us to become imaginatively involved in the life of an at once inspiring and humbling figure whom South Africa has for too long neglected: Robert Mangaliso Sobukwe.

Letters

[Received 2/5/69]

Robben Island Prison,
P. O Robben Island.
16th April, 1969.

Mrs V. Z. Sobukwe,
684 Mofolo Village,
P. O. Dube, Johannesburg.

Hullo Darling!

Some time ago I wrote to you but, of course, did not expect a reply. I hope you received the letter, though, because it had good news from Mrs Mokhele. Since then, I have heard from Mili as well – a very lovely letter!

Nenti and Mercy have been here. They spent about a week. Mercy is still as big as she was last year and Nenti looks just the same.

I asked Mercy to get me some stuff on Benjie's account – the same items as I discussed with you. She chose very expensive items and built up an account of R46 00

/2

A letter from Sobukwe to his wife Veronica with Robben Island postmark.

1960–1962

After Sobukwe's arrest on 21 March 1960, he was taken to the clinic where his wife worked, for a police search. The photograph shows Veronica and Robert Sobukwe, along with a security policeman, entering the clinic.

Robert Sobukwe
to Major-General C.I. Rademeyer,
Commissioner of Police,
Cape Town, 16 March 1960

Sir,

My organization, the Pan Africanist Congress, will be starting a sustained, disciplined, non-violent campaign against the Pass Laws on Monday the 21st March 1960. I have given strict instructions, not only to members of my organization but also to African people in general, that they should not allow themselves to be provoked into violent action by anyone. In a Press Statement I am releasing soon, I repeat that appeal and make one to the police too.

I am now writing to you to instruct the Police to refrain from actions that may lead to violence. It is unfortunately true that many white policemen, brought up in the racist hothouse of South Africa, regard themselves as champions of white supremacy and not as law officers. In the African they see an enemy, a threat, not to "law and order" but to their privileges as whites.

I therefore, appeal to you to instruct your men not to give impossible commands to my people. The usual mumbling by a police of an order requiring people to disperse within three minutes, and almost immediately ordering a baton charge, deceives nobody and shows the police up as sadistic bullies. I sincerely hope that such actions will not occur this time. If the police are interested in maintaining "law and order," they will have no difficulty at all. We will surrender ourselves to the police for arrest. If told to disperse, we will. But we cannot be expected to run helter-skelter because a trigger-happy, African-hating young white police officer has given hundreds of thousands of people three minutes within which to remove their bodies from [the] immediate environment.

Hoping you will cooperate to try and make this a most peaceful and disciplined campaign.

I remain

Yours faithfully,
Mangaliso R. Sobukwe
President
Pan Africanist Congress

PAC press release announcing
anti-pass campaign,
18 March 1960

CALL FOR POSITIVE ACTION

In accordance with a resolution adopted at our National Conference, held in Orlando on the 19th and 20th December, 1959, I have called on the African people to go with us into Positive Action against the Pass Laws. We launch our campaign on Monday, the 21st of March 1960, and circulars to that effect are already in the streets.

Meaning of campaign: I need not list the arguments against the Pass Laws. Their effects are well known. All the evidence of broken homes, tsotsism[1] and gangsterism, the regimentation, oppression and degradation of the African, together with the straight-jacketing of industry leads to one conclusion, that the Pass Laws must go. We cannot remain foreigners in our own land.

I have appealed to the African people to make sure that this campaign is conducted in a spirit of absolute non-violence, and I am quite certain that they will heed my call. I now wish to direct the same call to the police. If the intention is to "maintain law and order," I say, you can best do so by eschewing violence. Let the Saracens[2] have a holiday. The African people do not need to be controlled. They can control themselves. Please do not give my people impossible orders, such as "disperse within three minutes." Any such order we shall regard as merely an excuse for baton-charging and shooting the people. If the African people are asked to disperse, they will do so orderly and quietly. They have instructions from me to do so. But we will not run away! If the other side so desires, we will provide them with the opportunity to demonstrate to the world how brutal they can be. We are ready to die for our cause; we are not yet ready to kill for it.

Finally, I wish to offer all those non-African individuals and groups who have expressed themselves as bitterly opposed to the Pass Laws, an opportunity to participate in this noble campaign which is aimed at obtaining for the African people those things that the whole civilized world accepts unquestioningly as the right of every individual. Here is

1 Petty crime.

2 Military vehicles used by the South African Police.

an opportunity for you to create history. Be involved in this historical task; the noblest cause to which man can dedicate himself – the breaking asunder of the chains that bind your fellowmen.

Remember: "Every man's death diminishes me. For I am involved in mankind."[3]

Mangaliso R. Sobukwe
PRESIDENT
PAN AFRICANIST CONGRESS

3 From "No Man Is an Island" by John Donne.

Robert Sobukwe to the Registrar,
University of the Witwatersrand,
21 March 1960[4] (Aa11)

I hereby wish to tender my resignation from the position of Junior Language Assistant in the Department of Bantu Languages.

Circumstances have arisen which make it necessary, in the interests of the university, that I resign and that my resignation take effect from the earliest date the university may decide.

I wish to thank you for the attitude you adopted in refusing, in the face of terrific pressure, to interest yourself and the university in my political life.[5]

Thank you
Yours sincerely
R.M. Sobukwe

---

4 Monday, 21 March 1960, was the day that Sobukwe led the Pan Africanist Congress (PAC) in its anti-pass demonstrations. The restrictive and oppressive pass system, which required all black South Africans to carry an identity document (also known as the *dompas*), regulated and controlled movement, specifying whether a person was allowed to be in a particular area. To be found in an area not specified by one's pass – as, for example, in white residential areas – meant one could be immediately arrested. As Benjamin Pogrund (2015: 2) tells us: "The pass laws were hated as the tangible evidence of black subjugation, and for the ravaging effect on the lives of millions upon millions of people. Sobukwe had called on blacks to end the pass laws by making the system inoperable through mass arrests, thus clogging the courts and prisons by weight of numbers." This mass action resulted in the Sharpeville massacre – later that same day – in which at least 69 people were killed by the South African Police, who opened fire on a crowd of protesters outside the police station in the township of Sharpeville, near Vereeniging. This event, which drew international attention to the injustices and brutality of apartheid, was a turning point in the history of the country, and indeed, in the history of resistance to white supremacy.

5 A reference, no doubt, to the government threats the university would have faced once it became known that Sobukwe was the leader of the PAC.

The Registrar,
University of the
Witwatersrand,
to Robert Sobukwe,
22 March 1960 (Aa10)

Dear Mr. Sobukwe

I have to acknowledge receipt of your letter dated 21st March, 1960, wherein you tendered your resignation from the post of Junior African Language Assistant on the staff of the Department of Bantu Languages at this University.

I note that you wish your resignation to take effect from the earliest date that the University may decide, and I have to advise you that it will take effect as from 31st March, 1960, after which date you will no longer be a member of the University Staff.

Yours sincerely,
A. de V. Herholdt.
Registrar.

Robert Sobukwe,
Witbank Prison,
to Veronica Sobukwe,
[1961] (Bc43)

Darling,[6]

I am now at the Witbank Prison, as the address above indicates. I am quite well and would ask you not to be anxious about my health.

The distance from Johannesburg is much greater than it was to Stofberg [Prison] and you might find transport costs prohibitive. Don't strain your resources.

We are allowed to read approved books and I shall be glad if you will collect two books from Uncle which I left at his place.

We are in open country once more and for that I am thankful. One can see far into the distance.

Give my love to the kids, particularly to Zodwa,[7] the best of them all? Please inform me, when you reply, how Mili[8] is faring at school.

Cheerio Little Woman.

Your loving husband,
Mangaliso

---

6 Zondeni Veronica Sobukwe (1927–2018) married Robert Mangaliso Sobukwe on 6 June 1954 in a traditional African ceremony where she received the bridal name of Nosango. Veronica – as she is most frequently known in the letters – came later to be referred to variously as Mama Sobukwe and "the mother of Azania". She was honoured in a poem by Es'kia Mphahlele entitled "Tribute to Zodwa Veronica, a Great Woman". She worked for much of her life as a midwife and health practitioner. At the time of her husband's imprisonment, she was a midwife in Soweto.

7 Sobukwe often uses "Zodwa" to refer to Veronica in the letters.

8 Miliswa was the eldest of Sobukwe's four children. The letters contain frequent references also to Sobukwe's other children, Dinilesizwe and the twins, Dalindyebo and Dedanizizwe. Motsoko Pheko (1994) tells us that the name Dinilesizwe means "Sacrifice of the Nation", Dalindyebo "Create Wealth" and Dedanizizwe "Give Way, Imperialists".

Robert Sobukwe,
to Benjamin Pogrund,
Pretoria Gaol,
4 October 1961
(Ba1.1)

Dear Benjie,

I have about five letters to reply to and yours was the last to arrive. But I have decided to indulge in a bit of favouritism and write your letter first. Thanks indeed for your letter. It was a real pleasure to read it.

Through the kind permission of the prison authorities, I am able to write and receive one letter per week and have one visit per week. I have, therefore, been able to write regularly to my people in Graaff-Reinet and also to see my wife. Unfortunately children are not permitted inside the grounds, so I last saw my kids at Witbank [Prison].

Thanks for the news about Jennifer.[9] I had not received the glad tidings yet. I am glad to have got the news from the proud father himself. Since both of you are so easy to please I don't think Jennifer's task, to make you happy, should be a difficult one! I am sorry I cannot come and pay my respects in person to the lady, but hope to do so when I have left gaol.

My daughter is in Basutoland, attending school there. I learn that two weeks ago she was taken ill and that my wife has rushed to Basutoland to see her. Haven't heard any more since then.

Glad to learn you have taken up Zulu again – particularly Astrid. I was sorry when she had to give it up because of your interference.[10]

Thanks for remembering me, Benjie – and thank you also for your offer of help. As I said earlier, I am allowed a visit per week so that it should be possible to arrange for my wife to skip one week so that I may meet you.

---

9 Pogrund's daughter, born in July that year. She would go on to study at the University of Cape Town and then at Columbia University, New York, and gain a master's in international relations. Besides being a film-maker – between 1991 and 1992 she produced and directed a documentary film on Nelson Mandela entitled *The Last Mile* – she is today a member of the Department of International Relations and Cooperation (DIRCO) in Pretoria, where she is on the European Union desk.

10 Sobukwe's joking tone is obvious here. As Pogrund (2015) confirms, Sobukwe is referring here to Astrid's dropping out of university after her marriage to Pogrund.

Zeph[11] and Jacob[12] remained behind at Witbank. I am with P.K.[13] And we both would be happy to see you. You may perhaps be able to send me some books to read. We are allowed to receive *approved* literature – that EXCLUDES Westerns.

Give my greetings to Astrid and the kid. I wish them the very best. Remember me to Pat[14] and Dave[15] when you do write to them.

Salani kahle![16]

Yours very sincerely
Bob

---

11 Zephaniah Mothopeng (1913–90), like Sobukwe, had been a member of the Africanist faction of the ANC Youth League which broke from the ANC to form the PAC. Mothopeng was made chairman of the PAC on 6 April 1959, at the same inaugural conference at which Sobukwe was voted president. Like Sobukwe, he was arrested in 1960 for his part in organising the anti-pass campaign. He was subsequently sentenced to serve three years on Robben Island, although, because Sobukwe was kept apart from the rest of the prisoners, they had no contact during this time.

12 Jacob Dumdum Nyaose (1920–) became the secretary for labour in the PAC's national executive committee in April 1959. Later that same year he created the Federation of Free African Trade Unions of South Africa, an all-African non-Communist union.

13 Potlako Leballo (1924–86) had been a leader in the ANC Youth League (c.1954), who, like Sobukwe, was critical of the ANC's leadership, and who broke with the organisation to form the PAC. He was made national secretary at the PAC's inaugural conference (1959), and was sentenced to two years in prison following the declaration of a state of emergency in March 1960. Although a new banishment order was served on him when he was released in 1962, he escaped and fled to London. He subsequently established the PAC headquarters in Dar es Salaam, and served as leader of the PAC. (For more on Leballo, see Bolnick, 1991.)

14 Patrick Duncan (1918–67) had been owner and editor of the liberal magazine *Contact*, and was described by Pogrund (2015: 64) as "a man of intense sincerity and moral commitment to non-racialism". He participated in the Defiance Campaign of 1952. He acted as a national organiser for the new Liberal Party, from which he resigned in 1963 on the grounds that he no longer agreed with the party's policy of non-violence. Banned by the South African government, he escaped to Basutoland. He was accepted as a member of the PAC in 1963 and became its representative in North Africa, based in Algeria.

15 David Du Bois (1925–2005) was the director of the United States Information Service (USIS) in Johannesburg. He was known to Sobukwe through Potlako Leballo, who had found employment at the Johannesburg office of the USIS.

16 Keep well!

Robert Sobukwe, Pretoria Gaol,
to Veronica Sobukwe,
19 June 1962 (Bc1)

Darling,

Thank you for your note which I received on Friday. I was extremely sorry to learn that you had come here on the 11th and were turned away. The truth is, child, I have *NOT* had a visit this month. I do *not* know the Dan Mabena who is supposed to have visited me. I have never met him when outside or inside jail. I really cannot explain how the mistake occurred because whenever we receive visits we have to produce our tickets from which our particulars are taken. The person who had a visit on the 10th was Stanley but he, too, was not visited by a Dan Mabena. I reported the incident to the Chief and explained the error to him. Of course he, too, could not have done otherwise if it was recorded in the register that I had received a visit. He has, however, undertaken to have the matter put right, so that if you are able, you may still visit me before the end of the month.

I am quite aware, of course, of the difficulties facing you now, with schools about to close – the children's train fare and boarding fees to be paid and arrangements for their clothing and general comfort to be made. If then, you find it impossible to come this month, I will understand, Little Woman. I know what it feels like to undertake a journey full of hope and expectations only to meet disappointment. But as you will remember, I have often said to you that I shall not agree to see anybody unless they come with you, or, if you are for some reason or another unable to make the trip that month, you have informed me that somebody else will be coming to see me.[17] I abide by that decision.

I found myself thinking often about you and the children during these cold winter mornings, picturing you standing at [illegible] waiting for the bus. [Illegible] and back again in the afternoon. It has been a hard year, Little Woman, don't you think so? But please remember that "He who goes

---

17 Sobukwe's wording is a little confusing here. He is conveying his intent not to accept visitors unless they are accompanied by his wife, or unless his wife has informed him of who they are and given him advance warning.

out weeping to sow his seed comes back joyfully carrying his sheaves."[18] Happiness is achieved through suffering and struggling.

I received a letter from Mlamli.[19] He wrote from Cape Town and asked me to send the reply to his home in the Transkei. I have, unfortunately, forgotten his Transkeian address. I know it is P.O. St Mark's but I cannot recall the shop through which he receives his mail. Please ask Selby to find out from either Dennis or Fazzie. If neither of them knows it then he should try Nomvo Booi, P.O. Box 8, Engcobo. She will know.

How are the children getting on? I can imagine Dedani on a cold morning, reluctantly leaving the house for school. Where do you leave them on Saturdays and Sundays? And by the way, have you been on night duty already this year? I hope your turn does not come next month when the children are at home. Have the Mahlangus next door not yet added to their family after Thabo? What about Hilda?[20] She promised to drive up to Johburg in a Belaire or Biscayne[21] pretty soon – that was in 1959 when I was down in Durban. What is the news about the Varas? I wrote to Mercy last month. She has not replied yet. I want to write to Charles[22] next and ask him to make up his mind once and for all, whether he still wants his wife back or not. Their son is over fourteen years old now.

I am writing to Mam Tshawe[23] today. I have not written to her personally since I came to jail. I fear that she might feel hurt at the neglect. Buti hinted that she has a lot to tell me about Cape Town. But that, of course, will be when we meet.

Well, Greetings to Mama and the kids. How is Jabie[24] getting on? I enjoyed her book a great deal. Is Shadrach making any progress with the ceiling? Now that I remember, he is not fond of working alone you know.

---

18 Psalm 126: 6.

19 Clarence Mlamli Makwetu (1928–2016), who was secretary of the PAC in Langa, Cape Town, before the PAC was banned. He was imprisoned on Robben Island from 1963 to 1968 in the same jail as Nelson Mandela and other ANC members. When the PAC was unbanned in 1990, he became its president.

20 Veronica's older sister.

21 The Bel Air and the Biscayne were contemporary models of Chevrolet motor cars.

22 Robert Sobukwe's brother.

23 The wife of Sobukwe's brother Ernest.

24 Veronica's younger sister.

Even when we asked him to fit the doors and the skirting board it was only when Meshach assisted him that the job was completed. If he is slack, it might not be a bad idea to see his wife and first inform her about his negligence. She will undoubtedly get him to finish the job. Is Rosette back with Five Roses[25] or is he employed somewhere else?

Cheerio, Kid.

Your loving husband,
Mangi

25 The tea manufacturer.

1963

One of the few surviving pictures of Robert Sobukwe on Robben Island. The photograph was taken in 1965, recalls Benjamin Pogrund, as evidence of Sobukwe's good health.

Robert Sobukwe,
Pretoria Prison,
to Veronica Sobukwe,
26 March 1963 (Bc2)

Hello Darling,

Since my future is still so uncertain, I thought I should take this opportunity to tell you just how much your courage and love have meant to me during all these years of my imprisonment. Human nature is a queer thing, Darling. It is quite possible that after a time I may forget what you suffered on my behalf. That is why I want you to have this written testimony from me so that we both of us can go back to it in future. I just wish to say, Child, that you have been a magnificent wife and mother. You have been everything I could have wished my wife to be. And I mean that, Little Woman. And the children, too, will agree with me!

I received a letter from Buti.[1] He didn't have much to say except to express the hope that we will soon meet. By the way is J.D.[2] back yet or does he no longer intend to return to Joh'burg?

Then there is the question of my wood & coal business in Standerton. Segegede and I went 50-50 and money can be withdrawn from the bank only if the cheque bears the signatures of both of us. We placed some amount in fixed deposit, renewable every year in July. This was [illegible].

Please tell Stan that Emmanuel's wife has written to say she won't be coming to see him any further. She is employed and finds it impossible to come during the week. Will he please arrange that somebody else visit the boy? We would be extremely pleased if Z.B.[3] could do so even if it is just once. And of course Perry can do so – as a prospective sister-in-law.

---

1 "Buti" means brother, and it was Sobukwe's affectionate name for his brother Ernest.

2 "J.D." refers to Jacob Dumdum Nyaose (1920–), who often went by his initials. In Gail Gerhart's (1970) interview with Sobukwe (published in 2016), Sobukwe refers to Nyaose as "J.D.". Nyaose was made a member of the PAC's executive in 1959. Before this date he had argued for the formation of a PAC labour wing, and he came to assume this responsibility within the PAC when he became a member of the executive at the inaugural conference.

3 Z.B. Molete (1930–), who was made the PAC's Secretary for Publicity and Information at its inaugural conference in 1959. Molete was delegated by imprisoned PAC leaders in late

I shall be getting the next Reader's Digest early next month. You can write immediately to the Head Office in Cape Town to tell them to send the *May Issue* to 684 Mofolo and all the other issues from then on. You can forward them from Joh'burg to wherever I am or we can make further arrangements later. But please inform them, Sweet, of the change of address. It requires *six weeks* advance notice.

You can inform Benjie [Pogrund] too, to make arrangements for the May issue and subsequent issues of the English Digest to be mailed to Mofolo. I have not yet received the London Harper's magazine.

If Mercy[4] wishes to write please let her do so and if she can accompany you on your next visit let her do so. I would like to see her.

Well, Kid, give my love and greetings to the boys. If you do write to Mili and Dini tell them I shall reply to their letters. In the meantime let them study and behave as my children should!!

I'll [illegible]

1960 to head the PAC's underground organisation. Although he had been arrested in 1961 and sentences to a three-year jail term, he left the country – going to Basutoland – and subsequently worked with the PAC in Zambia and East Africa.

4 Mercy was the wife of Sobukwe's brother Charles.

Robert Sobukwe,
Robben Island,
to Veronica Sobukwe,
22 May 1963 (Bc3)

Darling,

I thought I would wait until I received one from you, informing me about your journey back. But I remembered that your hands are full and so is your heart.

I am still well though a bit lonely. I have derived great comfort and strength from Dr Peale's book[5] as well as from your visit. Your courage is magnificent, Little Woman. I thank God for a number of things and one of them, an important one for our earthly lives, is that he gave me you for a wife. I mean it. In one of his books, Robert Louis Stevenson writes of his wife that "She was as true to me as truest steel."[6] That is what I would say about you, too. Keep your chin up, Little Girl, and cling fast to your faith.

Thanks for the photos. I got them subsequently. How fine the children look! God and you have looked after them better than I could ever have done. I loved Dedani's smile. It is so open and fresh! Dali is either shy or extremely mischievous. In all the photos he is biting his lip. Mili and Dini have grown fast indeed.

I have not heard from Fabian[7] yet nor has the money come. I am hoping to get my lectures as soon as possible so that I can have something to tie me down to a fixed programme.

I had hoped to ask Dennis[8] to pay my fees. But I read recently that he had been sentenced to three years for continuing the activities of PAC. He was sentenced together with Mpumelelo [Mhlalisi], the boy who played with Dini

5 Norman Vincent Peale, *The Power of Positive Thinking* (1952).

6 In Robert Louis Stevenson's poem "My Wife"', he speaks about her as "Steel-true and blade-straight".

7 Dr Fabian Ribeiro (1933–86) was the husband of Veronica Sobukwe's sister Florence. He ran a general medical practice in Mamelodi township, Pretoria. Both were later assassinated by the apartheid regime.

8 Dennis Siwisa was a school and university friend of Sobukwe's, considered by Sobukwe as like a brother. He served three years on Robben Island for membership of the PAC.

when you visited Den[nis]. There were two others. They all got three years. I hope to write to his wife soon, to console her.

But this means that I shall have to depend on you then for the fees. I don't know what they will be, but I have a feeling that with books and all it won't work out at less than R80 (£40) a year. A very heavy bit, you will agree.

What papers did you arrange for and for how long? I received a letter from Prof Wellington[9] in which he stated a desire to pay me a visit. I asked him to send me his two volumes on Geography.

The cable from Cannon Collins[10] was forwarded to me from Pretoria. But I have not received the money. I do not know where they sent it. If you get it *you* will decide what to do with it.

By the way, you did not pack my black shoes, Darling. What you did pack were my slippers – black. And as you know this pair of brown shoes I have here needs immediate repair.

I wrote to Buti but I have not got his reply yet. I know they are worried. I told him in my letter that you would pass Graaff-Reinet if the detour was not too much, as the people who were driving you had to get back to work the following day and so did you.

Mercy[11] wrote, too, and her letter was re-directed from Pretoria. She commented on the health and activity of the twins.

Cheerio, darling. Love to the kids, Mama and friends.

Your loving husband,
Mangi

---

9 Professor J.H. Wellington was a retired head of the Geography Department in the University of the Witwatersrand, who had become friendly with Sobukwe during the time both were employed by the university. His two-volume book, *Southern Africa: A Geographical Study*, was first published in 1955.

10 Canon John Collins (1905–82) of St Paul's Cathedral played a crucial role in the International Defence and Aid Fund, thereby ensuring that those families who had been most detrimentally affected because of the anti-apartheid political activities of one or more members would be financially cared for.

11 Wife of Robert's brother Charles.

Robert Sobukwe
to Nell Marquard,
2 July 1963 (Bd2.10)

Dear Mrs Marquard,[12]

I received your letter on the 30th June and, as always, enjoyed it immensely. I am glad to know that Mr Marquard's condition has improved. *Asthma* can be very nasty and [illegible] customer. I hope he recovers completely because, like you, I am not yet ready to believe that climate is irrelevant to the condition.

Yes, I know Colesberg and I know Norvals Pont too.[13] Would your father by any means have been Rev. Andrew Murray, born in Graaff-Reinet 9th May 1828 and who died at Wellington January 18th 1919?[14] You did mention in one of your earlier letters that your Murrays were religious and were not engaged in farming, but you did not say you were the daughter of one of them! Incidentally the details I have quoted above I obtained from a book I am reading, *The Murray Tribute*, written by [illegible] Murray [illegible].[15]

With reference to your question about furring, the article merely states that "Armand[16] devised an ingenious additive to the water which prevented furring. It doubled the life of the train, allowed the railway to reduce its stock of engines and eliminated a thoroughly nasty job. It won him praise and, aged thirty-four, promotion to chief engineer." Very illuminating and helpful you'll agree.

---

12 Nellie Joan Marquard, born van der Merwe (1897–1981) was a liberal intellectual and a member of the Black Sash and of the Liberal Party, who taught English literature at the University of Stellenbosch for many years. In 1927 she married Leo Marquard. She was involved in many forms of public service. On her death her friend Moira Henderson wrote of her: "Her knowledge and wisdom ad her gift of interpreting the historical significance of current trends and policies were qualities which were of immense value to the [Black] Sash. But more than that, she was a shining example of gentleness and courage, of humility and forcefulness, of courtesy and conviction" (*Sash*, May 1981).

13 Small towns in the northern Cape Province.

14 Nell's mother was Jane Georgiana Murray and her father Petrus van der Merwe.

15 Perhaps *Chronicle of the Murray Family* by May Murray et al. (1913–20).

16 Louis Armand (1905–71), a French engineer who devised a means of preventing the calcification of railway engine boilers in steam locomotives.

No I haven't read Eugene Marais'[17] book. But the story is really delightful, though not very flattering to human beings.

Your story about Dr Adler[18] was very interesting indeed. And I agree that it is necessary to collect the medicine lore of our Africans as soon as possible. Witchdoctors are an interesting lot – outstanding psychologists. Some have a profound knowledge of herbs. There is a belief that those born to be "lingata" cannot escape their destiny. They become seriously ill and may even become insane if they do not heed the call. The lady who was my teacher in Sub A threw up teaching and joined this fraternity. I have been assured that she is a very competent practitioner. In Xhosa we distinguish between the Igqirha whose sole job is to "diagnose", which might include smelling out witches, and the ixhwele (with a lateral click) who prepares the potions. The Igqirha sends his patients to the ixhwele in the same way as some doctors send patients to the chemist.

I dislike "Hamlet", I believe, because from the first I was told that it was Shakespeare's greatest tragedy. My teachers waxed poetic when they discussed the play. I read "Julius Caesar", "Macbeth" "King Lear" and enjoyed them. I read "Hamlet" and, I am afraid, didn't feel that it was greater than the others, either in language or in construction. It is said that Sir Laurence Olivier's *"Othello"* is a masterpiece. I haven't seen any of Shakespeare's plays either in the theatre or on the screen. It is entirely through books that I have made his acquaintance.

In your reply please tell me what vegetable seeds can be sown and give me whatever information you can about water melons and sweet melons – when sown and how.

Again, thanks for your letter. Hoping for better news about Mr Marquard.

Yours sincerely,
RM Sobukwe

---

17 Eugene Marais (1871–1936) was a South African lawyer, naturalist and writer. He qualified as an advocate in London, and was one of the leaders of the Second Afrikaans Language Movement, hence his preference for writing in Afrikaans. He is considered the father of ethology, the scientific study of animal behaviour. The book referred to here is probably *Die Siel van die Mier* (*The Soul of the White Ant*), the book for which Marais is best known.

18 Dr Cyril Adler, who founded the Adler Museum of Medicine in 1962, now housed at the Wits University Medical School Campus.

P.S. With regard to Hamlet, then, I believe my dislike stems from sheer perverseness because all the others think highly of him, to show my independence of mind I have to class the play as indifferent. I'll try and find the reasons through ruthless self-analysis! RMS

Robert Sobukwe
to Veronica Sobukwe,
4 July 1963 (Bc4)

Hello Darling,

Thank you for both your letters, one dated 13th and the other 20th June.

I had also written to you, two weeks ago I think, suggesting that we hand over the money to the Defence and Aid Fund people. Then I received your letter to the effect that you had already fetched the money and placed it in the bank – fixed deposit. As I had said in an earlier letter, it is your money really, not mine. I won't press the point about Defence & Aid, then. You will do as you think best.

I have replied to Fabian's letter. I received the money and have already bought the kettle and iron. The radio is on the way. I have not bought a typewriter nor have I applied for an electric recorder.[19] These items are extremely expensive and will take up all that R100 and still leave us in debt. An electric recorder alone will work out at about R50 and a typewriter the same. Fabian has no experience of gaol life, Sweet. *You* have, through caring for me for these past three years. You will have to pull him up now and again. I have written to him, too, to acquaint him of the position.

I agree with you that you must be nearer either me or the children. And I want to say, Kid, that I shall be extremely happy if you can get a post nearer Mili and Dini. You will then have no worries either about Dedani and Dali. I am grown up, Child. I know you love me absolutely. I NEVER, even for a moment, doubt your love for me. But the kids need your presence. They must never lack mother-love if we can help it. So, please try for a post near them.

Thank you for the dates about the Papers. As you will have noticed in my earlier letter, I thought Pogrund was responsible for the Rand papers. Thank you, Kid.

I received the parcel, Darling. Thank you indeed. The pyjamas were the exact size and extremely welcome. So were the shoes. Incidentally, I don't remember the black shoes. The brown I recognised immediately. The sports shirts made my heart go around. They are lovely. Your choice of colours is wonderful. *BUT*, Darling, they are too small. Now please don't get

19 Presumably a record player.

disappointed. I would not have admitted that they are small. I do so because I fear you may buy others. These won't be wasted, Child. We will put them aside for Dini. Nothing that is done for love can ever be a mistake. Don't blame yourself. In shirts I buy 16½ collar. I don't know how one expresses that in sports shirts. Thank you for the jersey too. I now have three! There is the black one I had, then this green one you've sent. And this morning I received a fawn one from Mercy. She says she did not get a chance to show it to you before sending it off. She has some good things to say about you and the kids.

I have also received a warm vest, a pair of socks and a brown sports coat from Mam Tshawe. The coat sleeves are a little short and the jacket is a bit tight round the shoulders, but it is a lovely one. It appears I shall soon have to open a drapery shop around here.

Congrats to the kids. I pray for you all daily as I have done for the past three years. I am glad you have found them a place.[20] I am certain they'll be happy, particularly if you could soon be near them.

Thanks for the advice about soap flakes. I'll remember it. I have bought a lovely Picture Album – so let those snaps roll in! Father Webber[21] has sent me an expensive Bible. I am receiving Bibles & books all round. If you can make it down here, I'll be very pleased, of course, though in my last letter I pointed out that it would be an expensive journey.

Well, Good bye Little Woman. Love to the kids, Mama & friends.

Your loving husband,
Mangi

20 At a boarding school.

21 Father Reginald Webber was a Catholic chaplain at Pretoria Local Prison, who remained in contact with Sobukwe after he was moved from Pretoria by the prison authorities.

Robert Sobukwe
to Veronica Sobukwe,
29 July 1963 (Bc5)

My darling Mrs Sobukwe,

We've been having particularly cold weather this week with overcast, lowering skies, winds that howl like banshees and a tumultuous, obstreperous sea – altogether a picture which should be depressing but one that never fails to touch a chord in my heart.

It is said that our feelings are coloured, if not determined, by the state of the weather. To me, cold and rain have always been associated with a warm fire place and love and laughter. No wonder, therefore, that you have been particularly in my mind this week. And on Tuesday I celebrated your birthday with thanks and gratitude. I shall celebrate Mili's tomorrow in the same way. I am sorry I could not in person give you a birthday present that will in a very small way convey my esteem for you two girls and my gratitude for your love. I do hope my letter arrived in time to wish you a Happy Birthday.

I received, yesterday, a parcel of warm sheets, shirts, underwear, socks, trousers and hankies from Benjie. As usual they were beautiful patterns. I felt he had consulted you! He must have spent a very tidy sum indeed. I shall soon send you my measurements so that you should have my grey suit altered accordingly. The rest you can send to Charles.[22] I am sending my old stuff to Nenti[23] to dispose of as she pleases.

I received a letter from Fabian last week. He was in great form. I have been harangueing him on the Basutoland elections and the part played by the Roman Catholic Church to ensure the victory of Chief Leabua.[24] I told him a bit about Alice and how I met a certain lady during a [illegible] in 1949. I didn't

---

22 Charles Sobukwe was one of Sobukwe's two older brothers.

23 Sobukwe's mother.

24 Joseph Leabua Jonathan (1914–87) of Basutoland, great-grandson of King Moshoeshoe I, was a minor chief who converted to Catholicism in 1959 and founded the Canadian missionary-supported Basutoland National Party. His party won the pre-independence elections of 1965 and in 1966, as prime minister, he led Basutoland to independence as Lesotho. He faced opposition from the strongly Pan Africanist Basutoland Congress Party founded by Ntsu Mokhehle (1918–99).

tell him, of course, that one evening in the sitting room at Mary Balmer[25] I didn't hear a word of what my companion was saying because I was listening to a voice behind me! I don't think they should know that a little skinny girl shook my heart so.

I have also heard from Mrs Marquard. She spent a few weeks in Johannesburg and is now in P'Maritzburg. Her husband, she tells me, has had repeated severe attacks of asthma and their doctor advised them to try the drier air of the interior.

I have not received the "Cape Times" yet and now the "Sunday Times" too have begun to behave erratically. I did not receive the issue of the 13th & 20th June and the 20th July nor have I received this week's issue (25th July). I have written to the C.N.A.[26] in Joh'burg to enquire. But [illegible].

How were the kids? I wondered how you were faring with the coal shortage reportedly acute on the Reef. Graaff-Reinet, too, had severe snowfalls. The drifts between Graaff-Reinet and Middelburg were rendered impassable, the mountains were covered in layers of glistening crackling ice. The scenic beauty and grandeur are such as to fill an artist's heart to the brim. But there were practical problems of fuel and food which concern hundreds of thousands of non-artists. I have not heard yet from Buti. He is the one who gives the news in detail. Nenti and Tshawe are too immersed in Church affairs and the only people they write about are our Church friends.

Well, this is enough for the present. Cheerio Kid & love to the other kids.

Your loving husband,
Mangi

25 The Mary Balmer Nurses Home at Victoria Hospital, Alice, where Veronica trained and worked. Alice was also home to Lovedale College and Fort Hare University.

26 Central News Agency.

Eulalie Stott,
Newlands, Cape Town,
to Benjamin Pogrund,
11 August 1963 (Ba1.2)

Dear Benjamin,

Thank you for your letter of 23rd July and for the copies of certificates enclosed.

I have seen the Chief Magistrate, Mr. Wilman and he had agreed to give the necessary visitors permit to Mrs. Sobukwe. He says *she* must write *direct* to *him* and *ask him* to *send* the *permit to me.* Then when she arrives in Cape Town, if the Magistrate's Office is closed, it will not matter as I will have it and she will be able to take the boat to the Island in the Morning.

I asked for permission to visit myself – but was refused.

I shall almost certainly be able to arrange accommodation at an Hotel nearer town this time and will be able to do so as soon as you give me the word. I think that for all sorts of reasons it is best for the party to stay together and at an hotel, where they are quite independent.

Meanwhile I shall continue trying to find suitable employment. Has an official approach been made in this connection?

I suggest that I be sent a copy of the letter to the Chief Magistrate, Mr. Wilman, so that I know when to watch out for the permit and to make enquiries if it does not reach me by the Friday. Please do not forget to mention in the letter the reason for wanting the permit to be sent here, viz. that Mrs Sobukwe will be likely to arrive after the Magistrate's Office is closed.

Glad to help people in distress.

Sincerely,
Eulalie Stott[27]

P.S. Terribly busy fighting municipal election. Hold thumbs, please.

---

27 Eulalie Stott (1923–2010) was a founding member of the South African Liberal Party in 1953, and also a founding member of the Black Sash in 1955. The Black Sash was a group of white women who opposed apartheid laws and sought to provide assistance to African women in particular. Stott was president of the Black Sash when the organisation associated with the Pan Africanist Congress in the late 1950s and early 1960s. She was first elected as a councillor to the Cape Town City Council in 1961.

Veronica Sobukwe
to the Chief Magistrate,
Cape Town,
[1963] (Ba1.8)[28]

Sir,

I shall be privileged if you could, Sir, allow me an interview with you to discuss the possibility of my joining my husband, Robert Mangaliso Sobukwe during my forthcoming leave. He is detained on Robben Island.

I realise that you are very busy and that an interview may not be possible. If this is so, I shall be extremely happy to have your written permission allowing me to stay on Robben Island for the period of my leave.

My leave starts on the 22nd November, 1963 and is for a period of 28 days.

Wishing that my application will receive your favourable consideration.

Yours faithfully
Veronica Sobukwe

28 This letter is undated, and the recipient is not named, although it is presumably addressed to the magistrate mentioned in Eulalie Stott's letter of 11 August 1963.

Robert Sobukwe
to Veronica Sobukwe,
22 August 1963 (Bc6)

Hello Darling,

I haven't heard from you for quite a time now and was beginning to feel anxious, but Benjie's letter assured me you were all right. And I was happy. Benjie also informed me that you intended to pay me a visit this month and I presume that your failure to have done so before now has been caused by the formidable difficulties of transport.

I have heard from Wolsey Hall.[29] They received Fabian's cheque for £50. That settles the matter of my fees and textbooks. I have written to Fabian and he'll tell you what I said, I am sure.

Benjie sent me a good number of books and a photograph of their daughter, Jennifer. Quite a healthy and sweet little thing. Charles, too, has written and has sent me R1 (one). I appreciated the gesture because I know he just hasn't a penny to spare. He tells me they have reduced his salary to that of a female assistant – about £18! He assures me, however, that this time he means business about having Mercy back. He is saving toward his lobola[30] – so he says!

How are you, Little Woman? And what were the June holidays like with the kids around? You haven't reported anything about Mili's chest, so I take it she has got over her trouble completely now. I sincerely pray she does. She can't afford to be losing classes every year. I must say she looks excellent in the photographs – a real glamour girl!

By the way, Charles wishes to visit Joh'burg, but fears that in my absence there will be nobody to show him the sights. I have told him not to worry. First of all you will be happy to have him there and as for entertainment he won't lack it. Off-hand I can think of Matebula and Vara[31] who will be too happy to make him feel at home. He says he is keen to see the boys. Apparently Mercy has been sending them glowing reports about the twins.

---

29 Wolsey Hall, Oxford is one of the longest-established distance education institutions in the world. Between the 1930s and 1980s Wolsey Hall offered degree courses through the University of London external degrees programme.

30 The custom of bridewealth.

31 Neighbours and family friends of the Sobukwes.

Dini's report, of course, has sent Buti raving. He ran out of adjectives trying to describe his achievement. That boy has a very bright future, all right. And so has Mili. She is an intelligent kid, only very shy, as her mother is. And so was I too, before I started teaching.

I do hope you received my telegram asking you to send my Degree Certificates. One of them, I believe, is in your suitcase – the big one. Perhaps both are there, I am not sure.

I wrote to Dennis' wife[32] as I said I would, but I have not received any reply from her yet. I advised her to continue running the shop, if that were possible.

Did you manage to place the kids in a boarding school? I pray that you have, because that will relieve you of one cause of anxiety at least. And how is the work going on? When are you on night duty again? And which are your days off? I was doing some washing on Saturday and when I had finished, I found the smell of the soap on my hands so fresh and clean – just like you!

You have really made an impression on Mercy. She thinks the world of you as a nurse, a mother and a wife. So does Benjie. But your husband thinks that all they can say about you is but a pale reflection of the truth. Robert Louis Stevenson wrote about his wife in these words: "She was as true to me as truest steel." All I say about my wife is that she was God's gift to me.

Well, Kid, give my love to Dedani & Dali and all friends. Tell Mama I am all right. She should not worry.

God bless you child.

Your loving husband,
Mangi

32 Dennis Siwisa's wife.

Robert Sobukwe
to Veronica Sobukwe,
13 September 1963 (Bc7)

Hullo Little Woman!

What a pleasure it was to read your letter. Your voice rang through every sentence I read and for that reason I have read it over and over again.

I wrote to Mili last week. I hope she'll be able to read my Sotho. The trouble is we had evolved a new Sotho orthography at the Wits[33] and in my letter to Mili I used it here and there. It seems so childish to me to have to write *ke a tsamaea*[34] as three words when in fact it is one word *keatsamaea*. I give you your due there, Zulu is more logical in that direction, writing it *ngiyahamba*. Xhosa for no reason at all has decided to take the middle course with *ndiya hamba*.

I am glad you were able to have the kids placed, darling. I do hope Mili settles down and is successful in her exams. [...] Yes, you told me about Dlanga, Baby, and there is no fear of my becoming jealous. I know you too well to distrust you. I have told you time and again that you are a rare woman. I did not say that to flatter you. I mean it.

I have not yet received the certificates. Please send them as soon as you can, Child. I cannot register at the University until I have sent the certificates. And what about the photographs? I have the Album – all I lack are the pictures!

I received an interesting letter from Fabian. He told me [he] was going to see you that week. I have also received one from Buti. He is just as ignorant as Fabian is of Prison procedure!

The lectures might arrive any day now though no tuition is offered by Wolsey Hall in two of the subjects I have chosen. I hope to get information about the books I can read on them. The subjects are: Introduction to Scientific Method and Structure of International Society. If I can't get books on them I'll be compelled to take two others in their stead. I'd be sorry to do so because I really am interested in these two.

---

33 The University of the Witwatersrand.

34 I'm going.

By the way, Fabian tells me Hilda had a Caesarean. Is it a boy or girl? How many are there now? And what about Jimmy?[35] Isn't he a sub-inspector yet? And what about Tennyson Nyovane? Is he is still with the Joh'burg Municipality?

I have started work on the garden. The soil is extremely sandy and is infested with slugs and snails. I intend to lay out a vegetable garden and a small flower plot. How is your garden faring? If I have as much success with this one as we had with ours at home I'll be delirious with joy.

Tell Fabian I received the four records he ordered and I have acquired two more. I have looked through the papers, Kid: electric recorders are very dear – in the neighbourhood of R50. I can't afford that. Fabian has already spent over £100 on me. And, of course, you have borne the burden for years now, ALONE. And you need every penny for the kids. I wrote Mili that we wanted them to go as far with their education as they wished.

I shall not be able to send Birthday cards in time for the twins' birthday. Will you please buy them, Sweet, and present them on behalf of both of us? I may be able to send them a little birthday present later on. I'll send them a telegram, at least.

Where is Jabi working at present? Is she still with you or is she at Pimville? Give my greetings to her, please. She has been fond of me in her sulky way. How is Mama's arm?

I am O.K. Kid and thank you for the R10 you sent me through Benjie. He told me about the trousers and that the two of you thought that my taste in clothes is too conservative! Well I wonder what you'll feel like when you see me in the loud shirts and ties, the pointed shoes and narrow trousers sported by the fashionable crowd. I'll NEVER wear those things, Sweet. I am not going to be ordered about by fashion designers!

Well, cheerio Kid. God bless you. Love to the boys and to Mili & Dini when next you see them.

Your loving husband,
Mangi

P.S. I have just received the photographs. What a pleasure! Thanks a lot, Kid. Keep on sending them. You all haven't changed this bit!! "A thing of beauty is a joy for ever" says Keats. I agree. Mangi

---

35 Husband of Hilda, Veronica's older sister.

Robert Sobukwe
to Veronica Sobukwe,
28 September 1963 (Bc8)

Hello Darling!

I sent you a telegram last week asking you to forward the original certificates and to keep the copies. It is something we should have done earlier. But then I never could do things when they should have been done.

A copy of the Regulations I received from the University of London states that they will NOT accept copies from overseas students. They fear, probably, that students will forge copies, although, if they were to ask me, I could tell them that even originals are forged by some people.

I think I told you that I had written to Mili. My next letter will have to be addressed to Dini. I have ordered two "Junior" books from the Reader's Digest. I hope to give those to Dedani & Dali as their birthday gifts.

I read in the Press quite recently of a new method of teaching English that they have introduced into Kenya schools with spectacular results. As soon as I found out whether they have published any books on the subject I'll let you know so that you may start on the young fellows there at home.

Thank you for the photographs. They tell a whole story. They took me back to Lovedale, to Ladysmith, to Baragwanath[36] with Mili absolutely helpless in our hands, to Graaff-Reinet with a taxi rushing Dalindyebo to the doctor, to Ma Simelane pushing their prams to the clinic. I even remember you carrying Dini on your back every morning to White City.[37] What a life it has been!

When I saw your photograph with Dini in Durban and also at the clinic, memories came rushing back. And I remember our one table and one chair borrowed from Mama. We started right from the bottom, Little Girl, and turned a house into a home. Our one fault was that as we went forward, we tended to forget the One who had brought us together, and has blessed us with all we have! It will never happen again, I assure you.

The Defence and Aid people wrote me from their Cape Town offices asking if there was anything I needed. I asked them for vegetable and flower

---

36 Hospital in Soweto.

37 In Soweto.

seeds. I was hoping that by the time you visited me they would be ready so that you could take back with you, for Mama, flowers and vegetables from my own garden. I don't think that the hope will be realised. It is rather late now.

I have had my teeth attended to. That "gate" that they made at the Wits,[38] I have had filled up. You'll see the "bridge" when you come. It has not been fitted yet.

Father Webber of Pretoria has written to say he is very anxious to meet you and I have assured him that you are just as eager to make his acquaintance. When you visit Vemba[39] next, please ask them to take you to meet him.

The lectures still haven't come though I have received a letter informing me that they are on the way. All that remains now is for me to register with London University before the end of the year and then I'll be able to settle down to solid work.

I have plenty of reading matter and am receiving more week by week from people I have never met.

We are having glorious weather down here though the days can be depressingly hot.

The days I still find difficult are Saturday evenings and Sundays. They remind me too much of baking in the kitchen and that "Brunch" on Sunday between 11 and 12! And yet, when I was still a convict at Stofberg,[40] those were the days we looked forward to eagerly, because they were days of "rest" after a week of perpetual motion and weariness. How strange we human beings are, and how short our memories are, too, don't you think?

Lauretta [Ngcobo][41] too, has written. She says they are in Swaziland with Stanley and his wife. She has a teaching post at Manzini. Stanley's wife is a trained nurse. She'll probably find a post, too, though she's been working in a

---

38 A possible reference to the Dental School at the University of the Witwatersrand.

39 The name by which Florence Ribeiro was affectionately known.

40 Sobukwe was a prisoner at Stofberg, a farm prison, prior to being transferred to Robben Island. This period of Sobukwe's imprisonment had the advantages of him sharing a communal cell, and being among many other PAC men, but it also meant that all prisoners had to endure hard physical labour.

41 Lauretta Ngcobo, who later became well known as a novelist, was married to Abednego Ngcobo, a founding member of the PAC, who was sentenced to two years' imprisonment in 1961. Fearing arrest, Lauretta fled South Africa for Swaziland in 1963 and later moved to London.

factory in Johburg because of varicose veins. In a factory she can at least rest her legs whereas as a nurse she has to be on her feet the whole day! You girls have wonderful stamina, for sure!

Well, cheerio, Little Woman. Give my love to Dini's "dogs"? and to Mama, Jabi etc. Thank you for news about Vara and Mongeka.

Your loving husband,
Mangi

Robert Sobukwe
to Nell Marquard,
11 October 1963 (Bd1.1)

Dear Mrs Marquard,

Thank you for the magazines – The New Yorker, Life and The Listener.

Although I have listed The Listener last, it is the first on my list of preferences. It's the first time I have read it. I had heard of it, yes, most probably even seen it. But I had not read it until I got the copies you sent. And what a pleasure it was to read!

I have a further reason now for asking you to continue the "good work" you have started. I have registered with the University of London for the BSc. Econ. degree and my tutor in British Government has recommended the reading of good newspapers and journals. Among the many that he lists is "The Listener" (very good indeed). The brackets and comment are his!

I have quite a busy day. Besides studying and reading (I have quite a wide range of reading matter – from the Bible to G.B.S.[42]). At the moment I am reading [George] Orwell's 1984. I have just finished *The Ugly American*),[43] I also do some gardening. I have a fairly large garden, larger than my Mofolo one. But the soil in this part of the country is – I am sure you'll agree, patriotic Capetonian though you are – the despair of the amateur gardener. The vegetables (carrots, beetroot, beans) have somehow germinated but the flowers have not yet announced their arrival. Should both flowers and vegetables bear fruit, however, I'll undertake to make the Sahara blossom.

I have had trouble with some of my friends who seem to believe that I have become a tardy correspondent of late because I do not reply promptly to their letters. The Press apparently, gave the impression that I could write an unlimited number of letters. In fact I am allowed two a week and have to ration my replies on the strict basis of "First come, first serve" except, to be truthful, in the case of my wife who demands and to whom I have granted the right to jump the queue.

---

42 George Bernard Shaw.

43 *The Ugly American*, a political novel by Eugene Burdick and William Lederer depicting the failures of US diplomatic intervention in Southeast Asia, was published in 1958 and was made into a film in 1963 with Marlon Brando.

Again, thank you for the journals. Your choice of this issue of "Life" was a generous gesture to the Americans – proving to sceptics that they ARE capable of intellectual production!

Yours sincerely,
RM Sobukwe

Benjamin Pogrund,
105 Earls Court,
2nd Avenue, Killarney,
Johannesburg,
to Veronica Sobukwe,
25 October 1963 (Ba1.3)

Dear Mrs. Sobukwe,

I am sorry that I missed you yesterday afternoon. I waited until 4 p.m. and then decided that you must have been unable to get a lift into town.

I saw Mrs. Stott again and she has promised to go into the matter of a record player without delay. Should it prove impossible for you to stay on the Island with Bob, Mrs. Stott will arrange accommodation for you in Cape Town. Please let me know as soon as you receive a reply to your application to stay on the Island.

In the meantime, I hope you will not fail to contact me if you should need anything at all.

Best wishes,
Sincerely,

Robert Sobukwe
to Veronica Sobukwe,
7 November 1963 (Bc9)

Hello Darling!

Thank you for your letter. It was pleasantly surprising to note how alike our thoughts were about the books I sent the boys. As you will see in my letter preceding this one, I, too, referred to the interesting stories and games found in them. I am glad you think Dini and Mili will find the books useful.

I received a letter from Mili last week, just a day before I received yours and Mercy's and Bhuti's. Mili complains, Darling, that their school fees and book fees have not yet been paid and tells me rather sadly that if they are not settled in time, then she and Dini will not be allowed to go home.

I am, therefore, writing so that you may settle the matter quickly. I remember your telling me that you had sent their fees as well as some pocket money. Well, Mili tells me she would have written to me earlier but she did not have money for stamps! Please CHECK IMMEDIATELY whether the money you sent *did* reach the school authorities. I know you are busy with a thousand and one things, all demanding money and attention. But please, Child, attend to this matter immediately.

She tells me that she has done badly in Arithmetic in what she calls the August Test. [...] She says she is extremely disappointed! But I am not worried. I got 2/5 when I was doing Std II but went on to top the next few classes in Arithmetic. She must NEVER gain the impression that she is a dunce or that to fail even one subject is a disgrace. Churchill was mediocre at school and went into the Army because he was good for nothing else. But he was exceptionally good in English and history and he built his future on those two gifts.

I am looking forward with keen anticipation to your proposed visit – like a child in wild anticipation, waiting for a journey home!

Yes, darling, the lectures have come. There are two more subjects in which I have to receive lectures. Those should be done any time this month. The work is most interesting; but the notes are sketchy requiring wide reading. Of course they assume that their students have access to the libraries in Britain since the lectures are primarily meant for students resident there. I have no alternative but to get the books, although I am really sorry to have loaded you with this burden at this time of the year, when you need every penny for your journey and for Christmas.

Incidentally I notice that Mili's address, as given by her, is different from the one you sent me. She gives me her address as:

Emmanuel Mission School,
P.O. Box 274,
Ficksburg,
Orange Free State.

Just try this address when you write. Also please drop her a note too, to tell her everything is all right. If you find Sotho too tough you will have to write SIMPLE SENTENCES in English! [...]

Oh yes, Mili says she is looking well after Dini! But girls are not allowed to do washing for boys. So, she asks, who will do the washing for Dedani and Dali if you send them to school with her next year? She is quite a responsible girl, really.

Well, darling, so long for the time being. God bless you.

Your loving husband,
Mangi

Benjamin Pogrund
to Robert Sobukwe,
7 November 1963 (Ba1.4)

My dear Bob,

My deepest apologies for taking so long to answer your last most welcome letter.[44] I have been up to my ears in work as a result of leaving the [Rand Daily] Mail to undertake my research project. After more than five years on the paper, I am almost part of the furniture there, and leaving has been an almighty wrench. I am, however, receiving a monthly retainer and am also going in to work every Sunday night.

I saw your wife a few days ago and can report that she is keeping well. When I asked after the children, her face lit up – which is perhaps the best indication of their welfare that I can give you. I am sorry that her projected trip to Cape Town did not come off, but as you no doubt know, she will be down for several weeks from later this month. I shall be seeing her before her departure in case I can be of any assistance to her. Mrs. Eulalie Stott of Cape Town was up here recently. She is keen to give you all possible aid and I discussed ways and means with her.

As requested, I sent off the originals of your academic certificates to Oxford with a letter that the certificates should be returned to me. I was under the impression that you intended doing your studies through the University of South Africa. If this is in fact your intention and you are encountering any administrative difficulties, please let me know so that I can try to get them sorted out.

44 Given the volume of their subsequent correspondence, and the obvious closeness of their relationship, it is notable that there were not more letters exchanged between Sobukwe and Pogrund between 1960 and late 1963. This might be accounted for by the fact that Sobukwe was moved from one prison to another during the initial years of his sentence, and several letters may have been lost as a result. Pogrund (2015: 173–4) notes also, though, that there was a break in their contact after Sobukwe's arrest. "I cannot explain it, but remain ashamed of my behavior. I was badly shaken by my near-death after the shooting at Sharpeville and, looking back, perhaps unconsciously I linked Sobukwe personally with the episode."

I hope the parcel of books has now reached you and that they have given you some pleasure. Dr. Ellen Hellmann[45] has given me another batch of books and I will be sending this down to you soon. Also, Ernie Wentzel[46] is arranging for the London "Observer" to be sent to you, while I have arranged renewals of the "English Digest" and "John O'London".[47] Please let me know if the mix-up with the Reader's Digest has been sorted out yet and also whether there are any other papers or books you want. Mrs. Stott, by the way, will ensure that you continue to receive the Mail, the "Sunday Times" and "Sunday Express".

I am sorry that you have been caused distress in reading the Mail. When I read your statement ("I have had to bite my teeth at times as I read your views") I tried to think back to which of my articles could possibly have upset you so much.[48] I cannot recall any in the past few months in which I have

---

45 Ellen Hellmann (1908–82) was an anthropologist who studied at the University of the Witwatersrand – she was the first woman to obtain a DPhil from the university – where she subsequently worked at the Jan Hofmeyr School of Social Work. She was a vocal critic of the apartheid government, and a founding member of the Progressive Party, serving on the party's executive between 1959 and 1971. She served as the chairperson of the multiracial Joint Council of Europeans and Bantu, and was a prominent figure in the South African Institute of Race Relations, whose annual *Race Relations Survey* she edited for many years.

46 Ernie Wentzel (1933–86) was a founding member of the South African Liberal Party and an advocate who served as the chairman of the Johannesburg Bar Council. He was twice detained by the South African security police, in 1960 and 1964.

47 A weekly literary magazine, which ended in the 1950s but was revived for a short while in the early 1960s.

48 It is unclear which of Pogrund's articles Sobukwe may have taken exception to. It is worthwhile flagging a prospective ideological tension that may have been at play here. White South African liberals were, as a rule, opposed to *any* form of racial discrimination and committed to the ideals of non-racialism. Sobukwe, on the other hand, while maintaining a vision of a future Africa beyond the divisions of race, nonetheless favoured an explicitly Africanist agenda. As leader of the PAC, he had prioritised the immediate needs of the oppressed African majority. Doing so necessitated asserting independent African political agency and leadership beyond the scope of white influence. Hence, the PAC's policy of political non-collaboration with whites (an approach that would likewise be adopted by Steve Biko and the Black Consciousness Movement in the 1970s). Given that this has long been a contentious – and misrepresented – issue, it helps to cite Sobukwe directly. In an article he wrote for the liberal newspaper

expressed very strong views one way or the other – which might, of course, be an indication of how well-adjusted I am to the current South African situation.

Did you see our recent series of articles on the Churches, and if so, what did you think of them?[49]

I was in Basutoland recently and saw Z.B.[50] He is teaching there and keeping reasonably well. He sent you his best wishes.

I shall be in Cape Town in January or February for several weeks and am looking forward to being able to visit you, although I do earnestly hope that you will have been freed by then.

In the meantime, very warmest greetings to you from Astrid and me. We hope that your spirit remains as high as it has been and that your courage is not flagging. We pray for your welfare and that of your family.

Contact on 30 May 1959, Sobukwe says: "Our contention is that the Africans are the only people who, because of their material position, can be interested in the overhaul of the present structure of society. We have admitted that there are Europeans who are intellectually converts to Africa's cause, but, because they benefit materially from the present set-up, they cannot completely identify themselves with that cause... Politically we stand for government of the Africans for the Africans with everyone who owes his only loyalty to Africa and accepts the democratic rule of an African majority, being regarded as African." Contrary to those who accused Sobukwe and the PAC as racist for excluding whites, Sobukwe makes it clear that while his primary political loyalty is to Africa, *all* who share such a democratic political loyalty to Africa should be regarded as African and eligible to join the Pan Africanist struggle. Although Sobukwe's stance was politically defensible, it did earn him the suspicion of many whites (including liberals) who alleged that he was guilty of reverse discrimination. For more on Pogrund's discussions with Sobukwe on this – the dangers of a type of black racial exclusivity within the PAC, and the PAC being perceived as anti-white – see Pogrund's *Robert Sobukwe: How Can Man Die Better*, (2015: chs. 8 (p. 104 particularly) and 13 (pp. 204–5). For a helpful discussion of the ideas of non-racialism in the South African historical context inclusive of the perspectives of Sobukwe and the PAC, see Soske (2015).

49 Pogrund conducted a series of interviews for reports in the *Rand Daily Mail* in which he questioned a number of South African church leaders on their views on apartheid (see Pogrund, 2015: 195).

50 Z.B. Molete.

Robert Sobukwe
to Benjamin Pogrund,
20 November 1963 (Ba1.5)

Dear Benjie

Thank you for your interesting and most welcome letter. I was on the point of writing to thank you for the trousers. I just couldn't have chosen a better shade myself. If that is what you call breaking with conservatism, Benjie, then you are a first class gradualist![51]

Congratulations!!! Your interviews were superb. You discontinued them too soon. I could picture your victims squirming and ah-ah-ing, attempting to put you off with the usual meaningless pious platitudes.[52] But you brought them back to the point mercilessly. I felt like the small three-year old fellow whose mother woke up one night in the midst of a tremendous thunderstorm and hurried to his room fearing that she would find him terrified. But there he was at the window, jumping up and down and shouting with excited joy as each flash of lightning burst across the sky, "bang it again, Lord, bang it again!" I, too, felt like shouting, "hold him, there, Benjie, hold him there!" Thanks, old chap, it was a kingly banquet.

Incidentally, in the story of the little boy, are there any cultural points that suggest whether he is white or black? What are they? I'll be glad to get your answer and that of any "expert" you may feel inclined to sound.

Thank you for news about my wife and the many friends who have offered help. I wrote to my wife three weeks ago suggesting that we should discontinue subscription for the Rand papers. They arrive here rather late. For instance today is Tuesday (I have postdated the letter) and I received Saturday's Daily Mail and the two Sunday papers today. In addition I wanted today's Cape Times and yesterday's Cape Argus. And except for an odd item or two, the Cape Times, particularly, covers the same field as the Rand papers. And it isn't as if I lack reading material, Benjie. I have enough and to spare, thanks to you and my many friends.

---

51 A joking reference to a gradualist model of political change, one to which Sobukwe's own political activities within the PAC clearly did not adhere.

52 Sobukwe is referring to Pogrund's interviews with South African church leaders mentioned in Pogrund's letter of 7 November 1963.

I have renewed my subscriptions for the Reader's Digest. But I gave them a piece of my mind. They have continued sending my copies to Pretoria. I didn't receive the July issue. The Colonel, here, lent me his own copy. Then came the August issue. But not the September and October issues. The November issue has been sent here to me with the information that they have noted my change of address. Work efficiency, indeed!

I am doing Economics, Economic History, British Government, Introduction to International Law and Ethics as applied to Social Organisation as the five subjects required in the Part I of the B.Sc. Economics degree. But, oh, the amount of reading required! The books alone will cost over £110 or R80 in the new currency. Were I outside I would be able to borrow most of the books from the library, but being here, I have no option but to buy them. That is the reason I am cutting down on newspapers. One of the journals recommended is *The Listener* and Mrs Marquard, fortunately for me, keeps me supplied with copies of that.

Thank you for sending the certificate No,[53] Benjie. I did not intend you to make any other arrangements. I have applied to the University of London for registration and am awaiting their reply. The lectures I get from Wolsey Hall, Oxford, and have already received the first two. I am taking my time over this course and will write the Exam, Part I that is, in 1965 June. I felt that entering for the 1964 exams would entail high pressure swotting in a field that is absolutely new to me. In any event they demand that external students do the course in five years though, for one who has a degree, they are prepared to make concessions.

In one of her letters to me my wife told me I have a very good friend in you. I did not need her to tell me that. I knew it. But coming from her, it was quite a compliment. She has a very poor opinion of my sense of judgment, you see.

My thanks to Ernie [Wentzel] and Mrs Stott. I believe it was God's will that I should come here to realise how much Iove there is in the world and to get my sense of values right. Above all else I have had a chance to know myself – neither saint nor devil: just a bundle of capabilities in the hands of God.

I wish you every success in your project. I know you will enjoy the work.

My love to Astrid and Lady Jennifer.

Yours sincerely
Robert

---

53 Number.

Benjamin Pogrund
to Eulalie Stott,
25 November 1963 (Ba1.6)

Dear Eulalie,

Mrs Sobukwe did not telephone me before her departure, as I had arranged with her to do, and I was unable to see her again. I hope that, despite this, she did telephone you when she reached Cape Town and that there have been no difficulties about her accommodation.

As advised, please let me know if I can be of assistance during her stay down there.

With best wishes,
Sincerely,

Robert Sobukwe
to Nell Marquard,
6 December 1963 (Bd2.14)

Dear Mrs Marquard,

Thank you for your letter, the books and the regular flow of "The Listener".

I enjoyed the "conducted tour" through Greece very much indeed. When I was doing matric history, we had a section known as Ancient History in our syllabus. It dealt with the glorious past of Greece, among other things. And the Parthenon and the Areopagus featured prominently, and we enjoyed their sound! I can therefore appreciate your feelings when you saw them in the flesh, so to speak, battered though they are. And your description of the scene of the blind boy is most touching. Unfortunately I am not modern enough yet to be able to pretend indifference to an act of kindness.

Thank you, also, for the book. I have finished reading The Leopard.[54] I made the mistake of reading the critics' comments before reading the book with the result that when I had come to the last page I could not but feel, as some poet felt of the Skylark, I think, "Thou didst not sing to Shelley half so sweet a song, as Shelley sang of thee"[55] – with apologies to the literary figure I quote.

It is very kind of you to offer to send me "recreational" books. But it won't be necessary just yet. I have over a dozen books here that I haven't read yet and a friend in Johannesburg has written to say that more are on the way. Please believe me when I say that you couldn't have helped me more than by sending me "The Listener".

My wife was here last week with my little boys – the twins. She has gone back to fetch our two elder children who are at school in Basutoland. She'll be arriving back here late next week and will have to return to Joh'burg by the 11th to resume her duties. We spent some pleasant hours together. The twins were seventeen months old when I went to jail. They are five years two months exactly today (6th). I am looking forward to seeing them all next

54 Giuseppe Tomasi di Lampedusa, *The Leopard* (1958).

55 This is a quote drawn from an article by Israel Zangwill entitled "Without Prejudice" which appeared in the *Pall Mall* magazine in January 1894. The reference is to Percy Bysshe Shelley's famous poem "To a Skylark".

week. Incidentally, I celebrated my 39th birthday yesterday (5th, fifth) – my fourth in jail.

I shall not make this letter a long one, lest you feel you have to do the same! Unfortunately, my wife has not told me where she is staying in Nyanga East[56] and I cannot, therefore, give you her address. She has left the twins with friends in Cape Town.

Wishing you and your family a God-blessed Christmas.

I am,
Yours sincerely,
RM Sobukwe

56 A "location" in Cape Town.

Benjamin Pogrund
to Robert Sobukwe,
11 December 1963 (Ba1.7)

My dear Bob,

As always, your letter, which arrived last week, gave us great joy. In our concern for you we were glad to see that your letter reflected a spirit as cheerful and courageous as ever.

With your wife with you at the moment, I have no doubt that you are even happier. I am only sorry that it was not possible for her to spend more time with you. I had a note from Mrs. Stott yesterday saying that your wife and children were well settled in Cape Town and that they had not felt it necessary to take up the hotel accommodation which Mrs. Stott and I had arranged. I am looking forward to seeing your wife as soon as she returns, to have first-hand news of you and to learn whether there is anything we can do for you.

Your wife, by the way, worries us: despite my urgings, she so seldom asks for any assistance! My worry stems from my fear that she might be reluctant to ask. If you know of any such reluctance on her part, I do hope you will tell her not to hesitate to approach me at any time.

By now all the various papers should be reaching you and I trust they are a pleasurable means of whiling away the hours. Don't worry about getting the "Mail", "Times" and "Express" – they will be ordered for you all the same. Last week I sent you a copy of a booklet containing the series of articles on the Church which the Mail published.[57] After reading your kind words of praise about the series, I just had to send you the booklet! I cannot answer your question about the little boy – perhaps because I am too colour blind and only saw him as a little boy.

In regard to your University studies, why not send me a list of the books you need? I might be able to obtain at least some of them from friends and save you the expense of buying them. Also there is a government Library in Pretoria which lends books to students and sends the books through the post.[58] I think of this because some while ago I wrote a story about some

57 The series of articles was entitled "The Church and the Race Problem" and was based on interviews with a number of churchmen, white and black.

58 The State Library, now part of the National Library of South Africa.

prisoners who were studying in gaol, and the Library contacted me to advise me of the facilities they offered. If you are interested in finding out whether the Library has the books you require, let me know and I will get the address for you.

As I have previously told you, I shall be in Cape Town in January, working in local libraries etc., for my research project. I plan then to see you on a purely personal basis, as a friend. But, if possible, I would also like to be able to spend additional time with you discussing my research project which, as I think I have mentioned, is a study of Communist influence in Non-White politics. I have made tentative enquiries in Pretoria and believe that any formal application which I might make to the authorities for a formal interview with you for my research might be favourably considered. But before I make any such application, I obviously must first know if it meets with your approval. If you approve, I would be in Cape Town on January 15. Could you let me have your views on this as soon as possible so that, if necessary, I can arrange for travelling and accommodation?

Little else to tell you at the moment. I am fully immersed in my work and know little (and care less) of what goes on in the world around me. Zef [Mothopeng] has not been too well lately, but you will have seen reports about this in the newspapers.

Warmest good wishes to you from Astrid.

Robert Sobukwe
to Veronica Sobukwe,
December 1963 (Bc10)

Hello Darling,

I didn't think I should wait until I heard from you. I just had to "talk" to you!

I don't need to tell you that I miss you and the kids terribly and that all day Wednesday, Thursday and Friday I was following you in my mind from one station to another. I do hope you had a safe and comfortable journey. You should, though, because I entrusted you to the Everlasting. Amen!

Buti and Tshawe[59] have come to see me on Friday. They were both looking fine though they said Tshawe had been terribly sea-sick. You remembered that we discussed Buti's car and you were wondering whether he had changed it or not? Well, he has. And he has got himself a 1963 car straight from the box! In the excitement I forgot to ask him what make it was. They arrived at noon, in fact, at 1 p.m. and they had not yet got halfway with the things they wanted to tell me when the time came for them to go.

How [illegible] faring? Don't forget to send me those photographs now you have brought Dini and Mili back to their proper weights.

I have fought a roaring battle against the fruit you left and am just keeping a few oranges and one or two mangoes for Christmas Day.

Although Christmas Day will have passed when you receive this letter, believe that you are in my thoughts and I wish you the best Christmas you have ever had; rich and full with the love and peace of Christ, so that you will enter the New Year with your head high and your mouth filled with laughter and praise.

Cheerio Little Woman!

Love to the kids and Mama.

Your loving husband,
Mangi

59 Sobukwe's brother Ernest and his wife.

1964

Sobukwe's isolated living quarters during his time on Robben Island.

Robert Sobukwe
to Veronica Sobukwe,
23 January 1964 (Bc11)

Hello Darling!

Thank you for your most interesting and delightful letter. It was a pleasure to read, reminiscent of the 1950s when you were still a little girl jumping around the Tennis Court!

Benjie had already assured me that you were well. I had been worried by your silence particularly as you had been unable to secure bookings for you and the children. I should have known better, of course, but I did expect you to send a telegram if only to assure me you had arrived safely.

Thanks for news about the kids. They really are a bouncing & energetic lot! Dini will have his hands full disciplining those two. Incidentally I sent him a birthday card and have asked Benjie to buy him a book as a birthday gift from me.

Fabian has written and has promised to send R50 to cover the cost of the book I require. Benjie has taken the lists away with him to try and raise the books from friends. I am extremely fortunate really & am constantly reminded of God's challenge and promise. "Prove me now, says the Lord of hosts, if I will not open the windows of Heaven for you and pour out a blessing, that there shall not be room enough to receive it" (Malachi 3: 10).[1]

Thank you for your prayers, Kid. Keep on, do not despair. He is ever faithful to His word. We are in His hands and we are, therefore, safe. I was extremely pleased and happy to hear Mili and Dini pray so freely. After all prayers are conversation with a Father whose love for us is unmeasurable and who is so rich that there is nothing we can ask Him that He cannot give us provided it is for our good.

A lady in Cape Town sent me biscuits and sweets for Christmas and Buti and Fabian had also brought me some fruit, sweets and cakes. But I still had all the tinned stuff you had left and I almost overate during that week!

---

1 The full verse from Malachi 3 reads as follows: "Bring the full tithe into the storehouse, that there may be food in my house. And thereby put me to the test, says the Lord of hosts, if I will not open the windows of heaven for you and pour down for you a blessing until there is no more need."

Benjie complains that you do not ask him for assistance as often as he would like. And Professor Wellington has repeated his plea that I should ask you to see him because both he and his wife are anxious to meet you and to help in whatever way they can. I [illegible] have warned both him and Benjie that knowing you as I do you will have to be in real difficulty before you will ask anybody for assistance and that includes your husband!

I am glad to learn Mili and Dini are back to normal. By the way, I read that there is difficulty now in getting children to schools in the Protectorates.[2] How have you fared? I know you must be frantic with anxiety. Don't worry, darling, if you don't get your way. God is the only one who can see into the future. And nothing will interfere with His plan. I mean this. I am not just trying to console you. Do your best and He will show you the way.

Buti has written. He says they reached home safely. He left Cape Town before Tshawe. I was wrong. They both came by train. They left the car behind. He says [Charles?] arrived home penniless and gave me his excuse that he is saving for Mercy!

I am praying you get that week end.[3] To see you is to be back at Lovedale, "under the oaks". Cheerio Darling. Love to the kids, Mama & Jabie.

Your loving husband,
Mangi

2 Bechuanaland, Basutoland and Swaziland.

3 A possible reference to when Veronica might again be able to visit him at Robben Island.

Robert Sobukwe
to Nell Marquard,
23 January 1964 (Bd1.2)

Dear Mrs Marquard,

Thank you very much for the Christmas card, your letter, and the books. I have enjoyed the *Smith of Smiths*[4] immensely. I haven't had such entertainment for years! Not even [Jonathan] Swift with all of his dissections could so effectively ridicule and demolish dearly-held "convictions"!

What struck me most forcibly, of course, is how unoriginal the "mass-mind" is. The same arguments are used, generation after generation, to justify prejudice. What does "change" are the locale and the objects of prejudice. It does prove, doesn't it, that education as such is no cure for prejudice.

I must say that I was not a little surprised to learn that you were in your sixties. I met your husband[5] in Pretoria, in 1959 when we both attended the "Bantu Authors' Conference" and I put him down as an executive in his late forties. I haven't met you, of course, but whenever I read your letters I have a picture of a tall lady with nothing to suggest that she was a day older than thirty-five.

I had quite a pleasant time with my wife and the children. I had quite a few tales to tell them – in spite of the African taboo against relating folk tales during the day. The guilty party, it is said, will sprout horns. It is but a sign of the times that my kids laughed such ideas to scorn. The twins (boys) were a year and a half old when I left home and have now attained the manly age of five. Fortunately for me they were satisfied, at first sight, that I was the fellow their mother told them so much about.

---

4 Gerald Bullett, *Sydney Smith: A Biography and a Selection* (1951). Sydney Smith was an Anglican clergyman and noted wit. Sobukwe refers to this book in his letter to Mrs Marquard of 16 October 1968.

5 Leo Marquard (1897–1974) was a prominent figure in South African liberalism. He founded the National Union of South African Students (NUSAS) in 1924, and was likewise instrumental in establishing the South African Institute of Race Relations (1929) and was a leading figure in the founding of the South African Liberal Party in 1953. He was the author of *The Black Man's Burden* (1943), a commentary on South African politics published under the pseudonym John Burger, and *People and Policies of South Africa* (1950). He worked as head of the Oxford University Press in Cape Town during the 1950s and early 1960s.

I had to give up gardening because of the dry season which has hit our water resources very hard. My plants which were coming up most splendidly put up a prolonged and heroic resistance except for the carrots and beetroot and beans which threw up the sponge quite early in the fight. And yet they had been the most ostentatious.

Thank you for the copies of "The Listener." I am finding them very useful. My New Year resolution was to keep my letters short so that my friends would have a chance to read other matter. To prove that I am a man of integrity, I'll say "Tot siens".[6] Greetings to your family.

Yours sincerely,
RM Sobukwe

P.S. I shall let my wife know. Thank you.

6 Goodbye.

Benjamin Pogrund
to Robert Sobukwe,
24 January 1964 (Ba2.7)

My dear Bob,

I was happy to have the chance of seeing you again, and to find you in such good health and spirits. I am deeply grateful to you for your assistance in my research.[7] Quite apart from the detailed and authoritative background to events which you gave me, I found our general discussions stimulating and of tremendous value in gaining perspective. I can only repeat the assurance I gave you: the study will be as objective and balanced as any human-being can make it.

I saw your wife soon after my return and can report that she is keeping well. She also assured me that she was not in need of anything! She told me that the application for an exit permit has already been sent to the Minister of the Interior.[8] She is posting your spectacles to you as requested.

---

7 Pogrund is referring to his study on the Communist influence on black politics in South Africa (previously mentioned in his letter to Sobukwe of 11 December 1963), for which he secured a grant from Stanford University and a year's leave from the *Rand Daily Mail*. The influence of communists and white liberals in watering down the Africanist agendas of the African National Congress had been one of the crucial reasons that Sobukwe had broken with the ANC. Sobukwe was, as such, not only an expert but a historical participant within the broader topic of Pogrund's research. It is curious, given the monitoring of Sobukwe's letters, that this overtly political topic was not censored and that Pogrund had been granted permission to meet with Sobukwe to discuss this topic. Sobukwe and Pogrund were of course aware that this was an unusual concession. The government had perhaps hoped – so Pogrund (2015) speculates – that he would be able to bear witness to the fact that Sobukwe was being neither starved nor beaten, as was alleged by PAC leaders. Furthermore, given the inevitable monitoring and surveillance that took place in these meetings, they provided the government with a way of finding out what was on Sobukwe's mind. Sobukwe "understood the game as well as I did", reports Pogrund. "We worked on the premise that the room was bugged ... We spoke of personal matters and of our families and friends. We scribbled a few notes to each other when we had especially private details to convey" (2015: 199).

8 Sobukwe had been offered employment in the United States by the National Association for the Advancement of Colored People. An "exit permit" meant he would be entitled to leave South Africa but never to return.

Enclosed please find a clipping from the "Rand Daily Mail" of January 21. As you will see, the story was considered too long and was therefore reduced in length. Because of typographical errors – the bane of my existence – parts of it are nearly incomprehensible.

I am also returning to you the lists of books for your studies which you lent me. You need not worry about getting the books – I have been able to arrange for them and they should start reaching you shortly.

Recalling that, in May last year, the Minister of Justice announced that you would be able to receive visitors weekly, I wonder whether we could perhaps arrange for University of Cape Town lecturers in your various fields of study, to visit you regularly. A couple of hours discussion now and again with lecturers in economics, British Government, Public International Law, etc., would certainly, I think, be of immense value to you in doing your correspondence courses, which otherwise could be dry and barren. If you consider this idea worth pursuing, it might be best to approach the jail authorities first and ask whether they would be agreeable to allowing a selected panel of UCT[9] lecturers to visit you.

Incidentally, due to unforeseen circumstances, I have had to change my plans for visiting Cape Town. Instead of coming on February 1, I shall be there on March 1. All being well, I hope to see you then. I suggest you keep the notes you are working on for me until then. The month's delay will not affect me.

In the meantime, I have sent you, per passenger train, a batch of books for leisure time reading.

All for now, Bob. Look after yourself and let me know if there is anything you need.

Astrid sends her very best wishes.

Sincerely,

9 University of Cape Town.

Benjamin Pogrund
to Veronica Sobukwe,
5 February 1964 (Ba2.8)

Dear Mrs. Sobukwe,

I wonder whether you have now been able to obtain Dini's address? Even though his birthday is past, I am anxious to comply with Bob's wishes in sending him a present.

If you have the address, I shall be grateful if you will let me have it as soon as possible.

With best wishes,
Sincerely,

Robert Sobukwe
to Veronica Sobukwe,
12 February 1964 (Bc12)

Hullo Little Woman!

What did you mean I am quiet down here? I have written you two letters since your visit. The first I wrote even before I knew whether you had reached home safely or not!

Thanks for the news, Kid. I was particularly relieved to learn that Mili and Dini had gone back to school. Thanks also for news about the autochthons.[10] They are indeed a very lively lot. To which school have you sent them? If you've sent them to Mili's *Alma Mater* then you'll have to teach them English yourself. Otherwise they'll be writing you the type of incomprehensible letter that Mili's principal wrote to us – remember?

Yes, it was a pleasure to see and talk to Benjie, particularly as the subject on which he is working is one in which I am very interested. He hasn't changed a bit – except that he has lost some weight I think.

I am glad about the news concerning Mrs Pullen. She hasn't told me that she wrote to you. All she did was to ask me how old the children were, and to say how sorry she was at not being able to meet you. She thinks "Mrs Sobukwe must be a wonderful woman". You know my reply to that. She is one of the two Cape Town ladies I told you about who have "adopted" me spiritually. She has sent me a number of very valuable books on religion – books that have helped me to understand Christ better. She sent me cookies, sweets & fruit for Christmas. I'll write to her on your behalf.

Thank you also for the Twenty Rands. I didn't need the money really badly. You must need it more than I do. I'll use it to get some of the books or if friends can't [...] for me. Apart from those that Fabian undertook to get, Benjie has arranged with various friends that they provide me with as many of the books listed as they can.

What I said about registration, Darling, was that the fee was £10 (Ten pounds) and that I had to be registered before December (last year). I sent the money off immediately and received the Registration Certificate through the

10 That is, the children.

British Embassy. I have applied [illegible] to write the Part I Examinations next year. So you don't need to worry about that any more.

Nenti has written, too, complaining that she last saw the children in 1961. She has no idea, of course, of the expenses involved and the distance to be covered to make an annual trip home.

You don't know "Boy", by the way Buti's Mercy knows him. He is Sis [illegible]'s son and left home eleven years ago. Nenti writes to say he is visiting them – he has returned after these many years. She didn't say whether he has a wife or not.

Your friends have not yet sent the buttons I asked for. Did you get a chance to have the kids photographed? May I expect my photo?

Incidentally, among my files there are some ordinary KHAKI FILES with no clips to them. I need about six of them for my lectures. Could you give them to Benjie to bring along with him?

The nights of late are extremely lovely, just as they are at Graaff-Reinet in summer – cool and clear. Here there is the added attraction of the seagulls screaming like children just out from school. And waves lapping the seashore. All poetic – like you.

Who sent your telegram to Fabian? Didn't you do this yourself? He has written to me too. We have been exchanging views on poetry and music of late. But we are both of us stubborn. I think if we were to meet face to face we would argue until the following morning! I have asked him to collect folktales, proverbs, riddles and songs. If he had a tape recorder he could get the old men and old women to relate these and record them. I should like to get Northern Sotho ones particularly as well as Shangaan & Venda ones. You could also collect as many as you can from friends & others [illegible]. DO YOU HAVE THE TIME?

Give my love to the kids when you write to them. Did Dini receive his birthday card? I asked Benjie to send him a book and a birthday message on my behalf. God bless you, Child!

Love to Mama, Jabie & the kids.

Your loving husband,
Mangi

Robert Sobukwe
to Veronica Sobukwe,
6 March 1964 (Bc13)

Hello Darling,

Again I write before I have received a reply from you because, as I said before, it is a pleasure to do so.

Thank you for the R20 (Twenty Rands) and the interesting news. Fabian, too, has written and enclosed a cheque for R50 (Fifty). I am submitting my order for the books I require. I have been unable to do much in Economic History so far because the textbook deals in broad generalisations while the course, judging from the notes and the tests, requires a great deal of detail.

Benjie wrote to say he would be coming down on the 1st March. I have not heard from him yet. I don't know how he has succeeded in collecting the books he hoped to get for me.

I heard over the radio that there had been a train accident at New Canada. And I was relieved to learn there were no deaths. Human beings are selfish really because my first thoughts when I heard of the accident [illegible] yet the other men whose wives and children were on that train love their wives and children just as much as I love mine. We still have a very, very long way to go in our *spiritual* evolution to reach the stage Christ occupied over 2,000 years ago!

I miss you, of course, terribly, particularly on Sunday, when I know you are home – doing washing as usual!

[...]

I have written to Mrs Pullen to thank her on your behalf, but she will still expect and appreciate a direct letter from you. So when you do have a few minutes to spare do scribble a few lines to her, Child, please.

Have you heard from Den's wife?[11] She did not reply to my letter and I am just wondering where she is and what she is doing. I advised her to continue with the shop.

I do not know whether driver's licences are easy to come by in Cape Town or not, but the accident rate down here is phenomenal. I am sure I would spend sleepless nights if I knew you were coming down here by car. Almost every day someone dies in a road accident down here. At this rate they'll be forced

11 Dennis Siwisa's wife.

to increase public transport and ban private driving altogether, although of course the motor dealers will kick up a row if such a measure is as much as mentioned!

Do give my love to Mama and Jabie [illegible].

Thank you for your prayers, Kid. I, too, never forget to commend you and the children to His care and keeping. And up to now we can honestly say He has done for us more than we had ever hoped for. And He will continue to do so Darling. He *NEVER* breaks a promise. But we must keep our side of the bargain too – love and forgiveness. That is all He asks from us.

Give my love to Mili and Dini when you write to them. I am extremely proud of them all. And of *you* most of all. You're a rare girl – one who has taught me more about the love of God than all the books that I have read on the subject. And you've done it, Little Woman, just by being your natural self, without any pious talks or looks. God bless you, Child.

Your loving husband,
Mangi

Robert Sobukwe
to Veronica Sobukwe,
2 April 1964 (Bc14)

Hullo Darling!

Thank you for your letter. I had thought I had outgrown the "school boy" stage of excitement at receiving letters from you. But I haven't. I still find it a great comfort to read your letters over and over again.

Yes, it was a lovely time we had in our little cottage. I keep thinking about it – how we started off with exactly one chair in the kitchen and no furniture whatsoever in the Dining Room. It's been an uphill struggle, Little Woman. But, with the grace of God, we made it. Together, side by side, bit by bit, we converted those four walls into a home, fit for the children to grow up in.

[...]

Your telegram reached me a day before Benjie visited me. He promised to write to you immediately to tell you he had seen me and I was looking well. He appears to have put on weight since I saw him in January. He assured me that the books would be arriving any day and has undertaken to get the shoes, pyjamas and shirts I need. So don't worry about those. Only I didn't remember to tell him that the shoes should be broad-toed. Please advise him so if he comes to see you before buying them. I am also still well-off for cash. I won't be needing any just yet.

It's a pity you can't see my quarters. I have just been provided with curtains for the "kitchen" and the "lounge" – lovely mustard and orange curtains. The "kitchen" walls are a light blue and the lounge has a "modern" two-tone!

Winter is setting in and the rains will soon be falling. I'll be able, therefore, to take up gardening again. I feel so frustrated sometimes when I see lovely items in the Press advertisements that I would have liked to buy for you and the kids. But I'll have to resist the temptation because anyway I no longer know what sizes you and the kids now wear.

I wrote to Mrs Pullen and thanked her as you had asked me to do. I am glad you enjoy their fortnightly tracts. Benjie was rather annoyed when a friend told him you were being flooded with these tracts. I also receive them. We'll discuss them when next we meet.

Your remark about the kids playing in the mountains where their grandfather grew up was also made by Buti in a letter I received the same day as yours. Is it a case of two great minds thinking alike?

Yes Fabian told me they had named their son after me. I felt flattered and told him so. A pity about Jabi but I hope she'll settle down soon. Thanks for news about Mercy. Charles is absolutely quiet.

How are Dedani and Dali getting on? I miss those guys. They are irrepressible. I am glad you've managed to shake the cold off. Yes I remember the joke you mention. What a queer language English is!

I had a quiet Easter, but felt strangely elated. Sang some hymns on Good Friday & Easter Sunday, full-blast and was just short of audience (congregation is the word) to preach to. It is quite alright singing to oneself, but when one preaches to oneself one's sanity is immediately questioned. I am still sane enough to remember that!

[...] You remember Peter's sister?[12] Well I learn from Nenti that she too is at Healdtown[13] now. It is really surprising how these Graaff-Reinet people, poor as they are, still manage to give their children a tolerably good education.

How is Ma-Mpanza? Give my love to her please. I am sorry I did not know her when she was still younger. She must have been a very lovely girl. No wonder "indlondlo" fell for her so heavily!

Love to the kids and Jabi.

Cheerio darling.

Yours ever,
Mangi

---

12 This may have been a reference to Sobukwe's fellow PAC leader Peter Raboroko.

13 The famous Methodist school at Fort Beaufort, which Nelson Mandela had attended.

Robert Sobukwe
to Astrid Pogrund,
7 April 1964 (Ba2.11)

My dear Astrid,

Benjie has been twice to see me and assures me that both you and Jennifer are well and that you are back at varsity. I was really glad to know that you were able again to pursue your studies.

Benjie has also told me of the disgusting letter you received.[14] I am sorry that you have been caused so much pain and embarrassment. But I do hope that you will regard the letter as the malodorous product of a putrid mind and treat it with the contempt it deserves.

I was sorry I couldn't see you in Pretoria but I was happy that you had finally met the Zodwa[15] of your lectures!

Benjie told me he would be another week or so in Cape Town. Will you tell him from me that I am absolutely delighted with his choice of EVERY single item? In future I'll send him my size only and he can experiment to his heart's content with colour-combinations and fashions. Even the shoes which I first viewed with alarm (I am rather conservative, I admit!) are extremely comfortable and the pyjamas are a peach! The record player too, has arrived and I had a few turns on my creaky joints in the solitude of my room!

I do not know, though, what he would like me to do with the underwear. We had agreed on three sets. But when I opened the box I found they had sold him six briefs. There wasn't a single vest. Unfortunately I do not have his Cape Town address. I would then have contacted him immediately.

I must say you're looking well after Benjie. He's looking fine. And he assures me that he is a model husband and father. And knowing him as I do, I take him at his word, of course.

---

14 Pogrund (2015: 207) viewed this smear letter as the result of his reporting on the rise of black political power in Swaziland. His reporting "was not appreciated by … the white settlers there and I guessed the poison was from one or more of them". Pogrund notes also that he was touched that Sobukwe devoted one of his rationed letters to write a consoling note to Astrid.

15 Veronica Zodwa Sobukwe.

Wishing you every success in your studies and a happy and blessed re-union with Benjie.

I remain,
Yours very sincerely,
BOB

Robert Sobukwe
to Veronica Sobukwe,
13 April 1964 (Bc15)

Hullo Darling,

Thank you for both your letters although the last one was just a note really, and for the Ten Rands.

Before I proceed to our own "boloton" I should just like to let you know that Benjie has arranged that I get regular supplies of tobacco and fruit and has also purchased all the items of clothing I mentioned in my letter to you. It's all very expensive stuff he has bought and all of it top quality. So then, darling, there'll be no need for you to send any "allowance" in future. I'll let you know, Child, if there is anything else I need. The corduroy trousers, of course, are for someone with a waist twice the size of mine. But I am hoping to have that fixed. The shoes are very modern ones – a type I never thought I would wear. But they are extremely comfortable. He appears determined to wean me from what he terms my "conservative tastes"!

I remember you telling me when you visited Witbank that Theba was working on his car, but you did not tell me it had broken down, Sweet. How the blazes did you get back to Joh'burg? I don't think he'll ever buy a sound car. He just loves working with spanners and things. A sound car would leave him with no work to do.

Both Mercy and her husband are silent. I don't hear a word from them.

Thanks for news about the kids. How did Dini like the book he received for his Birthday? Incidentally, the record-player has arrived and more records will be coming soon. I have asked for the Messiah so that I may again conduct an invisible choir!

You can't imagine how proud Buti is that Mili and Dini can speak Sotho so fluently. If he had his way, you would be Mrs Rabohoe now. I can't agree to that, of course. I love the position as it is, where we are a mixture of all the major African tribes. We just need a Shangaan wife for Dini and perhaps a Venda one for Dedani and we will be all right.

In her letter to me, Nenti gave her address as 464. I do not know how to interpret this, whether as a mistake or whether as an indication that they have bought the house next door. If it is the latter, then they are definitely becoming bourgeoise.

Thanks for news about Den's wife. As you say, it is understandable that her in-laws should not favour the arrangement. But I agree with you that she will manage the shop well. And he, too, will be happy to know that his business is carrying on.

It was kind of you to write to Mrs Pullen. I haven't met her either. I don't know whether she has told you – her husband died suddenly about nine months ago. She still hasn't got over the shock apparently. But she is quite a brave lady.

Yes, Fabian told me they had named their son after me and that he was born on the 5th Dec. Father Webber, too, wrote to inform me that he was leaving for the U.S.A. on Good Friday.

Well, Little Woman, so long for now. God bless you and the children. Love to Mama and friends.

Your loving husband,
Mangi (I can HEAR you call me that!)

Robert Sobukwe
to Nell Marquard,
17 April 1964 (Bd1.3)

Dear Mrs Marquard,

I enjoyed your letter a great deal and can assure you that I didn't blame you at all for the delayed reply. I blamed the prison authorities – as I usually do. It provides me with something to grouse about. In any case I don't wish you to feel obliged to reply except at your convenience. Yes, my letters to and from my friends do take rather long.

Thank you for your comments on education, although I think you are being a little severe on the democratisation of education. In all ages, really, real thinkers or what sociologists call "opinion-holders" have been a miserable minority. What mass-education and the mass-media of communication have done has been to increase not only the numbers but also the absorptive ability of the opinion-followers. English visitors to America have often commented on the identity of views held by most Americans. But the phenomenon is universal really. It is not pleasant to hold an unpopular view as all communists in America, capitalists in Russia, Christians in Asia, and Protestants in Spain will bear out.

I, too, enjoyed Trevor Roper's[16] articles. In fact I have found "The Listener" extremely informative. Thank you indeed for the regular flow.

Oh yes there is a taboo on relating folk tales by day. Very little has been done to collect folk tales in this country. No, I have not read the book that you mention but I agree with you that folktales throughout the world are strikingly similar. In animal tales what generally differ are the "heroes" and the "dupes" with unpredictable Africa holding up the *tortoise* against

16 Hugh Trevor-Roper (1914–2003) was a renowned British historian and Oxford University professor. *The Listener* published his lectures on "The Rise of Christian Europe", later collected as a book, in November and December 1963. Trevor-Roper did not have a high opinion of African history, saying in 1963 that "Perhaps in the future there will be some African history to teach. But at present there is none, or very little: there is only the history of Europe in Africa. The rest is largely darkness." This is worth noting, because although Sobukwe evidently had much in common with Nell Marquard's reading interests, there would also have been ideological trends within some of this material that Sobukwe would have been opposed to.

all-comers! – transporting him to the USA in your Uncle Remus's stories.[17] There are certain experiences that appear to be common to peasants throughout the world and these experiences are reflected in their folklore. And, of course, stories "travel".

Thank you for your offer of seeds. I shall certainly need them. Onion and cabbage I still have but would be glad to have the others you listed. I do not know what type of fertiliser one would require for this soil and will leave the decision to you.

I have had two visits from Mr Pogrund this year and they were refreshing indeed, although I found myself groping desperately for words! Of course, I could remedy that by talking to myself regularly every day. But I am afraid that would alarm the prison officials who would most certainly conclude that I had taken leave of my senses. But of course I could do it indoors!

Again, thank you for the "little kindnesses".

Yours sincerely,
RM Sobukwe.

17 Uncle Remus is the narrator and eponymous character of Joel Chandler Harris's series of books (c.1881) based on African American folktales of the late 19th century and told in the genre of animal stories and songs. Harris was originally praised for telling the stories through the character – and in the Southern African American dialectic of – the fictitious kindly freeman Uncle Remus. By today's standards these stories – featuring the well-known characters Br'er Rabbit, Br'er Bear and Br'er Fox – are racist both in terms of the "old Uncle" stereotype and their patronising attitude to African Americans.

Robert Sobukwe
to Veronica Sobukwe,
8 May 1964 (Bc16)

Hullo Darling!

Bennie has by now been to see you, I think, and to assure you that I am well. He has probably informed you, too, about the numerous arrangements he has made for my care and comfort. I don't know what he would not have bought if I had allowed him!

I woke up this morning with our wedding anniversary in mind. It's quite a stretch, Little Girl. And you have become more marvellous, year by year. Of all God's blessings on me – and they have been very many – I thank Him most for you. Unfortunately I cannot send you any gift because I would like to choose it myself and it would be known only to us two! But my love and gratitude you have in plenty.

I received a letter from Lauretta [Ngcobo] the other day. She tells me they have a baby daughter – the third in an unbroken succession!

Mrs Pullen has written to inform me that she has received a letter from you and is about to answer it. Father Webber, too, sent me a card from England. He was in top form as usual.

When Benjie was here, I advised him to look up some of the Psalms of David. I mentioned particularly, Psalm 26. I had made a mistake. The Psalms I recommended stretch from Psalm 121 to Psalm 126. But the particular psalms are 126 and 91. Please tell him so. And about the shoes, Baby, the ones he bought are just perfect! They are, of course, "modern" and not at all the type *I* would have bought. But having worn them, I find I like them very much and will probably stick to that type in future.

I am bearing in mind that yours and Mili's birthdays are coming up soon. I hope to be able to get appropriate gifts for the occasions.

Well, Little Girl, this was merely to say "how do you do?" Just a phone call! I'll write again, soon. Remember, I am proud of you!

Love to Mama and the kids. I am writing to Fabian, too.

Your loving husband,
Mangi.

Robert Sobukwe
to Nell Marquard,
15 May1964 (Bd1.4)

Dear Mrs Marquard,

Your "note" arrived before I had answered your letter. Thank you for both of them. Particularly the letter. It was so AFRICAN! As Prof. Wilson[18] will tell you, when you ask an African how he is, you're in for it. You'll get a report on the weather and the state of the crops, the state of health of his family relatives friends, recent deaths and births and finally the assurance – with which, incidentally, the report was prefaced – that by and large things are not bad. A carry-over, most probably from the days when communications were primitive. Common, perhaps, to all peasant populations so that, strictly speaking, I have no right to make the chauvinistic claim that it is TYPICALLY AFRICAN!

Please say "thank you" for me to the person who has given you the money to buy me books. What I should like to have are the dramatic works of the younger English playwrights, particularly (John?) Osborne and Brendan Behan. ANY work of theirs will do, though *Borstal Boy* by the latter, judging by reviews, is a masterpiece.[19] The only stipulation I shall make then, with your gracious permission, is that the money be spent on the works of modern dramatists – excluding G.B.S.[20] (I have all his works). I still have plenty of reading material so that you can take your time over the bargaining.

No, I did not know Prof. [W.M.] Macmillan.[21] He was at Wits before my time. I have read his books though, including "The Cape Coloured

---

18 Professor Monica Wilson (1908–82), who was Professor of Social Anthropology at the University of Cape Town from 1952 to 1973. Previously she had taught at the University of Fort Hare and Rhodes University. Her famous monograph on the Mpondo was based on fieldwork for her Cambridge PhD and entitled *Reaction to Conquest.*

19 Published in 1958, *Borstal Boy* is an autobiographical coming-of-age account of Behan's three years of detention within a juvenile borstal during which time, despite his Irish republican allegiances, he comes to befriend a series of English inmates.

20 George Bernard Shaw.

21 W.M. Macmillan (1885–1974) was, in 1917, made the first professor of history at the Johannesburg School of Mines (later to become the University of the Witwatersrand). He

Question".[22] That was when I did "Native Administration" for my degree.[23] Nor is Governor Barkly[24] a complete stranger to me. I met him in that involved series of "Kaffir Wars".[25]

Yes, I read about Mary Harrison and her old friend at Paarl. It's not only been a pleasant friendship, though: it's been rewarding too. Thank you also for the spicy bit on Mrs Sigcau no. 5.[26] Talk of Hollywood!

I have been puzzling over the identity of Gladys Mgudlandlu.[27] I still am not sure whether it is the same woman as was at Healdtown at the time I was there 1940–46. She does appear to be making her mark in the art world which to me is an absolutely foreign one.

Thank you also for the garden stuff. I haven't received it yet but it most probably is on its way.

The Catholic priest, Father Webber, who cared for me while I was in Pretoria jail is on a fund-raising mission in the U.S.A. He spent a few days in Britain and while there sent me a postcard with a picture of Piccadilly Circus. He then passed on to New York from where he sent me another postcard, with

---

is regarded as the founder of the liberal school of South African historiography.

22 The title of Macmillan's book, first published in 1927, was *The Cape Colour Question* and was based on the papers of Dr John Philip.

23 Much is being left unsaid by Sobukwe here. It was while studying Native Administration at Fort Hare that the full extent of the injustices of apartheid became evident to him; this was a turning point in the development of his political consciousness and his commitment to the struggle against white supremacy.

24 Sir Henry Barkly (1815–98) served as the Governor of the Cape Colony and High Commissioner for Southern Africa between 1870 and 1877, and was notable (given the current context) not only for being a supporter of the Cape's non-racial constitution of the time – which he felt would not survive any negotiations with the Boer Republics for a confederation of South African states – but also because he played an important role in assisting the growth of the Cape liberal tradition.

25 Also known (in colonial historiography) as the frontier wars and (by critics of colonialism) the wars of dispossession. "Kaffir" was already in the 1960s a pejorative racial term.

26 Probably one of the wives of Botha Sigcau, a chief of Eastern Pondoland who was an early supporter of the National Party's Bantu Authorities policy. Later he became the first president of the so-called independent Transkei.

27 Gladys Mgudlandlu was a South African artist and educator (1917–79) who qualified as a teacher in 1941 at Lovedale College. She held a solo exhibition in Johannesburg in 1964.

a picture of Lower Manhattan & Brooklyn Bridge. What a contrast the two pictures present! Mature age and aggressive youth: culture and wealth.

I know this is not in your line but it is just possible that you have read in the papers about the decision of the Ghana Boxing Board to declare *their* boy the world champion.[28] I had a good laugh over that one. That's the Dark Continent for you – always something new! What an editorial I would have written on the subject! That's where Britain stands streets above us. The British can laugh very heartily at themselves. We're losing all sense of humour.

Thank you for the quotation from [W.B.] Yeats. We'll get there, don't you worry. "The cow and the bear shall feed: their young ones shall lie down together ..."[29] in this world of ours! God bless you.

Yours sincerely,
RM Sobukwe

---

28 Sugar Ramos of Cuba, the defending world featherweight champion, was initially awarded a split decision over Floyd Robertson on 10 May 1964 in the first world championship bout to be contended in Accra. The Ghanaian Boxing Authority subsequently over-ruled this decision, declaring Robertson the winner.

29 A quote from Isaiah 11: 17: "The cow will feed with the bear, their young will lie down together, and the lion will eat straw like the ox."

Robert Sobukwe
to Veronica Sobukwe,
22 May 1964 (Bc17)

Hullo Darling!

You've been complaining rather consistently about my silence and yet I know that I write at least two letters to your one, Child. For instance, I wrote you one on the 8th of this month. I have not yet received a reply to it but because it is a pleasure to me merely to write to you, I am writing this one.

If I did not thank you for the Easter card and the R10 (Ten Rands) please accept my most humble apologies, darling. Not only was the Easter message your card contained a lovely one but the very idea of your sending me one warmed my heart immensely. You belong to a rare class of women. I want you to know that and remember it, so that should I one day so forget myself as to hurt you in any way – I am mortal, after all, and "to err is human" – you will remind me of this, my testament!

Thanks for news about the kids. I need not tell you I miss you all. [...]

Mercy has written to tell me she failed. She is taking her failure very hard indeed and I really do sympathise with her. It can't be pleasant to think that she has to go back to Bara[30] when she thought she had finished with the place for good.

I shall be writing to Benjie next week. In the meantime, please tell him I have received the books he sent. I shall read the two that concern his subject very carefully and will make necessary comments. Tell him also that Father Flexmoor of the Roman Catholic Church came to see me on Sunday, 17th May. He has promised to call again.

Winter has set in with a vengeance and I am consuming gallons of coffee. I shall have to take your advice and alternate with tea, otherwise I'll end up with CCF[31] (that's the correct terminology, isn't it?)

---

30 Baragwanath Hospital, Soweto, where she was presumably studying as a nurse.

31 Congestive Cardiac Failure.

I am expecting some records of the "Messiah" and will be able to play and hear again "For Unto us a Child is Born"[32] which always reminds me of Dini's babyhood.

The fruit arrangements are working out fine and I am having plenty of fruit, so you need not worry over that score. I had intended, for your sake, to give up smoking. But I feel it will be too much of a strain just now. So I hope you won't feel I have let you down. Don't worry your head about cancer. I won't contract it. I'll die from old age, Little Girl, quietly, in a cool room with my children and great grandchildren around me. That's a promise!

I'll write again, very soon. Keep that head high, Sweet. "Underneath are the everlasting arms."[33]

Incidentally, I shall have to write to Mama and thank her for bringing you up. She did a splendid job!

Love to them all and particularly to Zodwa!

Your loving husband,
Mangi

32 The well-known chorus from Handel's *Messiah*.

33 Deuteronomy 33: 27 reads: "The eternal God is your refuge, and underneath are the everlasting arms. He will drive out your enemies before you, saying, 'Destroy them!'"

Robert Sobukwe
to Benjamin Pogrund,
30 May 1964 (Ba2.21)

Dear Benjie,

Thank you for the books, the needle, and the sponge. I am happy also about the arrangements you have made for fruit. What hasn't arrived yet is the tobacco assignment and I am just wondering whether you intend to make alternative arrangements about that also.

I have finished reading *An African Student in China*[34] and am now busy with *Africa and the Communist World*.[35] I am finding the latter most interesting. It is scholarly and well-documented and I am sure will provide you with a number of hints with regard to your own studies. Incidentally, I hope that the latter are going on well.

Father Flexmoor has been to see me since your last visit and has promised to come monthly. I asked my wife to refer you to Psalm 91 (ninety-one) specifically. That is the psalm I had in mind when I spoke to you.[36]

There is nothing new to report. The sea is still full and the wind still blowing which is proof, I am told, that no hydrogen bomb has been dropped anywhere.

My wife wrote to say she had received your letter and that, like me, she lacked for nothing – materially.

I know you are worried about me, particularly in the light of the latest "leakages".[37] But I think you should know me well enough by now to realize that when next you meet me you'll have no difficulty in recognizing the Bob you know. That is diplomatic language, isn't it? A lot of words uttered but nothing really concrete said.

---

34 *An African Student in China*, by Emmanuel John Hevi, was published in 1963.

35 *Africa in the Communist World*, a collection edited by Zbigniew K. Brzezinski (later, President Jimmy Carter's National Security Advisor), first appeared in 1963.

36 Psalm 91 (Qui habitat) is commonly invoked in times of hardship.

37 Sobukwe is referring to the constant surveillance of his communications and, presumably, those of his comrades and allies.

I'll write more next time. Am not feeling particularly bright today. Greetings to Astrid and Jennifer.

Yours sincerely,
Bob

Benjamin Pogrund,
213 Diamond Exchange Building,
De Villiers Street, Johannesburg,
to Robert Sobukwe,
11 June 1964 (Ba2.24)

My dear Bob,

Please forgive my delay in writing to you. I had to leave for Rhodesia unexpectedly soon after my return from Cape Town. In addition, at that time, I was reluctant to write to you as I would have had to give you news which I know would upset you. Astrid and I have separated and divorce proceedings are being instituted. At this stage, there is no hope of a reconciliation. Last night, however, she agreed with me that the divorce should be postponed for three months for a "cooling off" period, during which time she would also undertake psycho-therapy. The insoluble tragedy is our little daughter, to whom we are both passionately devoted. I am sorry to have to break this news to you, Bob, as I know it will distress you.

Before I left for Rhodesia, I made arrangements for your wife to visit Cape Town again to see you. She told me that she hoped to go during June. I have not yet been able to contact her since my return, but hope that she is already with you or on her way to see you.

By now, you should have received all the study books which you require. Last month I sent you four parcels of study books (I think four was the number) and I trust that they reached you safely. Friends of mine have confirmed also the consignment of books to you from overseas. I am glad that you have found the Hoover Institution book of value.[38] I haven't yet had a chance to read it myself, but plan to start on it during the next few days. Would you like me to send you other books of a similar nature? In addition to all these, there is a man up here who intends sending you a monthly supply of reading material

38 The Hoover Institution at Stanford University, California, is a conservative public policy think tank that also engages in publishing. The Hoover Institution would later produce a number of titles on South African politics, including a transcript of the Rivonia Trial. Pogrund is probably referring to *Africa in the Communist World*, edited by Zbigniew K. Brzezinski, which the Hoover Institution published in 1963.

and I have given him an outline of your tastes. This was easy in view of your catholic outlook!

Is the fruit of sufficient quality and quantity? Please reassure me on these points. In regard to the tobacco parcel, I have today written to the Defence and Aid Fund in Cape Town enquiring about it. As your letter was written on May 30th I think it likely that the parcel has now reached you.

I am still trying to discover what has happened to the subscription to the "Observer". Acting on the advice of the Robben Island authorities, I wrote to the Chief Magistrate in Cape Town enquiring about the matter. This has led to a protracted and confused correspondence in which letters are flowing in to me from the Magistrate and from the Secretary for Justice. I am not too sure why the Secretary is involved in the matter, and I don't think he is either. In any event, the gist of it all is that the Magistrate has not been receiving the newspaper and therefore has not been holding it back from you. I have arranged for the issue to be taken up with the CNA[39] and I hope that the paper will soon be arriving.

Is the clothing all right? Do you need more? You know that you must not hesitate to let me know your needs. The same, obviously applies to books and anything else that you may require.

I have had a hurried look through the notes you prepared for me and only wish I knew how to express my appreciation adequately. Thank you very, very much for your help, Bob. Your insight is penetrating, but above all you are fair and balanced throughout. As soon as I have the chance, I shall take up one or two points and ask you whether you would care to expand on them.

I had a good trip to Northern Rhodesia and gained quite a deal of valuable information. I saw a lot of Professor Z.K. Matthews[40]who reminisced about

---

39 Central News Agency.

40 Zachariah Keodirelang Matthews (1901–68) was one of South Africa's most distinguished intellectuals. He was admitted as an attorney to the Johannesburg Bar before leaving the country to study at Yale and the London School of Economics. He was affiliated with Fort Hare for many years, as lecturer and head of the African Studies Department. In his thirties he became increasingly involved in political activities, particularly within the ANC. He lent support to the 1949 Programme of Action, served as ANC provincial president of the Cape, and proposed the idea of the Congress of the People in 1953. Matthews was one of the accused in the infamous Treason Trial, which aimed to persecute all those involved with the Freedom Charter and its aims of ending racial discrimination. He was held in detention for six months in 1960, after he played a key role in the calling for consultations

your student days. He told me that he had predicted a brilliant future for you, but had warned you to be careful in using the power of your personality! He asked me to convey his warmest good wishes to you. The same regards come from Dr. Robert S. Bilheimer,[41] of whom I have previously told you. He remains a good friend. Also regards from other whom I saw – Lawrence Masinini, Mayekiso and Mike Mafase and others who were with him.

I have asked Julius Malie in Basutoland to arrange for photographs of your children to be taken and he has promised me that it will be done. I am writing to him again to check on the matter.

In accordance with our discussion on the last day we spent together, I took up the matter in Pretoria.[42] I did not do it in Cape Town simply because I was too scared! But I was well received and I was promised immediate action. I have not yet heard whether this was in fact carried out.

This is all for now. I hope that you have recovered from the depression which was so evident in your letter of the 30th.

My very warmest good wishes to you,

Sincerely,

---

among African leaders. In 1966 he was offered the post of Botswana's ambassador to the US, which he accepted.

41 Dr Robert S. Bilheimer (1917–2006) was an American Presbyterian theologian. He was one of the co-founders of the World Council of Churches (WCC), and it was in the capacity as WCC delegate that he met with representatives of the Christian denominations in South Africa to address the issue of apartheid in 1960.

42 Reflecting back on this comment, Pogrund (2015: 210) remarks: "I was still plugging away trying to bring about his release. At this distance of time I cannot remember exactly what I tried to do. Whatever it was, it was done in consultation with Sobukwe and must have been unorthodox and risky." A further point of contextualisation should be added. Pogrund (2015: 210) notes that as of May 1964 "the government's wooing of Sobukwe was at an end. Once the realization came that he was not going to change his ways and was not willing to be co-opted, the pleasantness and co-operation were replaced by increasing obstructionism."

Robert Sobukwe
to Nell Marquard,
19 June 1964 (Bd1.5)

Dear Mrs Marquard,

Thank you very much for your letter, the books and the edibles. I noticed, incidentally, that the chocolates were labelled "dark" and wondered whether you had made the choice in reference to my colour prejudices! They were a real and rare treat for my palate but I would hesitate at this stage to say that their palatal success was primarily due to their colour.

Your letter was not "scatty" at all: only it was a voice and not a pen – the kind of letter one reads with an ever-widening smile.

I enjoyed the plays – particularly [Brendan] Behan's. We belong to the same club, you know and share a common "historical experience". Laye's book was all you said it was – the work of an artist: an adult's tale told by a child.[43]

Thank you for the picture of Gladys Mgudlandlu. I am afraid, though, I still cannot say whether it is the same person. For one thing, she is carrying more than her fair share of weight and would probably look different from the sweet-sixteen I knew at Healdtown. This is no criticism. My wife is in the same position – a condition which would have reflected creditably on me if she had carried this poundage ("surplusage" is rather indelicate) while I was with her. But since the expansion has taken place in my absence it will most likely encourage the thought that the "poor child" is well-rid of this tyrant who starved her into unwifely proportions.

I am sorry I cannot provide you with the editorial on the Ghana Boxing Decision. Besides the fact that my letter would be too lengthy, such an editorial, I have decided after careful reflection, would be an act of disloyalty to the idea of an African Personality,[44] in vindication of which it was that

---

43 Camara Laye's novel *The African Child*, based largely on his own childhood in Guinea, was published in 1953, and is one of the earliest major works in francophone African literature.

44 The notion of an 'African personality' was invoked by African leaders and intellectuals such as Kwame Nkrumah and Kenneth Kaunda to refer to the cultural uniqueness among Africans as reflected in their attitudes, behaviour, beliefs, customs and societal norms. It referred also to the distinctiveness of explanatory frameworks – religious,

Floyd Robertson[45] entered the ring. And what a fine job he did of it! – as all the disinterested spectators who jammed the stadium and the impartial referee of international standard who, unlike the criminal judges at the fight, is not a lackey of the imperialists, so aptly decided. To add insult to injury, just a week or two thereafter, the pattern was repeated in Senegal where the local Boxing Board had to reverse the decision of the judges who had deprived the local hero of victory in spite of the fact that all who had paid money to see the fight (and that made it possible for these same criminal elements to be paid) were solidly behind the local boy!

I haven't had time yet to find out what "The Daily Graphic"[46] – an oppositionist propaganda sheet which calls itself an independent newspaper, has had to say on the matter. I'll pass its comments on to you. I won't be surprised if it ridicules the Board's decisions. It is an extremely unpatriotic paper whose task appears to be to belittle African achievement.

Thank you for your friend's offer of warm clothing. It couldn't have come at a more appropriate time! What I would be happy to have are blankets – two will do and, if it is not too much, a pullover. I am not sure that I appreciate the difference between a pullover and a slip over. However, what I would like in that line is a long-sleeved garment, whether V- or crew-necked. The size is 42.

Oh – the garden stuff arrived. I am sorry I did not inform you earlier. Thank you very much for it. I can't report anything yet. I am still watching to see what the infant mortality rate will be.

Thanks for reading so far!

Yours sincerely,
RM Sobukwe

---

cosmological – and the particular social and political systems that have developed historically across the African continent.

45 Floyd "Klutei" Robertson was a Ghanaian professional boxer. He fought Sugar Ramos on 9 May 1964. Although Robertson was initially awarded the fight, the decision was later reversed.

46 State-owned newspaper published in Ghana and established in 1950 by the London Daily Mirror Group.

Robert Sobukwe
to Veronica Sobukwe,
9 June 1964 (Bc42)

Hullo Darling,

You will by now have received the letter I wrote on the 22nd May, so that I am still ONE UP!

Thanks for the news. I am really glad you've been able to find time to go to the pictures, even if it were for only one day. I have heard that "The Ten Commandments" is an imposing picture.[47] But, of course, Hollywood can be relied on not to stick to the facts as they are, but to glamourise them. I won't be surprised if in this picture of Creation or something that they are making, Eve wears a bikini! Trust Hollywood to introduce an anachronism.

I am very eager to [illegible] about Mili and Dini. My girl is growing fast. It's time, I think, you got her a bicycle, even if it means digging into your savings! There's no better exercise for a growing girl – in the cities, that is.

Fabian has sent me a copy of an article of his which was published in the S.A. Medical Journal![48] It is quite an achievement, really, and I hope he maintains the intellectual interest in his profession which his article so clearly shows. I'll be writing to him next week.

I am extremely excited at the prospect of seeing you again soon. In fact, I am almost ashamed of my uncontrollable excitement. It does not become a man who is approaching FORTY and is the father of FOUR children into the bargain! It is almost schoolboyish excitement I am experiencing – the same as I felt in 1949 at Lovedale! I have been bewitched!

With regard to the boat's time-table I think the position remains unchanged viz that on Sunday, Monday, Thursday and Saturday, the boat arrives in the morning and returns in the afternoon.

On Wednesday, it arrives in the morning and returns at noon.

On Tuesday and Friday it arrives at 12.45 p.m. and returns in the afternoon.

---

47 The 1956 religious epic produced and directed by Cecil B. DeMille.

48 Fabian Ribeiro, "The incidence and treatment of iron-deficiency anaemia in an African general practice", *South African Medical Journal*, vol. 38, May 1964.

Now, darling, please remember the khaki files I asked for – five of them will do and my spectacles. If you can't find the spectacles, Kid, don't worry. I still can do without them.

I have been receiving postcards from Father Webber from all over America. He seems to be enjoying himself immensely.

Well, darling, love to the kids. I'll have quite a number of stories to tell them when next we meet. Love to Mama, Jabie and the rest.

Keep your chin up! Till we meet,

Your loving husband,
Mangi

Benjamin Pogrund
to Veronica Sobukwe,
1 July 1964 (Ba2.33)

Dear Mrs. Sobukwe,

Thank you very much for your letter of June 24. I was delighted to learn that you will soon be going to Cape Town to see Bob.

I have not been able to come and see you as I have been heavily involved preparing for another trip to Rhodesia. I am leaving tomorrow and will be back towards the end of July. So I shall probably not be able to see you before you go to Cape Town.

In regard to your accommodation in Cape Town, I have today written to Mrs. Stott advising her of the position. I suggest however, that you write to her direct as soon as you receive a decision from the Minister of Justice about your request to stay on the Island. As soon as you hear from the Minister, will you please confirm with Mrs. Stott that you will require accommodation at the Tafelberg Hotel?[49] Will you also advise her whether it is only for yourself or for the children also?

As my marriage has broken up, I am no longer staying at my previous address. The best way to contact me is at my office – telephone: 23-5714.

In regard to the school fees, I am sorry there has been a delay in repaying the money to you. Could you please send the receipt so that the exact amount can be known to: Miss Pike, P.O. Box 97, Johannesburg. I have spoken to Miss Pike, and she will send you the money as soon as she gets the receipt.

I look forward to seeing you again when you return from Cape Town. Please give Bob my very warmest good wishes.

Yours sincerely,

P.S. Mrs. Stott's address is:
c/o Cape Town City Council,
City Hall,
Darling Street,
Cape Town.

---

49 The hotel was in Constitution Street in District Six, then a largely "coloured" area of Cape Town.

Robert Sobukwe
to Nell Marquard,
22 July 1964 (Bd1.6)

Dear Mrs Marquard,

I read of your unpleasant experience, and I sympathize with you most sincerely. But then, as you know, the twentieth century has discovered a new deity – the State. And of course Africa, as you and I know, though lovable, has a madness all its own!

Thank you indeed for the blankets. They could not have arrived at a more opportune moment. And thank you for the jersey also. Were it not that I had feared the telegram would be too costly, I would have added "Cold where is thy sting, winter where thy bitterness?"[50]

My wife will be in Cape Town this Saturday and will be staying there for about a fortnight. I don't know yet where she'll be staying, but I shall ask her to contact you. She is, unfortunately, quite a stubborn little girl, quite unlike her very humble, docile husband! Incidentally, I read that she has applied for my release. Well, she told me nothing about it. The report was, however incorrect in one respect. – I have not made any personal (or non-personal even) request to the Cabinet for my release.[51] The only letters I have written are friendly ones, like this, to my friends.

---

50 See 1 Corinthians 15: 55: "Oh death, where is thy sting".

51 This was a point of considerable political importance for Sobukwe: he would not petition the apartheid government – which he viewed as wholly illegitimate – for release. To do so would be "to play their game", to cede them a degree of legitimacy. By the same token, Sobukwe was determined that he would not accept any form of "charity" from the apartheid state. Hence his insistence that his wife and children pay for their own meals on the island while visiting him, and the constant need – so evident in his correspondence with Pogrund – to raise money for books, clothes, a heater, etc.

Nelson Mandela and Sobukwe differed on this issue of petitioning prison authorities for better conditions or greater privileges, as Mandela (1994) describes in *Long Walk to Freedom*:

"I have always respected Sobukwe, and found him a balanced and reasonable man. But we differed markedly about...prison conditions. Sobukwe believed that to fight poor conditions would be to acknowledge the state's right to have him in prison in the first place. I responded that it was always unacceptable to live in degrading conditions and

Thank you, too, for the books. [John] Galsworthy and [George Bernard] Shaw have always been favourites of mine. And it was a real pleasure to make [John] Osborne's acquaintance as well as [Doris] Lessing's.

Please give my thanks to our mutual friend for the Yorkshire Products. The jersey was an aesthete's choice.

Have you read of the underground ocean of fresh water discovered in the Sahara? "And the desert shall blossom"![52]

I haven't heard from Graaff-Reinet yet – my home town, unfortunately! The place has always bred rebels it appears. I'm expecting my brother to tell me of the stock losses they have suffered. He thinks Graaff-Reinet is the capital of the Republic.

With best wishes,
Yours sincerely,
RM Sobukwe

---

that political prisoners throughout history had considered it part of their duty to fight to improve them. Sobukwe responded that prison conditions would not change until the country changed." (323)

52 Isaiah 35: 1: "the desert shall rejoice and blossom as the rose".

Robert Sobukwe
to Benjamin Pogrund,
6 August 1964 (Ba2.35)

My dear Benjie,

I am sorry I delayed my reply so much. But as you no doubt realize your news stunned me and I was hoping that my wife would be able to enlighten me so that I should know what unsolicited advice to give. Unfortunately she is as ignorant as I am of the circumstances surrounding the case. I can, therefore, only stupidly but sincerely advise, Benjie, that you do not allow your pride to make a reconciliation impossible. Please remember the long rough road you two have travelled together and then forget and forgive whatever wrongs you think you have suffered. So much for that.

My wife is around, Benjie and thank you for making it possible for her to come.

The tobacco supplies are coming in regularly with books and records. Also, I have received all the books pertaining to my studies, except books on Social Philosophy. Not one on this list has arrived. If it is because they are unobtainable, then don't worry, Benjie. The prescribed textbooks will do.

Thanks for news about Prof Matthews. He's right, he did give me some such advice.

Yes, I enjoyed the Hoover Institution books and will be happy indeed to get more.

I was surprised to learn you found my letter reflecting a mood of depression. I probably wrote it on a day I wasn't feeling too bright. But you can rest assured depression is not my regular mood.

I haven't received "The Observer" yet. But since so much trouble appears to be involved I don't think you should bother about it further.

Incidentally, I have just read Gordon Winter's report on the interview he had with me in Pretoria Prison in October 1962.[53] It was my first contact with it and I found it an outstanding piece of imaginative writing.

I am glad you found my [*The remainder of letter is missing.*]

53 The report entitled "Sobukwe Not Ill-treated" (*Sunday Express*, 28 October 1962) quoted Sobukwe describing his current physical condition as "Fit and well". In response to allegations made by his former PAC associate Potlako Leballo, according to which he (Sobukwe) was being subjected to horrifying and brutal conditions of imprisonment, the journalist Gordon Winter quoted Sobukwe as saying, "Leballo's report is entirely untrue and without foundation". It is perhaps this last statement that Sobukwe has foremost in mind when characterising Winter's writing as "imaginative". This being said, Pogrund (2015: 199) does note that Sobukwe "insisted on going public to repudiate the allegations of his poor conditions [on Robben Island]". Winter was later revealed to be a spy for BOSS, the Bureau for State Security. He later fled South Africa and published a book about his spying career, entitled *Inside BOSS*.

Benjamin Pogrund
to Robert Sobukwe,
1 September 1964 (Ba2.36)

My dear Bob,

I was so glad to hear from you again, and to know that you are keeping well and in good spirits.

Your concern about the divorce is much appreciated. I regretted having to break the news to you. But unfortunately it is a fact which cannot be avoided. One can only try and resolve not to make the same mistakes in the future.

The non-arrival of the London "Observer" is baffling. I have reported it to the donor who asks me to convey his apologies to you again. The subscription was definitely taken out months ago, and we are determined to ensure that the paper reaches you. The matter is again being taken up.

The non-arrival of the Social Philosophy books has also surprised me. My difficulty is that I no longer have the lists of subjects and books which you gave me, as I handed them out. But speaking from memory, wasn't your brother-in-law supposed to be getting these books? I seem to recall your telling me this. If I am wrong, can you please send me a list of the needed books and I will attend to it immediately.

Have all the other books arrived safely? And how are you doing with your studies? Are you able to concentrate on the books?

Also, how are you placed for reading material? You know that if you want more reading books, you have only to advise me and I will send down a carton-full.

I was glad to note that the cigarettes, records etc., are arriving regularly. Are the supplies of fruit also being maintained, and is the quality satisfactory? A few weeks ago I arranged for the fruit to be continued for another three month period and I trust that there have been no difficulties about this.

Can you also let me know how the record player is operating, what records you have and whether you want any others?

This is quite a list of questions I have put to you! I have omitted anything concerning your needs, *please* do not hesitate, as always, to let me know without delay.

My work has slumped badly recently. It has been a trying time.[54] An atmosphere of crisis, in which one is so deeply involved through close friends, is hardly conducive to sober, academic work! But I am now forcing myself back to my papers, and am having reasonable success in this.

Someone has sent me an article on you which appeared some while ago in the "Zambia News". I am enclosing it for your interest. Your comments, by the way, on the "Sunday Express" and "Sunday Times" reports have aroused great mirth among my friends.

I don't think I have told you about the results of the representations I said I would make. Coming at this stage, it will not surprise you to learn that they were turned down.

Since dictating all the above, I have seen your wife and was happy to find her well. She assures me that she is not in need of anything. While I was glad to have first hand news of you, I was distressed to learn that, apparently, you have not been receiving the supplies of fruit. I shall be writing direct to the Robben Island Officer Commanding about this. As you know, your wife will be able to take her annual leave at the end of December so that you will be able to look forward to seeing her again then.

There is little else to write about. What with personal difficulties and the general atmosphere at the moment, life is pretty strained.

Look after yourself. I pray for your continued welfare and for your courage and spirit to continue unabated.

Sincerely

---

54 Pogrund is referring to the detention without trial of a number of his friends and colleagues.

Robert Sobukwe
to Veronica Sobukwe,
17 September 1964 (Bc18)

Hullo Darling!

In my last letter I threatened to start divorce proceedings if by this date I had had no word from you yet. Well, I have NOT heard from you yet and it is exactly a month today since you left. But I'll withdraw my threat! My love for you grows with each day that passes. At this rate, by the time I am eighty I shall be kneeling to kiss your feet every time you enter the room! I am scared at the thought because I really would not like to be such a slave, not even of an extraordinary woman like Zodwa!

Well, Kid, how is the night-duty going? How many babies have you delivered already? You must be having your hands full, I believe, for sociologists report that the poor are prolific breeders.

I received a letter from Benjie two days ago – on the 14th to be exact and he tells me he saw you and you assured him that you were not in need of anything. Apparently, the question of his divorce is settled and there's nothing else we can do to help. It's a pity, though. It is always sad to see a marriage break up and all the high hopes with which the young couple started off dashed.

Have you done anything about the radiogram yet? It will be difficult, of course, now that you are on night duty unless your day off falls on a convenient week-day.

We have had bitterly cold weather – in fact we are still experiencing it and according to the radio the whole country is shivering.

How are the autochthons? I miss them a lot and still can't understand how Dali has changed in so short a time into a self-sufficient, confident little fellow.

This won't be a long letter darling. I feel much better after having written these few lines. Love to Mama and the kids. And God bless you Little Girl.

Your loving husband,
Mangi

Robert Sobukwe
to Nell Marquard,
17 September 1964 (Bd1.7)

Dear Mrs Marquard,

Thank you very much indeed for your letter – cheerful and quietly courageous as usual. And thank you also for the books which you choose with the uncanny skill of a mind-reader. I have always wanted to read [Henrik] Ibsen but just never got round to doing so. Now my education is complete!

I don't think you need fear that you are overloading me with plays. I have an insatiable appetite for them. And I find the modern dramatists an interesting lot. Incidentally, I really enjoyed [Eugene] O'Neill's "Ah! Wilderness." It could have been any home, anywhere. Truly, "There is only one man in all the world. And his name is All Men."[55]

My wife was very happy to have met you and thoroughly enjoyed the brief moments she spent in your company. Thank you very much for making her feel at home. I have not yet received a letter from her though she sent a telegram to inform me she had arrived safely. If all goes well, she should be down here again just before New Year's day. But she'll be accompanied by the children this time and will probably put up in the location. There is no room for children to play in a hotel: so she says at any rate.

Yes I was born and bred at Graaff-Reinet. And what memories I have of the place: still covered with thick bush and with the loveliest prickly pears imaginable. I saw the bush disappear and houses rise and streams run dry.

---

55 Sobukwe used these same words when he was president of the PAC. In his 2 August 1959 'State of the Nation' speech he intoned: "There is only one man in all the world, and his name is All men. / There is only one woman in all the world, And her name is All women!" In 1956 the poet Carl Sandburg (1878–1967) used these words – drawn from his own poem "Times Weep" (1963) – in introducing the "Family of Man" exhibition at the Museum of Modern Art in New York, adding a further sentence: "There is only one child in the world and the child's name is All children".

I know Reinet House very well[56] and "Werda" which we used to pass on our way to and from the rugby field near the Show Grounds. We used to fight daily running battles with the students who stayed there.

The "Murray" I know personally is "Bobbie" Murray of Broederstroom, who, in the 1930s was a young man who dominated the local Stock Market. Our auctioneers then were the Pohl Brothers. My father was employed by Jack Tilbrook & Co., the leading wool merchants in the town. And as he had passed Standard four, he was a registered voter![57]

There was also the shop of Kingwill and Murray, later known as "Kingray". But I never knew either Mr Kingwill or Mr Murray of Kingray.

I spoke Afrikaans fluently as a child though never so well as either my mother or my eldest brother both of whom, up to this day, can deliver an impromptu sermon in that language. My father, on the contrary, never learnt to speak Afrikaans but was recognized locally as an authority on Xhosa which he loved and spoke with a rare beauty.

Graaff-Reinet Xhosa, of course, is a species on its own, spoken in an area covering Nouwpoort & Hanover in the north and Aberdeen, Jansenville, Pearston etc in the S.W. It bristles with "maars" and "dans" and "togs", "assebliefs"[58] even having "ronanti" (goeie naand) and "rondara" (goeie dag)[59] as forms of greeting in place of the traditional "bhota" or the modern "molo" (môre). You'll excuse my spelling. I never *studied* Afrikaans.

I have read Mr V.G. Davies' complaints about the "incorrect" forms of Xhosa used in the Magistrates' Courts.[60] He makes the mistake many Europeans who know a Bantu language make. They not only think that the language they know is THE Bantu language but they are genuinely grieved

---

56 Reinet House was built between 1805 and 1812 as a Dutch Reformed Church parsonage. It and Werda were men's residences for the whites-only Graaff-Reinet Teachers Training College.

57 There was a system of qualified non-racial franchise in the Cape Province, which had been carried over from the Cape Colony, and was later abolished in 1936. This entitled suitably qualified Africans to vote in elections for the (largely white) Parliament.

58 That is, "buts", "thens", "after alls", "pleases". To avoid confusion: Sobukwe is noting how what he calls Graaff-Reinet Xhosa is populated with many Afrikaans phrases and conjunctions.

59 That is, good night and good day.

60 V.G. Davies was an inveterate writer of letters to the editors of Cape Town newspapers in the 1960s.

to note that it can stoop to *borrowing* as all other languages do! The modern approach to language study, however, is not prescriptive but *de*-scriptive. And the forms he complains of are widely used. Those he prefers are just NOT used by children. Unfortunately the Magistrate's clerk or interpreter who corrected him chose to demonstrate his knowledge of comparative philology and succeeded very brilliantly in demonstrating his ignorance. Why won't the shoemaker stick to his last?[61]

So should I. God bless you.

Yours sincerely,
RM Sobukwe

61 Or, in terms of a more current phrase: "Stick to what you know".

Robert Sobukwe
to Veronica Sobukwe,
24 September 1964 (Bc19)

Hullo Darling!

This is the fifth if not the sixth letter I am writing to you. Since you left, I have written you a letter EVERY week! I have not yet received the letter you said was "following" in your telegram.

I received an air mail letter from Benjie on the 14th (fourteenth) September. It had been posted on the 2nd (second). Another air mail letter from Lauretta [Ngcobo] in Swaziland reached me on the 21st (twenty-first) September. It had been posted on the 8th (eighth). An ordinary letter from Nenti posted on the 8th (eighth) reached me on the twenty-first. So even assuming you did not write immediately on your arrival, but waited until the end of the month, I should have received your letter by now unless:–

1. you have, for some reason or another, postponed writing the letter or
2. you wrote it and, like the children's letters, your letter has disappeared in one of the numerous offices [illegible]. It was to ascertain this that I sent you a telegram on Monday (21st). Unfortunately, I did not make it "Reply Paid" as I am certain you can afford the cost of a telegram.

I am writing this letter on Wednesday afternoon (4.15 p.m.) and I have not yet received a reply to the telegram I sent. I am really at a loss what to think, baby.

I had hoped to be able to write you a letter every week until, at least, the end of October. But there are a number of letters awaiting replies and I shall have to skip next week at any rate. However, I shall write again in the first week of October.

Nenti has asked me to thank you for the beautiful jersey you sent her. She says she would have written directly to you to thank you but she lacks your address. They tell me Fezile is back from the Circumcision School and is now in employment. It is a pity he could not proceed with his studies. Charles didn't go home for the June holidays.

Lauretta wants to know if you received the letter she wrote you some time back. They appear to use the initial "Z" for their daughters. The eldest daughter, I know, is Zabantu. I don't know the name of the second. But the latest addition to the family is "Zikhethiwe", reminding me of what an old preacher at Standerton said, when he heard I was about to get married. He told me my wife would have to be "a chosen among the chosen" (mokhethoa hara bakhethoa). I assured him that she was and I can assure him more than ever today – in spite of your quiet stubbornness!

I know, Child, how this separation affects you. There will be days when you feel absolutely hopeless and depressed. But please remember, darling, that the will of God ALWAYS prevails and try to live one day at a time. You cannot know what will happen tomorrow so you can't change it. Why worry about it then? I think you'll agree that God been very kind to us. Count his blessings and concentrate on THEM and thank him.

Mrs Marquard sent me a box of sweets early this month. I told you in my last letter that she was very sorry you did not have a chance for a tete-à-tete.

Fabian has been quiet, too, for some time now. They must be getting ready to welcome Father Webber, I think. He should be on his way back this month.

Well, Kid, so long for the time being. My love to Mama and the kids. And remember, Little Girl, I love you very much.

Your loving husband,
Mangi

Veronica Sobukwe
to Benjamin Pogrund,
24 September 1964 (Ba2.37)

Dear Mr. Pogrund,

I am extremely sorry to learn that you did not get my letter.

As I had explained in my last letter, I could not come to town.

I had to change my day off and take a weekend. Any-way, those people who promised me a lift did not turn up.

Please extend my apologies to her. I have received letters and a telegram from Bob. He says he gained three pounds during my visit. I phoned you on the 19th at 7.55 am but there was no reply.

Good-bye,

I am,

Yours sincerely,
Veronica Sobukwe

Telegram
from Robert Sobukwe
to Benjamin Pogrund,
5 October 1964 (Ba2.38)

Twins birthday tomorrow Tuesday have sent congratulations by telegram Can you procure cards please Bob

Benjamin Pogrund
to Robert Sobukwe,
12 October 1964 (Ba2.52)

My dear Bob,

Your letter arrived last week. I was, as always, happy to hear from you and to be reassured that you are keeping as well as possible in your somewhat extraordinary circumstances.

By now you will have received my telegram advising you that your wife and children are keeping well, and that there is no need for concern on your part on any account at all. Your wife has written two letters and intended writing to you again immediately I contacted her. As you no doubt know, she will be taking her annual leave in December so you have something good to look forward to again. She will not be short of anything for her trip, I promise you.

I am constantly amazed – although I shouldn't be – to find the number of friends you have here and in other parts of the world. There is a Mrs. Thomas C. Taylor (of 50, Plymouth Avenue North, Rochester, New York 14614), for example. I realise the pressures on your allocation of letters, Bob, but I wonder whether you could at some stage manage a few words to her? She is not after thanks for anything, but feels that some direct contact with you would enable her to put a little more reality and content into her prayers. She is, as you will gather, a very devout Christian, a Presbyterian, I believe.

I am enclosing an article from Saturday's "Mail" which might be of interest to you.[62] I will also send the original booklet to you. It is a completely factual account of the churches in South Africa, and the reader is left to draw his own conclusions. The conclusions which I have drawn in the enclosed article are probably controversial. Do you think I have painted too grim a picture?

I am going into the question of the missing books for your studies and will have them sent to you as soon as possible.

62 "The Christian Failure", *Rand Daily Mail,* 10 October 1964. This article was concerned with the way the church dealt with the "race problem".

In regard to Mrs Mittag,[63] I am writing to her to tell her about your letter to her. I shall, however, request her to continue sending you records. This is the arrangement I made when I was in Cape Town, and I can promise you that everyone concerned is only too delighted to assist you in this small way.

There is still complete confusion about the London "Observer" subscription, by the way. No-one can offer any kind of an explanation about it.

Can you send me the renewal notice for the "Reader's Digest" so that I can attend to it without delay? Frankly, after our other torturous dealings with the C.N.A. I would rather present them with a renewal notice than attempt to take out a new subscription!

Your telegram about the twins' birthday was received and was promptly acted upon. I sent out two birthday cards, inscribed "All my love, from your Tata", and I tried to make my handwriting as neat and small as possible to make it look at least something like yours. I also sent them some small presents. I hope my telegram acknowledging yours reached you safely. I must say that the Robben Island authorities are extremely helpful in enabling you to send and receive telegrams. I can't imagine that there is another prisoner in the country who has this facility.

How are you placed for clothing? Particularly with the coming of the summer, is there anything you need? Is there perhaps any chance of your being able to use that little beach near your bungalow for an occasional swim? If so, let me know and I shall send you a swimming costume.

What you wrote about my work is very true. I know that the desire within me to be academically honest and fair and to overcome my deep-rooted prejudices against the Communists can tend to push me into being over-fair towards them with equally disastrous results. On the other hand, I am applying uncompromising standards to the use or non-use of material, and unfortunately or otherwise, I am finding that a lot of the well-known allegations simply do not stand up to close scrutiny. Or is it that I am unable to track down the direct evidence? To cheer you up, though, let me add that I am digging up other previously unknown facts!

The work is going reasonably well, but I have had to resign myself to accepting that this cannot be the definitive study I had originally envisaged. We are still too close to events and it will be many years before we are able to

---

63 Sally Mittag, a friend of Benjamin Pogrund's who worked in the Cape Town office of the Defence and Aid Fund.

get hold of all the necessary information. Anyway, I hope that my study, broad as parts of it will necessarily have to be, will still be solid enough to be of some significance.

I am leaving at the end of this week for a trip to Natal and Basutoland in search of additional material. I will be away for about two weeks.

One final point: I was surprised to hear that you apparently have not been receiving the weekly parcels of fruit which I arranged, and for which I paid the jail authorities.

The authorities have not advised me of any change in the situation so I have naturally assumed that the arrangement was still being adhered to. Can you please let me know what is happening?

I have just had some photographs of Jenny taken, and I am enclosing a couple to show you why I am such a proud father.

My very warm greetings to you. I continue to pray for you.

Sincerely,

Robert Sobukwe
to Veronica Sobukwe,
20 October 1964 (Bc20)

Hullo Darling!

As I pointed out in the telegram I sent you, I haven't received your letter of the 10th September so I don't know why it took you so long in the first place to let me know about your journey.

Your letter of the 24th reached me on the 9th October. On the same day I received one from Fabian. He too had been quiet for some time.

I still can't understand, though, how after receiving my telegram seeking to know why you were quiet, you could calmly put it aside and write a letter thanking me for the telegram! Surely the telegram indicated that I was worried and anxious.

I have written to Benjie and have asked him to take up this matter of my mail with attorneys and I have told him that if he requires information about the contents of the Minister's[64] notices to me you'll be able to help him.

I received the watch. Thanks. And I hope you have received the "Book of the Human Body".

Mrs Marquard is keeping me supplied with plays by modern dramatists. She has also sent me a sizeable amount of sweets and nuts. She calls it "a hoard to draw from".

Mrs Pullen has written, too. She says she was sorry to read that refugees in Basutoland were all singing my praises as their leader.[65] She hopes I'll denounce them all and tell them I am now "a disciple of the Lord Jesus Christ".

---

64 The Minister of Justice.

65 Pullen probably had Poqo in mind here, a military offshoot of the PAC (in Xhosa, the phrase "Ama-Afrika Poqo" means "The original owners of Africa"). Potlako Leballo, Sobukwe's ally in the PAC, had called a press conference in Basutoland in March 1963 to announce that Poqo and the PAC were one and the same. He went on to assert the inevitability of African revolution in 1963, an event that would claim white lives. As Porgund (2015) argues, there is no evidence to suggest that Sobukwe was in any way involved with Poqo. Poqo's calls for violence would also have run counter to Sobukwe's Christian beliefs. All this being said, Sobukwe was clearly hesitant to denounce any of his Basutoland followers – seemingly inclusive of Poqo members – in the way that Pullen's letter demanded.

I suppose I'll have to take up ministry after that and be a good little Christian kaffir.[66] I don't think I'll answer the letter. I'll hurt her if I do.

Well, October is almost over. September was the longest month I have ever known. I didn't think it would ever end.

Well, the boys are six now! I hope they understood my messages. I decided to use idiomatic Xhosa to demonstrate to you that if I speak simple Xhosa it is not because I do not know the language well, but purely out of consideration for Joh'burg people! You wouldn't understand me if I were to employ Course Three Xhosa!

Incidentally, I do not know what message Fabian derived from the quotation from Job I sent him. I meant it as a straightforward quotation. However, if he detected a message in it which he found useful who am I to disillusion him? I haven't replied to his letter yet. I'll do so next week I hope.

Well, Cheerio Kid. Love to all.

Your loving husband,
Mangi

P.S. I read about the invitation to the Zambia Independence Celebrations.[67] Congrats! M

---

66 This is a powerful comment, and it stands out forcefully within the broader context of Sobukwe's prison correspondence which needed to be guarded in respect of more overtly political issues. It stands out for another reason also. The cordiality and politeness that so often characterised Sobukwe's letters with his correspondents – particularly those he didn't really know – may at times give the impression that the passion and conviction that animated his pan-Africanist politics had been subdued. This comment suggests the opposite.

67 Veronica Sobukwe was invited to the Zambian independence celebrations, but the South African government refused to give her a passport.

Robert Sobukwe
to Benjamin Pogrund,
20 October 1964 (Ba2.41)

My dear Benjie,

Thank you indeed for both your telegrams. I needed the assurance about my family and, as a father, I was happy to know you had succeeded in getting birthday cards for my autochthons.

I subsequently received a letter from my wife, dated the 24th September, followed by a telegram. But the letter of the 10th September to which she refers, I have not received.

And I want to take up this matter of my mail with you today with whatever matters may be relevant.

You will no doubt recall that I have been complaining ceaselessly about the (to me) inexplicable delay in my mail, almost from the very moment I got here. I thought I would stick it [out] for a while, believing the arrangements to be temporary in any event. But it has proved not to be. And now that letters from, first my children and then my wife, have for a reason unknown to me been apparently held up the possibilities are, to say the least, disturbing.

Now Benjie, it is my contention – and I have given the matter my most serious thought – that neither the Minister of Justice nor the Prison Authorities have the right, under any published law or regulations, deliberately to delay my mail as to render nugatory my right (granted under their own regulation!) to write and receive two letters a week.

The reason for their actions is not my concern. The Administrative arrangements they make to achieve their purpose are not my concern either. But I *do* want to be convinced by a Court of law that the rights I have referred to can be reconciled with such restriction. And it is not unavoidable, this delay, Benjie. I have been a convict, as you know. And I never had reason to complain about mail delays.

I, therefore, want you to please to take up the matter with Ernie [Wentzel] and get his opinion. My intention is to appeal to court for a "definition of rights." I don't know how one presents that in court. But the idea is to remove the caprice and whim that appear to define my relations here.

Any information you may require about the contents of the Minister of Justice's notices to me, my wife will, I am sure, be able to supply. And should you require an affidavit from me, on whatever aspects of my stay here you consider relevant, I shall of course, be only too happy to oblige.

I read that Ernie intended to leave the country but I believe it should be possible to get the services of somebody else equally good.

We have to establish the purpose of censorship and in the case of so-called subversive material, who is to decide whether words are subversive or not – a Court of Law or a civil servant? Has that civil servant a right to withhold my letter because *he* thinks it contains subversive material? These are but some of the questions one would like settled by a court.

I shall not comment on the events in Europe.[68] I want this letter to deal specifically and exclusively with a "definition of rights!"

Well, cheerio Benjie,

Yours sincerely,
BOB

P.S. Now that the Socialists are in Britain I am almost sorry I cancelled subscriptions for "Time and Tide."[69] It would be a pleasure to read their sputtering fulminations against Callaghan![70]

P.P.S. I received the watch – thanks. BOB.

---

68 Sobukwe is perhaps referring to the narrow election victory of Harold Wilson's Labour Party in the United Kingdom earlier that month.

69 *Time and Tide* was a British weekly political and literary review which started as left-wing but ended up being a conservative mouthpiece.

70 James Callaghan – future Labour Prime Minister of the UK (between 1976 and 1979) – had just been made Chancellor of the Exchequer.

Robert Sobukwe
to Nell Marquard,
28 October 1964 (Bd1.8)

Dear Mrs Marquard,

In my last letter I numbered you among mind-readers. In the light of later developments I am afraid I'll have to remove you from that company. Mind-reading and telepathy are out of it. You receive messages. That's the only explanation I find satisfactory. What I still have to decide is whether these messages come to you as "guidance" from God or whether they come through plain African witchcraft.

All the foregoing is to clear the ground for a sincere "thank you" for the hoard from which I still continue to draw and to tell you that I received the parcel the very week I had decided to give up smoking!! See the reference to witchcraft? I haven't told my wife the good news yet. I want to keep it as a pleasant surprise to spring on her when she comes down in December. She has, unfortunately, never believed that a pipe gave me a dignified and intellectual look. She has missed the poetry of it altogether and has stubbornly persisted in viewing the ancient briar from the Hippocratic angle.

Thank you for the latest batch of plays. I was quite thrilled the other day to see a picture of Arnold Wesker[71] in the "Cape Times", I think it was.

I know I haven't read enough of modern drama to be able to make a reasonable generalization. But would you agree that with many of these young writers it is as it was with "Westerns" – the characters were different but the ingredients of the plot came from the same pantry! Wesker's three plays[72] were clean and yet written in the tradition of "socialist realism". What does beat me is why realistic plays or novels must of necessity depict the seamy side of life. After all our pruderies and attempts at decency, even our notions of decency, are as realistic as the things we are ashamed of. I have read that Osborne's latest play[73] has been severely criticized for the occurrence of four letter words which do nothing to advance the play.

71 Arnold Wesker (1932–2016) was an English playwright, journalist, poet and essayist.

72 Probably the trilogy of *Chicken Soup with Barley*, *Roots* and *I'm Talking about Jerusalem*.

73 *Inadmissible Evidence* (1964).

To turn to more mundane things. May [I] again, please, presume upon your kindness and ask you to send me some D.D.T.[74] I have planted some cucumber and squash seeds and the packet containing the latter exhorts the gardener to "control fly infestation and sucking bugs". It doesn't say how this is to be done. But I believe that D.D.T. is as all-purpose as penicillin is in another field.

With best wishes,
I remain,
Yours sincerely,
RM Sobukwe

---

74 Although today it is banned in many countries, DDT was at the time a standard form of insecticide.

Benjamin Pogrund
to Robert Sobukwe,
6 November 1964 (Ba2.42)

My dear Bob,

Thank you for your letter of October 20 which reached me on November 3. I was distressed to read about the delays you are experiencing in receiving your letters and I quite understand your concern. I was, frankly, surprised about the delays: as we know, the Robben Island authorities have always done their best to ensure your comfort within the limits of your detention. Holding back letters from your wife seems pointless. At the same time, I recall that you have repeatedly told me about delays in letters reaching you. I assume that you have taken up the matter with the prison authorities, and that you have decided on court action after failing to achieve any satisfactory solution.

In accordance with your instructions, I have written to lawyers in Cape Town and have asked them to act on your behalf. It will be necessary for them to have your Power of Attorney and possibly also to see you. Could you therefore please write direct to Mr. Barney Zackon, Zackon and Birkan, Namaqua House, Burg Street, Cape Town.[75] He is a good friend of mine.

I have discussed the matter also with Ernie and he is drawing up an Opinion immediately. This will be sent to Barney Zackon.

My trip to Natal and Basutoland was a fiasco. A couple of days after reaching Durban I became ill, and had to leave my car there and fly back to Johannesburg. It was found that I had glandular fever and I have just got up after spending the last few weeks in bed. I am feeling much better but am still rather weak. I plan to leave again next week and will be away for up to three weeks. Any letters which come from you in that time will be forwarded to me by my office.

As you no doubt know, your wife was refused a passport to attend the Zambia independence celebration. I am sorry I could not give her any assistance in this. She telephoned me shortly after I returned to Johannesburg, but I was so ill that I was barely able to talk to her coherently.

75 In addition to being an attorney, Barney Zackon (1927–2009) was the Cape chairman of the Liberal Party.

In your letter you omitted two matters about which I had written to you: the non-delivery of the weekly fruit parcels to you, and the "Reader's Digest" renewal (I asked you to send me the subscription form). The subscription to the London "Observer" has been taken out anew and copies should start reaching you shortly.

There is little else to tell you. My work has taken a heavy knock because of this illness and I am trying to get on with it again.

I hope this letter finds you in better heart.

My warmest good wishes to you.

Sincerely,

Robert Sobukwe
to Veronica Sobukwe,
13 November 1964 (Bc21)

Hullo Darling,

Thank you for your letter dated 27th October. You thank me in your letter for my "last telegram and letter". You'll have to be more specific, child. I have written you over six letters, anyone of which could have been my "last letter".

Before I regale you with "boloton" let me settle a few business points. First of all, any day now, I shall be receiving Examination Entry forms from the British Embassy. I'll have to fill them and return them with £9 (nine pounds) – which is the examination fee. Will you please send me that amount urgently? Also could you get me Parker *Refills* – one red and two blue. They are about 4/6 each. So much for business!

I am sorry about the Zambia affair.[76] I would have been a C.C.F. victim[77] if you had been granted permission to go. I thought both you and Benjie were being extremely optimistic even to make the attempt. But I agree with you one can only know the reaction when one has MADE the attempt. Then there are no "ifs" or "perhapses", there is a definite, tangible result.

Oh yes, I answered Mili's letter immediately. In fact I am certain that in the letter I wrote to you I mentioned that I was writing to Mili at the same time!

Well I hope you are able to make suitable arrangements for Dini. Don't leave it until the last minute. I am glad to hear the autochthons are doing well at school. It should be interesting to see how they take to regular disciplined school life.

We've been having married men's weather for the last three days or so – cloudy with intermittent showers and drizzle. I know I used to be impatient to get home on days like that knowing that we had a fine excuse for remaining in-doors.

---

76 As noted in Sobukwe's letter to his wife of 20 October 1964, she had been invited to the country's independence celebrations, an event that she was evidently unable to attend. Zambia gained independence from Britain on 24 November 1964.

77 Perhaps a joking reference to Congestive Cardiac Failure.

There is quite a lot of talk about the population explosion. Drastic measures have been adopted in Asia and Latin America to keep the population down. In Japan over a million cases of legalized abortion have been recorded for a single year. The oral contraceptive pill is now the rage.

The fears are that if the present rate of population growth is maintained, pretty soon there will not be enough *room* for people to live and not enough food to feed them.

The latter fear is a little groundless. There will be enough food in the world for a long time to feed everybody well. Unfortunately, millions are overeating and have to go to hospital to reduce and take slimming pills and diets while others are perpetually *under*-weight, because they do not have enough to eat. Similarly with population figures: some countries are bursting at the seams while others are virtually "open spaces".

The world has to do some re-thinking. Working in co-operation, the nations of the world can tame the Equatorial forests and make them habitable and they could absorb and support thousands of millions. So too can the deserts be reclaimed and made productive and habitable. Our own Sahara can absorb hundreds of millions. Our continent can support ten times as many people as there are at the moment. The development of the continent is a glorious challenge, requiring bold vision and imagination. As you say, with such a task before us, hatred is a waste of time and energy.

Well it's good to learn that they have at last completed the clinic at Tladi.[78] When I went to gaol five years ago the impression prevailed that at any time the Tladi clinic would begin operations. I don't think you stand to benefit by applying for a post at Tladi. It's farther away from Mofolo and from town and will mean increased transport costs. It will be altogether inconvenient, I feel.

Well, cheerio Kid. Love to all.

Your loving husband,
Mangi

P.S. I love you VERY MUCH. Remember that always. RMS

---

78 A section of Soweto.

Robert Sobukwe
to Nell Marquard,
25 November 1964 (Bd1.9)

Dear Mrs Marquard,

Thank you for the sprayer and the powder which I received last week. I felt quite the progressive farmer as I moved round the garden spraying plants without fear or favour.

Thank you also for your most interesting letter. It was a bit cruel on Nixon, but I found the incident very amusing. After all, Nixon is an outstanding U.S. politician. And for him to be so effectively silenced by a "Negro boy" – from Alabama, at that!

Your references to the snobbery that attached to Nederlands[79] in the olden days reminded me of our Coloured preachers at Graaff-Reinet. The African and Coloured people constitute one congregation, in all denominations, so that services are conducted in both Xhosa and Afrikaans. In those days, the thirties, the Methodist Church seemed to believe that a preacher was a more reliable agent of God if he was uneducated. The emphasis was on the "indwelling Spirit". The result was that most of our preachers, African and Coloured, were barely literate. However, it was an unquestioned convention in those days that a preacher just could not see a word if he did not have his glasses on. And as most of them were labourers who had to change into their Sunday bests, it wasn't unusual for them to find they had left their glasses behind.

But, and this is what all this nonsense is leading up to, they had to create the impression that they *could* read. It was very important in those days to be thought able to read. Those of our Coloured preachers who could read, enjoyed their "zechenen tot hem".[80] One old man, who couldn't read, would invariably ask his congregation to sing "gesang 256 in die maXhosa taal" – for a very long time it was Kaffirstaal while the name used for the Coloured people by the Xhosa was as barbaric as the clicks it contained – "en 46 in Hollands:[81] Dag des

79 The language.

80 That is, blessing to him. Sobukwe's spelling conforms to neither Afrikaans nor contemporary Dutch; it is presumably a more traditional form of Dutch used in the church.

81 Hymn 256 in the Xhosa language and 46 in Dutch.

wonderen, dag des oordeel en al wat daar op volg."[82] And they would bring the roof down. For God was understood to be very indulgent. Some sinners had been known to go to heaven because they had used their musical talents for the glory of God. And musical talent meant lung-power, that's all.

Oh, but they were an imaginative lot! Here's one preaching on the "Fall of Man", painting a picture of God calling "Adam! Adam!" and Adam replying from the black recesses of some thick bush, "here am I". God then asks him if he has eaten of the fruit and he replies "It is this woman *You* gave me." God ignores the implied accusation, passes on to Eve and she blames the snake. God looked it up and down as it stood there in arrogant defiance. "It's these blinking legs that give you ideas" said God, and with that "whish", he cut off the legs and flat on its belly fell the snake. This, mind you, is given in onomatopoeic language, with appropriate gestures – faithfully reproduced by the interpreter – and when the snake falls "bhaxa", explosive consonants and clicks and gestures convey most vividly the precipitate prostration of the original snake.

I am sorry for this digression. Now for business. You ask what plays I should like to have. I have enjoyed Arnold Wesker's, [Doris] Lessing's and [John] Osborne's plays. Eugene O'Neill is, of course, outstanding. You sent me three plays of his: "Ah, Wilderness!", "The Hairy Ape" and "All God's Chillun Got Wings". As I said in my last letter, these people tend to be a movement, a school, rather than individual playwrights, so that the work of one is the work of all. I shall have to except O'Neill's and Brendan Behan whose works really stood apart from the rest. In short, then, Mrs Marquard, except for O'Neill and Behan I have no strong preferences. I am quite willing to have you guide my reading!

I am sorry, really, if I have not thanked you for "The New Yorker" in the past. It contains some interesting articles for light reading and relaxation. I enjoyed it.

My wife will be leaving Johburg on the 29th December and on the 5th (fifth) December, I'll be celebrating my *fortieth* birthday – entering into manhood!

With best wishes,
Yours sincerely,
RM Sobukwe

---

82 Day of miracles, day of judgement and all that follows.

Robert Sobukwe
to Nell Marquard,
30 November 1964 (Bd1.10)

Dear Mrs Marquard,

When I wrote my reply, I did not have your letter with me. I had misplaced it somewhere. But, yesterday, when I took up a book on Economics I came across your letter resting snugly between the pages. I read it over again and as a result, I am sending this postscript to you.

I wish you to know that I appreciate very much indeed and am grateful for the solicitude that prompted you to write despite your rheumatic hand. I felt very rotten when I realized how imperceptibly I was becoming selfish and callous. I wish you a speedy recovery and a pain-free and happy Christmas season.

Forgive me if I indulge in my usual reminiscences. But I can't help remarking that while the English pedantically wish one another a "Merry" Christmas and a happy New Year, we Graaff-Reineters – the location population – wish one another a "happy" Christmas and a "happy" New Year and we say it loudly, person to person. We aren't mercenary in outlook – far from it – but we do, all things considered, expect those on whom we confer the blessings of the gods to show their appreciation – a piece of cake, a cent piece or a bottle of beer, shall we say?

However, it often happens that our friends have nothing but good wishes to give us in return. The formula is "same to you", said indifferently or warmly, depending on our feelings toward our well-wishers. There are characters at Graaff-Reinet, however, who are known to hate having their good-wishes reciprocated, preferring a solid, tangible token of good-will. They are quick to follow their "happy Christmas" with "en moet my nie 'seventy-you' gee nie!"[83] – in the idiom of our location.

I was interested also in your account of the lecture on Galileo. I don't know what to think of the man. I happened to read, by accident really, Arthur Koestler's *The Sleepwalkers,* in which he traces the history of astronomy. For some reason or another he feels called upon to cut Galileo down to size and

83 And don't give me "seventy-you"!

to accord pre-eminence to his countryman, George Keppler.[84] Well, if there's one thing Koestler can do it is debunking theories and denigrating characters. He makes Galileo appear an arrogant, petulant, perfidious liar towards whom the Church showed unusual tolerance. He has marshalled his facts skilfully, but, as I say, he is arguing a case and has been too harsh on Galileo. But it is amazing how steadfastly scientists refused to make the assumptions that their observations should have led them to make, how they skirted the truth for centuries, making momentous discoveries and yet not realizing that they had. It's a fascinating story of how in his laborious serpentine climb man often goes off at a tangent, confidently: ends up in a *cul-de-sac* and has to retrace his steps!

Yes, a lot is happening on the world scene. I am happy about the outcome of the American elections because, whatever shady deals mar his past, [President Lyndon] Johnson, I believe, wants to and can fire the imagination of American youth. And I have a soft spot for Americans. Perhaps because they are so desperately anxious to be loved or because they are so vulnerable. There is one respect in which they resemble the Communists whom they loathe so much. In the days of Lenin, the Communists seemed to enjoy announcing their failures from the rooftops and going back to the job with the renewed vigour of those who have just returned from the confessional. The Americans, too, are extremely self-critical – a sign of strength.

I do not know the history of the crisis in South Vietnam, unfortunately. But I do believe that the Americans are allowing themselves to be blackmailed unnecessarily. There is not a single country in Africa, Asia or Latin America that would voluntarily go Communist. Of that I am certain. They'll all declare themselves *socialists*, yes, but it will be their brand of socialism. If America were to take up the attitude and let it be known, that she will assist to the best of her ability where her assistance is required, but that she will withdraw willingly where is not wanted, there would be no demonstrations, anywhere, against American embassies. Of course it is an unavoidable risk in democracies that some obscure paper will publish some uncomplimentary matter on some Asian or African country – something that State-controlled Communist papers can NEVER do – and that paper's sentiments are taken as representative of the country as a whole.

---

84 Johannes Kepler, a central figure in the 17th-century scientific revolution, best known for his theories of planetary motion.

In Europe, the situation is most intriguing. Professor Beloff[85] was of opinion that the Socialist parties of Europe would regard a Labour victory in Britain as a sign of a change in the international climate. Herr Willy Brandt, Signor Nenni and M. Gaston Defferre of Germany, Italy and France, respectively,[86] are going to be watched very closely in the coming months because socialist victories in these countries will give a fillip to the explosive though latent idea of a Socialist United States of Europe. What a mighty power that would be! And who knows, if liberalization were to continue behind the Iron Curtain, whether the Soviet Union and its satellites were not to be drawn into such a Union.

Strange as it may seem, I have no fear of a world conflagration. I have a strong consciousness of God's active intervention in the affairs of the world. We are moving towards God's solution.

I wish you and your family a God-blessed and memorable Christmas and New Year.

Yours very sincerely,
RM Sobukwe

In my previous letter, I spoke of bringing the roof down. As no applause was provided for it would have been more correct, perhaps, to have the roof blown off or the walls collapsing as they did in Jericho! RMS

85 Max Beloff was professor of government and public administration at Oxford University.

86 Willy Brandt was then leader of the German Social Democratic Party; Pietro Nenni national secretary of the Italian Socialist Party; and Gaston Defferre a French socialist politician.

Robert Sobukwe
to Benjamin Pogrund,
7 December 1964 (Ba2.48)

Hello Benjie!

You will probably have learnt by now that I have not yet written to Mr. Zackon. It isn't because I have misplaced your letter which, in the light of recent experiences, is likely to be your first thought. The reason, really, is that as my wife will soon be coming down and there is a strong probability that Dr. Ribeiro[87] will be joining her, I thought I would discuss the matter with them and see if the prayer or plea, whatever the thing is called, cannot be broadened. I felt that if they were to see Mr. Zackon themselves, then a lot of the preliminary ground can be prepared at no unnecessary cost.

I am glad you have got over your illness. By a strange coincidence Mr. and Mrs. Mittag were down with jaundice at about the same time. Fortunately, they too have recovered and have already been on picnic out in the Kalahari from whence they sent me some succulents and a lovely plant-pot, the work of the potter in Jeremiah![88] When I wrote to them, the plants and the pot had not arrived yet and I am afraid I may not be able to write to them again this year. Will you please, if you do write to them sooner than that, advise them that I have received the stuff and will write to thank them as soon as the queue clears.

A Mrs. Schonfield in Britain has sent me T.H. Green's *Political Obligations.*[89] And that is all in the line of Social Philosophy that has arrived. But don't worry, Benjie. The three books I have are enough for a pass: only the subject intrigues me and I feel I want to know as much about it as it is possible to know.

With regard to novels do you think that in the New Year it would be possible for you to get me books by the following authors:

---

87 Fabian Ribeiro, the husband of Veronica Sobukwe's sister Florence and thus Sobukwe's brother-in-law.

88 In Jeremiah 18, the prophet is instructed by God to visit a potter.

89 *Lectures on the Principles of Political Obligation* by the Oxford-based Idealist philosopher T.H. Green (1836–82). His ideas had a great influence on many social liberal politicians in England like Asquith.

1. C.P. Snow – I haven't read any of his works.
2. J.B. Priestley – have read "Let the People Sing" and "Midnight on the Desert".
3. [Antoine de] St-Exupery – Have read his Flight to Arras.
4. Goethe – Haven't read anything by him.
5. Balzac – Suspect his works will be banned, tho.

Am quite happy with [Harold] Wilson at the head of affairs in Britain and Johnson as boss in America. They'll complement each other with Wilson providing the ideas, the well-thought-out ideas of a critical, limpid intelligence and Johnson the persuasive skill that is his trade mark. Both have been shaped by [John F.] Kennedy in some way. Wilson hopes to provide the youthful inspiration and vision that Kennedy evoked. And he can: in Britain; where he will not be expected to be a romantic and athletic idol of teenagers. It is the intellectuals of Britain now who will have their chance as the American ones had under Kennedy.

Johnson, of course, has inherited Kennedy's mantle and programme. But he wants to be remembered as a great president in his own right. America has the resources to banish poverty completely from the States. And Johnson is going to strain every nerve to do it. He is also going to do everything in his power to implement the Civil Rights Act. In his domestic policy, he is going to be successful, I think. The weak spot in his foreign policy is the hostility towards Communist China which he has inherited. America has no intellectual case against Communist China. She is merely prejudiced. Nobody blames her for being prejudiced against China. She may even hate her if she feels like it. But it is a reflection on U.N.O. if China can be kept out simply because America does not like her policy. It tends to suggest that U.N.O. is America's club to which only those can belong who have America's blessing. And yet she could have China admitted to U.N.O. without in the least compromising her position.[90]

I have just laid hands on the "Reader's Digest" renewal form and am enclosing it in case you still need it, though I have received the December issue, which seems to suggest that the subscription has been renewed.

---

90 At that stage, China was represented at the UN by the nationalist, non-communist Republic of China (Taiwan). Only in 1971 did the People's Republic of China gain admission.

Without intending any insult may I wish you a peaceful Christmas season and a happy opportunity-filled New Year!

My love and very best wishes to Jennifer.

Yours sincerely,
Bob

Robert Sobukwe
to Veronica Sobukwe,
7 December 1964 (Bc22)

Hullo Darling,

Thank you indeed for the Birthday and Christmas cards. They were the sweetest and loveliest I have ever received. They made my day for me!

Thank you also for the Twenty Rands and the Parker refills. I am sorry to have been such a nuisance – at this time of all times. Unfortunately, I had not yet been informed that Fabian's money had arrived and I feared that when the Examination Entry Forms arrived I wouldn't have the money to pay. They haven't arrived yet: but the British Embassy promised to send them in good time. You know, I hope, that the examination is held in June, not in December. I still have a few months for concentrated revision. Lectures end in March!

I am rather glad you are coming by train and not by car. I fear the roads these days. Fabian has expressed a desire to come, but has not fixed a definite date. He did say though, that if he does not succeed in making the journey, Vemba[91] certainly will.

I'd be happy if you could bring a little Mist. Pot. Cit.[92] with you, not more than two bottles for a start and some of those pads for corns and callouses. I am trying to cut down on cakes and sweets but I certainly must have some scones baked by Mili and a cake or two baked by her mother!

Incidentally, thank them on my behalf for their touching Christmas card. I wish you all the loveliest and most satisfying Christmas imaginable.

I received a letter from Buti this morning, informing me, *inter alia,* that Zozo celebrated her twentieth birthday on the 12th November. How these children grow! Dorris then must be 22 or more. The tragedy is that they are merely sitting in mental idleness at home.

I received a telegram from Fabian this morning, wishing me a happy birthday.[93] He must have remembered rather late on Saturday that the great day had come!

---

91 Florence Ribeiro.

92 To treat urinary tract infections.

93 His birthday was on 5 December.

I am looking forward very keenly to your visit. Mam Tshawe is going to Queenstown for the N.C.A.W.[94] meeting this year, so they won't be coming down to Cape Town. Buti says they'll come down in two years' time when one of his boys is ordained as a priest.

Give my love and best wishes to Mama and the kids – as well as to the Varas and Matebulas.

Cheerio, little girl. God bless you richly.

Your loving husband,
Mangi

P.S. I have not yet renewed my subscription for the Cape Times and the Cape Argus. I don't know when the subscriptions expire. They haven't sent me any renewal forms. But the Cape Times did discontinue its deliveries from the 21st to the 27th November. If you haven't done so yet, don't pay any subscription until you've met me. I've already paid for the *Sunday Times* and the *Sunday Express*. Mangi

94 National Council of African Women.

1965

Sobukwe's desk, pictured alongside photographs of what it looked like when he used it daily during his time on the Island.

Benjamin Pogrund
to Robert Sobukwe,
19 January 1965 (Ba3.4)

My dear Bob,

This letter, I know, will be reaching you at a time of mixed emotions for you: joy at the reunion which you will recently have had with your wife and children; sadness that it has passed so quickly. My prayers, as always, are that the spirit and courage of both you and your family will be maintained, and that your ordeal will soon come to an end. These prayers are especially strong at the start of this New Year; 1964, thank God, is over and no year could be worse than it was.

I am now looking forward to your wife's return to Johannesburg to have first-hand news of you. I hope that, in seeing her, you found that neither she nor the children are lacking for anything.

Your letter of December 7 was gladly received. I have sent you the books you wanted, together with a few others, via Vanguard Books[1] of Johannesburg. The parcel of 20 books comprises:

1. [Giusesppe Tomasi di] Lampedusa: The Leopard
2. [William Golding]: Lord of the Flies
3. [Randall Jarrell]: Pictures from an Institution
4. Warren Commission Report
5. Priestley: Good Companions
6. Priestley: Angel Pavement
7. Priestley: Priestly Companion
8. Priestley: Bright Day
9. [Jean-Paul] Sartre: The Reprieve
10. [Joseph] Conrad: Lord Jim
11. [Roald] Dahl: Kiss Kiss
12. [Franz] Kafka: The Trial
13. [Honoré] Balzac: Droll Stories
14. Balzac: Country Doctor
15. [J.W. von] Goethe: Faust (I and II)

1 A famous left-wing bookstore run by Fanny Klenerman, a Trotskyist.

16. [Yevgeny] Yevtushenko: Selected Poems
17. [C.P.] Snow: Time of Hope
18. Snow: [The] Light and [the] Dark
19. Snow: The Affair
20. [Antoine de] St.-Exupéry: The Little Prince.

Please let me know whether the choices are suitable ones. As far as I can recall, I have not previously sent you any of these books. But if I have, try and return duplicates to me so that I can change them. In the meantime, much happy reading! Incidentally, I think you would like to know that the money for the books came from a variety of people, including Jill and Ernie Wentzel, Allister Sparks, Jill Chisholm, Terry Bell, Peter Hazelhurst, Lawrence Mayekiso, Terence Clarkson, Tim Rossi, Mike Phahlane and others (all newspaper colleagues of mine).

I shall probably be sending you a further parcel of books during this week. Of those in the list above, you will see that I have sent you Priestley, Snow, etc., as you requested. In addition, with your admiration for Kennedy I was sure you would be interested in seeing the Warren Commission report.[2] There has been quite a controversy since the report appeared – mainly in the U.K., I think – on the grounds that vital evidence was suppressed. Personally I think this is nonsense; there was no reason to do anything of the kind, and from my glance at the report it seems that the greatest possible pains were taken to investigate every tiny detail in a thoroughly judicial manner. You will, I hope, enjoy reading Yevtushenko's poetry; from the little I have read of him, he is among Russia's leading modern poets. Dahl's "Kiss Kiss" I have myself read and enjoyed thoroughly. He is not to everyone's liking – some find him "sick". Some of his themes undoubtedly are sick, but the beauty of his writing and his penetration of human character make, I find, exciting and entertaining reading.

For Xmas I sent you a large food parcel. This was from Mr. Fred van Wyk[3] and myself. I hope it reached you safely and in good time. I wrote to the Robben Island Officer Commanding advising that the parcel was on its way,

2 The Warren Commission or, more formally, the President's Commission on the Assassination of President Kennedy, presented its 888-page report to President Johnson in September 1964. It concluded that President Kennedy was assassinated by Lee Harvey Oswald, who had acted alone.

3 The assistant director of the South African Institute of Race Relations.

and, in view of its size, asking him to let me know that it had arrived. As I have not had a letter in reply I am somewhat anxious about it. I also hope that people in Cape Town were able to send you Xmas gifts.

This question of your Social Philosophy books is a complete mystery. I spoke to Professor Wellington about it but he has no list of books. I am pretty certain that you told me that your brother-in-law would be getting the books for you, and for this reason I did not keep a copy of the list. I know that I returned all the original lists to you. In any event, you clearly need the books so I suggest that you send me the Social Philosophy list if you have it. If you haven't, could you perhaps obtain another copy from the correspondence college or university?

Ernie [Wentzel] prepared an Opinion on your case and sent it, as arranged, to Barney Zackon. Frankly, Ernie's view is that the law is solid and there is probably little chance of succeeding with an appeal to court. But by now your wife will have spoken to Barney and you will have full details so I need not elaborate.

I had a letter from Mrs. Mittag last week and she mentions having heard from you that you had received the plants and the pot. She also said she was getting your Law books.

I harboured an initial mistrust of [Lyndon] Johnson – too much the slick political wire-puller, I thought. But recently, in reading detailed reports of his speeches and his attitudes, my views have changed. I admire his pragmatic approach coupled with his extraordinary drive to get things done. What I like most is his honest look at American society and his intention to eliminate ills, principally the Civil Rights problem, care of the aged and poverty and unemployment. Increasingly, I have come to feel that this is a sincere man, and that his obsessional idea to leave his mark on history will drive him to perform great positive and enduring feats. [Harold] Wilson, on the other hand, I have never felt all that warmly about and I still don't. Despite the election attempts to humanise him, I still regard him as a cold fish – and after his first few months in office, I still do not see any significant signs of his capability. The economic and other problems which he inherited seem to be tackled in a muddled, ill-thought out fashion.

There was a bit of a mess up about the continued payment of my research grant for the additional six month period which had been agreed to. As I could not live without an income, I returned to the "Mail" in December and am continuing work on the book in my spare time. My work on the "Mail" now consists of feature articles, the idea being for me to do intensive research and investigation. Basically, reporting in depth. At the moment I am working on a set of five major pieces on integration in industry. It will take many weeks of work to prepare.

Incidentally, you will I suppose remember Tommy Ngwenya of Cape Town.[4] He left for Rhodesia a year or so ago, entered politics through Sithole's organisation[5] and was placed in detention at Wha Wha[6] in October last year for a one year period. I have had letters from both him and his wife and have been glad to learn that he is at least keeping well.

I heard only yesterday that Lincoln University[7] in the United States wants to confer an honorary Doctor of Laws degree on you. Has this information reached you? The decision was taken last year and was conveyed to the South African Government with a request for information as to when you could attend to receive the degree. Apparently no reply was received.

I do not know if you have been able to spare one of your precious letter-writing opportunities to write to the Mrs. Taylor I told you about.[8] If you haven't written to her yet, you could perhaps, in your next letter to me, write a short message to her which I shall send on.

Enclosed please find copy of a letter I have sent to the Officer Commanding, Robben Island Gaol, inquiring about the delivery of fresh fruit to you each week. I am sorry I have taken so long to attend to this.

---

4 Ngwenya was a veteran trade unionist and ANC loyalist, described by Jonty Driver as more liberal than the Liberals.

5 Ndabaningi Sithole (1920–2000) was the founder, in July 1963, of the Zimbabwe African National Union (ZANU), a militant organisation that opposed the white government of Rhodesia.

6 A prison in Gwelo (now Gweru) in then Rhodesia.

7 Lincoln University in Pennsylvania was the first historically black US university to confer degrees. A number of Africans from South Africa had studied there since the early twentieth century.

8 Mrs Charlotte L. Taylor of New York was a parishioner of Robert S. Bilheimer, a US Presbyterian minister and co-founder of the World Council of Churches whom Pogrund had met. He had been involved in the preparations for the Cottesloe consultations with the churches in South Africa in 1960. Aware of Sobukwe's situation, Bilheimer had secured an offer of occasional funding from Mrs Taylor to help with various expenses associated with the Sobukwe family.

All for now. Let me hear from you soon and my very warmest greetings to you in the meantime.

Sincerely,

P.S. Am enclosing a London "Observer" article on Johnson which appeared in this morning's "Mail" – it will be of interest to you. Is the "Observer" reaching you now?

Robert Sobukwe
to Nell Marquard,
27 January 1965 (Bd1.11)

Dear Mrs Marquard,

I wish to say thank you first of all for your Christmas gifts both material and spiritual *id est*[9] both the sweets and the Christmas card as well as the unbroken flow of "The Listener". Thank you also for the Messiah programme[10] and this morning's parcel of pest killers. For all these "little acts of kindness", thank you!

My wife has been and gone. She came out with the kids on New Year's eve and so enabled me to enter the new year in a joyfully expectant frame of mind. The children have grown enormously, I think, particularly my daughter and they were so genuinely and uninhibitedly happy to see me that I began seriously to believe that I was (like Cassius Clay)[11] the greatest!

I was able to give them some squashes and cucumbers from my garden – the latter really outstanding specimens. The pumpkins have been disappointing, characterized by a plethora of foliage and a singular paucity of fruit.

The situation in Britain is most intriguing,[12] I see. It is rather frightening to face an electorate so unpredictable! If, however, the Wilson government has as rough a time as the Attlee government and fares as badly, I shall lose all my sympathies for the working classes of Britain and agree with Lenin that they have been bourgeoised by their environment! It's a pity about Gordon Walker.[13] He has quite advanced ideas about the future of the Commonwealth and one feels he would have been an intellectual foreign secretary. However

9 Latin for "that is".

10 Nell Marquard had sent Sobukwe the programme from a performance of Handel's *Messiah* that she had presumably attended in Cape Town.

11 The boxer Muhammad Ali.

12 In October 1964 the Labour Party won the general election and ended 13 years of Conservative Party rule.

13 It was widely anticipated that Gordon Walker would become the British Foreign Secretary after the Labour Party won the 1964 general election. He was, however, defeated in controversial circumstances by the Conservative Party candidate.

Michael Stewart[14] himself is a student of international politics with a thorough knowledge of both the American and Russian systems of government.

Sufficient unto the day!

With best wishes,
Yours sincerely,
RM Sobukwe

P.T.O.

"Dingaka" is a Sotho word, plural of *"ngaka"* (ŋ*aka*, phonetically), a "witchdoctor" in popular parlance. The Zulu variant is *inyanga* (iɲaŋga) spelt like the word for "moon" but with a different tone pattern. The plural is *izinyanga*. Xhosa has deviated from the proto-type and has adopted *ngqira* using *ukunyanga* (to heal) as a verb.

Unfortunately I do not know the African actors personally (i.e. Gumbi & friends), just as I do not know the members of the Johannesburg African Music Society. Like Job, "I had heard of [them] only by the hearing of the ear",[15] particularly Xatasi. RM Sobukwe

14 Michael Stewart was a Labour politician who served as Foreign Secretary in the cabinet of Harold Wilson from January 1965 to 1966 and again from 1968 to 1970.

15 See Job 42: 5, "I have heard of thee by the hearing of the ear, And now mine eye hath seen Thee".

Robert Sobukwe
to Benjamin Pogrund,
18 February 1965 (Ba3.9)

My dear Benjie,

Thank you for your letter dated 19th January which I received on the 5th of this month (February). I enjoy your letters immensely and feel refreshed after reading them. They are constant reminders that I have a self-respect to cherish!

The books arrived on the day that my wife was paying me her last visit and I asked her to advise you accordingly. They are an excellent lot of books, Benjie, the type I would like my children to know I read in my maturer years! Please give my thanks to the many friends who contributed towards the cost.

And will you, please, convey my thanks and gratitude to Jill and Ernie [Wentzel] for their exquisite Christmas gift. Unfortunately it got misplaced during the Christmas rush and I received it after I had sent off my letter to you. That is why I didn't mention it in my letter to you: and I believe they are anxious to know whether I received it or not. Well I did. And what a lovely gift it was! It couldn't have been selected by one of them alone; it could only have been chosen by *both* of them *together*.

I believe I have told you that "The Observer" has started arriving. Just before it came I received a book from Mrs Marquard titled "The Observer and J.L. Garvin"[16] – an outstanding book about an outstanding political journalist. So when "The Observer" arrived it found me kindly disposed towards it.

Most of the books on Social Philosophy are O P (out of print) and that is probably why I have not been able to get them. I told you, I think, that a Mrs Schofield had sent me T.H. Green's *Principles of Political Obligation*. I have the list here but I do not think it necessary to send it to you, Benjie, because the books are really not indispensable. The subject is one that requires *in*tensive rather than *ex*tensive reading. The textbooks are enough.

Didn't I tell you I had written to Mrs Taylor? I wrote within a week or two of receiving the letter in which you first mentioned her. And that is months

---

16 *'The Observer' and J.L. Garvin, 1908–1914: A Study in a Great Editorship* by A.M. Gollin, published in 1960 by Oxford University Press.

ago. To be exact, I wrote to Mrs Taylor on the 12th November 1964. Please find out if she has received my letter or not. If she has not then I'll do as you suggest, send her a letter through you.

Thanks for the piece on Johnson. I do not envy the man. His problems are immense; both domestic and international. Automation in the U S A is resulting in dramatically increasing wealth accompanied by increasing unemployment. A number of industries are featherbedding purely in order to keep fellows employed. And those whom automation is replacing are those who have no skills that can be put to other use. It is not *production* – increased production, that is his problem: it is *distribution*: equitable distribution of the common wealth of the U S A. But the problem has numerous ramifications and imponderables.

I am glad to learn you are back on the "Mail". I don't think you'll ever be happy away from "Fleet Street".

Thanks for the news about Tommy Ngwenya and wife. I don't know them personally, though – have merely heard of them.

No, I have had no information about Lincoln University at all. I don't think the Government should cause any difficulty over the matter. After all Lincoln is a *Negro* University: I won't be getting a *White* degree: I'll be getting a *Negro* degree!

Mrs Mittag has sent me the law books together with a valuable book on International Trade and Finance. I am getting quite learned!

With regard to the fruit, Benjie, the arrangements you had made were resumed some time back and I have been getting good fruit regularly.

I have been thinking about the project on which you are working. And at the risk of annoying your "bosses" I feel you should note in your conclusion that in spite of their unlimited propensity for mischief, it will be a sad day for the world if Communists were to disappear altogether. There are no people with such an imaginative disregard for the truth and a poetic genius for abuse as these guys. They have enriched the English language!

Thanks for Ernie's Opinion.

Cheerio, then, Sir,

Yours sincerely,
BOB

Robert Sobukwe
to Veronica Sobukwe,
25 February 1965 (Bc23)

My darling Mrs Sobukwe,

Thank you indeed for your very fresh and enjoyable letter! I was not unduly worried either when I did not hear from you for I knew you would have your hands full for a week or two. But your command concerning penicillin did alarm me a little. I thought that Dini's eye had become more inflamed as a result of the drops we had applied to it. But as you say nothing in your letter about the condition of his eye I assume that the inflammation was not aggravated and that the eye is normal once more.

I am glad to learn that you met Dini's ex-teacher and reached some agreement with her about his accommodation. I do hope he'll be able to settle down comfortably.

Yes, you *should* miss the autochthons. That house, without them, sounds like an empty dormitory I believe. I have not yet heard from Mili, either. But I know she will write soon – if she has stamps!

Thanks for the assurance that you found everything intact at home. Didn't you find my letter waiting? Benjie received his and I wrote them on the same day, the 7th December, hoping you would receive it before you came out here. By the way where is the Moroka Clinic[17] situated? In the area we call Maseru or is it near the Post Office? I am afraid I can't place it. I do wish and hope that you'll work happily there, too.

Both Fabian and Benjie have written. Fabian complained about my unbroken silence – "The Solitude of Alexander Selkirk".[18] But I already had a letter on the way to him when I received his. Benjie's was posted on the very day you left Cape Town for home. Both of them were looking forward to seeing you.

I have destroyed my pumpkin plants, darling. Like the fig tree in the bible they produced a plethora of foliage but no fruit.[19] The squashes behaved

17 In Soweto, Johannesburg, where Mrs Sobukwe worked.

18 Alexander Selkirk was a shipwrecked sailor who was the source of inspiration for Daniel Defoe's character Robinson Crusoe.

19 See Mark 11: 12-25.

admirably. They turned a brilliant gold and were a pleasure to behold. So too were the cucumbers.

I am quite proud to hear that your garden is supplying some of your needs. I am not surprised, though. You are, of course, a rare woman. I must make a special point of thanking my mother-in-law one day. She brought you up in the true African tradition!

If you miss me, Child, so do I you. I enjoyed your visit immensely. You grow lovelier, I feel, as you approach mature womanhood. As I don't see any signs of ageing in you I am afraid I can't speak of your growing older. But I certainly do see you maturing as a woman. And it is something I love to watch! The kids, too, were marvellous. They are a happy crowd.

You say I have never believed that you loved me on sight. I have, of course, felt flattered darling, ever since you told me so. If I appear reluctant to believe it the reason is not that I doubt your truthfulness. I know you to be a truthful little girl. The reason simply is that my mirror has never flattered me and I have, therefore, never been tempted to think that I am irresistible to the dusky daughters of Africa!!

What did you get Dini for his birthday? I had intended to give him the other flask on your final visit but it was really such a mixed-up day – I had even left my watch behind, remember? – I forgot all about it. He wanted some fancy shoes, though, if I remember well. He will have to improve his gait if he wants to wear such shoes!

We have been experiencing glorious weather lately. The days are clear and warm and the evenings clear and cool. There is a lovely moon in the sky, quite unlike the moon on which America's Ranger landed.[20] This is a silver moon with no craters and thick dust. And as it shines on the sea it transforms the latter into a wide stretch of polished glass. It is the type of evening in short that reminds me of you, because everything beautiful reminds me of you.

I certainly do pray for you and the children constantly, baby. And I know that no evil will befall you. God is great.

How are the physical exercises going? They can be extremely boring but I have come to enjoy them. Well cheerio Kid. Love to all.

Your loving husband,
Mangi

---

20 NASA's Ranger programme was a series of unmanned space missions to obtain close-up images of the moon.

Robert Sobukwe
to Nell Marquard,
25 February 1965 (Bd1.12)

Dear Mrs Marquard,

I have juggled the queue. I felt I couldn't wait another fortnight or so before telling you how immensely I enjoyed your letter of the 11th January.

It had an atmosphere of its own. If you don't mind my saying so, you appear to have been in a militant frame of mind and it was quite a pleasure watching you dancing circles around the philistines!

You didn't take long over Koestler.[21] You didn't exactly denounce him bell book and candle; but by judiciously contrasting a "sensuous scientist" with "the journalist in Koestler" you got the audience to cast rather hostile glares towards the unfortunate man. He has recently published a book on the Act of Creation[22] and there attacks viciously the theories of the behaviourist school of psychology. The dons and experts are after him with battle-axes and pangas. He is really unfortunate. Incidentally, he distinguishes between a reporter and a creative writer who is nonetheless a realist. He regards himself as the latter.

Then there was the slight jab you made at the writer of the article on automation. I think you presented your case beautifully. The facts are that in America today automation *is* increasing the National Product and the National Income. But a large percentage of the population constituting what is known as the "lowest third", earns a bare subsistence income and the middle classes whose incomes have increased, far from having more leisure are working harder than ever to maintain the standard of living to which they have now become accustomed.

And what *does* our much-vaunted efficiency consist in? Reducing the production costs of commodities and so reduce their price? But immediately the demand for them increases because of their cheapness, their price rises! Producing more cars for which roads and autobahns have to be built on which

21 Arthur Koestler (1905–83), a Hungarian-British writer and intellectual, was initially a member of the German Communist Party, before turning against the party in the era of Stalinism, and was known for his anti-totalitarian novels such as *Darkness at Noon* (1940).

22 *The Act of Creation* (1964).

more cars converge necessitating the employment of squads of traffic cops and Beeching reports?[23] America is at once the most efficient country in the world and the most wasteful.

But so long as we have the fears you express and realize that we are becoming "educated, skilled barbarians" our technological progress has not outpaced our mental development.

And then, towards the end of a hectic round you threw a thunderous right at the critics of today's youth. And again I am in complete agreement with you. I know the "Oxford"! I am not being original when I point out that our failure as a race is that we cannot strike the happy mean. In every aspect of our lives we push things to their logical extremes so that a reaction sets in and this movement takes us past the mean towards the logical extreme in the opposite direction. It is Hegel's thesis and antithesis all over again.

I have merely read reviews of Mutwa's[24] book and cannot comment authoritatively on it. But what I do know is that whatever the position might be in West Africa, in this part of the continent witchdoctors are *not* the custodians of tribal history. And certainly no witchdoctor knows anything about the Phoenicians! In short I am extremely suspicious of this witchdoctor and would be interested to know what his academic qualifications are. Africa is money nowadays and there is no lack of "marewu" (suurpap) experts to cater for that need.[25]

Thank you for the piece on Dr. Martin Luther King. There was something on him in the "New Yorker" you sent me.[26] He certainly is an intriguing person. And they do say that he is a powerful preacher. But he wouldn't be a Negro, of course, if he weren't!

---

23 A series of reports, first issued in 1963, on the rationalisation of the British railway system, involving closures of many lines.

24 Vusamazulu Credo Mutwa's *Indaba, My Children*, first published in 1964. It mixes traditional Zulu folklore with personal narratives and accounts of extraterrestrial encounters.

25 Sobukwe's implication is that there is no shortage of charlatans willing to fleece an international audience hungry to profit from Africa. *Suurpap* is porridge made with sour milk.

26 Perhaps the article "Martin Luther King Wins the Nobel Prize for Peace", *New Yorker*, 15 October 1964.

And your comments on "the Messiah" I appreciated. The "Hallelujah Chorus" was sung in almost every African college during my day. No student who came from a Training Institution could be ignorant of it. It has a basic folk-song rhythm and that's probably why it is so popular. I have read that tragedy purifies. But "King Lear" unlike "Macbeth" or "Hamlet" has always left me with a feeling of insupportable sorrow. It never can be a "bridal chamber of joy"[27] for me.

No, I do not play chess. How long does it take a reasonably intelligent human being to learn the game? I should like to learn it. I cannot say whether the M.G.[28] would be allowed in. Let's hold it for the moment.

Yours sincerely,
RM Sobukwe

27 Psalm 19: 5: "which comes out like a bridegroom leaving his chamber, and, like a strong man, runs its course with joy".

28 *Manchester Guardian*.

Benjamin Pogrund
to Robert Sobukwe,
17 March 1965 (Ba3.12)

My dear Bob,

I was delighted to receive such a cheerful letter from you. Your letter arrived this week when I was feeling depressed about my problems – and to receive such a letter from you in your circumstances was a tremendously elevating experience for me. My own problems paled into insignificance.

I saw your wife shortly after her return from Cape Town and spent some time with her getting full news about you and about the children. I was glad to know that all is well and I can again give you my absolute assurance that you need have no concern whatsoever about the welfare of your wife and children. As you know my only anxiety previously was that your wife would be reluctant to tell me of her needs, but I now know that we have got to know each other sufficiently well where this no longer arises.

I showed your letter to Jill and Ernie who were very happy that you liked the gift they sent you. Ernie is very keen to write to you but has not done so for fear of keeping away letters from your wife. I told him, however, that I thought you would like to have an occasional letter from him, so he will be writing soon.

I am not too clear what stage you have reached in your studies. I know that examination fees were paid a few months ago, but when will you be writing these exams? Also have all the books – apart from the Social Philosophy – reached you safely?

[...]

I see that fruit is still reaching you regularly. Can you please let me know who is paying for it. Because of the difficulties which arose last year I have not sent any money for this for some months. Have you been paying for it out of your personal funds? If you have please let me know and I will remedy the matter without delay.

I have applied to Pretoria for permission to visit you again and am awaiting an answer. Apparently it is not certain that I will be allowed in to see you because I am again a full-time newspaper man. I have however offered an assurance that if I am allowed in to see you, that I will not write anything for the Press about you. If permission is granted, I might be able to be in Cape

Town at the end of this month as I am going to East London on Sunday to attend a Trade Union Council Conference and could fly on to Cape Town from there. So it is possible that I will be seeing you within a day or so after this letter getting to you. I hope this will happen but we had better not bank on it.

I hope the books I sent continue to provide you with pleasant reading. Please let me know when you start approaching the end of them – if this has not already happened – so that I can send another batch down to you right away.

And as always, you must please let me know if there is anything at all which you need.

All for now. My very warmest good wishes to you and I hope that I will soon be seeing you again.

Sincerely,

Benjamin Pogrund
to Veronica Sobukwe,
30 March 1965 (Ba3.13)

Dear Mrs. Sobukwe,

I am sorry I have not replied earlier to your letter, but I have been away from Johannesburg.

I received a letter from Bob about two weeks ago and he was obviously keeping well and was in high spirits.

I have arranged for "Cape Argus" subscription to be renewed so you need not worry about this.

Please let me know if there is anything else that you require.

With best wishes,
Sincerely,

Robert Sobukwe
to Veronica Sobukwe,
31 March 1965 (Bc24)

Hullo Darling!

You should have received my letter by now, dated 25th February. I am writing merely to say "how are you"? and to tell you that you've been very much in my thoughts these last few days.

I wrote to Mrs Nkepu and she replied promptly. Her husband's case is still on though he is out on bail. They had the radio repaired and returned to me.

Mili has not written yet – most unusual! She probably has no stamps. Please do send her some cash or I could send her Two rands a month now that I have stopped smoking!

I told you when you were down here that Benjie had asked me to write to a Mrs Taylor in New York. I did: but evidently she did not receive the letter for Benjie has again urged me to write to her. You will have to do so, on my behalf, Child, not only in this case but in all cases where my quotas as a prisoner will interfere with my communications. You'll get her address from Benjie.

Fabian has written to tell me he'll be moving into his new house early in April. But he complains that I do not answer his letters. He is extremely interested in international politics of late and is remarkably well-informed.

Well, darling, it appears that pretty soon a journey to the moon will be possible. I have always wanted to take you there, of course. And if the fare is not exorbitant I'll take you there in 1980, I promise you.

How are the autochthons getting on? Oh, they're a lovely lot. I miss them intensely. [...]

We've been having rather unusually warm weather. Except for a biting wind in the morning and evening, the weather is still autumnal, what they call "bracing".

I came across some useful exercises in the *Sunday Express* the other day. I am forwarding them to you. They are specifically for women. I don't know when you can do them. The evening appears to be best. But you'll be too tired to be jumping around. The early morning will perhaps be best. But Jabi might know.

Well, Little girl, hold that head high! I am very proud of you and, of course, I love you very much.

Give my love to the kids when you write to them.

Your loving husband,
Mangi

P.S. How are you getting on with your reading? I am tempted to register you with Wolsey Hall. But I think we should discuss that when next we meet. RMS

Benjamin Pogrund
to the Minister of
Justice, B.J. Vorster,
9 April 1965 (Ba3.15)

Dear Sir,[29]

I have been advised by Security Police Headquarters in Pretoria that a request made by me to visit Mr. Robert Sobukwe on Robben Island has been refused.

While I realise that permission to visit Mr. Sobukwe is entirely within your discretion, I write to ask whether it is possible to reconsider the refusal, or else to advise me of the reason for the refusal.

During last year, I was given permission to see Mr. Sobukwe on six occasions. The first visit was for the purpose of conducting a newspaper interview, but the others were to enable me to interview Mr. Sobukwe for the private research on which I am engaged, and to see him as a friend.

I did not make use of these later visits for newspaper purposes. Although I am at present again a full-time member of the "Rand Daily Mail", my aim in seeking to see Mr. Sobukwe now is purely private in that I am a friend of his. There is no question of my attempting to make use of any opportunity I may have of seeing him for newspaper purposes.

Your kindness in allowing me access last year to Mr. Sobukwe was greatly appreciated by both him and me. I trust that you will find it possible to reconsider your refusal.

Yours faithfully,
BENJAMIN POGRUND

29 B.J. Vorster was the strongarm Minister of Justice in Prime Minister Hendrik Verwoerd's cabinet, a position that was combined with that of Minister of Police and Prisons in 1966. After Verwoerd's assassination in 1966, Vorster was chosen by the National Party to replace him as Prime Minister.

Robert Sobukwe
to Veronica Sobukwe,
14 April 1965 (Bc25)

My dear Mrs Sobukwe,

Thank you indeed for your letter and the Easter card, both of which I received on the 9th April. It was a real pleasure, a delight, to read your letter! I had already written a second letter to you when yours arrived.

I was particularly happy to hear about Dini. I am really relieved. I have no doubt that he will be happy with the Letlakas.

I have not yet received Mili's letter. But when you do write to her give her my love and ask her not to worry when she receives no reply from me. She can rest assured, though, that whenever I receive a letter from her I shall answer it immediately.

Thanks for news about the autochthons. I think of them continually and I really wonder how much trouble they are causing Mili in this new school.

Thanks also for the lawyers [illegible]. I know now where I stand. Thank you for all the trouble you have taken, Little Girl. You're a brick!

Yes, I received a letter from Fabian in which he complained about my silence. But I was of opinion that HE owed ME a letter not vice versa. He told me they would be moving into their house soon. He did not tell me, though, that they intend running a butchery. I'll have to write to him about it. I cannot understand how a medical doctor who, according to the principles of his profession, its ethics, is dedicated to the SAVING of life, should set up shop in a business that specialises in the murder of innocent cattle, sheep and goats.

Well, darling, if THAT is Moroka Clinic, then I know it. But I always thought that it was called *Jabavu* Clinic. That area is Jabavu, is it not? That's the area where Ismé Butelezi lives isn't it? How can you have Moroka Clinic in Jabavu Township? Where is the [illegible].

We had a touch of winter for a day or two this week. And what a taste it was!

In the letter before this one I sent you a few body exercises that are guaranteed to restore you to your Lovedale days! I also, I think, reported that I had received the radio from the Nkepus.

I understand about your financial troubles. I am in no screaming hurry for the goods either. But I shall be glad to receive the *Teelak, toothbrushes* &

Talcum as soon as possible. Incidentally, Benjie has written to ask if I need anything. I am not asking him for anything yet.

Well, Child, so long for now. The exams start on the 8th June. I haven't received the Time-table yet. I'll write again, soon. Mrs Marquard has asked to be remembered to you.

Love to Zodwa, Mama & the kids.

Your annoying husband,
Mangi

Robert Sobukwe
to Benjamin Pogrund,
14 April 1965 (Ba3.16)

Dear Benjie,

I received your letter on the 9th April and concluded that your application had failed as the weekend had already passed when you should have flown to Cape Town. I am sorry, really I should have liked to see you once more.

I hope you will have got over your depression by now. I appreciate your feelings very well indeed. I am extremely emotionally involved in the matter. You both are very dear to me and I hope I shall never be placed in a position where I have to take sides: though, mind you, if I were to get incontrovertible proof that you were to blame I would not hesitate, in fact I would be happy, to denounce you bell, book, and candle!

Thanks for news about Jill and Ernie and assurances about my wife.

In reply to your questions I have been receiving fruit regularly and paying for it out of my personal account, Benjie. I am afraid I don't know how my credit stands at the moment. It's not easy to obtain this information. But I do believe that my reserves are still some good way off from depletion.

With regard to the exams – I am writing them in June this year, Benjie. That'll be Part I of the Exam. They allowed me to do it in two years instead of three. The exams start on June 8th. I haven't received the Time-table yet, so I do not know on what days I write and what subjects I write on those days.

Now, please Benjie, this information is for you as a friend. "Tell it not in Gath, publish it not in the streets of Askelon"![30] Not that the results will embarrass me, whatever they are. Should they be unfavourable I can always pretend – and I think convincingly – that I deliberately worked towards that end as a patriotic South African who, respecting the traditional way of life of the country, did not want the black B.A. degree that I hold to be placed in immoral juxtaposition with an un-South African white degree! On the other hand, if the results are favourable, I can pretend that I toiled towards that end in order to defy the "fascist beasts". Incidentally, the latter is a Communist phrase. Do you now see what I meant about their poetic genius! If you term a fellow a "fascist" you merely attribute to him certain political

30 2 Samuel 1: 20.

attitudes and beliefs; one of which is that war "purifies" – it didn't seem to purify Italy's fascists, did it now? If you call him a "beast" you assign to him a brutish intelligence, manners & conduct. But call him a "fascist beast" then you conjure up a picture of the beast of the book of Revelations seen by St John in a vision on the island of Patmos, dinosaurian in proportions, moving in a murky fetid primeval jungle. You endow the fellow with a distinctive SMELL!!

I have all the books I need, Benjie. I have never failed an examination and I don't intend to start now. I had intended to major in Economic History but I have got so bored with the damn subject that I can't picture myself spending another two years over it. I may change my mind, of course. But at the moment I loathe all steel and railway cartels and rationalizations etc. Economics is interesting but my mind rebels against any subject that tells me that a thing is so because that is how it has been defined! I love Social Philosophy and British Government and enjoy International Law. That is my mental position briefly!

I'll discuss the books you sent me at some later date. I can assure you though that I have enjoyed them immensely, particularly Priestley & Snow.

With best wishes, Benjie,
I remain,
Your sincerely,
Bob

Veronica Sobukwe
to Helen Suzman, MP,
House of Assembly,
15 April 1965 (Ba3.17)

Dear Mrs. Suzman,[31]

I write this letter to you in your triple capacity as a woman, a mother and a parliamentarian of outstanding competence, whose integrity is unimpeachable and one who has made a name for herself as an untiring champion of liberty and justice for all men irrespective of race, colour or creed.

It is not my intention to go into the aspects of my husband's present position as this is well known to you, what I am writing to you about is to make certain requests concerning his future in Robben Island.

As you well know, the questions of my husband's detention comes up for yearly review in May and I wish to ask you to ask certain questions about him in Parliament.

First, how long it is intended to keep him *on the island*, and whether, in view of his conduct and his health, it would not be possible to transfer him to a place of detention on the main land.

Second, what the state of his health is and if it could be possible to arrange for regular visits by an independent doctor and reports submitted to the authorities and to his family.

I am aware of the prevailing atmosphere and that this stand will call for courage but I feel that this would be a humanitarian act of the highest order and I have confidence that you will not let me down at this time of hardships and trials for me and my children.

Please accept the considerations of my highest confidence.

Yours faithfully,
Veronica Sobukwe

31 Helen Suzman (1917–2009) was a parliamentarian, human rights activist and, for 13 years, the sole representative of the Progressive Party in South Africa's parliament in the apartheid era between 1961 and 1974. She made regular visits to Robben Island to enquire into the well-being of the political prisoners there.

Robert Sobukwe
to Nell Marquard,
29 April 1965 (Bd1.13)

Dear Mrs Marquard,

Thank you for your letter dated 13th March which I received on the 9th (ninth) April. I have not delayed unduly, therefore, in answering it!

I don't think I have ever thanked you for the book on J.L. Garvin.[32] It is a wonderful book with a great deal of information which is particularly relevant to my studies. I cannot help wondering what advice he would have given to the Lords today with regard to Wilson's intention to re-nationalize the Steel Industry and his threat to take action similar to that of 1911 should the Lords once more prove obdurate.[33] Thank you indeed.

I'll take up the question of chess at a later date. For the present I'll say thank you for the general picture and we'll let it be.

Thank you for the comments on "King Lear". I rely entirely on what I have read of Shakespeare's plays. I have never seen a performance of any play of his. Which might explain why I cannot share the enthusiasm of most students of English for Hamlet. I have never liked Hamlet and find it impossible to read any criticism that is favourable to the play: and which is not? What price, prejudice!

Your story of the Rhodesian boy is delightful. Children can be wonderful creatures. There's a story, which you probably know – it's a folktale – about little mice and little snakes which met at a stream, admired one another and swam together until evening when tired and happy they parted, promising to meet again the following day. When they got home the little snakes told their mother where they had been and with whom they had been playing. "Oh yes!" said the old lady indulgently, "then you most probably don't need any supper after such a glorious meal". Seeing their puzzled looks she asked, "Didn't you kill them and eat them?" "Of course not!" said the little fellows indignantly,

---

32 See Sobukwe's earlier letter of 18 February where he refers to the book on *'The Observer' and J.L. Garvin*.

33 The Parliament Act of 1911, passed on 19 August of that year by the British Parliament, deprived the House of Lords of its power of veto on legislation after the Conservative-dominated House of Lords had rejected the Liberal government's 'People's Budget'.

"one doesn't kill and eat one's friends!" The old lady's reply is better left to the imagination of the reader.

The little mice too, with beaming faces and "cheesy" fingers and mouths told their mother how they had played with the little snakes. Not only did she choke over her cheese but she also had a severe heart attack and had to be given what our people at Graaff-Reinet call "Harman's Druppels"[34] to bring her round.

When they met the next day, the young mice would not go into the river until the snakes had left. "What's the matter with you?" asked the snakes in disgust. "We also have a mother" was the reply.

I don't think it's indigenous. The moral is too obvious – which it is not, usually, in African folk tales. It sounds like one of Aesop's fables. But it's a story I love and have never forgotten.

Yes, I remember the article on Father de Chardin.[35] But have you seen an article in the April Digest (Reader's Digest) which suggests that plants and animals had the same origin! We now have not only monkeys for cousins but mimosa trees as well! "Jislaaik!"[36] to quote Dave Marais![37]

I don't think I'll comment on Wilson and Johnson just yet. I have too much to say about each of them. They are both outstanding, I think, in their domestic policies and will be popular leaders, nationally. With regard to Europe, their policies are sober and Wilson's might be dynamic. But they have not grasped the full meaning of the Afro-Asian revolution.

To negotiate from strength is to tell a man: "I am quite strong: and if you attack me there is no guarantee that you will win. Let us negotiate." But to tell him "I can annihilate you with one blow. The smack I gave you is nothing compared to what I can do to you when I set my mind to it. Come on, let

34 Harman's Druppels is an over-the-counter remedy ("Dutch remedy"), still available in South Africa, indicated to help with nervousness, restlessness and sleeplessness.

35 Pierre Teilhard de Chardin (1881–1955) was a French philosopher and Jesuit priest who also trained as a geologist and a palaeontologist, and who played a part in the excavations leading to the discovery of "Peking Man", a fossil of *Homo erectus pekinensis*, dated as being approximately 750,000 years old.

36 South African slang, *Jislaaik!* is an expression of surprise.

37 Dave Marais was the political cartoonist of the *Cape Times*.

us negotiate and stop your nonsense." That is bullying. And in the present temper of Asia doomed to failure from the start.

Let me call it a day. With kind regards.

Yours sincerely,
RM Sobukwe

Robert Sobukwe
to Veronica Sobukwe,
13 May 1965 (Bc26)

Hullo Darling!

I received your telegram, the Easter card and the Anniversary card – all most delightful and welcome. You will have realized now I think that I *did* receive your second letter and have replied to it.

I am writing this letter on the evening of the 12th and have post-dated it. It's bitterly cold but my heart is curiously warm because I received an extremely sweet letter from Mili this morning.

She wrote it on the 21st March but apparently it was only posted on the 7th (seventh) April. She acts as spokesman for all the Baboons[38] and obviously thought I would receive the letter long before Easter.

I am supposed to write to you and ask you to send Dali and Dede each a suit and a pair of shoes so that they, too, "like other children" should be decently clad during Easter. We know you are supposed to send Dini a pair of shoes like mine. I am urged to tell you not to waste time because the Easter holidays this year fall in April and these gentlemen must have these parcels before then!

Well, darling, I have done my duty. I wrote to you immediately I received Mili's letter. Please tell her that, although you will have to inform her that I received her letter in May and could not, therefore, carry out her request precisely.

She tells me she has been writing to you quite often, keeping you posted about the condition of the children and arrangements about Dini but has received no reply from you.

If this is a sample of the requests you receive from them then you really have my sympathy. My parcels can wait, Child. Do what you can for the autochthons and Dini. I'll ask Benjie to send me the articles you were to get me. Mili promises to send me a "lovely present" in June! She's got me excited, wondering what present she can AFFORD to send me!

She's very happy with her brothers around her and, of course, being Mili she wants to dress them up.

---

38 *Mfene* (Baboon) was the Sobukwe's clan name.

I sent Nenti one of the photographs of the children and she was extremely pleased though she wanted to know why I had not joined them. She tells me that Mercy is back in P.E.[39] and Archie is with her doing Standard Six. Dorris and Zozo are still at home sitting with folded arms.

Incidentally, Mili asked me in *ENGLISH* to "replay my letter pleace" – not too bad, considering that the sound "z" does not occur in Sotho so that "please" (pleez) is bound to be "pleace" (plees) just as "Mazibuko" is "Ma<u>s</u>ibuko" and "ci*v*ilization" is "ci*ph*ilisation". I have told her that I am going to write in English henceforth! She doesn't need to reply in English yet.

I have heard from Father Webber that Fabian went down to Durban and was fêted by the Medical Association for the article he wrote last year which won a prize. I wrote to him in March as I mentioned in my letter and have had no reply yet.

I have not yet received my time-table but I know the exams start on the 8th June. I am not feeling at my best either physically or mentally and cannot pretend to be very enthusiastic about the exams. But I intend to make it damn hard for them to fail me!!

Mrs Pullen has gone overseas on holiday and will also be attending a Temperance Conference. She asked me to give you her kindest regards and to say she is sorry she missed you.

Ntsu's defeat came as a surprise even if the vote was split between his party and the Marematlou.[40] I notice that Ellen lost and so did her brother. What about Khabella? Did he contest Maseru?

I won't be able to send you a card this time, Sweet. But I do want you to know when our anniversary comes round that I think you are an exceptionally wonderful woman whom I am extremely happy to call my wife and the mother of my children. [illegible] you are shockingly stubborn, but I have passed the stage where I am annoyed by such trifles. *Ndaawehla loo mgangatho.*[41]

---

39 Port Elizabeth.

40 Ntsu Mokhehle, a Pan Africanist trained at Healdtown and Fort Hare, was leader of the Basutoland Congress Party, which surprisingly lost the 1965 general elections in Basutoland to Chief Leabua Jonathan's Basutoland National Party and became the official opposition thereafter. The Marematlou Freedom Party came third in the contest.

41 I'm no longer bothered.

Well darling, God bless you. Please keep that chin high! How do you like the exercises I sent you?

Cheerio Kid!

Your loving husband,
Mangi

Robert Sobukwe
to Nell Marquard,
10 June 1965 (Bd1.14)

My dear Mrs Marquard,

I received four books of plays the other day and assume that they came from you. I thank you very much for them, though that is not the reason I am writing.

A week or so ago I received a letter from Benjamin Pogrund – almost a brother to me. He was extremely despondent and dejected at the news that my Napoleonic experience was to be extended.[42] I realized that many of my friends, among whom I include you very much, might be similarly afflicted. I am therefore, writing to administer a timely antidote. I'll say more at some later date.

I was reading the Acts of the Apostles the other night and enjoyed particularly chapter 19 from verse 24 dealing with what I can only describe as a near-riot as the silversmiths whose trade was threatened by Paul's teachings went through the streets shouting "Great is Artemis of Ephesus".[43] I read Moffat's translation and he really draws a vivid picture of confusion and reports that "the majority had no idea why they had met". But they roared and shouted *FOR TWO HOURS* – "Great is Artemis of Ephesus!" "Great is Artemis of Ephesus!" Talk of slogans and mob psychology! All these little tricks we so

---

42 A reference to Napoleon's detention on the islands of Elba and St Helena. Sobukwe's imprisonment was renewed year by year under a clause in the General Law Amendment Act, often referred to as the "Sobukwe Clause". There was, thus, considerable anxiety each year as the annual expiry date approached and Sobukwe's family, friends and fellow PAC members waited to learn whether he would be detained for another year. Nell Marquard in her article "Robert Sobukwe: A Personal Note" (1986) effectively describes the iniquity of the Sobukwe Clause when she noted that "I, like so many others, was deeply shocked, both at the injustice of it and at the thought of a man of his stature and integrity being condemned to the voiceless waste of solitary confinement".

43 Acts 19: 23–8 provides an account of the riot of Ephesus. A silversmith named Demetrius, who made silver shrines of the goddess Artemis, was outraged when Paul denounced these shrines as merely human (as opposed to godly) artefacts. Demetrius and fellow tradesmen who made good money from selling various depictions of Artemis whipped up broader public sentiment claiming that the widely worshipped goddess was being slandered.

fondly believe we are inventing have been used repeatedly in the past. And as you and I know, that two-hour roar and enthusiastic demonstration did not save "Artemis of Ephesus".

I do not know whether I still have a credit balance with you. If I do will you please try and get me a play or two by J.B. Priestley. I am almost ashamed to admit that I have only just discovered him and C.P. Snow and have enjoyed their novels immensely. Having read that Priestley has written some drama as well I am consequently eager to meet him in that field as well.

I am afraid I have nothing encouraging to report about my garden. I'll be starting work on it during the week-end. You'll appreciate, of course, that I did not want to leave fat, juicy cucumbers and beetroot behind to benefit the "enemy"! The "Scorched Earth" policy requires that we leave nothing behind on which the enemy may live. My supplies of fertilizers and insecticide are adequate!

My wife has written to say they are well and that the twins have lost their shoes at school. It beats me, of course, why natives want to wear shoes when they are obviously so much more comfortable going bare-foot and when we would give anything to change places with them and go barefoot without attracting curious stares.

I think this is enough for today. Benjie wrote to say he will be in Cape Town towards the end of May. I received his letter after he had returned to Joh'burg. He had hoped to be able to make certain purchases in Cape Town. I'll write again, soon.

Yours sincerely,
RM Sobukwe

Robert Sobukwe
to Veronica Sobukwe,
17 June 1965 (Bc27)

Hullo Darling!

Your letter written on the 10th May was only posted on the 15th May. So you are not outside the Bundu[44] either, are you now? I received the letter on the 4th June and enjoyed it immensely.

Before I forget: you write in your letter that: "This photo was sent by Sister Ger…". But no photo was enclosed. Are you sure you enclosed it?

As you will have read in the letter preceding this one, Mili did write, finally and put the case for her brothers very strongly. And I am really glad you were able to send the shoes in time.

Thank you, darling, for the telegrams and the good wishes for the exams. I am not too happy about my performance, but I should like to avoid any comment until the results are out. The papers were very fair.

Incidentally, with regard to that dentist's fee, thirty-three rands, sixty cents – R33.60 have been expended. And I have just been informed that you have sent Ten Rands. Thanks, Kid. I am quite flush, as you can see.

By the time you receive this letter the children will be back from school. And I pray that you have a very lovely holiday together, you, my "dusky, trusty, vivid and true"[45] wife and the lovely, joyful and playful children God has blessed us with.

You've been wonderful, Little Girl. And your courage is matchless. To be a Christian is not to go to Church in your "Sunday best" with a "Sunday" face – long and lugubrious. It is to suffer with God in a godless world. When Christ asked Peter, James and John: "Could you not watch with me one hour?"[46] He was expressing the loneliness and helplessness of God. And by this test, you are an outstanding Christian.

---

44 South African expression referring to the physical space of wilderness or – put in the terms of American English – the "boondocks".

45 The first line of Robert Louis Stevenson's poem "My Wife" reads: "Trusty, dusky, vivid, true".

46 See Matthew 26: 40.

It has become bitterly cold out here. I am thinking of getting a radiator so that I shall be able to work at my desk standing.

By the way, Sweet, have the "Cape Times" and the "Cape Argus" sent you reminders that your subscriptions are due for renewal? The "Cape Argus" cut off deliveries for two weeks or so and then, without a word either before or after, resumed deliveries. The "Cape Times" continued deliveries while the "Cape Argus" deliveries were suspended. But it has now suspended deliveries, too. And this is the fourth week. And they have sent no word to me.

I could have settled the accounts immediately. But I remembered that with the Sunday papers we had both paid the subscriptions, unknown to each other, and I did not want to risk the same thing happening here. But I certainly do not like the attitude of these papers in abruptly suspending deliveries without any warning whatsoever. I was almost tempted to tell them to cease deliveries for good. But we'll discuss that later. In the meantime tell me whether you'll pay the "Cape Times" subscriptions or whether I should.

Thank you for your generous comments about Winnie. That is, of course, what I expected from my wife. And I think I can guess who the neighbour was!

Now, Sweet, I have left this bit of bad news up to the last because I did not want to spoil your enjoyment of this letter. I have just read in the "Cape Argus" that Gideon Nkepu has been sentenced to twenty-five years. Yes, kid, TWENTY-FIVE YEARS! Apparently the Attorney-General had instructed that the death sentence be demanded. But since Gideon had only one previous conviction the Judge found it difficult to impose the death sentence. But even this which he had imposed is, I think, unique in the history of such cases in this country.

As I told you, I had written to his wife. I shall do so again. I should like you, too, to write to her and ask in what way you can help.

I'll write again, soon. Love to you all there and keep those heads high!

Your loving husband,
Mangi

Robert Sobukwe
to Benjamin Pogrund,
17 June 1965 (Ba3.18)

My dear Benjie,

I received your letter on the 4th June i.e. after you had returned to Johannesburg. In the circumstances, I could not contact you as you desired.

The exams are over Benjie and the papers on the whole were very fair. I made some very silly mistakes, however, with regard to the instructions. For one thing I did not start every answer on a new page as instructed and examiners can be very petulant. If, however, they concern themselves purely with the contents then I may just make it. However, I am quite satisfied now that I can pass this exam any time I wish, and whatever the results this year I am happily assured that there has not been an alarming deterioration in my mental capacities.

And I know that this is your chief fear. After I had read your letter I felt a heaviness of the soul. This is the first time I have felt sad after reading a letter from you. I detected a wee note of despair and dejection, Benjie, and I was deeply perturbed that my closest friends should feel this way.

Do you know that in 1937 my brother and I were the only two to pass Std Six, out of a class of thirteen, but we couldn't go to College until 1940 because our parents didn't have the cash ready? Even then the best we could aspire to was the 'Native Primary Lower Teacher's Certificate' – a three-year course after Standard Six. In 1943 I was granted permission to do J.C.[47] in one year. I topped the class in June but went down with T.B.[48] in August and so couldn't write the Exam. I had to repeat that class in 1944. But it was during my illness that I made friends with people who undertook to see me through Varsity.

In 1947 then I entered Fort Hare. At the Freshers' Social held in April, speaking on behalf of the Freshers of Wesley House – my residence – I unleashed a venomous attack on the attitudes of Wesley – its aggravated spirit of "hostelism" and the un-intellectual nature of its discussions.[49]

47 Junior Certificate.

48 Tuberculosis.

49 See Appendix 1 for a transcription of this speech.

Wesley House, of course, is arch-conservative and there were some outsiders present. The senior students were incensed and at a subsequent "House" meeting they decided, almost unanimously, that I be sent to Coventry for a month. We freshers didn't have the vote. So my friends and fellow-freshers could do nothing but merely sympathize. I was placed in a private bathroom, with the tub removed to make place for my bed. It was an isolation cell, all right. Within the precincts of Wesley House nobody was allowed to talk to me! It didn't bother me this much.

In June we were enfranchised and in the elections that were subsequently held to elect the House Committee for the ensuing year, I stood as a candidate for the Chairmanship. I won! You can't imagine the din and confusion. The elections were declared null and void and fresh elections ordered. All senior students were fetched wherever they were to cast their vote. I lost by about six votes. The next year I became a member of the House Committee with a room to myself!

In 1949 the new Fort Hare Constitution came into being whereby the SRC and the President of the SRC were to be elected by popular vote. I was the first President of the SRC to be elected according to that Constitution, Benjie, and the vote was as near unanimous as makes no difference. The moral? That I was born for better things, Benjie, than the Premiership of South Africa. Wesley House & South Africa are on a par!

In assessing our positions, Benjie, we must not lose sight of the fact that South Africa represents not even a thousandth-millionth of the world population. And the ruling caste represents an infinitesimal fraction. In being contemptuous of racial arrogance we represent the distilled product of Western intellectual thought.[50] And the greatest minds of both East and West say it is absolute rubbish to declare: "Du bist nichts, dein volk ist alles"[51]

50 In his review of the first edition of Pogrund's *How Can Man Die Better*, Tom Lodge (1991) drew particular attention to this assertion of Sobukwe's (Lodge, however, cites Sobukwe as saying that in the moral aversion to racism we see "the distilled essence of Western thought".) Lodge stressed furthermore that Sobukwe clearly had a degree of "admiration for Western culture". I note this simply to underline the fact that Sobukwe did not have a dismissive or wholly oppositional attitude towards "Western intellectual thought" as those who accused him of "anti-whiteism" all too frequently presumed.

51 "You are nothing, your people is everything".

as young Nazis were exhorted to do on waking up every morning. Because if *you* are nothing, your folk is nothing either.

And even in this country, the silent courage of thousands of men and women who VOLUNTARILY stand up to be counted is astounding testimony to the depths of human courage.

Then it is the brave man chooses,
While the coward stands aside
Till the multitudes make virtue
Of the faith they had denied.[52]

Now for the mundane. I am afraid my needs grow with the years. I certainly will wish to replace the sheets and the shirts and the pyjamas. They're all worn out. The shirts will be size 16½ collars and please make them striped or checked, Benjie, but *NOT* white! No, my friend, it is not a question of colour prejudice. Otherwise I'd ask for *Black* shirts, worn, as you will recall, by Mussolini's *Fascists,* while Hitler's blonde Aryans wore *BROWN* shirts!

I should also like trousers I can wear with my black shoes. My grey pair is giving in. I do not have my measurements but a size 5½ will not demand much by way of alterations.

I may later need a hot point and a radiator. But do not get these yet. I'll let you know later, in case permission has to be obtained to acquire them.

I saw in the Press that the Chairman of the Defence and Aid Fund in the Western Cape has been told to leave the country within ten days. Was that Mr [J.W.] Blundell? I haven't been getting the papers regularly – it's about three weeks now. I've not been getting the C. Times[53] – and I have missed some interesting news. I'll write to you soon. I have so much to say! By the way the pyjamas are size 42 as you know!

Love to Jenny! Yours sincerely, Bob

52 From James Russell Lowell's hymn "Once to Every Man and Nation" (1845).

53 *Cape Times.*

Robert Sobukwe
to Benjamin Pogrund,
1 July 1965 (Ba3.21)

My dear Benjie,

I really must thank you most sincerely for the heater. It put me right in the upper middle class. I wasn't surprised, though. It's what I expected from you.

In my last letter I attempted to persuade you to see the situation in South Africa against an international background. It then assumes its correct proportions. I intend to pursue this aim further in this letter.

I believe what strikes one in the Western world, particularly, is the emergence of, or desire for, the "strong leader", who is not only intensely patriotic, but is also master of the domestic situation. I have in my mind President Johnson & de Gaulle, particularly, and Harold Wilson. I am leaving out Franco and Salazar[54] for the moment. In Germany and Italy the systems have not yet fully recovered from the regimentation imposed by Nazism and Fascism, respectively.

Both Johnson and de Gaulle are dynamic in domestic issues. But the foreign policies of Franco appear to be more and more anti-American stances and posturings with no positive long-term synthesis. Johnson's foreign policy, on the other hand is extremely inept, particularly in relation to the Asian and Latin American countries.

Harold Wilson is dynamic too, in the domestic field particularly. But he faces tremendous problems. His image is blurred by the precariousness of his majority in Parliament, the delicacy of Britain's economic position and the British refusal to allow a Leader-Image to emerge. At a later stage I'll deal with Britain fully.

In the Communist world the dominant issue is the ideological schism between Peking & Moscow, reminiscent of the split between the Catholics & the Orthodox Church in the history of Christianity. The emphasis has been placed variously on Peking's "racialism", orthodox Communism or downright aggressiveness.

I think even Wilson, Socialist though he is, has failed to appreciate the revolution which Peking's intransigence reflects. It is possible to

54 The dictators of Spain and Portugal at the time.

explain it according to Djilas's[55] three stages of Communist government: (a) Revolutionary nationalist, (b) Administrative consolidatory, (c) Bureaucratic distributive, and to say Peking is in the first and Russia in the final stage.

But I believe that the fundamental factor is a re-appraisal of Western ideas. There was a time, Benjie, as you know (in fact as late as 1918), when the whole world was possessed by European powers. And since the ideas which prevail at any particular moment are those of the ruling or dominant classes, the ideas that prevailed in the world were those of Europe. All things were judged by European standards. Even human beings were divided into those of Europe and those not of Europe. The nomenclature was European. On the one side stood the "European" or "white" – on the other the "Non-European" or "Non-white". And what is significant is that this terminology has been used by the people of Africa, Asia and Latin America without any feeling of annoyance. We have described ourselves Benjie, as the *negative* of one third of the human race!! The revolution consists in this: that ⅔ of the human race are beginning to think of themselves POSITIVELY and MUST soon describe themselves POSITIVELY!!

China explodes her bomb and to protestations from the West she replies "Why is it 'fair' for de Gaulle to qualify as a nuclear man and bad for Chou en-Lai[56] to do so?" Why is it good for FOUR European powers to have nuclear arsenals and bad for ONE Asian power to have it? In other words, why should ⅔ of the human race be policed by ⅓?

Russia quarrels with China and withdraws all her aid. West Germany quarrels with Tanzania and withdraws her aid. China and Tanzania compare notes and needs must come to the conclusion that the "white imperialists" have behaved like this throughout the centuries.

But what moves me to the depths of my being, Benjie, is the love that Europe, America and the East bear for Africa, the missionary zeal with which the young people from these lands embrace any opportunity to be of service to the under-developed countries. I feel it, particularly when India and Pakistan, from their very limited resources, make available technicians for work in Africa and Latin America.

---

55 Milovan Djilas (1911–95) was a Yugoslav Communist theoretician and politician.

56 Chou En-lai was the first Premier of the People's Republic of China, serving from 1949 to 1976.

The youth of these countries have entered into the spirit of the revolution. They understand it; they share it. When they express disappointment or even disgust with certain aspects of African progress, I am grateful. You can only be disappointed by those you love and by those from whom you expect better things.

From my side then, I am excising from my dictionary the terms "Non-European", "Non-white" and "Coloured". I do not know yet how I shall refer to the groups traditionally so described. But the terms will emerge. Much more coming!

My love to Jenny and to friends.

Yours sincerely
Bob

Robert Sobukwe
to Veronica Sobukwe,
6 July 1965 (Bc28)

Hullo Darling!

This is a very short note to say "Happy Birthday" to both you and Mili. God bless you both "with length of days and show you His salvation".[57]

By the way, did I thank you for the anniversary card? Forgive me, if I did not, Kid. It's a sign of gross selfishness and [illegible] to take acts of kindness for granted. And selfishness is one weakness I would hate to be burdened with.

Benjie has sent me a magnificent radiator. I can now work at my desk till late instead of seeking the warmth of my blankets at such rural hours as 8 p.m. and 9 p.m.! Those are *your* hours, I know and though I respect you very much, Child, honesty compels me to say that those *are* rural hours!

How are you faring this winter? Reports of heavy snowfalls synchronizing with recent coal shortages have [illegible] my mind centred on Mofolo for where your treasure is there will your heart be also, say the Scriptures.[58] We had a few cold days. But on the whole, this has been an unusually warm winter.

Well, Cheerio [illegible]. I am looking forward to your visit and am trying to recollect as many folk-tales as possible for the entertainment of these gentlemen. It is time you introduced Mili and Dini to Scrabble so that we may have some "intellectual" amusement when you come down.

God bless you, Kid.

Your loving husband,
Mangi

57 The Christian author James M. Leckie used this phrase in his book *Consolation in Affliction* (1833).

58 Matthew 6: 21.

Robert Sobukwe
to Benjamin Pogrund,
4 August 1965 (Ba3.23)

My dear Benjie,

I received your letter this morning and enjoyed it immensely. Although this letter serves as a reply to yours of this morning, I had intended, in any event, to write to you today to thank you for the items of "cosiery" (derived from the adjective "cosy") all of which reached me safely and in sterling condition, and to unload a further consignment of half-baked political ideas.

Thank you indeed for the articles. They bore the unmistakeable print of a cultured mind! I hope you had as much pleasure in choosing them as I had in admiring them.

Yes I wrote to both you and Prof Wellington on the 30th June and I believe somewhere along the line the letters got mixed up. Fortunately I have no mistress with whom I correspond and my letter to whom might "accidentally" be directed to my wife.

Thank you for the story about Zululand. These tribesmen are extremely shrewd. They remind one of the Negro poet whose lines I think I have quoted to you before:

"The Indian stood, unyielding, still and grim:
We saw him perish; and we learnt from him
To mix a grain of philosophical mirth
With all the cruel injustices of earth."[59]

Reminds one, too, of the late S.E.K. Mqhayi,[60] the African "Poet Laureate" who, during the last war, attended the opening of the Ciskei Bunga[61] in King

59 From the poem "Self-Determination: The Philosophy of the American Negro' by Leslie Pinckney Hill in his collection *The Wings of Oppression* (1921).

60 Samuel Edward Krune Mqhayi (1875–1945) was a Xhosa biographer, dramatist, historian, poet and translator who is known among the Xhosa as "the poet of the nation".

61 The Bunga was a type of advisory council, made up of traditional authorities and the educated elite, which had little real power.

Williamstown clad in his regalia. When Van der Byl, then Minister of Native Affairs,[62] got out of his black Cabinet car, Mqhayi met him with the words:

> "Yehla, yehla, yehl' ingwe emthini"
> (Down comes the leopard from the tree).

Van der Byl & his retinue were flattered, even when the words were correctly interpreted. Van der Byl had come to press for the implementation of the "Rehabilitation scheme" strongly opposed by Africans. But the tribesmen were warned: When a leopard leaves the tree, while people are around, its purpose is to destroy!

It is only this week that the "Cape Argus" has finally reported on the furore your articles have caused.[63] I received the "Cape Times" for the last time two days before the Clay-Liston fight.[64] I have written to my wife to find out what is happening. So the only daily I receive is the "Cape Argus", which has been trying its damnedest to be "patriotic". The "Sunday Times" of the 13th (thirteenth) and 20th (twentieth) June and of the 4th (fourth) and 25th (twenty-fifth) July have for some reason or another gone astray. I haven't received them. It's only this week that I read that the "Sunday Times" also carried something about the Prisons. I am beginning to wonder whether there is some design in the non-delivery of these particular issues. I have, in fact, instructed my wife to ask you to find out about these issues. I have myself written to the C.N.A. but have had no reply yet.

---

62 P.V.G. van der Byl was the Minister of Native Affairs from 1943 to 1948 in Jan Smuts's United Party government. The rehabilitation schemes were meant to address problems of land usage in the African reserves but were bitterly opposed by many rural peasants.

63 In June and July of 1965 Pogrund published three reports in the *Rand Daily Mail* exposing the inhumane conditions – unjustified violence, abusive treatment, horrendous food, inadequate medical treatment – that those in South Africa's prisons (political and criminal prisoners alike) were subjected to. Both Laurence Gandar (1915–98), the editor of the *Rand Daily Mail*, and Pogrund were threatened, vilified and legally prosecuted by the apartheid government as a result. Each of Pogrund's informants was tracked down and likewise subjected to legal prosecution. Although the press had reported this extensively, it had all been kept from Sobukwe. Pogrund had sent the three reports he authored to Sobukwe, but Sobukwe, unsurprisingly, did not receive them.

64 Sonny Liston fought Cassius Clay (soon to change his name to Muhammad Ali) for the title of world heavyweight boxing champion on 25 February 1964.

After the fore-going, it will not surprise you to learn then that I have not yet received your copies of the "Rand Daily Mail". Strange as it may seem, I had intended to ask you to send me the relevant copies. I am keen to have these copies and suggest that you send me cuttings, preferably by Registered Post, so that the possibility of negligence on the part of the postal authorities will be ruled out.

I am afraid I haven't heard much even from the radio news broadcast as the only news I listen to is the 1 p.m. and 7 p.m. news on Springbok Radio. Otherwise I use the radio solely for music and drama.

You describe yourself as an anachronistic 19th Century liberal. And that is perhaps your greatest political asset, Benjie, excluding the "anachronistic"! For one thing, I *know* that you can never be used as a propagandist by any particular interest or constellation of interests. I *know* that what you write had received the most careful consideration the highest standards of journalistic ethics require. I want to assure you now that I admire greatly your personal courage, both physical and moral, and that of your illustrious editor, Mr Gandar.

I shall comment in a later letter on your remarks about the government's behaviour. But as you are a psychologist of no mean standing yourself, I think I may observe that:

(a) It was Hitler who remarked that faith is stronger than conviction because it persists in the face of irrefragable, irrefutable and overwhelming evidence to the contrary.
(b) Since faith is basically an emotional matter, irrational, it requires constant revival and replenishment.
(c) "No one likes to be alone with an unpopular opinion, and once people begin to relinquish an opinion because they feel isolated, the snowball can begin to roll."[65] More later.

I wrote the exams in one of the rooms in "my yard". A warder invigilated. I'll certainly let you know the results.

Thanks for news about Jenny. Have your parents seen her? Where's Astrid staying? With her parents?

---

65 Sobukwe is paraphrasing a comment by the British Tory politician David Windlesham (1932–2010), who remarked that "no one likes to be alone with an unpopular opinion".

The black shoes I haven't worn more than a dozen times and they are still virtually new. The brown, however, are beginning to show their age. I shall, therefore, be extremely happy if you will send me a similar pair so that I may rest them now and again. And with the shoes please send me Meltonian Dark Brown. The size is 9½.

I am enclosing a list of my sartorial statistics. I'll be pleased if you could make a copy and give it to my wife. I have a grey suit that I want altered. I have asked her to enlist your assistance. When she hands it over to you, Benjie, will you please send it straight to me. I would like to try it on as it is before suggesting alterations to it. You may tell my wife so, too, so that she shouldn't think we have fooled her.

Well, Benjie, so long for now. Thanks for everything and keep your courage high. "You are heir to the promises of God."[66]

Greetings to Ernie & Jill & others

Yours very sincerely,
Bob

PS Also please send me postage stamps – 2½ cent variety. Bob

66 See Romans 8: 17 and Galatians 3: 29.

Benjamin Pogrund
to Robert Sobukwe,
7 August 1965 (Ba3.24)

My dear Benjie,

In my letter of the 30th June I promised to continue the discussion I had begun in it, a discussion centring primarily on the international situation. Your letter of 20th July has forcibly brought me to realize how small our world is and how blurred the line is between international and domestic problems.

I had intended in this letter to examine the Afro-Asian-Latin American complex: to ask: What is its basis? Do the Latin-American states form part of this bloc? Will they in future? Is such a solidarity necessary? desirable? inevitable? Are regional-geographical loyalties and commitments destined to overshadow and replace biological-cultural associations? That is, for instance, are Australia and New Zealand to find their destiny and historical involvement in Asia rather than in the Commonwealth? Is Canada willy-nilly to be embraced by the U.S.A. or will she continue to seek her fulfilment in a Commonwealth to which she is attached by bonds of affinity and advantage? The same goes for the African and Asian members of the Commonwealth. Can Pan-Africanism permit the existence and continuance of "Former French colonies" and "Former British colonies" attached to France and Britain respectively?

But I think I must deal first with the problem you pose in your letter concerning "the dialogue between the deaf". You know, (this is by way of digression) one reason why I have a profound love and respect for the prophets of Judah is that they could look at contemporary history with eyes of ruthless and pitiless truth, even when it was most painful for them to do so. They also exposed the corruption of their times in words of rare poetry. *BUT*, and here lies their greatness, because they knew that besides the historical order there is what Paul Tillich,[67] an American theologian, calls the divine order, undergirding and supporting the historical, they were able, in spite of

67 Paul Tillich (1886–1965) was a German-born Lutheran theologian who taught at the Union Theological Seminary and Harvard Divinity School in the States, where he took up residence in 1933 after being dismissed from his German university post by the Nazis. He is best known for his books *The Courage to Be* and *Systematic Theology*. He is widely regarded as one of the most influential theologians of the twentieth century.

prophesying the destruction of the temple and the Holy City and the mass exile of the Jews, to sing out in triumph:

"Oh thou that bringest good tidings to Zion, get thee up into the high mountains:

Oh thou that bringest good tidings to Jerusalem, lift up thy voice with strength: lift it up, be not afraid. Say unto the cities of Judah, 'Behold your God.'"[68]

With similar unclouded vision let us examine the few instances you quote in illustration of Mr Gandar's thesis. Briefly, this is how I see the position. America and South Africa represent diametrically opposed, irreconcilable attitudes to the colour or "race" problem. If the apologists of apartheid are correct then wherever Negro Americans meet European Americans (incidentally, Negroes now term themselves Afro-Americans!) on terms of equality there must be friction. The only news that can please them, therefore, is news of "racial clashes" in the U.S.A. as this will "prove" the correctness of their thesis. President Johnson, however, is implementing his policy of complete equality determinedly and successfully: so successfully, in fact, that the African states, despite Afro-Asian solidarity, and despite this conviction that Johnson's Vietnam policy is wrong, will not condemn America because they appreciate Johnson's honesty in his domestic policy.

(2) The above analysis leads to an interesting point. The colour or Race issue is not, as such, a political issue. It is not confined within the political boundaries of a State. Whether they know it or not, Johnson and Verwoerd now serve as symbols of a divided conscience that spills over their territorial borders. All White Supremacists, all over the world, are extremely happy whenever the Verwoerd government takes a step that indicates or signifies its determination to "keep the Kaffir in his place". When he says he'll have no niggers working side by side with European scientists or flying jets, besides protecting his home crowd from shattering disillusionment regarding the inferiority of "black" men, he also rejoices the heart of klansmen in the U.S.A. who are happy to know that the nigger who is beginning to "give himself airs" in the U.S.A. has been put in his place by the S.A. govt. Johnson, on the other hand, is the hope of all who stand for non-racialism. His successes are theirs and they endorse his utterances on bigotry.

68 Isaiah 40: 9.

Both countries have to maintain a consistent, unbending attitude on matters of colour both for the sake of their domestic supporters and the international attitude they each represent. As a result, at U.N.O.[69] and elsewhere, the U.S.A. has had to take an uncompromising stand against Apartheid.

South Africa, i.e. the government, has of late turned almost gratefully to France as the one country that is sympathetic. At the same time, de Gaulle's France is extremely anti-Anglo-Saxon, touching a historical chord in the Afrikaner's breast. De Gaulle has been excelling at cocking a snook at the U.S.A. of late and, in fact, almost everybody has been of late. Verwoerd is not alone!

The Liberal in this country is in the same position as the White Supremacist in the U.S.A. in so far as the political climate is concerned.

I am not being original when I say that the race problem is to this century what the slave problem was to the last century. And it will be solved, because it has to. And to believe that the problem can be accommodated is to be naive. The government cannot but hot up the pace. Where the appeal is to emotion it has to be reduced to the lowest common denominator. Knuckling down solves nothing. For our own self-respect, we who oppose White Supremacy have to stand up to the forces representing it. I would rather die on my feet, Benjie, than live to a hundred crawling on my belly. And that is the only compromise possible.

If my argument does not hang together well, please excuse me. I do find that my concentration leaves a lot to be desired. I'll continue the argument later. Incidentally [I] haven't received this week's "Sunday Times" or "Express"!

Yours sincerely,
Bob

P.S. A logical exposition will require 20–30 pages! Have to truncate my argument! Bob

---

69 United Nations Organisation.

Robert Sobukwe
to Benjamin Pogrund,
11 August 1965 (Ba3.25)

My dear Benjie,

There are already two letters of mine on the way to you. Certain ideas in your letters act as irritants on my mind, compelling me to think them through. I am merely sharing my thinking with you.

I'll return to the International situation at a later date. At the moment I want to consider "liberalism" and "conservatism" which are very much in the news today.

They are, of course, not mutually exclusive at all; on the contrary they are complementary. Liberalism has been and continues to be the initiating and experimenting force. Without it there can be no progress whatsoever. This applies not only to politics but to all aspects of life. New ideas come exclusively from liberalism. In language, new expressions, words and styles are the product of liberalism: similarly in economics, religion and art. But liberalism unchallenged, undisciplined and uncontrolled cannot but lead to chaos because its very nature militates against equilibrium. And it can be challenged and stabilized only by conservatism. Take an example from language. If liberalism had unchallenged sway in language it would be impossible to communicate because words and expressions would be changing from day to day if not from hour to hour.

Conservatism, on the other hand, can never initiate or develop anything. It is, by definition, a force that CONSERVES: that preserves what already exists. It resists change and is synonymous with routine. And this applies not only to politics, but to all aspects of life. An example from language is not only the resistance to new words, expressions & forms but also attempts to keep the language "pure".

Because it preserves the familiar, conservatism has a stronger appeal to the ordinary man than liberalism has, for the ordinary man is a creature of routine. It is only the creative thinker – the artist – who cannot stand routine. He is the "unstable" element in society. Conservatism then, unchallenged, uncontrolled and undisciplined leads to stagnation and sterility. It has to be continually prodded by liberalism which in turn has to be continually restrained by conservatism. It is the continuous interaction between the two that maintains a "progressive equilibrium".

You will probably say that I am using "liberalism" in a special sense and that it refers to the political philosophy of the Nineteenth Century which was the counterpart of economic *laissez-faire*. But even then it would represent individual freedom and initiative as interacting with the inertia of the community.

If we believe, as Marx taught, that political and other ideas are mere reflections of the economic reality, then liberalism might be becoming a weaker force just as private enterprise is being replaced by public enterprise. Logically, then, we should expect an ever-increasing accretion of power to the State – a regimentation of thought congruous with the regimentation of the economy.

At the present moment, the Western democracies, particularly the Scandinavian countries, are attempting to complete the process of democratization. For years they have had political democracy but have not had social democracy as economic power and the social position that goes with it have been the privilege of a few. The Welfare State is an attempt to democratize wealth. In the Soviet Union and other Communist countries we have had social and economic democracy in so far as the wealth of the country ("means of production") is publicly-owned and differences in income are due to inequalities of contribution. But this social democracy operates in a framework of political oligarchy. Complete democracy here would require the implementation of political democracy.

Prof. Laski[70] argues, and I think convincingly, that in a capitalist country, political democracy is possible only so long as the economy prospers. Once the economy contracts, the contradiction between the political power of the working man and his economic dependence is exposed. The worker will want to use his political power to improve his economic condition; and this he can do while the economy prospers. But once it contracts, his interests clash with those of the owners of wealth who, generally, never number more than one per cent of the community. A government in a capitalist country then has no option but to protect the interests of the employers (the owners

70 Harold Joseph Laski (1893–1950), British author, economist and political theorist, taught at the London School of Economics and exerted great influence through his teaching and prolific writing.

of wealth). It must take a stand against the workers. That is how he explains the emergence of Fascist regimes in Italy, Germany, Spain and Portugal in the 'thirties during the depression. His thesis is that fascism is inevitable in periods of capitalist contraction. But U.S.A., Britain??

Incidentally, political philosophers recognize that in organization and structure, fascist and communist regimes are identical. The only difference is that fascist regimes protect the interests of the few owners of wealth in the employing class – while Communist regimes protect the interests of the working class. Whether this is how things turn out in practice is a matter to be empirically ascertained. Further, political philosophers do not regard communism and fascism as either left or right: they are off the spectrum!

Whether it is possible to have states whose economy is "planned" without ultimately having their politics "planned" is a matter on which I have severe doubts. However, the de-freezing in Russia and the countries of Eastern Europe reminds us of the eternal cycle of human development and behaviour. Nature is nicely balanced and the exclusive pursuit of a particular programme or idea leads to an imbalance, the correction of which leads to further imbalance.

So much for now. To turn to the poetic a little. Thanks for the assurance about my wife and children and for news about little Jenny. And may I suggest that I shall feel happier and easier in my mind if you take lessons in karate purely as a precautionary measure. The newspapers are beginning to cause me some concern, particularly as "The Observer" too has now failed to arrive for three weeks running. It's my wasted money that grieves me!

Best wishes, Benjie.

Yours sincerely,
Bob

Robert Sobukwe
to Benjamin Pogrund,
25 August 1965 (Ba3.26)

My dear Benjie,

I saw your photograph in the Sunday papers and remarked, not only that you were looking surprisingly fit and well but that you were becoming handsomer by the day – as, of course, Jenny's father should!

I have also read Dr Yutar's[71] remarks made both in court and within the congenial atmosphere of Pretoria University. I fumed at the time, but the editorial in the "Sunday Times" does indicate that if he decides to be a politician he will be dealt with as such. I feel reassured and am only sorry D.G. Lowen[72] cannot be brought into the fray to face him. He relishes encounters with Yutar and, of course, doesn't know how to pull punches.

It was you who drew my attention to this dialogue of the deaf: the calcification and ossification of attitudes on either side. In the present case, those who instinctively either disbelieved or resented your articles still do and will continue to do so whatever the verdict of the courts. Similarly, those who instinctively believed or welcomed your articles still do and will continue so to do irrespective of what the courts say or do. The former group sees in Van Schalkwyk's recantation[73] a "rebuttal" of your case – to quote the "zealous" Dr Yutar; the latter group, unimpressed, will cynically refer to the 1938 "confessions" in Stalin's courts.

I am, therefore, not unduly concerned about the court proceedings except only in so far as your integrity, both as a person and as a journalist, is being

71 Percy Yutar (1911–2002) was the first Jewish attorney-general in South Africa, and prosecutor of Nelson Mandela in the 1963 Rivonia Trial. Pogrund (2015: 224) notes that Sobukwe was "contemptuous of ... State prosecutor, Dr. Percy Yutar, known for fervently carrying out Security Police briefs".

72 D.G. Lowen was a distinguished German-born barrister in Johannesburg who was well known for defending apartheid dissidents in court.

73 Pogrund (2015: 224) notes that Warden G. van Schalkwyk, one of his informants in the prisons exposé, "was railroaded into repudiating his statement to me [concerning the abusive circumstances within prisons], only to find his retraction was then used against him to convict and jail him for lying".

impugned. That is the object Yutar has in view; and on that score alone I would have him fought every inch of the way to hell and back. I think I am satisfied now that that will be done.

There is, of course, the whispering campaign that will be directed against you and for which you must be fully prepared. It is going to be "discovered", Benjie, that you are of Jewish extraction. And racists loathe a fearless Jew. It is going to be "discovered" that you are a very close friend of mine. In a sense I am glad your divorce is through because Astrid would be getting more of the type of letter you told me about last year. All the advice I could give you on this kind of warfare is contained in *Hornstein's Boy* by Robert Traver,[74] who observes that McCarthy was challenged and routed by a very gentle old Senator, Joe Walsch[75] I think the name is: that, quoting Holmes, "as life is action and passion, it is required of a man that he should share the passion and action of his time, at the peril of being judged not to have lived."

The mundane. I have been informed that "The Observer" has been received and is being withheld because the Minister's order provides that I should receive *only* South African newspapers. Of course, what Prison Regulations permit, I am entitled to have. And I know that *Life, Time* and a host of magazines from overseas are allowed into jail under Prison Regulations. I'll have to check the list again. In any event, I know that Ernie and you entered into a great deal of correspondence before you made the order. You wrote to the Chief Magistrate in Cape Town, I remember. Could you tell me what he and Pretoria said in reply to your enquiries?

In the meantime, as Ernie has paid a year's subscription in advance, the paper is being presumably regularly sent here and being withheld from me – a state of affairs most unsatisfactory to both Ernie and me. I suggest he arrange for the suspension of deliveries until we have ascertained what ruling the Chief Magistrate gave on the matter, if he did give any and whether, in fact, the "Observer" can legitimately be withheld from me.

---

74 A 1962 novel by the lawyer John D. Voelker, who used the pen name of Robert Traver.

75 Joseph Nye Welch served as chief counsel for the US Army when it was under investigation for Communist activities by Senator Joseph McCarthy. He quoted from the eminent US Supreme Court justice Oliver Wendell Holmes.

I am O.K. don't worry. And as for your question whether I require further funds for my studies, I shall know the answer when the results are out and will let you know. Part 2 promises to be much more interesting.

Give my greetings to Ernie and the rest and my love to Jenny.

Yours sincerely,
Bob

Benjamin Pogrund
to Veronica Sobukwe,
3 September 1965 (Ba3.28)

Dear Mrs Sobukwe,

I am sorry I missed you when you came to see me this afternoon. I would have liked to have had the chance of talking to you as it has been a long time since we saw each other. For this I apologise, but as you will have seen from reports in the Press, I have been extremely busy with reports about the jails.

I shall take up without delay the question of the children's schooling, and you need not worry about this. Let me contact you again, however, about the matter of your next visit to Cape Town as I must investigate the position first.

Bob has written to me several times lately. On Saturday alone I received three letters from him. I was glad to know that the clothing had reached him safely and that it was to his taste. I shall be sending him two pairs of shoes tomorrow, as well as extra shirts, etc. He has asked me to let you have the size in suits he takes, and I shall send this out to you early next week.

If you are in need of anything, or if I can be of any help to you, please do not hesitate to let me know immediately.

All good wishes,

Sincerely,

Robert Sobukwe
to Nell Marquard,
7 September 1965 (Bd1.15)

Dear Mrs Marquard,

This, I am afraid, is going to be a letter of "requests". I have a number of favours to ask of you.

First of all, you asked me, in your last letter, what books by C.P. Snow I had read. As I had asked you for some of J.B. Priestley's plays as well, I think I should give you a complete list of the works of both authors that I have read. These are:

C.P. Snow – Time of Hope
The Light and the Dark
The Affair

J.B. Priestley – The Good Companions
The Priestley Companions
Angel Pavement
Bright Day
Midnight on the Desert
Let the People Sing

Secondly, as you know, I receive a parcel of fruit weekly from Stuttafords[76] in Cape Town. I have recently arranged that the fruit be sent fortnightly. For reasons of security it was agreed that the parcel be addressed to Major Visser, but it is now no secret on the island and probably in other circles off the island, that the parcel is meant for me.

The practice, up to about two months ago, was for the mouth of the box which contained the fruit to be sealed with a strip of brown paper. Of late, however, the flaps have merely been pushed in as though the parcel was meant for personal delivery by Stuttafords van in one of the suburbs. I have found it difficult to believe that a firm of Stuttafords' reputation could be so incredibly irresponsible and rude: but I have been assured by the Prison Authorities that that is how the box is delivered at the docks in Cape Town.

76 A leading department store in Cape Town.

My request, then, is that you please find out from the management why there has been this change. I am sorry to cause you so much trouble. I know a Mrs Henderson[77] had a hand in the arrangements but I do not know what her address is.

Finally, may I please ask you to send me some foot powder? Two tins should see me through the remaining months of the year. I hope to make arrangements for regular supplies when my wife visits me early in January.

That is all for requests. Now may I thank you for the "resumed" issues of "The Listener". They have been a rich lot indeed. The articles on Africa by Margery Perham,[78] and Judith Listowel[79] I found very reassuring. They were rather too sympathetic I thought and tended to play down the warts. I enjoyed George Bennett's article on the socialisms of Ghana and Kenya, while the articles on the BBC and on "inequality" were typical of the ruthless self-criticism so characteristic of the British: a kind of pure air in an atmosphere of drum-beating, adulation, and hypersensitiveness.

I was also suitably impressed by the pipe-smoking women of the Transkei and the serious factory girls of Ghana. My weakness, of course, is that I love the continent – warts and all. But I am not blind to the warts.

I hope you enjoyed your stay in Natal. Your letter from Pietermaritzburg was quite intriguing. It contained a lot of suppressed irrepressible laughter – know what I mean? It had the air about it of Churchill glowering at his opponent after a foreign affairs debate in which he had received a hammering, and then suddenly putting out his tongue at the man!

Thank you for explaining why you used red ink. Without the explanation I most probably would have seen red. And may I also explain that I am not a fan of Mrs Malaprop[80] nor do I regard you as a pagan.

With best wishes to you and Mr Marquard.
I remain,
Yours sincerely,
RM Sobukwe

---

77 Moira Henderson was a friend of Eulalie Stott's and also a Black Sash member.

78 Margery Perham, "Britain's Role in a World of Racial Challenge", *The Listener*, 3 June 1965.

79 The journalist Judith Hare, Countess of Listowel, gave a series of broadcasts on the BBC in June 1965 on her visits to four African countries, including Rhodesia and Tanzania.

80 Mrs Malaprop was a character in Richard Sheridan's play *The Rivals* who was fond of using words that sounded similar to the ones she intended; from her habit comes the word "malapropism".

Benjamin Pogrund
to Robert S. Bilheimer,
22 September 1965 (Ba3.32)

My dear Rob

Your letter, cable, and finally your cheque have all been safely received. And once again I am deeply indebted to you for your generosity.[81] The best way in which I can express my thanks is to let you have copies of the latest batch of letters from Bob. As you will see from the letters, his stature grows in adversity. Whatever the depths of his troubles, he is always more concerned with the problems of the outside.

My deepest and sincerest gratitude to you,

Yours sincerely,

81 Bilheimer arranged for one of his parishioners, Mrs Taylor, to help with occasional funding for Sobukwe.

Benjamin Pogrund
to Robert Sobukwe,
22 September 1965 (Ba3.31)

My dear Bob,

You've given me a real treat – four letters within a fortnight, three of them arriving on one day! Apart from the talk about serious things – I'll return to these later – I am delighted just to have so much news of you, and to know that your spirits are high. Your letters reached me in full. Also, as a welcome change, it was nice to receive your letters a reasonable time after the writing of them. I must apologise for my delay in replying. I have wanted to give thought to what I write, and I have had to wait until enough quiet time was available.

Your wife came to see me recently, but missed me. She left a letter for me in connection with the children's schooling and her next visit to you. All this is O.K., and by the time you read this I shall have contacted her. So you can start looking forward to seeing her again before not too long. This will be possible because your friends have again given solid support.

Before I forget, I should mention that Mrs. Taylor will probably soon be writing to you again. The week before last I arranged for another parcel to be posted to you, consisting of:

1 pair brown shoes (very good and to be used when receiving International Red Cross and "Sunday Tribune" representatives)

1 pair "huskies" for leisurewear (I overcame my religious scruples and bought shoes with pigskin uppers)

1 dacron/cotton shirt

1 light-weight jersey

(note that, to maintain my image in your mind of a "cultured mind", I made sure that shirt and jersey are matching colours).

I was happy to know that the last parcels of clothing reached you safely and were to your taste. I hope the same will apply to this batch – which is, by the way, a gift from an articulate lady.

By the time you read this, the announcement will have been made that I am suing Yutar for defamation.[82] Two prominent advocates (one a Q.C.) have unanimously recommended the action. There are a couple of other defamation actions which the Editor and I will be instituting shortly in addition to this one. In fact, we have submitted a large number of "possibles" to counsel, in each case stipulating that we want as much of a 100% guarantee of success as possible, otherwise we are not interested. The Yutar action falls into this category.

I need not conceal from you that Yutar's remarks in court hurt me deeply. It is one level – the integrity with which I try to approach my work – at which I never thought to be attacked in such a vicious way. Perhaps I was naive in this respect. I had, of course, fully anticipated a smear campaign against me – what an easy way to try and answer what I wrote! – but still, this particular attack threw me off balance, at least for a while. But I sat down, looked at what was behind the attack, and forced it into perspective. My initial dismay had been transformed into a cold determination to expose the lies – and the defamation action (plus a couple of other things which are on the go) will meet this aim.

Bob, my friend, in the meantime, your words of support have meant a great, great deal to me.

Your perceptiveness about what I should watch out for has been well-grounded: even before your letters came, I had already been the target of large numbers of abusive and threatening phone-calls, as well as a few letters. A rather amusing (sick-amusing, that is) side-issue is that the bulk of the phone-calls have been received by Astrid because her telephone is still registered under my name. Apparently, crazy characters have phoned her until late at night, demanding to know where I am, saying they want to kill me, that they are coming to blow up her flat, etc. etc. Last week she was in a distraught state about all this, and finally accepted my advice that she should complain to the police. I have naturally taken proper precautions to protect myself, one of these being that a Karate expert on the "Mail" acts as a bodyguard whenever necessary!

---

82 Pogrund was to sue the Deputy Attorney General of the Transvaal, Dr Percy Yutar, for defamation action arising from remarks Yutar had made about Pogrund in a trial connected with the *Rand Daily Mail*'s exposé of prison conditions.

I have also been the recipient of a particularly nasty and scurrilous circular letter (in duplicated form). You refer to the Swaziland letter – well, how right you were, because it features in this latest effort. I didn't broadcast the news of the Swaziland letter at the time, but I did lodge complaints and handed copies of the letter to both the South African and Swaziland Security police. So I wonder who is responsible for this latest scurrilous piece? Please be assured, Bob, that none of this bothers me. It is what I anticipated, and it has not, and will not, deter me in the slightest from going on. If anything, the feeling of sickness I get that people should descend to this low level, serves to spur me on.

At times in these past couple of months, I have come close to despairing of my basic belief in the ultimate triumph of the truth. There have been occasions when I have felt depressed, and have thought that the forces against us were too well-organised, too determined to conceal and to cover-up, whatever lengths they had to go to. But these moods of depression do not last long, and I can only tell you that, whether I am being naive or not, I believe firmly that the truth here will prevail. It is too big a truth and has been going on for too long and in too many places, for attempts at concealment to have any hope of final success. I am not being starry-eyed in this because I know and accept that difficult and even perhaps terrible days are still ahead. But as the Editor wrote, we have opened a chink in the curtain of secrecy – and we are determined to bust it wide open.

I am sorry that you have not been receiving the newspapers regularly. I suppose you have taken up the matter with the officials immediate to you. If so, hasn't any explanation been given? So much has been appearing on the jails issue[83] that non-delivery of those copies containing news of it would mean that you are receiving hardly any newspapers at all!

I would like to send you another batch of the original reports. Unfortunately, because of Strachan's banning, I cannot do this.[84]

---

83 The "jails issue" refers to three articles that Pogrund wrote in the *Rand Daily Mail* between June and July 1965 exposing the inhumane and abusive conditions within South African prisons.

84 Harold Strachan (1925–), a former political prisoner, was Pogrund's chief source for the reports he wrote about prisons in South Africa. Strachan was subsequently tried under the Prisons Act and sentenced in May 1966 for a term in prison.

I am just reading your letters as I write, and I'll deal with points seriatim as they arise.

Jenny continues as lovely and joyful as ever – and to prove it, I am enclosing pictures I took of her over the weekend. I still see as much of her as I possibly can, between four and five times a week.

Astrid is still staying in the flat which we occupied last year. Didn't I tell you that she remarried last December? Communication between us is virtually non-existent, and is confined to formalities about when I can fetch Jenny. As I have indicated to you previously, it is not a particularly pleasant story and the details can wait until we next see each other.

I am sorry, Bob, but in ordering the shoes I overlooked your request for Meltonian. I shall attend to this without delay, and it will be posted to you this week.

The postage stamps you need are enclosed herewith. R1 worth should keep your letters flowing for a while – and please let me know when the supply starts running low.

I have taken too long already to get this letter off to you. So let me end now and I shall write again in a couple of days.

In the hope that this letter will be handed to you before my New Year[85] starts on September 27, let me wish you security of spirit, greater happiness, freedom and reunion with your loved family and the friends who cherish you, in the year ahead.

My prayers, as always, are with you and for you.

Sincerely,

85 The Jewish New Year.

Benjamin Pogrund
to Veronica Sobukwe,
24 September 1965 (Ba3.33)

Dear Mrs Sobukwe,

I am glad to be able to let you know that I have been able to raise the money for your visit to Cape Town. Will you please let me know how much you need so that I can send it out to you?

The only difficulty is that I am leaving for Durban on Tuesday and will be away for about ten days. The best thing might be for us to wait until I return to Johannesburg so that I can come out and see you. Will you, in the meantime, send me a letter to let know what time of the day you are usually at home at present?

I have had several letters from Bob lately, and there is no doubt that he is keeping well. His spirits are high and he is cheerful.

In one of his letters he asked me to send you the list of his measurements, and I am enclosing this herewith. Bob said in his letter that he would like me to help you to arrange alterations to his grey suit. He said, however, that I should send the suit to him *before* any alterations are made, as he would first like to try on the suit. It might be best again to wait until my return from Durban so that I can collect the suit from you and attend to sending it down to Bob.

Please forgive me not having been to see you for so long. But I am afraid that this jails business has kept me under extremely heavy pressure, and I have not been able to give my friends the time that I would have liked to have given them.

In any event, I look forward to seeing you again soon.

I hope that you and the children are keeping well. Their school fees, by the way, have been paid so you need not worry yourself about this.

All good wishes,

Sincerely,
BENJAMIN POGRUND

Robert Sobukwe
to Benjamin Pogrund,
30 September 1965 (Ba3.34)

My dear Benjie,

I intend this to be a short letter, uncluttered by vulgar displays of questionable erudition and political sagacity. There was enough of that in my letters of the 5th, 7th, 11th, and 25th August. That is enough of a lambasting for anybody though I must admit you've taken your punishment bravely!

Thanks a lot for the shoes, the shirt and the jersey. They were, as usual, what my butler had recommended. Thank you also for the New Year good wishes. I am sorry I did not send you a card. I came to know about this holiday only on Saturday, 25th when I read about [it] in the "Cape Argus".

I read in the "Sunday Times" of the 26th September about the civil actions pending – yours included.[86] You know, of course, that if I can be of assistance in any way I shall be happy to oblige. Just you say the word!

With reference to the fruit: For some time now Stuttafords have been sending it in an open carton with the flaps tucked in to prevent the fruit from falling out. I have asked Mrs Marquard to take up the matter with the management. I just can't understand how they dare to send food across the ocean in an unsealed carton. How the harbour officials are persuaded to accept the consignment I fail to understand. If they are recalcitrant I shall cancel the order immediately, Benjie. We can then arrange, when my wife comes down, to have somebody make the purchases and deliver the parcel at the docks, as Mrs Mittag did with the Defence and Aid packages.

I received a letter from AB's[87] wife, Lauretta, a psychology graduate of Natal University. She is now teaching in Zambia, went up there in March, she tells me and earns £120 a month (R240.00). She complains, of course, that the cost of living is high and that she hasn't met her husband yet. They have been parted for over two years now.

Finally, when next you send me books – any time, even next year – will you please include the following:

---

86 Pogrund was to sue Percy Yutar for defamation. Although Pogrund eventually had to go to the Appellate Court, he won the case, and legal precedent was created.

87 A.B. Ngcobo was a PAC member, and a member of the original PAC national executive.

1. Literature on Judaism – particularly the Jewish case against the Christian faith.
2. Works by Somerset Maugham– *any* of his works.
3. Plays by J.B. Priestley
4. *African Socialism* by Leopold Senghor– if it is not banned, and any other topical books that have escaped the ire of our censors.

Keep well and keep your courage high.
Love to Jenny and greetings to friends.

Your sincerely,
Bob

P.S. Since August, I have arranged to have the fruit sent *fortnightly* to avoid waste. Bob.

Veronica Sobukwe
to Benjamin Pogrund,
1 October 1965 (Ba3.35)

Dear Mr. Pogrund,

Thank you for your letter which I received yesterday.

Thanks a lot for the help you have given me in connection with my trip to Cape Town.

I have calculated the train-fare for the four of us. It will amount to R77.79.

I was pleased to learn from your letter that Bob was keeping well. I have not heard from him for a month.

Thanks for all the trouble you have taken to make us happy.

Good-bye,

Yours sincerely,
Veronica

Benjamin Pogrund
to Eulalie Stott,
8 October 1965 (Ba3.37)

Dear Eulalie,

Mrs Sobukwe will be arriving in Cape Town on about January 1, 1966, in order to visit her husband. I have asked her to make a point of contacting you when she gets there in case you wish to see her about anything.

In the event of her requiring any cash or whatever it may be, could you perhaps also assist her? I am providing her with funds for the trip but am concerned lest she run short. If you do have to lay out any money, please let me know and I shall refund it.

I hope you will not mind my burdening you with this. I am writing to you early as I shall be away from Johannesburg a great deal in the next month or so and I don't want to forget to ask you for this help.

Hope you are keeping well,

Sincerely,

Telegram from
Benjamin Pogrund
to Robert Sobukwe,
9 October 1965 (Ba3.39)

Delighted news your examination success stop I will now also call you Prof[88]
Regards Benjamin

88 A joking reference – Sobukwe's followers in the PAC called him "Prof" both because of his evident intellectual prowess and his former position at the University of the Witwatersrand.

Robert Sobukwe
to Nell Marquard,
13 October 1965 (Bd1.16)

Dear Mrs Marquard,

I have a lot to thank you for: your letter of the 26th August, the plays, C.P. Snow's book and the foot powder. For all these, thank you very much indeed.

But I am afraid I still have more favours to ask. And this time, if you refuse, I shall understand. It is, I agree, rather asking too much of a friend. But please hear me patiently.

You have perhaps read the bit about me in the "Sunday Tribune" of 22nd August.[89] I am quoted as saying, *inter alia*, that among my regular correspondents are ... "two ladies whose interest in me is purely Christian".

You will admit that there is the suggestion of a sneer in that sentence: an implication that they do not see me as a person but as a prospective convert or prodigal son.

Now, the two ladies live in Cape Town, and what I said was that my correspondence with them is confined to purely religious matters.

I know that if they interpret this sentence as I do they will be deeply hurt. We have kept up regular correspondence since 1963 and they have tried to cheer me up as best they could.

Both ladies are Baptists and both are widows. They are elderly. I have never met them but one of them has constantly reminded me that she is not highly educated. And I fear that she, at least, may regard my reprinted remarks as a deliberate attempt to hold them up to ridicule, particularly as you and Prof Wellington, the other correspondents mentioned, are recognized intellectuals. I have written to both of them, but I fear they may think I am being hypocritical. After all, before this report appeared, all my letters to them gave the impression that I valued the shared Christian experience.

In short, Mrs Marquard, I am going to ask you and Prof Wellington, individually to contact these ladies in whatever manner you deem best and assure them, from me, that my remark was very unfortunately reported. I thought it necessary to make the qualification about the content of our

89 The newspaper had been given access to Sobukwe as part of the government's attempt to discredit the prisons exposé.

correspondence because I had given their names. Incidentally they are: Mrs Catherine D. Pullen, Garthpool, 4 Nares Road, Claremont; and Mrs Dorothy MacBride, 14 Vredenhof, Mouille Point. They wrote to me independently but I was able to bring them together. Mrs Pullen strikes me as a timid and very sensitive person. I shall really be grateful if you were only to ring them and pass on that message from me.[90]

I am not going to write anything else. I shall comment on your Hamlet article in a subsequent letter. I have enjoyed it immensely and would certainly be happy to receive more from the same pen.

Thank you also for information about water-melons. Unfortunately I won't be growing them this year. I am not growing anything at all. Our water supply is very low. I'll have to be satisfied with a Japanese garden.

I am sorry if I have appeared to be kindly disposed towards Dave Marais. I didn't know, of course, that you belonged to the great family he has been systematically maligning.[91] I shall know, in future, how to view his despicable cartoons.

And, finally, thank you for the story of the crossing of the Red Sea. I admire the young fellow's considerateness. I hope Mr Marquard is feeling himself again.

God bless you both.

Yours sincerely,
RM Sobukwe

---

90 Marquard later reflected on Sobukwe's request, noting that he feared that the ladies in question "might be deeply hurt", stressing that his considerateness in asking her to "get in touch with them and assure them of his sincerity ... was of a piece with his concern for his friends" (1986, p. 8).

91 Nell Marquard had been born a Van der Merwe, a family name that is regarded as stereotypically Afrikaans. Van der Merwe is a stock figure, a representative of Afrikaners, in South African humour and was the butt of David Marais's cartoons.

Robert Sobukwe
to Nell Marquard,
21 October 1965 (Bd1.17)

Dear Mrs Marquard,

Your letter of the 30th September reached me on the 12th of this month (October). Two days previously I had written to thank you for the books and the footpowder. I also wrote to ask you to soothe some Christian feelings. I realize now, though, that I should have made the proviso – if you feel such an interpretation of the statement is likely.

Again thank you for the foot powder. My trouble appears to be purely one of very free perspiration for which any footpowder will do. I have used both kinds outside(!) indiscriminately.

Thank you also for the trouble you have taken to enable me to get books from the Provincial Library Service. I'll certainly make use of the service.

Touching the fruit it would appear that a new man has taken over that department. I had arranged at the beginning that they should not send me any avocado pears (my figure, you know) and they have observed that taboo for two years, until last week to be precise. It must be a fresher who's responsible for this confusion.

It does appear that the "Sunday Tribune" article to which I referred in my letter of the 13th has caused some mischief. Prof Wellington has written to say that a certain lady had, after reading the article, offered to help with my wife's fare so that she may visit me more often. But it's not just the money, you know. My friends would be prepared to finance six trips a year if I so desired. However, my wife is employed as a nurse and she does not want to be taking unpaid leave every now and then, getting on and off trains, just to see a husband! But the poor dear does not know that. Oom Danie Nel[92] would tell her she does not know the "Bantu". They are happiest when they are away

92 A joking reference to "Danie" de Wet Nel, Minister of Bantu Administration and Development and Bantu Education, 1958–1966. The "Oom" ("Uncle") is used with ironic familiarity.

from their wives; the longer the separation the merrier! Please point that out to any prospective good Samaritans who may come to your door.[93]

I was amused by a piece I read in "Life" magazine a month or so ago. An article dealing with the Los Angeles riots reports that a number of shops hurriedly put up signs: "Blood Brother", "Negro owned, please, thank you," "Negro owned and operated – we shall overcome".

It was this last that I found most amusing. It is so opportunistic! But there is a bit of pathos in it too. How many throughout the world are compelled to pronounce "shibboleth" to safeguard their lives, homes and businesses.

I am not commenting on Hamlet yet. I am reading the play over once more in the hope that I shall achieve Arnold's "willing suspension of disbelief".[94]

Yours sincerely,
RM Sobukwe

I have passed Part I of the BSc Econ. exams. No class or grade given in Part I. But I know it was J-U-S-T! All set for 2nd leg of the Double! RMS

93 Reflecting back on the letters she received from Sobukwe, Marquard (1986) wrote of Sobukwe that "he never complained … [although] sometimes he found an outlet in irony … Only once did his irony have a bitter tang" (p. 8). Referring to the "Oom Danie" comment above, elicited by the offer of a woman to pay for more frequent visits by Veronica to the Island, Marquard states that this "touch of bitterness was an exception".

94 The term was in fact coined by S.T. Coleridge, not Matthew Arnold.

Benjamin Pogrund,
804 Doromo,
Van der Merwe St,
Hillbrow, Johannesburg,
to Robert Sobukwe,
21 October 1965 (Ba3.41)

My dear Bob,

I arrived back in Johannesburg the night before last, after an absence of a week or so, to find your letter of September 30 waiting for me. From your letter I see that you had not yet received the letter I sent to you some weeks ago in which I enclosed some photographs of Jenny. I hope you have it by now.

I saw your wife just before I went away and can report that she is looking well. She assured me that she is not in need of anything, and as usual, I extracted a promise from her that she would contact me without delay should she require anything at all. I discussed with her the arrangements for her travelling to see you and she told me she proposes to go down on about December 30, taking the four children with her. Not so long for you to wait for this! I have, in the meantime, also made arrangements for a friend in Cape Town to give her assistance if required while she is there.

Immediately after learning about your examination success I sent a telegram to you and I hope this arrived safely. I was truly delighted with the news – not that I had really had any fears about the outcome. Will you let me know the exact details of your passes? And what now? Are you going to treat yourself to the normal university three month summer vacation, doing some quiet sunbathing and swimming on the beach near your bungalow, or do you want to start the next year's work immediately? As before, you need not worry about your tuition fees or your books. Please merely let me know what the fees are, and send me a list of the books.

I have noted what you want in the way of both serious and light reading and will start collecting these straight away. It will take me a while to get together a good assortment, but I promise it will be reaching you long before next year.

Thanks for letting me have the details about the fruit. But what you haven't told me is who has been paying for it. If you are paying yourself, please let me know as I have had an offer from some people to take over on a regular basis.

Just let me have the amount needed and who must receive it. I am surprised that Stuttafords has been sending it in an unsealed carton. From what I was told when I last visited the Island last year, I would have thought that, for obvious reasons, the prison authorities would have been the first to insist on a sealed package. But I do not think this presents any great problem and I am sure Stuttafords will rectify the position once it is drawn to their attention. I will take up the matter also from this end.

I said earlier I had just returned to Johannesburg. I was in Durban – I have been there on and off for the Strachan case[95] – and on my latest trip, also found myself in Cape Town for a day. That was on Tuesday this week. My thoughts were particularly with you on that day, I wished we could see each other again. We must wait for happier, freer, times …

Half my clothing is still in Durban as I shall be returning there sometime next week. Also there is the batch of letters received from you – the ones, to use your phrase (which needless to say, I reject outright), of "questionable erudition". I want to continue the dialogue with you but I want to have the letters in front of me as I write. So I'll have to delay answering until I go back to Durban.

The Strachan trial, by the way, is going well. For reasons of tact and good manners, you will forgive me if I do not write frankly about my feelings regarding the conduct of the trial. That too will have to wait for another day. Let me merely say that I have yet to see any evidence produced which disproves what I wrote. I would like to be able to send you the "Mail" for the period of the trial as we are carrying tremendously full reports – six to eight columns each day. This is probably the most well-reported case this country has ever had. But I fear that it would be pointless sending you the papers as, judging from past experience, they would not be allowed through to you. But perhaps you could check this point with the officials. If they say it is O.K., I will gladly post the full set of reports to you.

---

95 In an attempt to challenge Pogrund's reports on conditions within prisons, Vorster and the government sought to discredit Pogrund's sources. Pogrund tells us that the government had framed charges against Strachan, which thus put the onus on Pogrund and Gandar to prove the truth of the reports. For a short time it appeared that Sobukwe might be given the chance to act as a witness in the case, to testify about the physical assaults and atrocious conditions of prisons. Ultimately Pogrund's lawyers decided against this plan of action. For more details see Pogrund's *How Can Man Die Better* (2015: 221–5).

All for now. I regularly give Jenny greetings from "Uncle Bob", whom she knows to be a good friend who stays far away. I must tell you, by the way, that on the New Year, I took her to a synagogue for the first time. Previously, she had only been to a synagogue for a wedding. But when we walked in and sat down, she looked with awe at the chazan (cantor),[96] who dressed in his white robes, stood in the middle of the congregation leading the prayers. After a few minutes of intent gazing, all four years of her turned to me and whispered: "Daddy, is that God?" When I told her it wasn't she promptly lost interest in the proceedings and soon began clamouring to be taken home! When I asked her the next day whether she had liked going to "shul" with me, she pulled a face and said she far preferred a "bride's shul". So I am afraid my little daughter is not taking well to the religion of her forefathers. Jewish religious services can of course be somewhat arduous, and to one who does not know what is happening, I suppose they must be boring in the extreme. Thinking back to my own childhood, I grew up in a highly orthodox home where religion was part and parcel of growing up. There was the regular lighting of the Sabbath candles, and on the Festivals, the saying of prayers on Fridays and on Festivals, and the fact that from my very earliest years, my sister and I went with my Parents to "shul" as a matter of course. It is true that, at a later age, I rebelled against this. I rejected it simply because I felt I had merely been dragged into it all, and it was something I was observing because it was customary and not because I really knew what it was all about. But then I went back again, when within myself I decided this was something I wanted and I knew what it was about. So the process of rejection was, in the long run, a positive phenomenon, and I cannot really say that the childhood years' experience was a bad thing. In fact, if anything, I would regret the fact that I was not given a more positive guidance than I was given – that I received religion just as an everyday thing, without more meaning being imparted to it.

The relevance of all this is that I am worried about Jenny on this score because she has no religion in her background at present. Astrid and I never really saw eye to eye on this point. I believe in children getting a religious background in the home. I think it gives them a sheet anchor, and when they reach the age of maturity, they can decide themselves what they wish to do with their religion. But the background must be imparted to them, otherwise they can prove to be rudderless, with no basis for morality or for their attitude

96 A person who leads synagogue services.

towards their fellows. As I say, with me no longer in the home, there is none of this for Jenny and it worries me and perplexes me because I do not know how to fill the gap. Jenny knows herself as a "shul girl", and gradually I suppose, as she grows up, she will learn that this means she has a particular religion. But I wonder whether this will go any further within her. [...]

A page ago I wrote "All for now", and then rambled into this discussion. Hope it's been of some interest to you.

With great affection,

Veronica Sobukwe
to Benjamin Pogrund,
25 October 1965 (Ba3.42)

Dear Mr. Pogrund,

Thanks for your help. I bought the ticket on the very day I left your office.

The children will be coming home I think in the second week of December.

I think sixteen rand will be enough for their trip home.

I have not received any letter from Bob for some time.

With best regards,
Sincerely,
Veronica

Benjamin Pogrund
to Veronica Sobukwe,
3 November 1965 (Ba3.44)

Dear Mrs Sobukwe,

I have pleasure in enclosing herewith R16.00 to pay for bringing the children home from school. As always, it comes with all good wishes.

Mrs. Eulalie Stott has replied to the letter I wrote to her and she says that she will be delighted to help you in any way possible when you visit Cape Town. She is trying to get you permission to visit Bob every day while you are there and to have lunches with him, but so far she has not succeeded in this.

Mrs Stott asks that you contact her as soon as you reach Cape Town so that she can give you any help you may need. Her address is: "Lunesdale", 6 Bishopscourt Road, Newlands, Cape Town; telephone: 77.3368.

With all good wishes,
Sincerely,

Robert Sobukwe
to Benjamin Pogrund,
9 November 1965 (Ba3.47)

My dear Benjie,

Your Mr Walters interviewed me some time last week. I commented as fully and as objectively as I could on the Strachan article which he read to me. At the end he felt, however, that my evidence would not materially assist the defence and informed me that I would, therefore, not be called as a witness by the defence.[97]

I am sorry he thought that way because I was rather persuaded that there was a lot I could substantiate. But then, Mr Walters is an advocate and knows best, presumably, what is relevant and material in a court of law.

I want to assure you that I am quite aware of the political implications of this case. And I do not wish history *ever* to record that for some opportunistic reason or other, I kept mum like Brer Rabbit, when I should have spoken, at the same time being quite voluble when I should have held my peace.

If then, at any time in the future, at any stage of the case, you should like me to testify please don't fear that your calling me as a witness will jeopardize my position. We have become so anxious to shield and spare our friends that we are virtual "collaborators"!

Thank you for your letter of 21st October, received on the 2nd November. Thanks for news about my wife. Am looking forward to the visit. Around this time of the year I miss the children a lot.

As my letter of the 21st October indicated, I received your telegram. Apparently they do not give details for Part I unless specifically requested. In fact the Pass List wasn't sent to me at all, but to the "appropriate overseas authorities". In South Africa it is I and a certain Nisbet of Natal who passed Part I of the Econ. course.

Thanks for the offer regarding tuition fees and books. I believe the fees are settled. I paid £34 at the beginning of the course. I have written to Wolsey Hall and am awaiting word from them. I'll let you know what the sharks demand.

---

97 Tom Walters was a Cape Town attorney who gained access to Sobukwe on behalf of Pogrund, in connection with the Strachan case.

The books have arrived safely. I have already read and have been moved to the depths of my being by "The Representatives".[98] The least said about the "Vicar of Christ" the better. In fact I have been thinking, over the past few months, about the total absurdity of a solemn conference of over two thousand educated and responsible cardinals and bishops discussing whether or not the Jews killed God. How arrogantly stupid can Europe get?

I am glad to report that Stuttafords have reverted to the *status quo ante* (It's not my fault if you chose science instead of the classics!). I have been paying for the fruit myself and have arranged for deliveries to be made FORTNIGHTLY instead of weekly. I am getting on in years, young man, and have to regulate my calorie intake! I believe R28 (twenty-eight rands) should cover a year's supply. The best would still be to send the amount to the Commanding Officer with the requisite instructions that it be used solely for fruit.

I'll be glad to get the "Mail" reports of the case.[99] As I said earlier the trouble arose because of an interpretation of instructions which was unfortunately restrictive. I am certain there'll be no trouble this time. The matter has been resolved even if there still are hedgings and provisos.[100]

Thanks for the bit about Jenny. The sight of her tears at my heart. I am not going to comment on the bit about your faith except to say that I am glad you have on your own found your way back to the Holy One of Israel. I am not a racialist, Benjie, as you know very well. But if I were to be any one other than who and what I am, I would choose to be a Jew. With all those solemn promises and assurances from God I would walk on air, absolutely certain that "underneath are the everlasting arms."[101]

With best wishes,
Yours sincerely,
Bob

---

98 A play in English translation, by the German author Rolf Hochhuth, which was highly critical of Pope Pius XII's role during the Second World War in abetting the Nazis.

99 The Strachan case was first discussed in Pogrund's letter of 22 September. This letter is a response to Pogrund's letter of 21 October.

100 Sobukwe is referring here to the conditions of censorship governing what he was allowed and not allowed to receive – conditions that he was actively challenging.

101 Deuteronomy 33: 27: "The eternal God is your refuge, and underneath are the everlasting arms".

Robert Sobukwe
to Nell Marquard,
14 November 1965 (Bd1.18)

Dear Mrs Marquard,

This is not intended as a letter. Not even as a note.

Attached is a newspaper cutting which will thrill you as a student of Shakespeare. I should have liked to send the cutting without comment except, perhaps, for a caption reading "Asserting the African Personality"!

I was thrilled, I can assure you. Coming close upon the heels of the furore caused by the bare-bosomed duskies from Sierra Leone it provided me with the assurance I needed that Africa continues to embarrass and bewilder Europe.[102] Incidentally, Soyinka whose picture appears on the other side and who is described as "immensely intelligent" made some rather unpatriotic comments about the ladies. He is reported as saying, "They don't dance bare at home – not beyond a certain stage of puberty"; which is quite true but should not be published in the streets of Askelon.[103]

Thank you for your representations to Stuttafords. They have borne fruit. The cartons are now sealed once more.

I didn't tell you that I had written Part I Econ. examination in June. I was quite certain I had failed and I didn't want to embarrass my friends. But God is very partial to his idiots, and as one of them I have been informed that I have been successful.

With best wishes,
Yours sincerely,
RM Sobukwe

---

102 This refers to performances by the Sierra Leone National Dance Troupe at the Commonwealth Festival held in the UK in September and October 1965. Wole Soyinka, the Nigerian author, poet and playwright, was also present in England as his new play *The Road* was being staged in London at the time.

103 2 Samuel 1: 20.

Robert Sobukwe
to Nell Marquard,
21 November 1965 (Bd1.19)

Dear Mrs Marquard,

Thank you for your letter dated 7th November which I received on the 19th. And thank you also for *The Shoes of the Fisherman*[104] into which I have already got stuck!

I believe I have already told you that Stuttafords have once more reverted to sending the fruit cartons. I have also heard from Mrs Pullen that you have been to see her. I have put you to a lot of trouble indeed and I thank you for the willingness with which you went even beyond what I had expected or hoped for. It was very kind indeed of you to see Mrs Pullen personally – although she is a Baptist!

I have not yet started on Snow's *The Masters*: not because I do not have time or am not interested, but because I am afraid. There is a thin, choking pain that runs through Snow's novels – a kind of primeval, community pain, unaccountable and incurable – that I find difficult to bear. Roy Calvert and Sheila Knight[105] leave me limp with pain. They seem to suffer purely and simply because they are themselves; their suffering is written into the code of their personality. There is nothing they can do to avoid it and there is nothing their friends can do to help. I could not contain their pain and I am intellectually unprepared at the moment to expose myself to similar suffering.[106]

When we were boys at Graaff-Reinet we used to hunt snakes, lizzards, butterflies etc for our zoo-museum. Whenever a snake entered a hole our leader, older and bolder than the rest of us, used to smoke it out after placing a razor blade on the ground. I never saw this happen, but I was assured by the

---

104 *The Shoes of the Fisherman*, by Australian author Morris West, was published to great popular acclaim in 1963. The novel recounts events following the election of a Ukrainian Pope.

105 Characters in C.P. Snow's Strangers and Brothers series.

106 Nell Marquard (1986) reflected on this passage, some twenty years after receiving this letter observing – accurately, I believe – that "Suffering in others hurt him deeply ... he found Snow's *The Masters* [1951] almost insupportable because of [the] pain that runs through [it]".

others that when the snake left in that direction, the blade would cut into its soft belly and as it felt the pain it would push forward more firmly, hoping to escape the pain but merely succeeding to disembowel itself. That is how I feel Snow's tragic characters behave. I should like to hear your comments.

I have read Hamlet over again as well as your article on "The Graveyard Scene".[107] You have, of course, a much wider and profounder knowledge of Shakespeare than I have and can relate one play to another. You also have practical experience of the theatre and can see the play in your mind. I am, nonetheless, going to give you my impressions for what they're worth. Unfortunately I shall not be able to compress the whole of my "essay" into the "regulation" pages.[108] I hope I'll be able to continue the discussion in my next letter.

You start off by saying that the idea of vengeance disturbs our modern minds. I wonder if I can agree. I should have thought that the impatience of audiences with Hamlet stems from his tardiness to exact vengeance. I remember reading, in the fifties I think, that when the play was staged somewhere in Italy, an irate member of the audience stood up and shot "Hamlet" dead because he would not kill Claudius "in the purging of his soul ...". No, I do not think that vengeance poses any difficulty for us.

I agree completely that when Hamlet kills Claudius at the end of the play he does not do so in vengeance. You say Hamlet does so as a judge; that he is now fully integrated. I have my doubts.

I get the overall impression that Hamlet did not hate Claudius: he could not hate him. He despised him, perhaps, although even that I would not accept too readily. What is certain is that he had the greatest respect for his father and, in his eyes, no man could have been his father's equal. He loathes and abhors his mother's "overhasty" marriage and incestuous bed even before he learns of Claudius's guilt.

What baffles him is how his mother could possibly fall for another man – whoever he may be: that she should do so with such indecent haste and with his father's brother increases his disgust. If the Queen feels that the lady "protests too much", Hamlet does not. He believes that this is how his mother would have spoken to his father. And the ghost's concern for Gertrude does

107 N.J. Marquard, "The Meaning of the Graveyard Scene in 'Hamlet'", *Theoria*, no. 7 (1955).

108 There were limits to the number of letters that Sobukwe could send and receive and to the length of the letters he was permitted to write.

suggest that they had been a devoted couple. In his talk with his mother what Hamlet emphasizes is that he cannot understand why his mother does not feel as strong a repugnance toward Claudius as he does; that she continues to live

"In the rank sweat of an incestuous bed, stew'd in corruption"[109]

He is quite tender with her when he believes she has seen the folly of her ways.

I'll continue from here next time. Lest I do not get the chance again, please let me wish you a blessed and fruitful Christmas and a happy New Year. God's blessing on you all.

Yours sincerely,
RM Sobukwe

---

109 Act 3, Scene 4, line 104.

Benjamin Pogrund
to Robert Sobukwe,
7 December 1965 (Ba3.51)

My dear Bob,

Your most welcome letter of November 9 was received on November 27. I can only say a humble "thank you" for your continued willingness to assist in proving the truth in the jail cases. There is a Talmudic saying to the effect that it is a "mitzvah" (a blessing) for a rich man to give to charity; when a poor man gives, the blessing is increased a thousand-fold. Because of your current confined situation, and the possibility of your future being affected, I see you as the poor man. Having written this, however, I am not so sure that I appreciate describing myself as "charity"!

I am glad that Stuttafords is now sealing your fruit parcels. I have had a letter – just a few days ago – from a friend in Cape Town who took up the matter with Stuttafords. The letter says they were only too pleased to assist. I have already taken up the question of the needed R28 for fruit and hope to have the cash very soon. I shall send it direct to the Officer Commanding, as you suggest.

I sent off several parcels of books to you. To ensure that they all arrived safely, I think it best as well to give you a list:

[Upton] Sinclair: The Jungle
[Joseph] Conrad: Three short novels.
[Vance] Packard: Status Seekers
[W. Somerset] Maugham: Collected Short Stories: Vol. 3
Maugham: Collected Short Stories: Vol. 4
Maugham: The Narrow Corner
[E.M.] Forster: The Longest Journey
[André] Gide: Symphonie Pastorale and Isabelle
Koestler: Darkness at Noon
Hochhuth: The Representative
[Boris] Pasternak: The Last Summer
[Christopher] Isherwood: Goodbye to Berlin
[Wallace] Stevens: [Collected] Poems

[Leo] Baeck: The Essence of Judaism
[Trude] Weiss Rosmarin: Judaism and Christianity: The Differences
[Isidore] Epstein: Judaism
[Martin] Buber: Two types of faith
[Ludwig] Lewisohn: Selection of Jewish Short Stories
[Ghita] Ionescu: The Reluctant Ally (study of Communist neo-colonialism)
[Robert] Conquest: Marxism Today
[Percival] Griffiths: The Road to Freedom
[P.J.] Honey: Communism in North Vietnam
[Kurt] London: New nations in a divided world
[Vernon] McKay: Africa in World Politics
Senghor: On African Socialism
[Leopold] Labedz and [G.R.] Urban: The Sino-Soviet Conflict
[Sven] Hamrell and [C.G.] Widstrand: The Soviet Bloc, China and Africa
[Jan] Carew: Moscow is not my Mecca
[William] Appleton: The Student Trap
[Dietrich] Bonhoeffer: Letters and Papers from Prison

As you see, this is a very mixed bag. The literature, I hope, has been to your taste. I particularly recommend Koestler's "Darkness at Noon" which I first read as a teenager. I have just been rereading it and have been in the happy position of finding that I can barely recall a single detail of it so that I can enjoy it anew. Whether the word "enjoy" is appropriate I am not so sure: as you will discover, it is a study of horror, written in brilliantly concise language. You asked for books on Judaism and I trust I haven't flooded you out! As light relief, I also put in the selection of Jewish short stories. The one I particularly commend to you is "Bontsche the Silent". I have read and reread and loved this story ever since I was a child, and I have no doubt it will have the same appeal for you. For the rest, the books on Communism are all written from the Western side of the fence so I cannot see that there will be any difficulty in their getting through to you. The quality of quite a few of these is rather suspect, I am afraid, so don't hesitate to throw them aside if the opening few pages bore you. But McKay and Senghor should at least give you good reading. And, of course, the prize in all this is Bonhoeffer's book which came to you, by the way, as a special gift from your friend Mrs Taylor.

In my contact with churchmen, I have found that Bonhoeffer[110] has become the conscience-prodder of Christians who find themselves in parallel situations. Whether his example should be followed is a problem which many Christians I have encountered torture themselves about.[111]

Another friend in the United States has just let me have another batch of books and these will be going off to you this week:

Irving Stone: Lust for Life
[David] Krech, etc: The Individual in Society
[Booth] Mooney: The Lyndon Johnson Story
Webster's Dictionary
[Robert E.] Thompson and [Hortense] Myers: Robert F. Kennedy
[John] Herling: Labor Unions in America
[Robert] Ruark: The old man and the boy
Benjamin Franklin: Autobiography
[James McNab] McCrimmon: Writing with a purpose
K.E. Priestley: China's Men of Letters
Pearl S. Buck: Escape at Midnight and other stories
[Werner] Klatt: The Chinese Model
[Thomas R.] Brooks: Toil and Trouble
[Francis] Harper: This is China
[J. Arthur] Thomson: Riddles of Science
[Eileen] Chang: The Rice Sprout Song
Tennessee Williams: Summer and Smoke
[Chandler Whipple]: John F. Kennedy: Expendable

---

110 Dietrich Bonhoeffer (1906–45) was a German pastor, theologian and dissident, who spoke out against the Nazi's genocidal persecution of the Jews. He was arrested in 1943 by the Gestapo, accused of being associated with a plot to assassinate Adolf Hitler, subsequently found guilty and executed by hanging on 9 April 1945. His writings on the role of Christianity in the secular world were highly influential, and his book *The Cost of Discipleship* (1937) is considered a classic.

111 In respect of this letter, Pogrund (2015) notes that he wanted very much to alert Sobukwe to the debates that were underway among Christians in South Africa as to how Christianity might be used as a means of standing up to tyranny, that is, to apartheid. He hoped that he had used "enough circumspection to get around the censors" he adds (p. 235). Evidently not, as the letter did not reach Sobukwe.

[U.T.] Hsu: The Invisible Conflict
Lyndon B. Johnson: My hope for America
American Politics and Government
[Betty] Schechter: The Peaceable Revolution
William James: Selected Letters
Joyce [Cary]: Mister Johnson
[Janet] O'Daniel: The Cliff Hangers

Again, as you see, very much of an assortment of literature, current affairs, biography, and books both good and possibly not so good.

In addition, I am sending you a copy of Sorensen's biography of Kennedy, which has just been published.[112] As an equal admirer, with you, of Kennedy, I am being selfish in trying to read through the 700 plus pages before sending it to you. Hope you don't mind! I shall get it to you in the post by next week.

I have renewed your "Reader's Digest" subscription for next year so it should continue to reach you without interruption.

For Xmas, I have arranged for a parcel of good things to eat to be sent to you via Thrupps of Johannesburg.[113] I wish you well with it and I hope my choice of foods will be to your taste. As with last year, I included a few decorations so that you could brighten up your room (rooms?). This is one time when, if I had been able to sit down to Xmas dinner with you, I would have been willing to put aside my normal religious scruples about this sort of thing!

Earlier today I posted off to you two parcels of records, a total of seven records. Four, in one parcel, consist of American folk songs. The other parcel contains music from Porgy and Bess, and a George Gershwin operetta. Also, "Zorba the Greek", from the soundtrack of a film which has been showing this year. This latter record is my personal Xmas gift to you, and it comes with my warm and affectionate good wishes. The record has some rather delightful passages of philosophical dialogue interspersed between the music; as for the music, well, I am sure it will captivate you and I recommend letting yourself go as you listen to it; you'll find yourself stamping and swaying around the room. The food parcel I mentioned earlier you should regard as a token of good wishes from the many who hold you in high esteem.

---

112 Theodore (Ted) Sorensen, *Kennedy* (1965).

113 An upmarket grocer in Johannesburg.

Accepting, as you say, that the jail authorities will not refuse to allow you to read[114] about the Strachan trial, I have posted the complete set of reports which have appeared in the Rand Daily Mail. As you will see, the reports are probably the most extensive ever published of a court case in this country. Because of the bulk of the papers, they have been posted to you in seven separate parcels. From now, I shall also be sending the reports as they appear, and in fact, the first couple have already been put in the post.

Mrs Taylor recently wrote to me and asked that a letter be forwarded on to you. I am enclosing it herewith.

While I think of it: I gave the measurements for your suit to your wife, and we have arranged that she will take the suit with her when she travels to Cape Town later this month. I saw her just the other day, incidentally, and can report that she is well. She told me that the children too were all right. All are looking forward with great eagerness to seeing you again. I arranged at the same time for the children to receive toys for Xmas.

Whew! This seems to cover all the subjects which we usually refer to as the "mundane". If there is anything I have omitted, or anything which you need, then as usual do not hesitate to let me know.

In recent months I have become increasingly despondent about the course of affairs in this country. I need not, I know, go into details with you. Let me only say that, as I feel at the moment, I just do not wish to go on living here. I have a growing feeling of sheer physical illness at what I see. It goes without saying that I shall see out the end of the jails issue – whatever happens or is likely to happen to me. But once it is all over, I want to go. When this will be I cannot know for certain, but it should be within the next six to 12 months.

In the meantime, I have begun to look out for suitable work overseas, either somewhere else in Africa, or in the United Kingdom or the United States. I am not sure yet just what I shall do, but it will be either in journalism or academic work within a university. I am obtaining "testimonials" from people whom I know well, and I wonder whether you feel able to write one for me also?

---

114 One becomes aware in lines such as these that Pogrund's letters are addressed also to the Security Branch censors who would be reading the letters. By noting that "the jail authorities will not refuse you to read", Pogrund is justifying his inclusion of material that might otherwise have been censored.

It has been a painful decision to have to take: my emotional roots are sunk deep in this country. And most terrible of all, I have to accept that I shall have to leave Jenny behind. My friend, we are, I know, close enough to each other for me not to have to write anything more.

A full week has passed since I began writing this letter. There was a sudden rush of work and I could not get back to writing to you. There were a number of other matters which I wanted to go into, but I shall now leave these for a later letter.

Life is good at the moment because I have Jenny staying with me for three weeks. Astrid went away on holiday and hence the present situation. We have had a lot of joy in each other's company since she came to stay with me last week. On Friday we are flying to Cape Town to spend a week with my Parents. I shall be looking across the bay and thinking of you. I shall be staying in Sea Point, right across from you![115]

I hope this letter will reach you before Xmas, and I take the opportunity of wishing you well for then and for the New Year. I hope the visit of your family will lift up your heart – and I pray for your release in the New Year.

With affectionate greetings,

P.S. I am enclosing a photostat of the goods ordered from Thrupps.

115 The suburb of Cape Town that looks out across the sea to Robben Island. Pogrund reflected on the experience of taking the road above Sea Point on Signal Hill: "I always chose to drive on this ... mountain road as it gave me a few minutes of quiet reflection about my friends on the island – Sobukwe ... and others" (2015: 235).

Robert Sobukwe
to Benjamin Pogrund,
8 December 1965 (Ba3.52)

My dear Benjie,

I am sending you the book lists which arrived with my first lessons!

Those books I have ticked (√) I already have.

The books I need urgently, of course, are the textbooks. In some subjects, as you will note, I have the necessary textbooks. However, I am sending you all the lists for all the subjects so that you may be able to find out from friends which are the most desirable supplementaries.

My special period is economic history 1820–1886 on which I am expected to write authoritatively. I shall, therefore be grateful if you could get me the supplementaries there noted.*

The lessons are arranged so as to enable me to write the exams in 1967. I am going to work as though that is when I sit for the exam and if by October *next year* I am tempted to take the plunge, I'll apply for a change in the examination date. I am tempted to get the damn thing out of the way. I have always hated exams.

That is all for now. Will write again in the new year.

With best wishes,
Bob

*After consultations, of course.

Benjamin Pogrund
to Officer Commanding,
Robben Island Gaol,
28 December 1965 (Ba3.54)

Dear Sir,

A few weeks ago I arranged, through a firm of Johannesburg grocers, Thrupp and Co., for a parcel of food and Xmas decorations to be sent to Mr Robert Sobukwe. Thrupp and Co. have today advised me that the parcel has been returned to them marked, "Not allowed to receive any parcels containing eatables".

In view of the fact that Mr Sobukwe has previously regularly received food parcels, I thought I should write to you to inquire about the matter. Last Xmas I sent a similar parcel to Mr Sobukwe and he was allowed to receive it. For the past eighteen months or so he has been receiving regular parcels of fresh fruit as well as biscuits.

In these circumstances, I wonder whether you would be good enough to allow Mr Sobukwe to receive the Xmas food parcel which I had arranged for him? If you advise me that it is in order, I shall request Thrupp and Co. to arrange for immediate delivery of the parcel.

I trust that it will be possible for Mr Sobukwe to receive this Xmas gift.

Thanking you,
Yours faithfully,
BENJAMIN POGRUND

1966

Sobukwe at his work desk.

Robert Sobukwe
to Benjamin Pogrund,
3 January 1966 (Ba4.1)

My dear Benjie,

I am not writing because I have some great news that will not keep. As you know my wife and the kids haven't arrived yet so I can't entertain you to even a bit of psycho-analysis. I am writing, really, because I want my first letter in the New Year to be for you.

As usual, I have to say 'Thank you' for kindnesses done. My wife has told me a little of what you've done for them and will no doubt have plenty to add when we meet. I know you are happy to do so much for me and mine and do not wish to be thanked for it. But I am an African, Benjie, and one thing we can do is to say "Thank you". And at my home I was taught to say "thank you" whenever the opportunity offered.

So, speaking as one African to another, permit me to thank you for:

(a) *The Records.* I had a real hootenanny on New Year's day. I played every one of them and enjoyed them immensely. I realize that you young fellows are trying to "modernize" me and I believe you are succeeding. It was a pleasure to hear Miriam[1] again. She bowled me over the very first time I heard her and I have been her fan ever since. The opera pieces were marvellous. It was a real musical extravaganza. Yesaah!

(b) *The books.* I went into the Sino-Soviet dispute boots and all and was quiveringly indignant and happily amused in quick succession. There's no doubt about it, these boys are experts in their field and it was intellectually stimulating to follow their discussions and papers. I enjoyed Legum's article (paper) in spite of his obvious sympathies.[2]

I haven't read far into the "consignment"[3] yet but the little I have read convinces me that your research must be published, Benjie. Even if you were to draw

1 Miriam Makeba, the renowned South African singer.

2 Colin Legum, who was born in South Africa, was the London *Observer*'s African correspondent.

3 Of Pogrund's research.

the conclusion that there is no unmistakeable evidence of overt Communist activity, the bare, unadorned facts will make interesting reading, I am certain.

I have been thinking of Dave Du Bois[4] a lot of late, remembering how at times we despaired of countering Communist propaganda against the U.S.A.

Jill and Ernie [Wentzel] have once more sent me a lovely Christmas gift. As I say, you young people are trying to modernize me. I don't even know the name of the article. It is a kind of cravat. I'll have to ask my wife to show me how it is worn.

I have made heavy demands on your purse of late, Benjie, I know. And whatever you feel about it, I am sorry. But I hope the pressure will ease this year. You should have received the book lists by now. The lectures are continuing to arrive but Wolsey Hall has now effected some changes in the dispatch dates to make the spacing between lessons to conform to my desire to write in 1968.

Just before the end of the year Prof Wellington wrote to say he was looking forward to meeting my wife and the children. I hope they met. And Mrs Marquard has been making enquiries about them, too.

And how did you and Jenny spend the New Year? By the way, I think it's time you bought a home in the posh suburbs with a heated swimming pool etc. etc. so that at week-ends I can have somewhere to luxuriate!

Well Benjie, may the Holy One of Israel make His face to shine upon you and give you and yours peace. As for you, 1966, look out, here we come. *Quid vobis videtur?*[5]

Yours very sincerely,
Bob.

---

4 He was director of the United States Information Service (USIS) in Johannesburg.

5 What do you think?

Robert Sobukwe
to Nell Marquard,
3 January 1966 (Bd1.20)

Dear Mrs Marquard,

Thank you for the Christmas card and your letter of November 24.

This writing by instalments is unfortunate because it interferes with one's moments of inspiration. I find now, in spite of my promises, that I am unable to control the discussion on Hamlet. With your permission I shall, therefore, effect a disengagement of my forces.

May I, however, make one or two slight observations. First of all, don't we all have a Hamlet in our personalities? Don't we require regular conferences, services, parties, talks, discussions etc. to "whet (our) almost blunted purpose"?[6] Again on page 66 of your pamphlet you quote Hamlet:

"He that hath killed my king",[7] etc. and suggest that here he speaks with assurance. I get the impression, on the contrary, that he is seeking assurance from Horatio, a further whetting of purpose. And Horatio's words on page 67, "Why, what a king is this!"[8] I accept as an unambiguous reference to Claudius. They are the equivalent of "What is this that we have for a king?"[9] It is because of this remark that Hamlet utters the words you quote on page 66. So much for that.

In your letter you enquire about my children's ages. Well, the girl, my first-born, is eleven now, the boy who comes after her is nine and the twins are seven. They are all now attending school in Basutoland. The twins have just started and are at what we term "Form A", the "African" equivalent for Sub-Standard A. The older children, if they've been successful last year, should be starting Standard 4 this year. They'll be arriving in Cape Town on the 8th January after having spent a week at Graaff-Reinet with my parents.

---

6 The quote is from Scene 3 Act 4, where the ghost reprimands Hamlet, telling him to redirect his energies away from his mother and, instead, against Claudius: "Do not forget. This visitation is but to whet your blunted purpose."

7 Act 5 Scene 2.

8 Act 5 Scene 2.

9 Act 4 Scene 3.

They will have only two weeks to spend here. However, I am looking forward to the visit very keenly and I thank you for your kind wishes.

Thank you also for assurances about the fruit. Yes, the matter of the avocado has been attended to.

I, too, enjoyed "A grain of mustard seed".[10] Incidentally, have you read that Soyinka went and took over the broadcasting station in Western Nigeria and called Chief Akintola a thief and a robber?[11] He is now facing charges of theft. Africa compels her intellectuals to be involved: no neutralism.

By the way, you wrote to say you were sending sweets etc. I am afraid I have not received them. I thought I should let you know in case the parcel has gone astray: you are in a better position to make inquiries in that event than I am.

With best wishes for a happy and blessed New Year,
I remain,
Yours very sincerely,
RM Sobukwe

---

10 Perhaps *The Grain of Mustard Seed* by Brother Mandus (1955).

11 On 15 October 1965 an armed Wole Soyinka broke into the Western Nigeria Broadcasting Corporation's radio station in Ibadan and broadcast a statement denouncing the corruption of political leaders and demanding the cancellation of the forthcoming regional elections. Chief Samuel Akintola was Premier of the Western Region from 1963.

Benjamin Pogrund
to Robert Sobukwe,
6 January 1966 (Ba4.2)

My dear Bob,

This will be a quick reply to your letter of December 8 which reached me on December 30. That's quite a formidable list of books you have to read!

I have consulted an academic friend about the list of books from Wolsey Hall and he feels strongly that you should not be drowned in a flood of material. He has marked books which he considers are needed for proper study of your subjects, and I am setting out to obtain them.

As a start, I am today posting the following books to you:

Dobb, M.: Studies in the development of capitalism
Cole, G.D.H.: A short history of the British Working-class movement, 1789–1947
Ashton, T.S.: The Industrial Revolution, 1760–1830
Beales, H.L.: The Industrial Revolution, 1750–1850
Halevy, E.: A history of the English people (1)
Halevy, E.: A history of the English people in 1815 (3)
Halevy, E.: History of the English People, Epilogue: Book 1: Imperialism
Cole, G.D.H.: Persons and Periods
Hammond, J.L. and B.: The Town Labourer: Vol. 1
Hammond, J.L. and B.: The Town Labourer: Vol. 2
[G.D.H.] Cole and [Raymond] Postgate: The Common People, 1746–1938

These books, by the way, are a gift from a friend. As I finished typing this last sentence, Lewis Sowden[12] came in to see me and reminded me that, some time ago, I had told him you wanted books by Priestley. He has just given me the following four, which will also be posted today:

Priestley: All about ourselves and other essays
Journey down a rainbow

12 Lewis Sowden (1903–74) was the *Rand Daily Mail* assistant editor and book review editor.

Midnight on the desert
The other place

The Priestley books look a bit weather-beaten, but I hope you will find them acceptable.

I was extremely upset because a Xmas food parcel I sent to you, as described in my last letter, was returned by the authorities. I immediately wrote to the Officer Commanding asking him to be good enough to allow the parcel to reach you. For your information, I am attaching a copy of my letter to the Officer Commanding. I am now awaiting his reply. I am also attaching a copy of a letter I have sent to Stuttafords in Cape Town making arrangements for paying the fortnightly fruit parcels which they send you.

I went to Cape Town for six days and had Jenny with me. We had a lovely time together, on the beach every day, very warm and close in enjoying being together all the time. She had previously stayed with me – at the home of a friend – for two weeks. These were golden days, and I don't suppose they will ever occur again [...] I was gloriously happy having Jenny with me all day long.

Your wife and children will be with you at present. I know how much happiness you will all be deriving from this. I had heard that the authorities intended allowing your wife to visit you each weekday, instead of the previous three days a week only. I hope this story is correct. I am looking forward to having first-hand news of you when your wife returns.

While in Cape Town, I saw Mrs. Eulalie Stott, who as you know has been a good and consistent friend. She feels that the chair she gave you in 1964 is probably wearing out by now, so she proposes to have a new one delivered to you shortly. She told me that she had made arrangements with the Cape Town Municipal Library Services for you to borrow books and records. On checking recently, she discovered you had not made use of this service and she was wondering whether there was any special reason for this on your part. Also, she is very keen to write to you, and I took the liberty of telling her that I was sure you would be glad to hear from her.

All for now. My warmest good wishes for the coming year. I trust there will be a drastic change in your circumstances this year!

Sincerely,

Officer Commanding,
Robben Island,
to Benjamin Pogrund,
10 January 1966 (Ba4.4.1)

Dear Sir,

RE: ROBERT SOBUKWE: FOOD PARCELS.

1. Your letter of the 28th December 1965 refers.
2. Mr. Sobukwe may receive food parcels from relatives only under very exceptional circumstances.
3. He may however purchase a reasonable amount of eatables out of his available funds.

Yours faithfully,
OFFICER COMMANDING

Robert Sobukwe
to Nell Marquard,
16 January 1966 (Bd1.21)

Dear Mrs Marquard,

Your letter dated 28th December arrived after I had written mine of the 3rd January. We are both clear now, I think, on the question of food parcels. Benjamin Pogrund also had the same painful lesson to learn.

Thank you for the piece on the Irish Protestant. It is rich.

I do not know whether to agree with you or not about [C.P.] Snow. I read "The Masters" early this month and once more my heart was lacerated. Some would say he is a realist. I suppose there is no doubt about it that the intrigues he depicts are characteristic of most if not all contests. And yet, evil though we are, in our sober moments we find the suffering of a good man insupportable. And Snow does not spare his readers. He lays bare the weaknesses of his characters with clinical detachment; and one feels Jago's[13] pain more because of his earlier confession that "one's dreadfully vulnerable through those one loves."

Yes I have read "The Shoes of the Fisherman". I devoured it on receipt. I realized that the priest depicted was Teilhard de Chardin. I have read quite a bit *about* him but haven't come across any of his works which are said to be "difficult". I shall not just yet ask for "The Future of Man"[14] but I'll keep the offer in mind and do thank you for it.

Your letter of the 3rd February came through rather quickly and was most welcome. One appreciates the truth of Snow's words again … "we are vulnerable …".

Yes my wife and the kids arrived. They arrived on the 8th January and left on the 19th. Fortunately they got permission to visit me every week-day, so I saw them from the 10th–14th and from the 17th–19th January.

---

13 Jago is a character in Snow's *The Masters*.

14 Teilhard de Chardin's collection of essays on theology, philosophy and science, first published in 1959.

My wife's address is
684 Mofolo Village,
P.O. Dube,
Johannesburg.

Thank you for the Commonwealth Journal.[15] It is a treasure. I had thought I would comment on Robert Gardiner's Reith Lectures.[16] He handled his subject with brilliant delicacy, I think. It had both breadth and compassion. Even Prof Manning found it possible to praise him.[17]

Yes, I have made use of the library service and have found it quite adequate so far. I am going to use it fully and will be prepared for the delays.

I am afraid I haven't read any of Vera Brittain's[18] books (Is she Mrs?) and cannot, therefore, comment on her *weakness*. Yes, the Nehrus certainly are gifted.[19] They are a kind of Indian Royalty. The lack of bitterness you note has been commented upon by many, and with wonder. Somebody has, in fact, remarked that in some respects the Indians are more English than the English. However, I don't envy Mrs Gandhi[20] her task. It is formidable. The question has to be answered in India whether democracy and rapid economic development are incompatible and, if they are, which is preferable. And all the time there will be the menace, ideologically and militarily, of China.

I haven't grown anything in my garden this summer. Our water-shortage is acute. For some reason or other somebody has sent me a copy of Rachel Carson's "Silent Spring", the blurb on which reads:

---

15 *The Round Table: The Commonwealth Journal of International Affairs.*

16 Robert Gardiner (1914–94) was the Ghanaian-born executive secretary of the United Nations Economic Commission. His Reith lectures, entitled "A World of Peoples", discussed questions of race.

17 Charles Anthony Woodward Manning (1894–1978), a South African-born professor of international relations at the LSE until 1962.

18 Vera Brittain (1893–1970), writer, feminist and pacifist. Her 1933 autobiography, *Testament of Youth*, told of her experiences during the First World War.

19 Jawaharlal Nehru (1889–1964), first Prime Minister of India (1947–64), played a crucial role in Indian politics before and after the country gained independence.

20 Mrs Indira Gandhi, Prime Minister of India from January 1966 to March 1977.

> "What we have to face is not *an occasional dose of poison* which has accidentally got into some article of food, but a *persistent* and *continuous poisoning* of the *whole human environment.*"

The underlined words appear in RED PRINT! And the book deals with the use of insecticides.

I am all right. Please don't worry.

With best wishes
Yours very sincerely,
RM Sobukwe

Veronica Sobukwe
to Benjamin Pogrund,
1 February 1966 (Ba4.6)

Dear Mr Pogrund,

We returned on the 21st from Cape Town.

The children left for school this last week end.

I am enclosing in the total amount of their school and hostel fees. I wrote a letter to the Sister in charge that their fees will be sent in as soon as possible.

Bob asked me to give his best regards to you. He also asked me to tell you that the Christmas food parcel you sent him was never given to him. He wrote to the Commanding Officer asking if you didn't send any parcel. He was told that he could receive food from his relatives only under special circumstances. He himself was not informed that these parcels had arrived.

Before I came, he was warned by the Special Branch not to express political opinion in his letters. They quoted the following extract from a letter he had written to a friend, "If I had failed, the enemy would have rejoiced and my friends would have been grieved".

He has lost weight. I took most of his trousers to the tailors for alterations. He is complaining of painful joints, severe back-ache and fibrositis. For all these which had been diagnosed by the Prison Doctor, he is receiving no treatment what so ever. He is in the first stages of Arthritis. His fingers are disfigured.

For two years he has suffered from Prostatitis. Except a 10 day massage of the gland in the 1st year and a bottle of tabs in the 2nd year he has received no treatment for this illness. He has also complained about his eyes and teeth. Truly speaking, I did not like his health's condition this time.

I think that is the only way they can get rid of him, by neglecting his health. He told me that they were thinking of making arrangements to take him to hospital for his Prostate Gland complaint. But I think it has long been neglected.

Despite the fact that he has paid in advance for the newspapers, the Prison Authorities have withheld copies of the Sunday Times which carried news they did not approve of. Issues of the Rand Daily Mail sent by you were confiscated by Prison Authorities and it was only after months that he learnt about this.

Bob did not ask me to tell you all this. But please write an article about everything.

I am really sick and tired about these glorious reports we continue to read about his health's condition on Robben Island.

Newspaper men or Reporters meet my husband in his room. But I have never been inside the yard in which he is confined. I don't even know what his living quarters look like.

On our way back to Johannesburg we met Mary [Moeng], your former domestic servant. She was very kind to us. She gave the kids a lot of sweets.

With best wishes,
Sincerely,
Veronica Sobukwe.

Benjamin Pogrund
to Veronica Sobukwe,
3 February 1966 (Ba4.7)

Dear Mrs Sobukwe,

I have just received your letter of February 1, and am writing immediately to assure you that I am taking up the question of Bob's health without delay. I was most distressed to read your letter.

What I have done is to write direct to the Minister of Justice telling him that, after seeing Bob, you have reported to me on Bob's condition and that there is cause for concern. I have outlined to the Minister everything that you write about, and have asked him to have it all attended to as quickly as possible.

I received the account for the children's school fees and am paying this without delay. You need not worry any further about the fees.

I was glad to hear from you and to know that you are safely back in Johannesburg again. If there is anything I can do at any time, remember – as always – that you should not hesitate to contact me.

With all good wishes,

Sincerely,

Benjamin Pogrund
to the Minister of Justice,
B.J. Vorster,
3 February 1966 (Ba4.8.1)

Dear Sir,

I am taking the liberty of writing direct to you in connection with the conditions of detention on Robben Island of Mr Robert M. Sobukwe. As you may be aware, I am an old and close friend of his. I am addressing this letter to you without his prior knowledge, and I am doing so because of the deep concern I feel on his behalf.

His wife, who is a qualified nurse, paid a visit to him last month and has reported to me as follows on Mr Sobukwe's condition:

1. He has lost weight to the extent that Mrs Sobukwe had to take most of his trousers to a tailor for alteration while she was in Cape Town.
2. He is complaining of painful joints, severe back-ache and fibrositis. His fingers are disfigured from arthritis. He is apparently not receiving any treatment for these complaints.
3. For the past two years he has suffered from prostatitis. Except for a ten day massage of the gland in the first year of his detention and a bottle of tablets in the second year, he has not received other treatment for this condition. The jail authorities are apparently at present considering removing him to hospital for proper treatment, but the matter seems to have been long neglected.
4. He is having difficulties with his eyes and his teeth. Mrs Sobukwe also states that, despite the fact that Mr Sobukwe had paid in advance for a subscription to the "Sunday Times" (which must obviously have been with the approval of the jail authorities), copies of the newspaper have been withheld from him. Copies of the "Rand Daily Mail" which were sent to him were also withheld, and it was only some months later that he was advised of this.

Mrs Sobukwe also states that, while newspapermen and other visitors have been allowed to see her husband in his living quarters, this privilege has never been allowed her.

In addition, I sent Mr Sobukwe a Xmas food parcel through the agency of a leading Johannesburg firm of grocers. It was returned by the jail authorities, although a similar parcel had been accepted the previous Xmas, and other gifts of food and fruit have been allowed in freely. I took up the matter with the Officer Commanding and was advised that only his relatives could send him food parcels, and then only in exceptional circumstances. This is clearly a departure from the previous situation. To add to it, Mr Sobukwe was not even told that a parcel had come and was only advised of it when he approached the authorities.

There has also been great difficulty in the past in the supply of the London "Observer" to Mr Sobukwe. After the approval of the jail authorities had first been obtained, a subscription was paid for this newspaper. It was delivered at first and then, apparently, Mr Sobukwe did not receive further copies. I do not know whether the distributors are at fault here or whether the newspaper was withheld by the jail authorities.

I have written this letter in the belief that details of this kind would not perhaps normally come to your attention, but that once you are aware of them, something will be done to rectify the situation, should this be necessary.

Yours faithfully,
BENJAMIN POGRUND

Benjamin Pogrund
to Sister-in-charge,
St Mary's Hostel,
Leribe, Basutoland,
4 February 1966 (Ba4.9)

Dear Madam,

I have pleasure in enclosing my cheque in an amount of R138.00 (plus bank exchange), to cover the fees for the whole of 1966 for Miliswa, Dalindyebo and Dedanizizwe Sobukwe. Your statement of account for the children is also enclosed.

Thanking you,
Yours truly,
BENJAMIN POGRUND

Benjamin Pogrund
to Robert Sobukwe,
5 February 1966 (Ba4.10)

My dear Bob,

I was most distressed to hear from your wife this week that you are not well. Your wife explained that, apparently you did not wish her to tell me about it, but she is so upset that she felt she had to advise me of the situation. After thinking it over I decided that the best thing to do would be to write direct to the Minister of Justice. I am enclosing a copy of the letter I have sent to him. I hope you will not be angry with me for having done this. I can only say that I share your wife's concern, and that, as far as I am concerned, the paramount consideration is that you should receive whatever medical treatment you need with the least delay.

Also enclosed is the list of the study books which you sent me. As stated in my last letter to you, written last month, some of these books have already been posted to you and I hope they have reached you safely. The books you already have (i.e. from your previous year of study), I have marked with an "S". I have also marked off the ones sent to you last month. The ones I have placed on order for you are marked with an "O" and a "D" (the difference in marking is because I did it at different times and forgot what symbol I had used). All being well, these books should be getting to you quite shortly. Will you let me know if the choice of books has your approval? I had difficulties in deciding what to select in the special studies of particular subjects. I thought it best here to return the list to you and to ask you to decide which special studies you wished to undertake and to advise me which of the listed books you wanted. So will you let me know about this as soon as possible? I have kept a copy of the lists so don't worry about returning the original to me.

I have not yet, at the time of writing, heard from you about my letter of December 7. Did it reach you?

My friend, there is little I need say about the Government's announced decision this week to detain you for a further year. You know my feelings. I pray only that the courage and strength of heart and will which have sustained you up to now, are still with you. Those of us who know you and cherish you know the truth.

Coming at a time of bad news about you, your letter of January 3 gave me great joy. Reading your first page, I clucked my tongue in displeasure when I came to your reference to yourself as an "African" – and the one thing Africans could do was to say thank you. But I chuckled when I turned the page and read ... "speaking as one African to another" ... and saw that you had neatly trapped me into a line of racial thinking. No thanks needed, as you know. I am only delighted that the records and books have given you pleasure. I hope to send some more records soon.

Forgive me if I do not write any more in this letter. I was anxious to let you know about my letter to the Minister and to return your book lists and I shall write at greater length when I next hear from you.

You are in my nightly prayers.

G-d bless you.

Veronica Sobukwe
to Benjamin Pogrund,
14 February 1966 (Ba4.12)

Dear Mr Pogrund,

Thank you for your letter of the 3rd February which I received on the 8th.

Thank you very much for sending in the children's school fees account. I am really relieved.

I haven't been well these last days but I am now much better.

Thank you for writing to the Minister of Justice about Bob's condition.

I think we should write another letter to him owing to Bob's health's condition which has deteriorated.

I think we should be given an exit permit. After all, he need not be afraid of him any more, he is finished physically.

It will be better if we get a lawyer, because if we write direct to them we will not get any reply.

I know your hands are full but I know you will try your best.

With best wishes,
Sincerely,
Veronica

Robert Sobukwe
to Benjamin Pogrund,
16 February 1966 (Ba4.13)

My dear Benjie,

In your letter dated 6th January, 1966 you refer to an earlier letter in which you had apprised me of a Xmas food parcel you were sending. Your last letter to me, prior to that of the 6th January, was dated 21st October, 1965. I received it on the 2nd November and you made no mention in it of anything pertaining to Xmas.

I was, however, sure in my mind that you would send me a parcel and when by New Year's day I had not received it I made inquiries and was informed of the new ukase.

I asked my wife to tell you about the warning I have received from the S.B.[21] I hope you won't find my letters "dry" as a result.

The books you listed in your letter have arrived, so have the Priestley books (for which, incidentally, I am very grateful) and a number of Penguin books on the Roman end of my "Political Thought" subject.

Stuttaford's have begun sending the fruit according to the new arrangements. Thanks a lot.

I hope Mrs Stott has not been hurt by my failure to make use of the Library facilities she had arranged. With regard to the Records I felt I shouldn't borrow those because they scratch and break easily and in any event I had enough of my own. As for the books, I discovered that the books I requested urgently were also in demand, apparently, in Cape Town and when I did finally receive them, because of postal delays, I could keep them for only two or three days. Mrs Marquard has made fresh arrangements which appear to be more satisfactory, employing as they do the services of the local library. You were right, I certainly would be glad to hear from Mrs Stott. She can describe the workings of the Cape Town City Council for me.

I have received a letter from Mrs G. Taylor. But she writes from England and not from the States. Can you explain? A Mr Hill of Somerset, England also sent me a Christmas card. I appreciated their messages.

---

21 Special Branch.

Finally, Benjie, thanks to you and my friends for making my family's trip possible. I am glad the kids were able to visit my parents and they, too, enjoyed the experience. And my people, I am certain, were happy to see them.

Oh, by the way, I was admitted to hospital, Karl Bremer,[22] on the 31st January, operated upon on the 1st February, discharged on the 8th February and have been in my quarters ever since. Am all right.

Best wishes to you all,
Bob

22 Hospital in Bellville, Cape Town.

Robert S. Bilheimer,
Central Presbyterian Church,
North Rochester, New York,
to Benjamin Pogrund,
17 February 1966 (Ba4.14)

Dear Benjamin:

This will introduce to you Mr. and Mrs. Thomas C. Taylor of Rochester. Mrs. Taylor is the one who sent money to help the Sobukwes. They are very good friends of mine and I hope they will have an opportunity to talk with you. I trust them completely and know that you can also. They will both have many questions and I hope that you will help them to understand the situation.

I am very grateful for your letter of September 22nd and hope that you received my acknowledgement of it. All that you sent to me of your correspondence with Robert Sobukwe is most enlightening. Did I tell you that I took opportunity of sending a paragraph from one of Sobukwe's letters to Mr. McGeorge Bundy,[23] a Special Assistant in the White House who is a friend of mine, with the suggestion that he call the attention of the President to it? This was a paragraph in which Mr. Sobukwe commended the President for his measures concerning race relations, commented upon their effect in Africa and also had a sentence which raised question about the U.S. policy in Vietnam. It seemed to me an altogether excellent paragraph for the President to see. Mr. Bundy replied that he was grateful for this and that he thought it would be worthy of showing to Mr. Johnson.

We are all, of course, alarmed at the reports which appear frequently in our press, concerning government action against the newspaper, its editors and you. I shall be very anxious for word from the Taylors as to how the matter stands. You, of course, have our deepest sympathy and encouragement.

I could not help but notice in your correspondence with Mr. Sobukwe references to your personal situation. You have had my deepest sympathy in all of this, as indeed you do now. Ever since Cottesloe,[24] not to mention

---

23 McGeorge Bundy (1919–96) was special assistant on national security in both the Kennedy and Johnson administrations.

24 A conference organised by Bilheimer on behalf of the World Council of Churches and held at Cottesloe, Johannesburg in December 1960, in the wake of the Sharpeville Massacre.

the Mindolo Conference,[25] I have most greatly admired your sensitivity and integrity, both of which have been a source of inspiration to me. May God bless you and be with you in all that you are doing.

With best wishes,
Sincerely,
Robert S. Bilheimer

The Dutch Reformed Church representatives, under pressure from the government, withdrew from the conference.

25 A conference on "Christians and Race Relations in Southern Africa" organised by the World Council of Churches and held at Mindolo in Zambia in May–June 1964.

Robert Sobukwe
to Veronica Sobukwe,
2 March 1966 (Bc33)

Hullo Darling:

Thanks for both your telegram and your letter dated 5th February. I can appreciate how busy you must have been preparing for the children's return to school.

[...]

It is fortunate that you could not get the kettle connection because the ones you brought fit perfectly.

You will remember I suggested that you get a diary to note down these thousand and one little responsibilities and items that a responsible wife and mother has to [illegible]. Well, darling, in your letter dated *5th February*, you tell me you haven't been able to contact Benjie and Fabian yet. I do not know about Fabian. It is possible you had not met him yet when you wrote. But Benjie you certainly had: because he wrote me on the *5th February* and attached to his letter a copy of a letter he had written to the Minister of Justice based on talks he had had with you.

You have probably read in the papers by now – most certainly someone has come to inform you – that I have had the operation I told you about. I have been out of hospital for three weeks now. I am quite fine, Kid: drinking plenty of water and looking forward to the time when I shall be able to resume my daily exercises. Whether you like it or not you will have to admit finally that I am tough, Kid. I may not look it but I prove it!

Mrs. Marquard asked me for your address. She will most probably write to you soon. Prof Wellington, too, has repeated his desire to meet you. As I have said before, darling, you are you. You have your own personality. You are not a carbon copy of your husband. And I don't want you to be. I have great faith in your intelligence and common sense.

Give my love to the children when next you write to them. Sorry about the flu.

Please keep your head high, little girl. I am proud of you. And of course I love you VERY MUCH.

Your loving husband,
Mangi

Robert Sobukwe
to Benjamin Pogrund,
2 March 1966 (Ba4.17)

Dear Benjie,

Thank you for your letter dated 5th February. I intend to make this a brief note and to comment seriatim on the points raised in that letter.

First of all let me say I am very sorry you wrote to the Minister of Justice. I really am. And the reasons are purely and exclusively personal. You will forgive me then if I do not make any comment whatsoever on the subject.[26]

The list of the study books arrived safely and I notice you have bought almost every book in spite of your earlier remark that I should not be burdened with a lot of unessential reading matter! Your choice of books has been perfect, Benjie. I can't improve on it. Incidentally, under the subject titled *Great Powers,* you have arranged to get me the two volumes on *The Growth of the American Republic* by [Samuel Eliot] Morison and [Henry Steele] Commager. I am sorry I missed that, Benjie. But I had expected such to appear under American Economic History. I *HAVE* both volumes. And they are darned expensive. If you can prevent their purchase, please do so. I really regret the oversight.

Your letter of December 7 has not reached me. As I said in my earlier letter your last letter to me, last year, was dated 22nd October. Around that period I wrote to you on the 13th and 21st October, the 9th and 29th November and finally on the 7th December. I hope you received all these.

You haven't said anything about Jenny in your last letter. I am always anxious to get news of her.

That's all for today. Greetings & love to friends.

Yours most sincerely,
Bob

P.S. In one of my letters to you I enclosed a subscription form to *Economica,* a British journal on economics. Did you receive it? Bob

---

26 As noted earlier, Sobukwe did not wish to receive any concessions or special treatment from the apartheid government, lest it should in any way grant them a semblance of legitimacy.

Veronica Sobukwe
to the Minister of Justice,
B.J. Vorster, 4 March 1966 (Bc34)

Dear Sir,

I wish to write to you as I am worried about the health of my husband, Robert Mangaliso Sobukwe.

When I visited him on Robben Island in January, I saw that his health had deteriorated. I know his health better than anybody else.

I have reports that he has now had an operation for his prostate gland. Normally prostate glands give trouble after the 50th year. In my husband's case age has not been the predominant cause of the enlargement or otherwise of the gland. It can be due to many other causes.

When I saw my husband, he was complaining also of other aspects of his health. He has developed rheumatism. His eyes and teeth were giving him trouble. His finger joints are swollen and disfigured.

My great fears are complications. What tactful and sympathetic treatment is he receiving? He is no longer a prisoner. He finished his sentence nearly three years ago. In all respects, because of his health, if for no other reason, he requires special treatment and attention.

I can not accept that he is receiving the best possible medical and other treatment. If he was, his prostate gland trouble would not have gone unchecked and he would not be suffering from his other complaints.

For two years he has suffered from Prostatitis. Except a ten day massage of his gland in the first year and a bottle of tablets in the second year he has received no treatment for this illness. Then it was only in the third year that he was sent to hospital.

I wish again to ask that you allow him to leave South Africa on an exit permit together with his family. There is no reason to keep him locked up on Robben Island.

If you will not let him leave, I ask you to have him moved to some other place where I can look after him properly. I want to make sure that his health is good.

Thanking you,
Yours faithfully
Veronica Sobukwe

Robert Sobukwe
to Nell Marquard,
16 March 1966 (Bd1.22)

Dear Mrs Marquard,

There was a time at Graaff-Reinet when it was fashionable for the ladies of our location – the less inhibited ladies – to declare:- "Of course, ja, dit pak op my bors ja"[27] whenever they intended "om iemand te skel" or "om iemand to shout",[28] both expressions referring to a deplorable practice whereby the deformities and deficiencies of the "iemand", real and imaginary, mental, physical and spiritual were loudly and eloquently enumerated, to the delight and/or embarrassment of the ever-present crowd.

We had experts, of course, poetic geniuses with amazing powers of observation and description. In those days, ladies were on the plumpish side and small waists and foundation garments were, by the class I am dealing with, looked upon with scorn. Men were terrified of such women, oh but terrified! And who wouldn't be, of people who on the spur of the moment could describe the physiognomy of a rival as an *"afdrant gevreet"* simply because the individual concerned had a rather broadish and flattish nose![29]

I could write pages about them, the darlings who brought me up. But I mention them because I believe you, too, have nearly reached a stage where it begins to "pak op die bors" and has to be got off. And I am trying to suggest that you can get it off quite as effectively by laughing as by "shouting"!

You will forgive me if in my letters I sometimes fail to thank you for gifts you've sent: the truth is that because of this writing "by instalments", by the time I answer your letters I am beholden to you for so much that it would take a page mentioning the articles, provided, that is, I had taken the precaution of

27 "Of course, yes, it's rising in my chest", or "the bile is rising". This could also be expressed in more idiomatic terms as: "I'm reaching boiling point!", "I'm about to explode!"

28 To reprimand ... to shout at someone.

29 "Gevreet" is crude slang for "face". In effect, "afrandt [strictly, afdraand] gevreet" is something like 'downhill face', but that phrase is without the insulting valence of the Afrikaans. The point is to convey that someone's face looks like the downside of a hill – hence "sloping mug". An equivalent insult in English might be: "a face like the back of a bus".

recording them. However, thank you very much for the postal order as well as for the other articles which I presume were returned to you. It was kind and considerate of you merely to *think* I might read these things, let alone sending them.

It did occur to me, too, to inform you that I was "in town" and to arrange for you to visit me. But I knew the attempt would be futile. I spent exactly a week in hospital and it would have taken at least ten days to get the information to you.

There is a story I have been wanting to tell you for some time reflecting on the Xhosa reputation for thieving and lying; an unfortunate reputation indeed. So bad were things at one time that in Joh'burg, in order to get a job, the poor fellows had to pretend to be Zulu and Location Superintendents refused to hear any cases in which Xhosas were involved saying they knew the damn things were going to lie.

Well, then, the story goes that one of them stole a hen, was arrested and charged with theft. His defence was that the hen was his and called his pal as a witness. The latter, when asked if he knew the hen before the event asked, "this hen?" and was told "yes, this hen". "This black one with …" "Yes, this one, man. There is only one hen here." "You want to know whether I know this hen, this black hen …" and so on. And he was examining it all the time. Finally he admitted that he knew the hen and was able to describe it in fine detail when asked to do so. But, of course, there were many hens like that, he conceded. This one he knew particularly well because he had known it when it was still an egg. "When that egg hatched, I was there: As the chick emerges, I am there: As it grows I am there, watching it: until it became this beautiful hen which today has owners who did not own the egg from which it hatched." His evidence, we are told, clinched the case and his friend was acquitted.

Some time later, the witness was arrested and accused of having stolen a gun. He claimed the gun was his and called his friend as a witness. The latter confirmed that the gun belonged to his friend. "How did he know?" He could pick out this gun anywhere. Why, he knew it when it was still a revolver, so big. As it grew into the huge rifle now on display he was there, watching it.

Thank you for the books and copies of "The Listener". I have been reading Gardiner's articles[30] over and am impressed by his intellectual probity.

30 The Reith lectures, referred to in his letter of 16 January.

In my previous letter I asked you not to worry. I am getting on well, really. In fact I have never felt like an invalid. I was a little weak for a few days or so but my strength is back. You can, with a clear conscience, re-assure my friends.

With best wishes to both you and Mr Marquard.
Yours sincerely,
RM Sobukwe

Benjamin Pogrund
to the Minister of Justice,
23 March 1966 (Ba4.8.2)

Dear Sir,

On February 3, 1966 I addressed a letter to you dealing with the state of health of Mr Robert Mangaliso Sobukwe who is detained on Robben Island.

As I have not had an acknowledgement of this letter, I shall be grateful if you will advise me whether it reached you safely.

Yours faithfully,
BENJAMIN POGRUND

Benjamin Pogrund
to Robert Sobukwe,
23 March 1966 (Ba4.18)

My dear Bob,

We seem to be having some difficulties with our post. I wrote to you on December 7, January 6 and February 5 (this last letter by registered post). Letters from you were written on January 3 and February 16 (the last received a matter of about ten days ago). Will you let me know whether any of my letters have failed to reach you?

I am sorry I have not replied earlier to your latest letter, but there have been a lot of difficulties to contend with recently, and I have been hard-pressed each day. [...]

Under separate post I am sending you another batch of books. So that you can check their safe arrival, I am as usual setting out a list of the books: happy reading!

[Eric] Bentley: The storm over The Deputy
[Frederick J.] Hoffman: The 20's
[Harvey] Breit: The writer observed
[James Thomas] Flexner: The Benedict Arnold case
[Stephen] Coulter: Threshold
[Louisa May] Alcott: Little men
[Ivar] Lissner: The living past
[Herbert] Mitgang: Lincoln as they saw him
[Moses Coit] Tyler: History of American literature
[Mark] Twain: The adventures of Tom Sawyer
[Emily] Brontë: Wuthering Heights
[Henry C.] Wallich: The cost of freedom
[Burton] Crane: The practical economist
[William] Saroyan: The daring young man on the flying trapeze
[Alistair] Maclean: The guns of Navarone
[Anthony] Thorne: Fruit in season
[C.S.] Forester: Death to the French
[Charles] Dickens: A tale of two cities
[H.E.] Bates: A moment in time

[Massimo] Salvadori: The American economic system
[Albert] Fried: The essential Jefferson
Twain: Tom Sawyer abroad
[Lew] Wallace: Ben-Hur
[Earl Schenck] Miers: Mark Twain on the Mississippi
[Graham] Greene: Stamboul Train
[Preserved] Smith: A History of Modern Culture: Vol. 1
Smith: A History of Modern Culture: Vol. 2
[Groff and Lucy] Conklin: The supernatural reader
[Francis] Parkman: The conspiracy of Pontiac
[Nathanael] West: The day of the locust
[Robert Allen] Rutland: The birth of the Bill of Rights
[Max] Weber: General economic history
[Richard] Condon: An infinity of mirrors
[James Fennimore] Cooper: The last of the Mohicans
"Argosy" short story magazine: seven back numbers

In addition, I am at long last keeping my promise to send you Sorensen's biography of John Kennedy. My deepest apologies for taking so long to get this to you.

As you see, again very much a mixed bag, ranging from books for your studies to serious and light fiction.

In regard to your study books, as they reach you, will you please let me know so that I can keep track of what you have? I have just had a letter from Dr Marvin Wachman, president of Lincoln University, advising that they will be glad to assist in ensuring that you get the books you need. They will be posting a batch of books direct to you care of the Officer Commanding.

Incidentally, there was an unexpected difficulty in regard to a book which I sent you in about October last year. It was Professor Vernon McKay (of Johns Hopkins University) on "Africa and World Politics". The book was published in 1963, and unknown to me it was banned last June. In due course, I was called in by the Special Branch and advised that I was facing a possible charge of distributing objectionable literature. I was invited to make a statement which, of course, I did. I pointed out that Professor McKay enjoyed an international reputation as a scholar, and that, to my knowledge, his book was a serious and academic study of the subject. Apart from this, I said that I had no knowledge of the banning and sending a book to you care of the Officer Commanding was hardly an attempt to get the book to you illegally. The police officer was very helpful about the matter. My statement was submitted to the Public Prosecutor and I was later advised that there would not be any prosecution.

Within a couple of weeks from now, I hope to be able to send you more records, so don't worry anymore about not using the Cape Town library services. Is your record-player playing all right, by the way?

I have seen your wife several times lately, and we have both been concerned about the state of your health. I read the Press reports about your operation and I hope you are now fully recovered. *Please* let me know how you are.

Regarding "Mrs G. Taylor": I do not know who this can be. Under cover of my letter of December 7, I sent you a letter from Mrs Charlotte Taylor of Rochester in the United States. Has this reached you? We seem to be dealing with two Mrs Taylors.

All for now. Let me hear from you soon.

Affectionate good wishes,

Benjamin Pogrund
to Robert Sobukwe,
28 March 1966 (Ba4.20)

My dear Bob,

Your letter of March 2 reached me on Friday. I am sorry that I opposed your wishes, and have upset you, by writing to the Minister of Justice about your state of health. When your wife and I discussed the matter, we realised that it would probably be contrary to your desires for such a letter to be sent. But we decided that it should be done. The only excuse I can offer is the deep concern which your wife and I have about you.

In my last letter, of March 23, I detailed the dates of the letters I had sent you and those received from you. Your latest letter gives information of letters which I just did not receive, namely, your letters of October 13 and 21, and November 29. In regard to my letter of December 7, which you did not get, I have found a copy of it and am enclosing it with this letter.[31]

This morning I sent off to you per passenger train the carton of books which I detailed in my letter of March 23. To enable you to take delivery, I am enclosing the railways consignment note.

I am, at the moment, reading Howard Fast's "Spartacus",[32] and have rarely been excited so much by a book as I am by this one. Some of the writing, I find, is a bit "unstylish", with clumsy sentence construction which tends to jar. But the presentation of ideas is readable and profound while the story itself unfolds on a gigantic scale. Let me know if you haven't read the book and I shall gladly send you a copy.

Jenny is as lovely as ever, and as proof of this, I am enclosing a picture I took of her recently. I continue to see as much of her as possible. [...] We see each other every Saturday afternoon, every second Sunday for the day, and three times during the week, when I fetch her during lunch-time. Of course, she knows about her Daddy's friend, "Uncle Bob", and whenever I tell her

31 The importance of this letter, which Pogrund asked Sobukwe about on 5 February, and which, on 2 March, Sobukwe confirmed he had not received, is that it was the letter that informed Sobukwe of Pogrund's decision to leave the country.

32 The novel is discussed in more detail by Sobukwe in his letters of 20 April and 1 June 1966 (below).

about you, she wants to know when you are coming to see her. So both of you have something to look forward to!

I have noted that you already have "The Growth of the American Republic", and will try to stop another set being sent to you. Have any of your study books reached you yet? Please let me have a list as the books arrive so that I can keep a check on it.

As always, you are much in my thoughts and in my prayers.

God bless you,

Robert Sobukwe
to Benjamin Pogrund,
30 March 1966 (Ba4.21)

My dear Benjie,

In your letter of the 5th February you state that you were happy to note that my use of the term "African", in an earlier letter, had no racist connotation or signification.

Imagine my joy then when I received a letter from my daughter informing me that on their way to Joh'burg from Cape Town they met someone she calls "Ausi Mary" ("ausi" being the Sotho equivalent of the Afrikaans "ou sis" = elder sister) who had for some time been employed by "Ntate Pogrund". Now "Ntate" – for the benefit of you Zulus – is the Sotho term for "father".

I have been rather strict, Benjie, in bringing up my children. I have stressed that their responses must always be accompanied by a polite "father" or "mother". In other words I want "yes, father", "no, mother", "thank you, father" from them and not just "yes", "no", or "thank you" etc.

I need not tell you, of course, that I have been hard put to it to decide how I can train them to show this politeness to *all* people irrespective of colour, without making them colour-conscious. And lo and behold, my child, most naturally, without any self-consciousness, writes of "Ntate Pogrund" as she has written of "Ntate Mothopeng" (Zeph) before.

She reads me like a book, of course, that little girl. And I am afraid she is going to make me dance to her tune!

Mrs Marquard has sent me a lovely, warm jersey – RED. I am writing to thank her and to point out the sinister associations of the colour.

I am sorry to introduce a note of squealing in a letter I had intended to be cheerful. But I am getting a little worried that not a single *textbook* has reached me so far i.e. the *prescribed textbooks*: more so when in some of my subjects I have already received notes for Lesson Five and have been unable to do the tests set as I have been able to do no reading outside of the notes. Otherwise I am enjoying my studies immensely.

Among the books you've sent me is one, "Writing with a Purpose". I have not had time to read it yet – the fiction and the non-fiction are equally enthralling – but are you hinting that I might consider serious writing like the witchdoctor on the Rand – Mr Mutwa.[33]

I have received letters from a Mrs G Taylor and a Mr G Hill both of Britain. Both contained messages of sympathy.

So much for now, Benjie. I'll write again soon.

Love to Jenny.

Yours sincerely,
Bob

P.S. I am fine, don't worry.

33 Credo Mutwa, author of the book *Indaba, My Children*. For Sobukwe's thoughts on Mutwa, see his letter of 25 February 1965 to Nell Marquard.

Robert Sobukwe
to Veronica Sobukwe,
3 April 1966 (Bc35)

Hullo Darling,

You have been particularly in my thoughts of late. Your Ten Rands and "Get Well" card arrived after I had written to you. Thank you for them, Kid. I know you have been very anxious but I hope my letter has served to set your mind at rest.

I received a lovely letter from Mili. She told me about your journey from Cape Town. She will make a first-class letter-writer. I sent her a little cash to buy stamps. [...]

Tell me, Little Girl, what are you doing these days? What shift are you on? What is the weather like out there? Have you met Fabian yet? What has he to say about his sustained silence?

Mrs Marquard has sent me a very warm and beautiful jersey while Professor Wellington has been writing a letter every week irrespective of whether I answer or not!

Buti has written too, and tells me Zozo has gone to the Secondary School at Somerset East to complete J.C.[34] Dorris is, apparently, not bothered at all.

Didiza and her husband are in Cape Town I learn. The husband is a D.V.T. (District Visiting Teacher) – what we call a Supervisor of schools in the Transvaal. It is a rank below that of Sub-Inspector. You have to be a graduate, I think, like Jimmy, to qualify for the position of Sub-Inspector.

We have had some lovely rains and in spite of the fact that crops are wasted, I am tempted to start a garden again.

I notice that the subscriptions for the "Cape Argus" and the Sunday papers all expire in May. Please DO NOT RENEW the subscription for the "*Sunday Express*". It has deteriorated alarmingly; contains jejune and puerile material. But I'll like to have the "Sunday Times" just to get news about Joh'burg.

You remember the fawn shirt similar to your blouse? Well it is already frayed at the edges. So when your finances permit I shall be glad if you could get me two shirts of that kind – size *16½* collar, remember (sixteen and a half). Please Madam!

34 Junior Certificate.

I have not heard from Linda Nkepu yet nor have I written to them. I wrote to Tukani but he has not answered yet. I hope my writing to him did not introduce him to the attentions of the S.B.[35]

Well, darling, so much for now.

When you write to the kids give them my love. I have resumed my exercises but have not pulled out all the stops yet.

I read in the Press that Mpehle,[36] too, has left the country! And yet you'll remember that I told you someone had warned me to be careful and beware of him. It is a confused and amusing situation isn't it?

Lauretta [Ngcobo] writes to say she has taken driving lessons, has bought herself a small car, has already smashed it in an accident so that it has been consigned to the scrap-yard – all in just a year's time!

Well, cheerio my girl.

Your loving husband,
Mangi

35 Security Branch.

36 A reference to longtime ANC member Mtutuzeli Mpehle, who left South Africa in 1962, going first to Ghana and then Zambia, where he worked as a school teacher and became involved in the political education of young ANC cadres in Lusaka.

Robert Sobukwe
to Nell Marquard,
11 April 1966 (Bd1.23)

Dear Mrs Marquard,

My "thank you's" are assuming a ritualistic pattern, I believe. But they are sincerely meant. As I observed in my last letter, I find myself ever beholden to you. Please accept another "thank you" for the jersey. It's a real *yum-yum* according to the "with it" colloquialism.

I was a little worried about the colour but I consoled myself with the thought that you wouldn't have made the purchase until and unless you had satisfied yourself that no suspicion of "un-South Africanism" could attach to the transaction.

We have had some soaking rains since I last wrote to you and I find myself tempted to go in for gardening in a big way. I am, therefore, going to bother you for some seed. I shall be grateful for any vegetable seed you care to send but should like to have beetroot, carrots and onions included.

With regard to flowers I do not know what to ask for. In the early years of my settlement I tried verbenas, lupins, stocks, the lot. The infant mortality was horrible. 100% still-births. I do not know whether the mistake was planting the seed in the ground instead of first cultivating it in boxes. But I am getting cultured again and should like to see some flowers growing. Could you please send me some seed. I leave the choice to you though I have a weakness for zinnias and stocks.

I notice that there has been a gathering of the clan; and quite a mighty clan it is. But I wish to assure you that when I sent you the little piece about the expanding or growing gun I had no idea that such a gathering was in the offing and did not, therefore, intend the piece as a contribution.[37]

Letters from my wife and Prof Wellington seem to suggest my letters – so far this year – have not been reaching them. I find the news perturbing and in the hope that you do not have a similar experience to report I should like

37 This could be a reference to one of several trials of PAC members or prisoners at this time, such as the trial of 56 men alleged to have been involved in PAC activities in Steynsburg in the Eastern Cape, as reported in the *Rand Daily Mail*, 8 February 1966.

to ask you please to assure my wife that I *have* written to her and that I am making favourable progress.

I wrote also to Benjie i.e. Mr Benjamin Pogrund to inform him that I haven't received a single textbook to date. In case he is having an experience similar to that of the others will you please convey this information to him? As it is I am already five lessons behind with my work; and unless he receives this information the position will get worse.

Incidentally, could you please, when you send the seeds also send me a rake? Yes, a rake, the garden instrument: All the other instruments or, rather, implements, I have but this one appears to be in very short supply and yet it is the one I need most for tidying "my place".

With best wishes to you and Mr Marquard,
I remain,
Yours very sincerely,
RM Sobukwe

P.S. I note that the witchdoctor has been at it again. Has produced a second book.[38] Well, well. Has anybody ever taken the trouble to interview the gentleman or has any society invited him to lecture on his subject? It should be an interesting experience.

RMS

---

38 Credo Mutwa, *Africa Is My Witness* (1966).

Robert Sobukwe
to Benjamin Pogrund,
20 April 1966 (Ba4.26)

My dear Benjie,

I received both your letters – of the 23rd and 28th March – on Monday, 18th April. As usual I wish to make a point by point reply.

23rd March

1) I received your letters of January 6 and February 5. As I said earlier, December 7 not received.

2) I received all the books listed except Vol 2 of [Preserved] Smith's *A History of Modern Culture.*

I received volume one only, covering the period 1543 to 1687. Thank you for Kennedy's book. I have read raving reviews of it.

3) With regard to my study books, as I have observed in an earlier letter, none of the relevant and immediately necessary books have reached me. I shall spell it out in more detail:–

Applied Economics: NOT ONE of the books listed.
History of Political Thought: NOT ONE of the books listed. Under *Texts* I have received

[Niccolò] Machiavelli – *The Prince*
[Jean-Jacques] Rousseau – *Confessions*

Great Powers in International History:–

I have received: Halevy – *History of the English People* vols. 1, 3 and Epilogue

As I pointed out I already have *Growth of the American Republic*

American Economic History: NOT ONE of the books listed.
English Economic History 1485–1716: NOT ONE of the books listed.
English Economic History 1760–1939:
Received:-
Ashton. *Industrial Revolution*
J.L. & Barbara Hammond: *The Town Labourer* vols 1 & 2
Cole & Postgate. *The Common People.*

I notice that I did not tick [J.H.] Clapham's *An Economic History of Modern Britain*. I have two volumes of this and I believe they are sufficient. They cover the period from 1850–1886, 1887–1914.

Economic History: Special
Have received:–
G.D.H. Cole. *Short History of the Working Class Movement*
As you notice, NOT *ONE* textbook on Main Supplementary!

28th March:

I realize that you wrote out of concern for me, Benjie. No further comment.

I am sorry I cannot remember what I wrote in the letters of October 15, 21 and Nov. 29, and unlike you I have no copies that I can send. Of course, the last quarter of last year was a very unpleasant and trying period for me. No further comment.

I have read *Spartacus*. In fact, Howard Fast and Arthur Koestler are favourite authors of mine. I still do not believe that "Spartacus" can compare with *My Glorious Brothers*,[39] describing the struggle of the Maccabees. My wife and I read it together, page by page from beginning to end. And we wept as we read.

I had already read *Darkness at Noon* twice and have read it again. Incidentally it was Koestler who provided me with ammunition to fight the Reds. His "The God that Failed"[40] – he is *one* of the contributors. *The Yogi and the Commissar* and *Darkness at Noon* as well as *Arrow in the Blue* I got at a time when I was ready for their message.[41]

What I enjoy in Fast is just his "unstylish" style. It has a biblical simplicity.

Thanks for Jenny's photograph and for news about her. She's a lovely little darling.

With regard to the letter of the 7th December, I did *not* receive:–

---

39 Howard Fast, *My Glorious Brothers* (1948). See also his letter of 1 June 1966.

40 *The God That Failed*, edited by Richard H. Crossman and David C. Engerman (1950), collected the essays of six influential ex-Communist writers and journalists who described their disillusionment with Communism.

41 Arthur Koestler, *Darkness at Noon* (1940); *The Yogi and the Commissar* (1945); *Arrow in the Blue* (1952).

(a) The letter itself
(b) Mrs Taylor's attached letter
(c) The following books:–
    (i) Weiss Rosmarin: Judaism & Christianity: The Differences
    (ii) Epstein: Judaism
    (iii) Lewisohn: Selection of Jewish Short Stories
    (iv) Conquest: Marxism Today
    (v) Griffiths: The Road to Freedom
    (vi) Storey: Communism in North Vietnam
    (vii) London: New Nations in a divided world
    (viii) McKay – I noted what you said about this one
    (ix) Carew: Moscow is not my Mecca
    Appleton: The Student Trap

As they are not banned, you will, I expect, ask to have them sent back to you.

(d) I also did not receive the Strachan articles. Again, as they are your personal property, I expect you to ask to have them returned to you.

I need not tell you, of course, that not only were these books, articles and letters withheld but I was denied even the elementary courtesy of being informed that they had arrived and were being withheld.

I understand your desire to leave this country. But I am afraid I cannot give you a testimonial, Benjie. Such an act would be unethical. I cannot write a testimonial for my brother.

I'll write again soon. Thanks for the telegram about the kettle. I am all right.

Yours affectionately,
Bob

P.S. In one of the letters that did not reach you I had enclosed an order form for *Economica,* a journal recommended by the University and made available to students at reduced prices. What can we do about it?

Benjamin Pogrund
to Robert Sobukwe,
25 April 1966 (Ba4.28)

My dear Bob,

Your letter of March 30 reached me on Friday. I was surprised to learn that none of your text books had reached you yet. I have gone into the matter without delay. Will you let me know as soon as the books get to you? They will be arriving in different batches. Actually, this whole question of whether books get to you or not is a frustrating one as I am never certain whether anything has gone astray in the post. Whenever books reach you, can you please send me a complete list so that I can know what is happening? In my letters of March 23 and 28 I referred to a carton of books which I had just sent to you per passenger train, and I trust that this has now arrived.

Your telegram asking for an electric kettle was received, and on April 15 I wired you advising that Stuttafords were posting a kettle to you that day. I hope that this too has arrived and that it is OK.

While I think of it, how are you placed for winter clothing? Sheets, blankets, a heater, trousers, jerseys, pyjamas, socks, shoes, shirts, underwear, etc? You notice that I carefully specify each possible item because long experience of you has shown me that you are reluctant to tell me of your needs unless I pinpoint each article! Whatever you need, *please* let me know so that I can have it sent to you.

I was delighted by your story of Miliswa's letter to you … and very flattered also by it. There is nothing more honest than a child, and I am glad to know that I am accepted by her. I had heard that "Ausi Mary" had met your wife and kids on the train – also that she spoilt them outrageously by plying them with sweets.

When I sent you "Writing with a purpose", there was no hidden motive in my mind. But now that you mention it, I have been wanting to write to you for some time to urge you to have a stab at some serious writing. If you feel able to write some kind of a "witchdoctor" tale, you'll make a lot of money … I'll gladly act as your agent so that I can share the spoils with you. But apart from any such straightforward commercial venture, I have for long wondered why we have not yet produced any great story about African existence. I am thinking of the African in the city: the amount of material exists on a vast scale, with every conceivable aspect of human suffering and emotion waiting to be set down on paper. There is of course Alan Paton's "Cry the beloved country", which I admire intensely. But without, I hope, being racialistic, I have always been surprised at the lack of penetrative writing by Africans themselves. Zeke Mphahlele,[42] Bloke Modisane[43] and others have written on the subject, but none in my view comes anywhere near the power and insight which Paton displayed. Now how about you dashing off the "great South African novel"?

I'm not being flippant about this: for a variety of highly complimentary reasons – with which I shall not embarrass you – I have always looked forward to your producing some outstanding fictional writing about people. I remember, when I first met you, that you told me that you wrote poetry. Are you still doing this, and if so, wouldn't you send up some of your writing to me?

There is another point, although I am not too certain whether this is the best time and place to raise the question. What about some autobiographical writing? You have reached a sufficiently advanced stage in your life where you can attempt such a work without running the risk of being accused of overweening vanity! Wasn't it Randolph Churchill[44] who wrote his first autobiography at the age of about 21? I warn you: if you don't do it, I shall have to do it for you! And I promise you that it will not be nearly as sympathetic a

---

42 Es'Kia Mphahlele (1919–2008) was one of South Africa's most celebrated authors. He produced poetry, plays, non-fiction (including two highly regarded autobiographies) as well as short stories. In a long career he worked as a teacher, as a contributor to *Drum* magazine, and, during his twenty years in exile, he played an instrumental role in establishing the Chemchemi Creative Centre in Kenya and the Mbari Club in Nigeria. Some of his most famous works include *Man Must Live* (1946), *Down Second Avenue* (1957) and *The Living and the Dead* (1961). He was nominated for the Nobel Prize in literature, and was awarded the Order of the Baobab by Nelson Mandela in 1998.

43 William "Bloke" Modisane (1923–86) was a South African writer, actor and journalist. During the 1950s he was a contributor both to *Drum* magazine and the *Golden City Post* (the latter as a jazz critic). In addition to his journalism, he was an actor, and a member of the African Theatre Workshop (featuring in the 1958 production of Athol Fugard's *No Good Friday*). He shared writing credits on the film *Come Back, Africa* which was filmed largely in Sophiatown. Angered by apartheid, Modisane left South Africa in 1959 for England. His famous autobiography, *Blame Me on History*, was published in 1963. In the 1960s Modisane settled in Germany.

44 Winston Churchill's son.

portrait as if you had done it yourself. I hope this dire warning will frighten you into getting down to the job without any further delay.

Thank you for the love for Jenny, which she heartily reciprocates. She continues as adorable as ever. In my letter of March 28 I sent you a picture of her and I hope this has reached you safely.

You will be observing your "anniversary" on May 3.[45] My thoughts and my prayers, as always, will be with you.

God bless you.

With great affection,

---

45 The date on which the "Sobukwe clause" was reconsidered.

Robert Sobukwe
to Veronica Sobukwe,
29 April 1966 (Bc36)

Hullo Darling!

If I had a postcard I should use that because I do not have any worthwhile news. Only I woke up feeling I had to write and tell you that you are a wonderful woman and that I love you immensely – both of which I have said times without number.

I received both the Ten Rands and the Twenty Rands, Kid. Thank you so much. I am sorry to alarm you with telegrams but I learnt rather suddenly that I had not a cent to my name. Please inform Benjie that I have received the kettle and I thank him for it. I have written to him about my textbooks etc.

If there are people who are offering to help with books please consult Benjie, Baby. He has the list of the books I require.

I was shocked to learn that you had been actually confined to bed for two weeks with flu. When you wrote to say you had had a touch of flu I thought you had perhaps been feverish and had developed a cough but had, as usual, merely taken some sulphatriads and gone on. When you remain in bed I know it must be something serious. I am really relieved and glad you are up. I just cannot stand to think you are ill little girl.

Fabian has written from Rome – sent me a postcard. They had had an audience with the Pope and had then gone out to sample life in Rome. He quotes Martin Luther: "Let him who would love a Holy life stay away from Rome". He'll be excommunicated for quoting a "renegade, lascivious and lecherous liar". That is how for years the Roman Catholic Church has described Luther. Things must really be changing if he can be quoted now by self-respecting Catholics.

We are still having warm weather down here. Winter has not yet set in. I have asked Mrs Marquard for some flower and some vegetable seeds. I am hoping to do some decent gardening once more.

I have had my eyes tested quite recently and will be having new glasses pretty soon I hope. I may have to send you another S.O.S. to pay for the glasses. But I hope I shall be able to pay for them from the Twenty Rands you have sent. I have to learn to economize and do without the non-essential as you are doing.

Buti has written to ask what caused Prostatitis in my case. I replied that you suspect cancer. But I think you are wrong, darling. It is purely a strepto-coccal or gonococcal infection. I am not yet *losing* weight; and I am certain I could put on extra pounds of lard if I allowed myself to do so.

I told you Mili had written me a lovely letter. I sent her Two Rands and asked her to send me Dini's address. It is high time he began writing letters too.

I had said this was a brief note and then I go filling page after page! And "how do you savengamize"? as Brer Rabbit said to Tar Baby. How are your midwifery sessions going? Have you thought what to do about Fezile yet?

Well, darling, cheerio. Let me call it a day. I haven't heard from the Nkepus yet and I have not written to them again. I wrote to Tukani but he has not answered. I sincerely hope my writing to him has not jeopardized his job.

God bless you Child. Love to Mama and to the children when you write.

Your loving and proud husband,
Mangi

P.S. I have suggested to Tshawe that she should visit Joh'burg and let the Baragwanath doctors give her a thorough examination. Also I am thinking of having "The World"[46] daily instead of the "Cape Argus". But I'll discuss it with you. It's too late now to do anything about it. RMS.

46 *The World* (formerly the *Bantu World*), was the leading black newspaper of the day, edited by M.T. Moerane.

Minister of Justice
to Benjamin Pogrund,
3 May 1966 (Ba4.8.3)

Dear Sir,

RE: CONDITIONS OF DETENTION: ROBERT M. SOBUKWE.

With reference to your letters of the 3rd February and 23rd March, 1966, I have been instructed by the Honourable the Minister of Justice to reply to your representations as follows:

(a) *Loss of weight.*
Sobukwe has lost eleven pounds of weight in two years. According to the District Medical Officer, this loss of weight can be explained by the chronic infection of his prostrate gland.

(b) *Painful joints, etc.*
The District Medical Officer states that chronic prostatitis has been the cause of some minimal arthritic pains but there is no evidence of true Rheumatoid arthritis or joint deformity. This view is confirmed by physician specialist Dr. Barry Kaplan who examined Sobukwe on the 16th October, 1965. Dr. B. Kaplan assured Sobukwe that he is not suffering from arthritis. Sobukwe has received various analgesics for mild pains that he complained about.

(c) *Chronic Prostatitis*
On October, 1964, Sobukwe has been treated for chronic prostatitis by the District Surgeon, urologist and by a physician specialist. He has been examined whenever he complained but at least monthly and his complaints have been treated. His case was finally assessed and surgery was recommended in December 1965. However, due to his wife's visit it was decided to postpone his operation until after her visit.

As you are probably aware, Sobukwe has had a prostatectomy and, according to the urologist who performed the operation, the operation has been successful.

(*d*) *Teeth and eyes*

His teeth have given trouble at times but on each occasion a dentist attended to him.

Sobukwe has complained about his eyes and arrangements have been made for an eye specialist to test his eyes.

(*e*) *"Sunday Times" and "Rand Daily Mail"*

Copies of both the abovementioned newspapers have, on occasions, arrived late on the Island.

(*f*) *Visits in living quarters*

Facilities for visitors exist at Robben Island Harbour.

(*g*) *Food Parcels*

Only relatives are permitted to send food parcels to Sobukwe.

(*h*) *London "Observer"*

Sobukwe is entitled to receive South African newspapers and periodicals only.

Yours faithfully,

Benjamin Pogrund
to the Minister of Justice,
7 May 1966 (Ba4.8.4)

Dear Sir,

I am in receipt of your letter of May 3, 1966 (Your Reference: MJ21) dealing with the conditions of detention of Mr Robert M. Sobukwe.

I write to say that your actions in investigating my representations and advising me of the result thereof, are much appreciated.

Yours faithfully,
BENJAMIN POGRUND

Benjamin Pogrund
to Veronica Sobukwe,
8 May 1966 (Ba4.8.5)

Dear Mrs Sobukwe,

I have just had a reply from the Minister of Justice, Mr Vorster, to my letter (which I wrote on February) about Bob's conditions of detention. I am sending you herewith a copy of Mr Vorster's reply for your information. If there are any matters arising out of it, will you please let me know?

Tomorrow I am going in to the Brenthurst Clinic for a period of three weeks for treatment for my ulcer. I am looking forward to having a good rest. In case there is anything urgent which you wish to discuss with me, please do not hesitate to telephone me – I shall have a phone next to my bed. The number is 441041.

I had a letter from Bob recently – a most cheerful letter in which he reported that he was keeping well.

My very warmest good wishes to you.

Sincerely,
BENJAMIN POGRUND

Benjamin Pogrund
to Robert Sobukwe,
14 May 1966 (Ba4.33)

My dear Bob,

As you see – and as my telegram sent yesterday indicated – I am in hospital at present. So if nothing else, you will have to endure my handwriting while I lie in bed! I came in on Monday because I have been feeling ill for some time with ulcer trouble. I came in originally for rest, diet and medication for three weeks. But the X-rays taken at the start of the week look so bad that it seems surgery is indicated. I am now being subjected to an entire battery of tests before a final decision is taken.

Lying here, with friends with me a great deal of the time, I have thought back to when you had your operation earlier this year, and how lonely and cut-off you must have felt. Those in whose care you were, were hardly close or dear to you.

One of the primary reasons of course for my deciding to come into hospital, apart from the fact that I have been feeling so ill and run-down – is that I want to be 100 percent fit in the coming months. You know […] I mean to put up a big, big fight. I've learned a lot since June last year, Bob. I've learned more about evil and corruption than I had dreamed was possible. And I have had to test myself and examine myself to see how far I was prepared to stand up for what I believe. I would like you to know that in the agony of spirit which I have gone through, the thought of you has been a primary factor. I have looked at your example of courage and integrity and I have drawn strength from it. And underlying it all, I have so often put the question to myself: If I do this – or don't do that – can I look Bob squarely in the face again?

It was against this background that your letter of April 20 reached me the day before yesterday. As I always do, I opened it and read it joyfully, happy to have word from you. When I reached your last few paragraphs – when you wrote about the testimonial – I am not ashamed to confess that I started weeping and I could not stop weeping. Thank you, Bob. I despair only because I cannot do enough for you and your wife and children. You deserve so much.

To the mundane again: I am enclosing a copy of a letter I have had from the Minister of Justice, Mr Vorster. Both in regard to the letter, and in regard to the non arrival of the books listed in your April 20 letter, I intend taking up in official quarters. If you wish to make any comments on the letter, please let me know. I agree with you that, if nothing else, it is grossly discourteous not to advise either you or me that books etc sent to you have been withheld. Other considerations apart, also there is also the financial one – for example, the large Xmas food parcel which I sent – unsuccessfully – to you. There is the funny side to it: the title "Marxism Today" (one of the books held back from you) happens to be a strongly anti-Communist work; the one on North Vietnam is also anti-Red, and by no stretch of the imagination could it be considered subversive even in our fair land. Anyway I intend taking up these matters.

The subscription form to the "Economica" did not reach me. Why? Your guess is as good as mine. If you look at the Minister's letter you will see that overseas publications are verboten (careful choice of word?), but I simply don't see how this could or should apply to a reputable academic journal. I will take up the matter here again, but I suggest that you also ascertain the position from your immediate guardians.

In regard to your study books I deeply regret the delay. I can promise you that I have been pushing things as hard as possible. I did this again after receiving your last letter, and have since had a reply from Professor Wachman, president of Lincoln University (which has, you will recall, awarded you an honorary degree – now your followers can really call you "Prof"!) to the effect that a batch is on its way. It should have reached you by the time you receive this letter – I hope. Other books I am trying to rush to you as rapidly as possible.

Incidentally, I must tell you that being in hospital is a most comfortable experience. I had great difficulty in getting a bed and had to accept a luxury ward here – at a price which makes my ulcer twitch whenever I think of it. Next to my bed (with padded headboard) is a panel of switches, controlling sundry lights to give strong or soothing illumination, air conditioning, etc. I have brought with me my record player and a tape recorder and I spent most of the time transcribing my records onto tape. I have decided to go "modern" and anyway, tapes are easier to cart around the world than stacks of records so it is being done too with an eye to the future. Most important of all I am eating regularly and well – something as a bachelor, which I haven't been able to do for a long, long time. The food here is outstanding as the Brenthurst prides itself on providing anything a patient wants. I believe the only time the chef was stumped was when a Frenchwoman ordered snake. Somehow I feel the food I am getting now is even better than what you eat.

And joy of joys, the kind-hearted Matron has agreed to allow Jenny to come and see me tomorrow. So I am looking forward to a great treat. The other day I was talking to Jenny about her "Uncle Bob", and I found it interesting that she repeated a question she has repeatedly asked – whether you had ever seen her. I told her no, as you have been living a long way away but that you had seen her pictures, and that you are a close friend of her Daddy's and therefore a friend of hers. This she happily accepts – and sends you her love.

I am both happy and sad that you have read "Spartacus" – sad because I so much wanted to send it to you. "My glorious brothers"[47] I have just got and will be reading it in the next few days.

If I have to undergo an operation I shall send you a telegram the day before and will ask you to bear me in your thoughts and to pray for me. It would mean much to me to know that you were thinking of me then.

God bless you and maintain your spirit.

With great affection,
Benjamin

---

47 See Pogrund's letter of 20 April.

Robert Sobukwe
to Veronica Sobukwe,
19 May 1966 (Bc37)

Hullo Darling,

Thanks for renewing the subscriptions to the various newspapers. I have cost you quite a lot of money this month.

In my last letter I told you I had had my eyes examined. I received the new glasses yesterday (Wednesday, 18th) and they cost me R12.40 (Twelve Rands forty cents). They have made a tremendous gap in the Twenty Rands you sent, but I am not asking for any more dough.

Benjie has written to ask if I require anything by way of clothing. But I am quite all right for the winter and perhaps even for the year. I don't think I'll be needing anything for some time.

Mrs Marquard wrote to me recently to console with me over the death of my uncle. But I don't know which uncle it is, where and when he died. I have not received any information to that effect nor have I read about any death of a relative of mine. Have you heard anything?

What is the news about the children? Has snow fallen already on the mountains of Lesotho? I told you Mili had written me a lovely letter. I asked her, in my reply, to send me Dini's address. She has not yet answered that letter.

This one is certainly going to be a brief note. How are you keeping, girl? What shift are you on? I haven't forgotten our wedding anniversary. I'll celebrate it here appropriately with coffee instead of wine.

Give my love to Mama and friends.

Cheerio Darling. God bless you.

Your loving husband,
Mangi

Robert Sobukwe
to Nell Marquard,
19 May 1966 (Bd1.24)

Dear Mrs Marquard,

Thank you for both your letters; that of 3rd April and that of 1st May.

But first let me say I was rather shaken when I read in the press that Mr Marquard was ill. Your letter calmed me a little, though I must say I am still sorry to learn he is keeping [to] his bed. His professorial comments on Rich Tulbagh[48] and the various problems as well as the causes and sequence of the Kaffir Wars[49] are of great interest and assistance to us students of history and make "Passing Show"[50] one of the most delightful columns to read. It has a "traditional" flavour about it.

You will pardon my saying so but your letter of the 3rd April breathed an air of aggressive impatience as though you had just been listening to "Current Affairs" or "Africa Survey"![51] I was tempted to reply immediately and ask you to give the budding Bob Hopes a chance. But I realized that it is good for one at some moments to stamp one's foot and shake one's mane in righteous wrath and indignation. "Blessed are the meek".[52] Yes: But the man who said that told the High Priest – "If there's anything wrong in what I've said, tell me what it is: if there's not, then why do you strike me"[53] – some meekness!

I have just realized that I have not thanked you for the books you sent. Please forgive me. As I said earlier, unless I write immediately I receive your letters and parcels – impossible under the circumstances – there'll be a lot I forget to thank you for.

---

48 Rijk Tulbagh (1699–1771), Governor of the Dutch Cape Colony between 1751 and 1771.

49 The frontier wars between the Colony and the Xhosa, often referred to collectively as the Hundred Years War.

50 A humorous column that appeared regularly in the *Sunday Times*, written by the editor, Joel Mervis. But Marquard seems to have also been involved, at times perhaps. Marquard and Mervis had jointly produced a humorous book, referred to elsewhere in these letters.

51 These were current affairs programmes on the SABC, which firmly toed the National Party government line.

52 Matthew 5: 5.

53 John 18: 23.

Yes, *The Listener* does carry some touching stories and the piece on the soldiers and the mob showed, as you say, a sense both of humour and of human nature.

Oh no, the Xhosas accept the charge of being thieves and liars. In turn they accuse the Zulu and Fingo[54] groups of being "ja baas"[55] types – the "good boys" of the white man. All sheer prejudice, of course.

In the case of the Fingo whom in their better moments they refer to as *aba-Mbo*, the hostility of the Xhosa dates back to the period when the British government placed the Fingo in the area around Peddie to form a buffer between the colonists and the Xhosa.

It is said that when the Fingo were removed from among the Xhosa (and Rev Shaw of the Methodist Church presented this as the equivalent of the trek of the children of Israel out of the bondage of Egypt) they, protected by the guns of British soldiers, took with them the cattle of their masters and neighbours.

It is something for which one is ever thankful that the bitterness thus created (and it was intense!) through, at least in part, the good offices of the missionaries was completely wiped out through the efforts of the same missionaries in their schools like Lovedale, Healdtown, Fort Hare, etc where Xhosa, Sotho, Zulu, Fingo, Ndebele, Shona, etc met and learnt that they were all African.[56] Thus it was that my brother married a so-called Fingo woman who became my father's darling and I fell in love with and married my wife without knowing and without caring to know to what ethnic group she belonged.

I am glad to hear about this relative of mine whose acquaintance you have made. Broadly speaking, in this clan of mine (the Baboons) it is the men who, tall, very dark and rather ugly, are gentle and even sheepish. The women, who are on the whole beautiful and lovely physical specimens of womanhood, tend to be vile-tempered vixens. I am glad this one had an engaging smile. But, of course, they are perfect hypocrites!

---

54 The Fingo (Mfengu) were regarded by many Xhosa as collaborators with the Colony. In 1835, under the direction of the Rev. John Ayliff (not the Rev. William Shaw, as Sobukwe has it), they were settled at Peddie and became loyal subjects of the British.

55 "Yes, sir."

56 A central tenet of Sobukwe's Pan-Africanism was to contest the tribal conflicts and identities fostered by the divide and conquer tactics of white supremacy in its various forms of colonialism and apartheid.

Do you see what I mean? I am just remembering that I haven't thanked you yet for the rake, the fertilizer, the seeds and the Sluggem.[57] Thank you for them all. And thank you also for conveying my messages to Johannesburg.

Your comments on the play "The Lion and the Jewel"[58] are very generous. My weakness, I think, is that though I bitterly resent the sneering remarks of the ill-disposed, I am, with my friends, brutally and ruthlessly critical of African efforts. And with regard to the theatre I think, besides the reasons you mention, we suffer from the fact that our middle class is still very puritan and regards the theatre and cinema and dances as evil – things with which only "fast" women are associated. As a result, dramatic societies and the entertainment world in general do not attract the best socially and intellectually: a very grave handicap. Secondly, our actors, perhaps because of this puritanism, appear anxious to convey the idea that they are *acting a part*. They do not want to be identified with the character they are acting. The "willing suspension of disbelief" is thus made difficult. Our women, in particular, have a stereotyped impersonal "stage" voice.

But, of course, these are the beginnings. Hamlet, too, had a lot of complaints about the actors of his day!

I see that Sir Laurence Olivier's "Othello"[59] will be showing soon. It is the one piece I should have liked to see either in the theatre or in the cinema. Critics say he excels not only those who have played the part before him but he excels anything he himself has done before. A very tall claim that. I shall be most interested to get your impressions when the film comes round.

Finally, lest I forget. The 27th (twenty-seventh) July is my wife's birthday. She'll be forty then. I am told it is a difficult age for women. Could you please send her a message when the time comes. She'll appreciate it.

With best wishes to you and Mr Marquard,
I remain,
Yours sincerely,
RM Sobukwe

---

57 A proprietary brand of insecticide.

58 A play written by Wole Soyinka, first performed in 1959.

59 The 1965 film adaptation of Shakespeare's tragedy.

Benjamin Pogrund
to the Minister of Justice,
26 May 1966 (Ba4.8.6)

Dear Sir,

With further reference to the correspondence which I have had with you in regard with Mr Robert Mangaliso Sobukwe (Your Reference: MJ.21), I wonder whether I may ask if it would be possible for you to grant me an interview.

I ask for the favour of an interview on two bases, namely:

(a) To take up various matters which have come to my attention in a letter recently received from Mr Sobukwe.
(b) In order to submit certain representations which I am certain you will be willing to consider.

Should you be willing to grant me an interview, I am available virtually at any time.

Yours faithfully,
BENJAMIN POGRUND

Robert Sobukwe
to Benjamin Pogrund,
1 June 1966 (Ba4.34)

My dear Benjie,

Thank you for your very enjoyable letter which reached me on the 27th May. I had to take it in instalments in order to preserve my manly integrity. C.P. Snow makes one of his characters observe that "somehow one's dreadfully vulnerable through those one loves."[60] I like that – we are vulnerable!

When my wife was down here she told me you were not well but I did not want to raise the matter in my letters. I hope you recover completely and soon, Benjie. Mind you, bearing in mind the pace you've been maintaining ever since I knew you – and I am told you've stepped it up even more – you sure have lasted fellah.

In my childhood I was a bit of a coward, and my father who was no mean psychologist repeatedly advised me, "if you can avoid a fight, then avoid it. Apologize, if that will prevent a fight, even if you are in the right. But if you *must* fight, then make a complete job of it so that even if you have to be carried unconscious from the field, your adversary should most decidedly *not* wish for a second encounter." Years later I found Polonius giving the same advice to Laertes (in "Hamlet") though not in so many words, proof, if any were needed, that Shakespeare was related to my father. I give you the same advice, Benjie. Choose your ground carefully, don't dissipate your energies. I have never been worried about you. I've always known you cannot be untrue to yourself. A man must live with himself. And to live with someone you despise is hell.

In your reading of "*My Glorious Brothers*"[61] you presumably have by now reached what to me is the whole message of the book: "Tell Ragesh that the

60 Sobukwe remarked on the same line from C.S. Snow's *The Masters*, in his letter of 16 January 1966 to Nell Marquard.

61 *My Glorious Brothers* is a novelistic account of the (Jewish) Maccabean revolt against the Greek-Syrian Empire in 167 BC. Howard Fast, the author of the novel, was a committed anti-fascist, and the book recounts the heroic account of the Maccabees who, although confronted with a superior military force, opted to stand fast in resisting the tyranny of Greek-Syrian religious and political oppression.

Maccabee is in Judaea; the Maccabee and his brother Simon etc etc".[62] A similar configuration appears in *Spartacus* – "Tell the Senate ..."[63] And what a message! And yet I've always felt that the message in *Spartacus* was a political testament. The message to Ragesh was in the genre of the great utterances of the prophets – a timeless message for all oppressed. And when Ragesh, the High Priest, received it, he wept. It reminded him of what he was. I can never forget that passage, Benjie. You give it to Jenny, on the night of the Passover to remind her that "once we were slaves in Egypt, and we shall never be slaves again".

I am not going to comment on the letter from the Minister of Justice. It's the typical bureaucratic reply and I am not interested in scoring debating points. However, with regard to (e) you have my letter (I hope!) informing you that these were *officially withheld*. After all, as you know, I have not been receiving the "Rand Daily Mail" for over two years now so that for copies of it to "arrive late" is absolutely out of the question. With regard to (h) my wife has the Minister's original order. There you will see that Mr Sobukwe is entitled to receive South African newspapers *in addition* to literature permitted under the Prison Regulations. There is a long list of "verboten" literature (in jail) (including "The Golden City Post" and "Drum") and "Economica" is certainly not on it. In fact what is specified in the Minister's order is *news*papers and the "Observer", I believe, is a newspaper and can, therefore, be regarded as verboten in the same way as the BBC and other radio *news* is verboten as far as I am concerned. It is with regard to *news* that I must be confined to a South

---

62 The novel deals with how the Maccabees respond, when the Greek king of Syria, Antiochus, orders the Jews, under threat of death, to abandon their religious practices and worship Greek gods. After a series of assaults on the Maccabees, Judas, the man who will go on to become a hero in the Maccabees' struggle, roams across Judaea, seeing what can be done. It is only through the efforts of Rabi Ragesh and Judas that the Maccabee villagers forge weapons and prepare themselves to fight, and resistance to the might of the Greek-Syrian empire becomes a possibility. The resonance between this material and Sobukwe's own political struggle is obvious.

63 Spartacus (111–71 BC), a Thracian gladiator and escaped slave leader, was a major figure in the slave uprising against the Roman Republic. The moment that Sobukwe refers to occurs when Spartacus warns the Roman Senate that the slaves – of whom he was so prominent a leader – would not surrender but continue to fight the Republic, even in the face of seemingly insurmountable odds. Sobukwe seems particularly fascinated by such moments of courageous resistance, and the accompanying sense of political agency associated with them, even when the prospect of overturning tyranny was at best remote.

African diet. The "Economica" dealing with balance of payments etc cannot by any stretch of the imagination be regarded as verboten EVEN IN TERMS OF THE MINISTER'S Order. It is just as much a part of my lessons as *The Listener* which I continue to receive. Its suppression belongs to the last quarter of last year – the troubled and unpleasant period I wrote you about. Please arrange immediately for copies of "Economica" to be sent, Benjie. I have a lot to catch up with in practical economics. Incidentally, in the "Observer", there is a column on Economics written by Professor Allen of London University. Ernie Wentzel receives the "Observer", do you think he could send me cuttings of those articles?

I received a letter from Lincoln University on the 3rd May, informing me that books were on the way by surface mail. The airmail letter was dated 29th (twenty ninth) April. I haven't received the books yet.

The [Harold] Strachan articles[64] I am talking about are those you said you would send – the Press reports on the case in Durban. After your letter saying you would send them, I heard nothing further. I didn't even know you had sent them!!

Glad to know you are enjoying your hospital rest. I had the delightful company of a warder and an S.B., one on each side of my bed for twenty-four hours a day. And, of course, the "Medicine for Rhodesia" campaign was launched at the hospital on my fourth day there.[65] Very congenial surroundings indeed!

Finally, Benjie, on the 27th July is my wife's fortieth birthday. I should like her to know she is highly appreciated. Do you think you could organize a present from me and the kids? I am writing early so that you may consult me if you wish. I leave the choice of a present to you. I am writing to Miliswa, too, to apprise her of the great event.

As for myself I am afraid I shall have to bother you again for a rand's postage stamps (2½ cents) and a further rand's 6d (is it 5 cents?) postage stamps for my Wolsey Hall assignments.

---

64 As noted earlier, Harold Strachan was Pogrund's chief source in the prison exposé articles he published in the *Rand Daily Mail*. See Pogrund's letter to Sobukwe of 7 December 1965.

65 Apparently a campaign to raise medicines for embattled Rhodesia after UDI and the outbreak of guerrilla warfare with Zimbabwean nationalists. Karl Bremer was a white hospital catering mainly to Afrikaner patients and staffed mainly by Afrikaner doctors and nurses.

Love to Jenny and friends. Incidentally thanks for her photo. Did I thank you for it? No harm in repeating the pleasure. I am rather suspicious of the "kind-hearted" matrons and nurses. However, best wishes and enjoy your rattlesnake puddings.

Yours affectionately,
Bob

P.S. No books have arrived yet. Will inform you when and as they do. Bob

Private Secretary,
Minister of Justice,
to Benjamin Pogrund,
7 June 1966 (Ba4.8.7)

Dear Sir,

RE: ROBERT M. SOBUKWE

The Honourable the Minister of Justice and of Prisons has instructed me to acknowledge the receipt of your letter of the 26th May, 1966, and to inform you that he is not prepared to grant you an interview.

Any representations which you may wish to make must be done in writing.

Yours faithfully,
PRIVATE SECRETARY

Robert Sobukwe
to Veronica Sobukwe,
23 June 1966 (Bc38)

Hullo Darling!

I should perhaps have waited until next month before writing this type of letter. But the future is not in our hands and I do want to make sure this letter reaches you in time.

I have been conscious for months that on the 27th July you celebrate a rather special birthday in so far as years are recorded according to the calendar.

Mili and I have exchanged some ideas about it: rather I have suggested a few things to Mili. I have also told Benjie about it. I hope you won't mind.

This is the one time I am indeed grieved that I am not around to express my thanks to and appreciation of you as a wife and mother. I have said it before and I repeat it boldly and gratefully that you are a chosen among the chosen (mokhethoa hara bakhoelhoa).

We have come a long way together Little Girl and we have watched each other grow and mature. And we have watched the children God has blessed us with grow. We occupied a building at Mofolo and we turned it into a home. You denied yourself a lot of luxuries and worked uncomplainingly to achieve this. The children and I thank you and bless you.

You've been a widow now for over six years. But you have been father and mother both to our children and they have grown up like other children lacking nothing that you could give them.

You've been regular in your visits to me throughout my years as a convict right up to the present day; ever dignified, calm and cool, ever uncomplaining, never whining. The children and I thank you and bless you.

I have said that according to the calendar you will be forty this year. But to me you will always remain the young girl I saw at Victoria hospital[66] and at Fort Hare: the young wife with whom I dug out stones at Mofolo and created a lovely garden.

You have had your share of sorrow. But it has not been in vain. You have discovered new and true friends in quarters that you did not suspect. You

66 The Victoria Hospital in Alice, where Fort Hare is situated, trained nurses like Veronica Sobukwe.

have come to know yourself: to know what you can bear. And that is a great lesson to learn. Among the Xhosa, as you know, when men doubt each other, they go for a swim in the river so that they may see whether the other fellow has been through the Initiation School. It is a great thing to be able to say "I have been through it. I know what it is like".

I'll say more to you, personally, when we meet. My heart is full because I have come to know what a great woman you are – the true embodiment of African womanhood.

Well, darling, I wish you a very happy birthday and I know that you will be spared to see many many more. I shall get myself a special cake for the occasion and will celebrate. I'll do no work that day either physical or mental. I'll just celebrate.

I have remembered that on the 30th July is Mili's birthday. I have told her she'll get her present in December. I'll discuss it with you later.

Have the "Reader's Digest" people sent you these three volumes of their new dictionary, selling at R10.00 (Ten Rands)? It's a lovely set and I was sorely tempted to keep it. But I have to watch my budget carefully now – so back they have to go.

The Radio reports that you have been having very cold weather up there of late. We have a curious set up down here. The days are gloriously warm. You can move around in your shirtsleeves. But the nights are bitterly cold – real Antarctic weather.

I received a letter from Nenti some time back. She thoroughly enjoyed your visit. Again, thanks little girl.

Tshawe, too, has written and she tells me that Charles is on sick leave for six months. He went up to Nelspoort[67] for tests early this year. I pray that he does not have a relapse.

Well, Darling, so much for now. God bless you. Ukhule ntombazana uze ukhokhobe, bakusingathi abadala bazikhangeze izinyembezi zakho.[68]

Your grateful and fortunate husband,
Mangi

67 A small town near Beaufort West with a hospital.

68 Girl, my wish is that you will live, enjoy life and grow as old as possible, and that the ancestors who look after you will wipe away your tears.

Nana Mahomo,
607A Grand Buildings,
Trafalgar Square,
London,
to Benjamin Pogrund,
28 June 1966 (Ba4.40)

Dear Ben

Many thanks for your letter of June 24th.

My note was intended to convey that you can call upon us for future study books for Robert whenever necessary.

We would appreciate it, however, if you would give us more time so as to enable us to arrange for cheaper means of postage. We will try to find the balance of the books requested and forward them to you as soon as possible.

We have placed an order for a year's subscription to "Economica" and have instructed the publishers to forward the issues to you direct, beginning with the first number this year.

Your comments regarding Bob and the need for discretion in this matter have been noted.

We are pleased to learn that Bob is in good shape and good heart. We shall always welcome any news you may have regarding Bob and do let us hear how you yourself are getting on. You should be hearing from us soon.

Yours sincerely
Nana[69]

---

69 Nelson "Nana" Mahomo (1930–2014) was a former member of the Transvaal Youth League who sided with Africanists within the ANC and subsequently left that party to join the PAC. He was elected secretary for culture in the PAC in 1959, and was in addition a member of the organisation's national executive committee. Mahomo did much to build the PAC in the Western Cape. He had been delegated to leave South Africa before the anti-pass campaign in 1960, and went on to act as one of the organisation's chief representatives abroad.

Robert Sobukwe
to Benjamin Pogrund,
29 June 1966 (Ba4.41)

My dear Benjie,

You will pardon me if this letter appears "official". I have discovered that whenever I write as I feel I seldom say all that I should have like to say. Good.

First of all, then, I received three books early this week which, I was informed, had been sent by you. The bore the ff[70] titles:-

Economics of Industrial Organization – [Arthur] Beacham
Capitalism, Socialism and Democracy – [Joseph] Schumpeter
The Heavenly City of the 18th Century Philosophers – Carl L. Becker.

Yesterday I received a further batch which, I presume, is from Lincoln University. These are the books:–

Medieval Thought: St. Augustine to Ockham – G. Leff
Essays in Economic History Vol I and II (ed) E.M. Carus-Wilson
Chartist Portraits – G.D.H. Cole
The International Economy since 1850 – W. Ashworth
The Structure of Industry in Britain – G.C. Allen.

Since the President of Lincoln said he was sending about a dozen books I suppose the rest are still being censored.

You can't imagine how happy I was to receive these books. I felt like reading them all at once. I never dreamt I would come to enjoy Economics like this.

Thank you for your telegram which I received this morning (Incidentally I have not yet received your letter which I presume accompanied the books. This is, therefore, not a reply to it). I had been afraid that by writing to you so early on the matter of the Birthday I might give you the impression that I had written July by mistake and that the great day was in fact June 27th. Your telegram set my mind at rest.

70 That is, following.

As I stated in my replying telegram your choice of gifts suited me just fine. I know it will suit my wife too. Will use the set when we are entertaining on a grand scale at some future date.

I have written to Miliswa about this event and told her that Ntate Benjie will be consulting her. She's the most sensitive of my children, I think, and will relish being drawn into the conspiracy. To heighten the drama, therefore, I suggest that when you visit Mofolo, you call her aside, away from her mother and tell her what presents we are planning to make.

I told her that the two of you would have to get a cake (but this is really for *them* to eat that a "Birthday" cake with candles etc) and that each one of them will have to present their mother with a bunch of flowers on the 27th July. If you can arrange the details for those two items with Miliswa you'll have given her the responsibility she is in such a hurry to shoulder.

As I say, I have not yet received your letter and do not know what comments you have made on the Kennedy visit.[71] I assume that you have commented and expect your comment to be favourable seeing that you are an "ultra-liberal", to borrow a term from the eminent Prof. Logan of the Hague Case fame.[72] By the way I have been following the discussions in the Geography Teachers' Symposium being held at Stellenbosch University and am suitably impressed by the unanimity of thought, attitude and vision exhibited by the eminent academicians who have presented papers there. The only foreigner, I think, is the eminent American Prof. Logan, who, to my knowledge, has never been in this country before.

Oh yes, you remarked in an earlier letter that no African has produced a great social novel in this country. I agree with you. But I want to suggest to you, as a verifiable fact of history, that an oppressed people or class has never

---

71 Robert Kennedy visited South Africa in June 1966 at the invitation of the National Union of South African Students and gave a memorable speech at the University of Cape Town, regarded as one of his finest.

72 In 1960, Ethiopia and Liberia filed a case against South Africa – the 'South West Africa Case' – claiming that the country had not fulfilled its mandatory duties in its governance of South West Africa (which South Africa had acquired as a mandated territory from the League of Nations after the end of the First World War). In 1966, the International Court of Justice at The Hague finally gave judgment in this case, ruling that the applicants, Ethiopia and Liberia, had no standing to bring their suit against the Republic of South Africa. As a result, South Africa continued its rule over the former German colony. Professor R.F. Logan of the University of California gave evidence on behalf of the South African government.

produced great literature or art. When we read that such and such an artist was a peasant or worker, what in fact is meant is that he was of peasant or worker *origin*. He himself was no longer that. It is the middle class that idealizes the worker or the peasant or that writes indignantly on his behalf. As Bernard Shaw says, "The worker is concerned with the drudgery of earning a living" and has no time to appreciate the nobility of character assigned to him. Marx spoke of the "stupidity" of the peasant. He, of course, belonged to the middle class.

Do you know that at Fort Hare we loathed "Cry the Beloved Country"? The Rev. Nxumalo[73] typified for us the "Uncle Tom" mentality which we abhorred. In other words no one of us could ever have had such a character as a hero. And yet he is a typical missionary-school product. And Paton took him as he found him. What the oppressed produce is propaganda. If they attempt to be detached, they write superficially.

This is a subject requiring a letter by itself, Benjie. An exuberant literature is coming out of Nigeria. And in America the complaint is that Baldwin[74] is over-concerned with race – he feels, therefore he produces propaganda. The same was said about Richard Wright.[75]

As for me – well, perhaps I'll take your advice. But I'll never write an autobiography, Benjie. I think this form of writing is being overdone. Yes I wrote some poems and short stories, but they were in Xhosa. Remember I asked you what I could do when the late Mosaku confiscated my manuscripts from his typist who was typing them during office hours. You wanted me to get Ernie [Wentzel] to sue for their return. I recited some of them in jail and the natives were suitably impressed.

Love to Jennie. Will write again, soon.

Bob

---

73 Sobukwe appears to be consciously avoiding the anglicised spelling used in Alan Paton's *Cry, the Beloved Country*, referring to the novel's 'Reverend Kumalo' instead as 'Nxumalo'.

74 James Baldwin (1924–87), influential American novelist, social critic and often associated with the Harlem Renaissance. Baldwin published his first novel, *Go Tell It on the Mountain*, in 1953; it was followed by *Giovanni's Room*, *Another Country* and *Tell Me How Long the Train's Been Gone*.

75 Richard Wright (1908–60), noted American author, often associated – like James Baldwin – with the Harlem Renaissance. Wright's first novel was *Native Son* (1940), which shared the predominant concern of much of his fiction, namely that of themes of racial discrimination and inequality in the United States.

Benjamin Pogrund
to Veronica Sobukwe,
12 July 1966 (Ba4.43)

Dear Mrs Sobukwe,

I would be most grateful if you would contact me as soon as possible as there are some matters which I would like to discuss with you.

Unfortunately, I no longer have a permit to enter Soweto,[76] so I wonder whether we could perhaps meet at the "Mail", in my office? Could you please telephone me as soon as you know you will be coming into town? You can get me at my flat (449030) in the mornings (and you can telephone as early as you wish), or at the "Mail" after 5 pm as I am now doing night-duty.

I trust that you are keeping well.

Sincerely,
BENJAMIN POGRUND

76 Whites were required to have a permit to enter African townships or locations.

Benjamin Pogrund
to Robert Sobukwe,
20 July 1966 (Ba4.51)

My dear Bob,

Thank you for your letters of June 1 (which arrived on June 16) and June 29 (which arrived on July 16). I can hardly believe that more than a full month has passed since your first letter arrived. I am sorry I have been so slow in replying.

I have been delighted to share in the surprises for your wife's birthday, and happy also that my suggestions for gifts are acceptable to you. I saw your wife yesterday and can report that she is keeping very well indeed. All being well, I hope that she will be visiting you next month. We worked out the details of a visit and she is now going to find out when she can take leave from the clinic. She will travel to Cape Town for about two weeks just as soon as this can be arranged. So something good for you to look forward to.

I was upset yesterday, however, to discover that I had just missed the children, as they had returned to school the previous day. The new term apparently starts unexpectedly early. Your wife assured me that they are well, and are also doing well at school this year, Miliswa in particular (she has come second in class).

Naturally I did not let on to your wife as to what is in store for the 27th. But I shall be seeing her on that day and will have pleasure in handing her the various presents. My only regret is that you will not also be there.

I have also, today, written to Miliswa telling her how sorry I was that I did not see her. I have sent some money to the school for pocket money for the children, and have told Miliswa that, should she wish to send her mother a telegram, or even a small gift, she should go ahead and make use of this money. I see also that it is Miliswa's birthday on July 30: I shall be sending her a small gift for this.

Enclosed please find copy of a letter which I have sent to the Officer Commanding, Robben Island Gaol. As you will see from the letter, I have deposited R15.00 to be used by you on whatever purchases you may wish to make. I did this after seeing your wife, and have arranged with her that any future monies which you may need will be channelled through me. So when this amount runs short, will you please let me know? Another idea which strikes me: in the past, whenever you have needed a kettle or a heater or anything like that, we have had to go through the process of your advising me, etc. Wouldn't it be simpler if you were to purchase the goods from Stuttafords in Cape Town and have it charged to me? I have an account with them, both in Cape Town and up here, so there is no problem about the accounts side. All you would then have to do would be to let me know whatever you buy so that I could check the accounts. Can you find out from the jail authorities if this will be in order for you to do? And if it is, please let me know and I shall drop a line to Stuttafords asking them to give you all cooperation in making purchases. The fruit parcels, by the way, have been extended and I hope that they are still reaching you safely and that you are enjoying them.

Also enclosed is R2.00 of 2½c and R2.00 of 5c stamps, as requested by you. Sorry I have taken so long to get them to you.

I note that, this year, you have not replied to my inquiries about your need for jerseys, other clothing, blankets, etc. Are you *quite* sure that you do not need anything?

I am tremendously relieved that, at long, long last, the study books are beginning to reach you. I am deeply sorry about the length of delays, but they were virtually unavoidable. There are still quite a lot more to come so will you please continue to let me know as they arrive? Also, I am at present putting together a bundle of lighter reading material for you and this will be sent down, I hope, within the next few days.

Re my illness: I had a narrow escape from an operation which apparently would have been an unnecessary one. My doctor had flatly told me that I had to have an operation, and I was reconciled to this. The surgeon, etc had already been chosen. Then I insisted on getting an opinion from Dr Mozie Suzman (Helen's husband), who is probably the top man in this country. He came to see me and ruled out an operation entirely. He took over my treatment, and although I am on a daily diet of tablets, I am feeling pretty well – in fact, far, far better than I have for a long time past. I stayed in hospital only for about ten days, but the rest and good food (I never did get round to asking for that snake) did me a world of good. It was just what I needed to get me on my feet again. On doctor's orders – and also because I have long felt the need of it – I now also do a lot of exercise. I go to horse-riding twice a week, and this is magnificent fun, although I think you would split your sides if you saw me in my jodhpurs and black riding hat cantering along. Ernie and Jill [Wentzel] have joined me in this and we go out first thing on Sunday mornings for an hour riding around the Bryanston countryside. I also took up judo but soon had to retire temporarily when I tore a ligament in my chest. I fear I am just too old for this particular violent game, Bob, but I'm determined to go on pretending that I am still a young man and I intend resuming classes again next week. Sometimes, when I had first started, I wasn't too sure whether the cure was not worse than the illness: I just never knew which part of my body was aching more!

Then, at the office, since the start of June, I have been doing sub-editing. It had long been thought a good idea for me to gain this experience – it is all to do with making up a newspaper – and advantage has been taken of the current "lull" to get me in there. I shall probably be doing subbing until the end of August, and will then, I hope, go back to writing, all else being equal. I find subbing absolutely dreadful, and am bored to tears by it. Knocking what other people have written into shape seems to me to be a particularly pointless way to spend an evening. One little side-effect is that the so-called work hardly taxes my abundant energies at all, with the result that when I come off duty at midnight or 1 am, I am usually still wide awake … so I tend to drift round, at that time of the night or sit and read until the early hours, wake up early and am thoroughly tired by late afternoon when the working day is just starting! It must sound rather mad to you, and I assure you that it is.

Thank you for your message for Jenny, who is as adorable as ever. We were in Cape Town together over the long weekend at the end of May, and walking along the Sea Point beachfront, I used to point out the Island as the place where her Uncle Bob lived.

Her latest nursery school report, for the end of June, has filled me with delight. After noting that her temperamental outbursts have ceased, it continues: "In the school situation she has become cooperative and reasonable and much more emotionally self-reliant. She responds best to positive suggestion and is not so prickly to criticism. This warm and affectionate little girl shows increased maturation emotionally and socially." What pleases me here is the fact that Jenny has come through the trying period of the separation, and is showing herself to be a remarkably adjustable child. And above all, she is the "warm and affectionate little girl", as the report describes her. She celebrated her fifth birthday this month, by the way, and is quite the young lady.

On your remarks about Africans producing a great social novel: I don't class you – at the present time – as either a "peasant" or a "worker" (whatever other phrases others might use about you!) This is so whatever your origins in the past. And to take it a step further, even after allowing for the restrictions of existence in our country, there are many Africans – to be counted in their thousands or even tens of thousands – who despite their peasant or worker origin, have through education and economic advancement become middle class in their mode of living and in their outlook. This being so, surely the fact that an oppressed people are too busy merely keeping their bodies together, does not explain the lack of good writing in South Africa? Particularly when the process of numbers of people breaking out of and away from their origins has been going on at an accelerating tempo since well before the turn of the century (although – to anticipate your retort – at that stage, only a handful was involved. But during the last 20 years, you would surely agree that a great many in number have been involved in this changing process?)

This is all for now. I shall be writing again soon. In the meantime, look after yourself, and study hard.

God bless you,

Robert Sobukwe
to Benjamin Pogrund,
21 July 1966 (Ba4.52)

Dear Benjie,

This is merely intended to inform you that the books from Lincoln University have arrived. There were ten in all and these are the titles:-

1. An Economic Interpretation of the history of the U.S.A. by Charles Beard.
2. Nationalized Industry and Public Ownership – [William A.] Robson.
3. A history of American Economic Life – [Edward C.] Kirkland.
4. The Civil War and Reconstruction – [David H.] Donald.
5. The Turner Thesis – Role of the Frontier in American history.
6. The Wealth of Nations Vols I and II – Adam Smith.
7. The Great Experiment – [Frank] Thistlethwaite.
8. The Frontier in American History – J.F. Turner.
9. The Structure of Competitive Industry – [E.A.G.] Robinson.

The ones I need desperately are [G.H.] Sabine's on Political Theory and [A.J.] Grant and [H.M.V.] Temperley's on International history. As you will recall theirs are the sole textbooks in their respective subjects. The notes are based almost exclusively on them.

I have just received a letter from Miliswa in which she informs me that their schools re-open on the 18th July. I realize then that our plans for bouquets by the children will have to be dropped. I hope she received my letter before she left so that she should know, at least, that we had intended her to play an important part in the festivities.

Benjie, I realise that I have never thanked you for renewing my "Reader's Digest" subscription. I do so now. We tend to take the kindness and sacrifices of our friends for granted.

I hope you have recovered completely and are up and about.

Love to Jenny

With best wises
BOB

P.S. I have written to Lincoln University, but will appreciate it if you could do the same, listing the books – Bob.

Benjamin Pogrund
to Robert Sobukwe,
28 July 1966 (Ba4.55)

My dear Bob,

I am hastening to write this short letter to you to let you know that all went well on your wife's birthday yesterday. I delivered to her, as a personal gift from you, sweetpeas, and from you and the children, a tea service as we arranged. This is a set of "Royal Standard" English bone china, and I think your wife liked it a great deal. My own gift was a black leather handbag, while my girlfriend presented a box of toilet soaps. One thing on which you and I slipped up: you should have sent me a little note to include with the tea service. As we had not done this, I had to improvise, and the note I delivered from you and the children read: "To a wife and mother. For your courage and devotion".

Good news for you: your wife will be making a trip to Cape Town during the first week of September. She has taken a week off work, and we are making the necessary arrangements at this moment. All being well, you should be seeing her on September 6 or 7.

Under separate cover, am sending you another batch of study books. They are:

[P.T.] Bauer and [B.S.] Yamey: The economics of under-developed countries
[J.P.T.] Bury: France: 1814-1940
[C.R.] Fay: Great Britain from Adam Smith to the present day
[David] Thomson: England in the 19th century
[E.H. Phelps] Brown and [J.] Wiseman: A course in applied economics
Grant and Temperley: Europe in the 19th and 20th centuries

Did I tell you that I was in touch with Nana [Mahomo] in London? He is proving himself a good friend of yours, and has undertaken to obtain whatever other books may be needed by you.

All for now. I want to rush this letter to you.

God bless you

Benjamin Pogrund
to Veronica Sobukwe,
2 September 1966 (Ba4.59)

Dear Mrs Sobukwe,

I am glad to let you know that Mrs Stott has advised me that she has attended to your booking at the Hotel Tafelberg in Cape Town. She will also attend to the account, so we shan't have to worry about this.

I am advising her by telegram today that you will be arriving in Cape Town at 2 pm on Monday, September 5. I am certain that she will be at the station to meet you. Just in case there is some slip-up, her address is: 6, Bishopscourt Road, Newlands, Cape Town, telephone 77.3368.

To cover incidental expenses for your trip, I have pleasure in enclosing R20. Should this prove to be insufficient, will you perhaps ask Mrs Stott to lend you whatever you need, and to let me know the amount so that I can refund it to her?

I know how much this trip will mean both to you and to Bob, and I am glad to have been able to help in bringing it about. Naturally, my warmest affections to Bob. I hope he is well, and that his spirit and courage continue at the same high level. I only wish that I could also go and see him — or even better, that we could see him off the Island.

Best wishes for a happy visit.

Sincerely,
BENJAMIN POGRUND

Robert Sobukwe
to Benjamin Pogrund,
14 September 1966 (Ba4.60)

Dear Benjie,

Thank you for your letters of the 20th and 28th of July. I thought I should wait till after my wife's visit before replying to them.

I just could not start thanking you, Benjie, for all you have done. My wife has told me of your unfailing solicitude and your palpable love and concern for me. She has told me of how you came in, on her birthday, happily staggering under a load of parcels. I do not wish to embarrass you. I know you enjoy doing all you can for me and mine, but I can assure you it is much more than I would have expected even from one who had shared the same womb with me. Thanks a lot. I'll get the opportunity to thank you most appropriately one day.

Incidentally, your message accompanying the gifts was, as to be expected, most appropriate. My wife was thrilled and arrived here still walking on air.

We had a very lovely time together and she laughed just a little more often and more loudly than she usually does. She was quite happy at the hotel too. She is very reticent, of course, perhaps typically African. But she is thawing, Benjie, she is thawing.

I am, of course, typically un-African (But oh' well it not in Gath!). I grew up in an environment where African women (my "African" as you know includes so-called "coloureds"), young and old, felt quite at liberty to pick up any child they met in the street, dangle it in the air, plant a resounding kiss on its lips and let it go its way. I have never thought, consequently, that strength of character and dignity cannot be found apart from a grim, unsmiling visage.

The six books you listed in your letter of the 28th all reached me safely. Thanks. And thank you for news about Nana [Mahomo]. As I have said to you before, no friend of mine has ever proved and can ever prove untrue to me. That is my blessing!

Thank you for the R15.00 (Fifteen Rands) and the generous offer re Stuttafords. I have not taken the matter up with the Prison authorities yet but they will have no objection, I am certain. You can go ahead then with the arrangements.

Thank you also for the stamps and the fruit parcels which continue to arrive, neatly and securely packed.

I am glad to learn you are taking riding lessons. I envy you them. I never went beyond riding a donkey bare-back. Your judo experiences I find very amusing indeed, perhaps because they tally so with mine. It got so that I became worried if there were no part of my body aching!

Glad to learn an operation wasn't necessary. You had a narrow escape though.

Yes, Jenny's report is very encouraging. And like you, I am very glad that she has come through the experience so well.

In your letter you let fall, most casually, the precious news that your girl-friend had given my wife a parcel of toilet soap. And here I had been, deceiving myself that you were living in monastic innocence! But my wife whispered the name to me and I was excited as a schoolboy. I know nothing about the lady in question except that I love her even "*in absentia*". Congrats!!

With regard to my remarks about the social novel, I believe I expressed myself badly. The point is, Benjie, when we talk of European experiences, we talk in terms of class. Except for the great national struggles of the mid-19th century, the dichotomy in Europe has been a class one. But in Africa, particularly, though I believe this goes for Asia, too, to a large extent, class interests are either non-existent or irrelevant or muted. The oppression and the struggles are *group* oppression and *group* struggles. In Europe, when a member of the middle class wrote about the lower classes he was writing about a *different* people. In this country the dichotomy is a colour one. Class distinctions within the group are muted and perhaps even discouraged and emphasis is placed on the solidarity and unity of the *group*.

Do you think that "Exodus" and "My Glorious Brothers" could have been written by Jews in Hitler's Germany? But your needling is just about getting under my skin and you may irritate me just enough to make me accept your challenge and write this novel if only to see whether and how far I can be truly honest as a writer.

Oh, by the way, I am sorry you lost the case against Yutar.[77] I should have enjoyed squandering his millions! Will write again soon. Love to the ladies!! i.e. M. and J.![78]

Yours affectionately,
Bob

77 Pogrund sued the Deputy Attorney-General of the Transvaal, Dr Percy Yutar, for R10,000 in a defamation action arising from remarks Yutar had made at the trial of the prison warder G. van Schalkwyk, but the action was dismissed with costs in June.

78 Margie and Jennifer.

Robert Sobukwe
to Nell Marquard,
14 September 1966 (Bd1.25)

Dear Mrs Marquard,

It is almost hard to believe that I have had your letter of the 20th July for more than a month. When your letter arrived I had heard that my wife would be visiting me for a couple of days and I thought I should delay my reply until I had had the visit.

Well, I have had the visit. My wife came to see me from the 6th to the 9th. She told me she had gone to see you on Monday, 5th, but had found that you had visitors. It does serve her right, though, I feel, because she surely could have written to you in time, to tell you she was visiting Cape Town. Had it not been for Benjie I should not have known either that she was coming that week to see me.

However, I am sorry she did not see you because she wanted to thank you for your letter and your gift. In her letter to me she had written to say she was glad that about your sincere friendship she had never had any doubts.

Thank you for the news in your letter, particularly about Graaff-Reinet. I am sorry you did not meet my brother. He would have been very happy to make your acquaintance. He is absolutely harmless. The Special Branch can vouch for that. The farthest he can go is the Progressive Party and he would feel extremely conspicuous in that company. He belongs heart and soul to the "establishment". If he were in Britain he would vote Conservative consistently!

In your letter you say "much has happened since last we wrote".[79] And of course, much more has happened since. Events have come fast and furious and oh with what unpredictability! I am afraid I cannot detect a clear pattern or trend yet, particularly on the international plane. Some terrible explosion appears imminent in China – if press reports are to be believed – and one wonders what effect it will have on Asia and the world.

Through some misunderstanding my wife did not renew my subscriptions to the "Sunday Times" so that from March to the end of August I did not

79 Sobukwe is referring obliquely to the assassination of Prime Minister Hendrik Verwoerd in Parliament on 6 September.

receive my copy. And when I looked this week the causes of the Xhosa Wars had disappeared. Oh yes I enjoyed the instalments I read.

My birthday occurs on the 5th December, on the same day as that of Mr C.R. Swart, the State President! I am rather upset to learn that he will be retiring soon because I have always felt flattered to think that the SABC[80] and numerous other institutions and persons who probably loathe me were nonetheless celebrating *my* birthday.

I call my clan "Baboons" because that is the totem of my clan. As you know, the Sotho adopt animals as totems of their various clans. There are thus crocodiles, baboons, monkeys, lions etc. You'll, therefore, realize that those who claim to know me do not in fact know me because, if I am not mistaken, I have been described as a Xhosa: I am not, as you can see.

Thank you for the interesting stories about the Bushmen. They are called *"abathwa"* in Xhosa and Zulu and a phonological variant in Sotho. One common story about them is that whenever they met a Xhosa hunter they would pose the question "when did you see me?" and since they were very touchy about their size one had to be careful to have seen them a long distance away. Unfortunately one did not always know from what direction they had come and it was quite a risky job answering the question. The Xhosa being experienced liars lied their way out. One of them is said to have replied: "I saw you when you were still over there on that mountain over the---re!" He pointed to a mountain in the South only to be told by the *um-thwa* that in fact he had approached from the North. "Then it was your shadow I saw" was the reply.

Thank you for the story about the bishops. It is the type of thing one would expect from the Anglican bishops. The word that comes to my mind when I think about them is "obstreperous".

I hope Mr Marquard has recovered completely and that you are enjoying the Spring. I'll write again to report on my garden.

With best wishes to you both.
I am,
Yours very sincerely,
RM Sobukwe

---

80 South African Broadcasting Corporation.

Robert Sobukwe
to Nell Marquard,
5 October 1966 (Bd1.26)

Dear Mrs Marquard,

Thank you very much for the books. I read the poems and the Life of Azikiwe[81] there and then and enjoyed both immensely.

There were a number of poems, of course, that I just couldn't understand. Modern poetry baffles me; and that grieves me because I have always enjoyed poetry – Pope, Shelley, Tennyson, Keats, Wordsworth, Spenser – the whole lot. I have enjoyed Walter de la Mare and some of [T.S.] Eliot and [C.S.] Lewis. I have been able to enjoy Roy Campbell too. But Guy Butler and Dorothy Spears[82] and this whole crowd of poets who have no sentences, no (to me) observable continuity of imagery; no punctuation marks, no (to me) discernible theme, no meaning even – I find quite baffling. I certainly don't enjoy their poetry. If they say it's because I am a fool, I'll accept that. I admit that I haven't kept up with the times.

I was particularly interested in Azikiwe's biography. I have read "*Without Bitterness*"[83] which sets out the "Zikist philosophy" – lovely language and enthusiastic rather emotional nationalism. I used to read the "West African Pilot" at Fort Hare and enjoyed Zik's "Inside Stuff".

His was the only party which was truly national; and he has been severely criticized by George Padmore[84] and the Ghanaian Africanists for his

81 *A Life of Azikiwe*, written by K.A.B. Jones-Quartey, was published in 1965 by Penguin Books. Nnamdi Azikiwe (1904–96) was the first president of Nigeria and was considered "the father of Nigerian nationalism". As a young man he edited a daily newspaper in Accra, Ghana, in which he wrote a column "Inside Stuff by Zik", which promoted black pride and African nationalism. After returning to Nigeria, he started the newspaper the *West African Pilot*. An inspirational figure for Pan Africanists, Azikiwe was a prolific author and poet who took to politics after a successful journalism career.

82 Guy Butler was Professor of English at Rhodes University and a poet. Dorothy Spears, who was born in Iowa but lived most of her life at the Cape, was also a poet.

83 *Without Bitterness: Western Nations in Postwar Africa*, by Akweke Orizu, was published in 1944.

84 George Padmore (1903–59) was a leading Pan Africanist, author and journalist who left his native Trinidad to study medicine in the US, where he joined the Communist Party. Padmore moved to the Soviet Union, and was an active Communist Party member, but

reactionary return to the "Witch of Endor" – the tribal crutch.[85] And events would seem to justify their criticism.

Did you see [Malcolm] Muggeridge's article on H.G. [Wells] in the Sunday Times? Typically iconoclastic! And what do you think of the Churchill series in the Argus? It's so pathetic isn't it? One is glad that he got from his wife the love he was denied by his parents. And to think that but for the Second World War he would have been written off as his father was before him.

Once more my plants have been a disappointment. There were such a variety of insects that attacked the cabbage and the flowers and they were so stubborn that, having exhausted the insect killer pesticide, I gave in. The beetroot and the carrots flowered but would form no crop. Furthermore, whatever cabbage threatened to grow was cropped by rabbits which wander rather freely around my yard.

Then suddenly, after the past few rains the cabbage seemed to make up for lost time, came out in majestic splendour, throwing out voluminous and succulent leaves and even attempted to form heads. But it was too late.

It's been a pleasure, though, just to see them grow. And the petunias and the stocks are beginning to flower, too. It is they that have made me feel that the trouble and the heartache have been worthwhile!

We do not have an abundance of fresh water here so that a summer crop is out of the question.

I was sorry to read about the death of C. Justice Centlivres.[86] Makes you feel the ancient landmarks have been removed. You know, I have always found Lord Bedivere's[87] cry singularly forlorn: –

"And I the last go forth companionless
"Among new men, strange faces, other minds"[88]

---

broke with the Party in 1935, when it became clear that his support of African liberation was in direction opposition to Soviet foreign policy of the day.

85 The Witch of Endor appears in the Old Testament, where she summons the spirit of Samuel from the dead.

86 The liberal-minded Albert van der Sandt Centlivres (1887–1966) was Chief Justice of South Africa from 1950 to 1957 and served as Chancellor of the University of Cape Town between 1950 and the year of his death, 1966.

87 The fictional knight of the Round Table of King Arthur who returns the sword Excalibur to the Lady of the Lake.

88 From Alfred Tennyson's poem "The Passing of Arthur".

I hope the quotation is correct. You experience a loneliness of the soul, a kind of nostalgia for a life you do not know, you cannot describe but which you feel you have known before.

My wife has not written yet. She probably won't write at all until just a few weeks before she comes down in January. One wonders why their parents bother to educate these native girls.

I do hope Mr Marquard has recovered.

With best wishes.
Yours sincerely,
RM Sobukwe

Veronica Sobukwe
to Benjamin Pogrund,
11 October 1966 (Ba4.67)

Dear Mr Pogrund,

Thank you for your letter which I received on the 6th October.

I am really sorry for having delayed in telling you about my trip to Cape Town.

We had a wonderful time with Bob. I am very much relieved for having been able to see him after his operation. Once again, I thank you so much for your kindness.

I would also be very grateful if we could meet as there are some matters worrying me concerning Bob.

I am on night duty. Will Thursday morning be convenient to you [illegible] to contact you by phone?

Good-bye.

Sincerely,
Veronica Sobukwe

Robert Sobukwe
to Veronica Sobukwe,
13 October 1966 (Bc39)

Hullo Darling!

As I did not read of any train accidents during the week you left for Joh'burg I am constrained to believe that you reached home safely. It is on the basis of that assumption that I write this letter.

The Sixteen Rands you sent from Cape Town and the note that accompanied them reached me on the 26th September. I thank you for both.

I heard over the radio that Den's mother had died. That was about three weeks ago and the announcement had been entered by Den.[89] I wasn't too sure whether I had heard correctly. Will you please find out whether it is so or not.

With the schools about to close you must be frantic with worry, I know, as you attempt to find accommodation for the twins. Best of luck.

Mili wrote to me towards the end of last month and already gave the name of their country as *Lesotho*.[90] I replied immediately and asked her to go steady with the propaganda – the country would be known as "Lesotho" from the 4th October! Incidentally, I wrote to her in English this time. She wanted to know whether she should write in English or not when she answered Benjie's letter. I advised her to write in Sotho until we had straightened out her spelling a little.

Well cheerio, darling. Until I hear whether you are still in the land of the living or not.

Your loving husband,
Mangi

89 Dennis Siwisa.

90 Basutoland acquired independence from Britain on 4 October 1966 and became known as Lesotho.

Robert Sobukwe
to Veronica Sobukwe,
14 October 1966 (Bc40)

Hullo Darling!

Your letter, which I received yesterday after I had already dispatched one to you, was one of the loveliest I have ever received from you. It was simple, sincere and affectionate. If I had received it in September, when I was looking forward with trembling excitement to receiving a letter from you, I would have been drunk with joy. But as it arrived five weeks after your departure, the effect was less drastic. I was just happy.

The moral then is that if you have the wherewithal to make somebody happy – whether it be news, a message or a gift – don't keep on putting it off. Like medicine [illegible]. I think that's one of the reasons why we so often fail to thank God for answering our prayers. By the time He answers we have already forgotten that we had ever asked for the thing he gives us. The devil, on the other hand is prompt. It guarantees immediate delivery!

Well, Little Girl, after this sermon, which I just *HAD* to get off my chest or I would burst, let me again say thank you for your letter.

I am glad to hear you arrived safely home. Life has become very risky these days. "In the midst of life we are in death", says one of those great men of the Bible.[91] That is why, incidentally, I am happy to hear that Fabian escaped injury in his encounter with the hold-up gentlemen.

I am sorry to hear about Vusi's illness. Please let me know how he fares.

Mili mentioned the twins' birthday to me, too, but made a mistake about their age. She said they would be nine. She has a wonderful heart, that child, and would make a first-class kindergarten teacher.

I am always uneasy about these night-duty shifts. When I saw you in the Jabavu clinic, sitting alone in a vast, cold hall, with any and every ragamuffin having free access to you, I shuddered inwardly. I have never forgotten that night. And yet you've never complained. You are a rare jewel indeed.

91 "In the midst of life we are in death" is to be found in the Book of Common Prayer, in the section on Burial of the Dead.

But then in midwifery you won't be receiving calls. You'll be going around in your jeep bringing young Africa into the world: a noble job though rather messy, if you ask me.

I wrote to Benjie soon after your departure, thanking him for everything. He hasn't answered yet. But I realize that he has been very busy attending meetings and celebrations, fighting Yutar in court, collecting books for me and entertaining his lady and his daughter. It is a busy life indeed – no wonder he suffers from ulcers.

And how are you getting on my lady? I had hoped that in your letter you would say you enjoyed the visit because my company is thrilling and what not. Instead you say I am a tonic for your nerves. What an unromantic thing to say about your husband, woman! Am I nothing more than a sedative?

You laughed much more on this visit than I have heard you laugh for a long time. And it was a sweet sound, the kind of laughter that comes from deep down in the stomach.

How is the migraine? Remember, you can beat it without tablets. I suppose it will be worse now that you have to arrange for the twins' accommodation. I wish you best of luck.

Well, darling, so much for now.

Keep that head high!

Your loving husband,
Mangi

Robert Sobukwe
to Benjamin Pogrund,
2 November 1966 (Ba4.71)

Dear Benjie,

Thank you for the two volumes of Lipson's *Economic History of England*, Sabine's *Political Theory* and the seven superb records.

I received all these on the 17th October but thought I would wait until I had received the letter which I believed had accompanied them. Incidentally, on the same day, I received a book on African myths and legends, from Lauretta and A.B. Ngcobo who are now in Lusaka. Lauretta teaches in a Secondary School there and tells me she earns £120 a month. She complains, however, that the cost of living is high, which might mean a lot or nothing.

Miliswa wrote to ask whether she should write to you in English or in Sotho. Her spelling is, unfortunately, very poor and I accordingly advised her to write in Sotho which she writes beautifully.

In one of the letters which you did not receive last year, I had suggested that you buy yourself a house in one of the posh suburbs – complete with warm-water swimming pools and what have you – where I could "luxuriate" over week-ends. I still think you should try to get your own house to enable Jenny to run freely and kick and laugh without the constant fear of upsetting some fastidious, grumpy fellow-tenant.

I have been wondering whether you attended the independence celebrations of Botswana[92] and Lesotho and what you thought of the whole play. What message did you get from the Grecian chorus? "And may the gods spare us or forever cast us down" (Oedipus).

Prof Wellington has made detailed studies of the drainage systems of the Zambezi and has made valuable suggestions for the development of the Okavango area. I read the articles a while ago and not only enjoyed them but found the project so practicable and the homework so well-done that I felt I could assume personal responsibility for it. There is so much to be done and so many willing hands and brains to do it. All that is lacking I think is the *correct appeal* – bold, daring and imaginative; an invitation to meaningful occupation, to meaningful sacrifice!

92 Bechuanaland became independent on 30 September 1966 as Botswana.

I have received all three issues of the "Economica", Benjie, thank you. Some articles, while interesting, contain so much maths, that they leave huge gaps in my understanding. When I have finished this course I'll have to settle down and learn the ABC of maths, physics and chemistry. Without these one's education is not complete these days.

Mrs Marquard has sent me a book on the Life of Azikiwe written by a Ghanian University lecturer. I used to read his "West African Pilot"[93] at Fort Hare and I admired him immensely. At that time he could have united Nigeria solidly behind him and his NCAC party.[94] But to do that he had to sever his tribal umbilical cord. He wasn't big enough to do that. Padmore never forgave him for returning to the tribal fire. "There is a tide…".[95]

I should like your opinion on three books about which I have read "raving" reviews of late. From all reports they are literary gems. One, I think, is titled *Selma*[96] and deals most aesthetically with the Civil Rights movement in the U.S.A. The other is written by a number of Europeans in South Africa, among them Gertrude Millin and Stuart Cloete. It is titled *We are also People* or something like that.[97] I am told it is very warm and compassionate. A third is by South Africa's brilliant golfer, Gary Player.[98] I haven't seen the title anywhere but I am told it is very original and makes some profound sociological observations.

Well Benjie, cheerio for now. My warmest greetings and love to the ladies.

Yours sincerely,
Bob

---

93 *West African Pilot* was a Nigerian newspaper launched by the future President Nnamdi Azikiwe in 1937, dedicated to the cause of independence from British colonial rule.

94 National Council of Nigeria and the Cameroons, a Nigerian political party which existed from 1944 to 1966.

95 In *I Speak of Freedom: A Statement of African Ideology* (1961), Kwame Nkrumah asserted: "There is a tide in the affairs of every people when the moment strikes for political action."

96 *Selma, 1965*, by Charles Fager, published the previous year, and still an important reference text fifty years after first appearing.

97 *White Africans Are Also People* was the title of a book by Sarah Gertrude Millin, published in 1966.

98 Gary Player, *Grand Slam Golf* (1966).

Robert Sobukwe
to Nell Marquard,
23 November 1966 (Bd1.27)

Dear Mrs Marquard,

Thank you for your letter dated 16th October, the books sent under separate cover and the very handsome "celebration vote".

I enjoyed your letter immensely, particularly what you term a "travelogue". The Fort Beaufort-Alice complex is like home to me. I spent seven years at Healdtown (shopping at Fort Beaufort) and three years at Fort Hare (shopping at Alice). As students at Healdtown we used to go out on "hunting expeditions" in the Hogsback and as Fort Hare students we visited the neighbouring villages (up to Middledrift) in search of linguistic and anthropological material. I had the pleasure, therefore, of following you all the way from East London to Grahamstown.

Thank you for news about your garden. It strikes me as a very lively and lovely little spot with all the fusses and airs of someone who knows she is loved.

As I said in my previous letter, mine has been a bit of a disappointment and because of the drought I have had to watch the flowers wither and die.

I have really enjoyed [H.G.] Wells's "The History of Mr Polly". I had heard a great deal about it but hadn't read it. The same with "Good-bye Mr Chips"[99] which I have just read, and enjoyed. The ignorance that lurks under these know-all exteriors is truly astounding!

And then, of course, there is "Blame it on Van Riebeeck".[100] Hilarious! Riotous! I laughed as I have not laughed since George Formby's[101] days.

If all goes well my wife and children should be here again early in January. The children will be back from school round about the 10th December but my wife's leave starts only in January.

---

99 James Hilton, *Goodbye, Mr Chips* (1934).

100 *Blame it on Van Riebeeck* is the title of a short book published by Nell Marquard's husband, Leo, and Joel Mervis, the editor of the *Sunday Times*, in 1952. The authors – a historian and a humourist respectively – offered a farcical perspective on South African history.

101 An English actor (1904–61), singer and comedian famous for his comical songs typically performed on a ukulele.

My mother, too, who had hinted that she might visit me this year has written to say she will do so early next year – around April – accompanied by my sister-in-law who is a nursing sister at the Livingstone hospital in Port Elizabeth. It's her favourite daughter-in-law she'll be travelling with (incidentally she is "Fingo"), so I have no anxieties on that score. They'll spend about three weeks in Cape Town. It is just possible that my mother may stay longer. But I'll send you the low-down when the time comes.

As I may not write to you again before Christmas, please let me wish you and yours a blessed and joyful Christmas and New Year.

Yours very sincerely,
RM Sobukwe

P.S. I wish to observe the proprieties. The name obviously has very revolutionary associations and might be embarrassing. But if you so wish, I could address you as Mrs N.J. Marquard von Tecklenburg![102] Just a suggestion. RMS

---

102 The Marquard family came originally from the county of Tecklenburg in Germany.

Robert Sobukwe
to Benjamin Pogrund,
23 November 1966 (Ba4.77)

My dear Benjie,

Three more books arrived last week and I am writing to acquaint you of the fact. They are:

[L.C.A.] Knowles: *Industrial and Commercial Revolutions*
[J.W.] Allen: *Political Thought in the 16th Century*
[Pauline] Gregg: *A Social and Economic History of Britain*

Pace University, in New York, also sent me a couple of interesting books:-

Yes & No (African Folktales) by Alta Jablow
The Benin Kingdom (Anthropological work on Nigeria) [by R.E. Bradbury]
The Heart of the Hunter (novel) by Laurens van der Post
The Prehistory of Africa by H. Alimen
Elements of General Linguistics by [André] Martinet.

I told you, didn't I, that Miliswa had written to ask whether she should write to you in Sotho or English. I advised Sotho. But I wrote to her in English and hope she understood what her father said.

My mother may be visiting me next year. She writes to say that my sister-in-law will have three weeks' leave in April next year (she's a nursing sister at Port Elizabeth's Livingstone Hospital, a real "bright spark") and has suggested that they visit me together. Here's hoping!

I notice that a book by a certain Mr Jacobs of Johannesburg has been banned.[103] You know a report appeared in Life magazine last year describing the Afro-American riots in Harlem. A number of businessmen in Harlem put up notices to the effect that they were one with the rioters. One which read "We shall overcome!" I remember thinking, as I read the article, that these businessmen had probably never bothered about anything except making profits. Tomorrow they would be on the side of the police. I don't think

103 Anthony Jacobs, *White Man Think Again* (1965). Hence "Jacobian" later in the paragraph.

climbers on to bandwagons are contemptible: they are pathetic. I have never despised anybody who cringes. I have felt sorry for them. I never like to see anybody humiliated – not even by himself! And the "summer soldiers and sunshine patriots"[104] of the Jacobean ilk deserve pity not contempt.

If the papers are to be believed, Robert Kennedy will be in a position to challenge L.B.J. in 1968.[105] I'll be sorry if he does. I like Johnson. I don't think he is devious. I don't think he is very complex either. He isn't an intellectual, but then there are very few in the political field. His touch is very deft in domestic matters and I believe that if, in Vietnam, he had followed his own bent, if he had been true to himself, he would have chosen to negotiate right from the start. He has one outstanding virtue for which I like him. He *feels*. Some have said he is sentimental. And that is the man for me any day: a man who can be moved: a man who can feel anger, who can feel deep compassion. But above all a man who can *weep* in the presence of great sorrow and suffering.

The tragedy of our day is the inability of politicians to read the signs of the times. In the 20th Century we are faced with a situation where "negotiating from strength" is an outmoded maxim – if it were ever valid! It has always been true, I think, and it is more so today, that the person who can afford to lose face is the strong person – provided he does so of his own free will. "Don't crowd me" is a very vivid English expression and it is more apt on the lips of the weak.

After Nehru's death I wrote to a friend of mine that Shastri[106] could achieve much more than Nehru because the latter's reputed brilliance was a handicap. If he had achieved a settlement of the Kashmir problem the Pakistanis would be looking for a catch all the time. It is a pleasure to submit to persuasion. But somehow it seems to be humiliating to be reduced to silence by Socratic logic.

---

104 The phrase comes from Thomas Paine, who, in *The Crisis*, speaks of the American Revolution, saying: "The summer soldier and the sunshine patriot will, in this crisis, shrink from the service of their country; but he that stands it now, deserves the love and thanks of man and woman."

105 A reference to the 1968 US presidential elections. Lyndon Johnson decided not to stand again and withdrew from the race. Robert Kennedy was assassinated during his election campaign in that year.

106 Lal Bahadur Shastri was the second Prime Minister of India, from 1964 to 1966, and led the country during the Indo-Pakistan war of 1965.

Of course, Kennedy stands a better chance to start negotiations with China and North Vietnam. He has not committed himself as Johnson has done. He would be able to withdraw American troops from Vietnam and win American support for the action. But what Americans term the "domino theory" would remain valid. We shouldn't kid ourselves. Cambodia, Thailand and the rest of the archipelago would face Communist bids for power. The most powerful state in Asia is China and she is Communist. Co-existence will be on her terms, just as co-existence in Europe will be on Russia's terms and in America on the terms of the U.S.A.

Oh I could write pages on this, Benjie. But it wouldn't solve a thing. One thing, however, can be said about the U.S.A. and it is that she is not in Vietnam for any imperialist purpose. On that both friend and foe are agreed.

How is it with Jennie? There's a programme on Springbok Radio – an ad really – where a woman complains that nothing has gone right that morning and while she is complaining she hears the piano playing. "And now listen to that!" she says. "Jennie: stop that noise. My nerves just won't stand it!" she screams. And I always picture Jenny sliding off her stool with a kindly smile on her face.

Well, Benjie, look after yourself and look after the ladies.

With best wishes.
Yours sincerely,
Bob

P.S. Wishing you and yours a blessed New Year. Bob.

Benjamin Pogrund
to Robert Sobukwe,
1 December 1966 (Ba4.79)

My dear Bob,

Thank you for your letter of November 2 which reached me last week. Looking at your letter I can hardly credit that all these days have passed since it arrived. I have been on leave for the past three weeks, working on my thesis,[107] and I have become very much the academic, oblivious to the passing of time and to events around me. Despite my delayed reply to your letter I have, however, been active on your account in other spheres as I shall outline later, so I hope you will forgive me.

Earlier today I posted off to you a carton of books for your leisure moments. They are:

[Pamela] Frankau: The devil we know
[David] Attenborough: Zoo quest for a dragon
[Elizabeth Jane] Howard: The long view
[R.B.] Robertson: Of whales and men
[David] Walker: Harry Black
Ellery Queen's 1963 anthology
[John] Harris: The sleeping mountain
[Hammond] Innes: The land God gave to Cain
[Guy de] Maupassant: Harriet and other stories
[Eric] Linklater: Juan in America
[Jean-Baptiste] Molière: The Miser and other plays
Three Restoration Comedies
Sophocles: The Theban plays
Two Satyr plays
[Compton] Mackenzie: The rival monster
The Thurber carnival
Ibsen: Three plays
[William] Faulkner: The unvanquished

107 Preparatory work for a PhD on the history of Communism in South Africa, undertaken at Wits University.

[William] Faulkner: The sound and the fury
Balzac: Eugénie Grandet
Short stories from America
[Thorne] Smith: The night life of the gods
[Samuel] Butler: The way of all flesh
[Ian] Fleming: Goldfinger
[Len] Deighton: Funeral in Berlin
Great English short stories
[John] Braine: Room at the top
[Hammond] Innes: Campbell's kingdom
[G.B.] Shaw: Major Barbara
[Nicholas] Monsarrat: Three corvettes
[C.S.] Forester: The captain from Connecticut
Argosy short story magazine: three issues

The books come to you with best wishes from Jill, Ernie and myself. They are a pretty wide cross-section of reading and we hope will meet any mood in which you happen to be. Some of them are unlikely to be to your taste but I thought I would rather err on the side of sending books which you might not wish to read than possibly deprive you in any way. I don't know whether you have ready any of Ian Fleming's James Bond books (Goldfinger is in the batch). Like the late President Kennedy, I am an avid Bond fan, and if you turn out to be the same, please let me know and I shall send other books on Bond. Also, in case you have not previously read Thurber, there is a great treat in store for you. But I must tell you that, from my own experience, Thurber has to be read at least ten to twelve times before one properly begins to savour his delicious humour. My favourite stories are "The night the bed fell" and "The day the dam broke". For best results, they should be read aloud! Deighton's "Funeral in Berlin" represents the current popularity of high-class thriller stories. Again, if it's to your taste, I'll be happy to send down some more.

Also sent to you recently, after arriving from London, were further study books:

P. Gregg: A social and economic history of Britain
L.A.C. Knowles: Industrial and commercial revolutions in Great Britain
J.W. Allen: A history of political thought in the 16th cent.

Will you let me know when all these books reach you so that I can check that there are no postal delays? I should be sending you some more study books soon – I am awaiting the arrival of some from the U.K.

Incidentally, I have been meaning to ask you for some while: do you have access to any library down there, either for study or reading books?

With the carton of books posted today was included a bottle of ink. In case it has reached you before this letter I hope it did not cause you to fear that I had gone off my head. It is, in fact, part of my personal Xmas gift to you – a Sheaffer fountain pen. I vouch for the pen: I was given one as a present some months ago and have been delighted with it after years of writing with a ball-point. I chose a medium nib for you as it seems best to suit your handwriting. I shall be sending the pen off shortly, as your name is being engraved on it at the moment. I decided to get it away early to ensure that it reaches you by Xmas. And, of course, it comes to you with my heartfelt good wishes and affectionate greetings. You know that during the Passover festival Jews wish each other the blessing: "Next year in Jerusalem", and Passover is indeed a festival of freedom, commemorating the escape from Egypt. For you my wish is simply: "Next year at home".

I have also renewed your "Cape Argus" subscription and I hope there has not been any delay in it reaching you. During the next few days I shall be seeing your wife to make arrangements for her visit to you next month, so once more there is great joy for you to look forward to.

I haven't yet heard from Miliswa but I am looking forward to getting a letter from her, in whatever language she prefers to use!

About your remarks about my getting a house-cum-swimming-pool: I am afraid you are getting me mixed up with other, moneyed friends of yours. I doubt that I shall ever be able to aspire to such delights. I was simply born to be poor. I am constantly oppressed by a feeling that I am letting down the traditions of my people because I am such a lousy businessman. It's not that I don't want money, but I just don't have the slightest idea of how to go about getting it! Despite my lack of a swimming-pool, both now and in the future, I hope we can still be friends.

Actually, now that it is summer-time, I do have problems with Jenny over a hot weekend. She's an active, energetic little thing so I have to try and find a pool to take her to so that she can keep amused. If the weather is unpleasant, and we retire to my flat, I ply her with paints and books and other occupational therapy – and within the half hour I usually retire to a couch feeling limp and exhausted in trying to keep up with her. She continues, by the way, to be a glorious little girl, full of charm and warmth. She will be starting school next year. A new age restriction has just been introduced here, whereby children must be five at least six months before December 31 if they are to be allowed to start school. Jenny misses this deadline by eight days. Representations on her behalf are at present with the Education Department, because she is undoubtedly ready for school and has a tremendous desire to learn. In fact, I think the suddenness with which this departmental ruling has been sprung on parents has been rather unfair to children, but then, what can one do? If the department won't accept her, she will start at a private school as these are unaffected by the new ruling.

To answer your query about attending the various independence celebrations: unhappily, I am passportless, but then I love my country so I don't really mind not being able to visit other strange, foreign lands.

About the three books you mentioned: I had not intended reading them. But your comments have thrown new light on them, and one of these days – perhaps in twenty years' time – I must rush out and buy them.

At the start of this letter I referred to being on leave. I have taken a month's leave to concentrate on my thesis, as I had been neglecting it – which is probably the under-statement of the year. But now I have been going flat out on it and it is moving quite well, although I am constantly dismayed by the amount of work still to be done. There are hundreds of tiny points which have to be meticulously checked and followed up, and I find myself spending hour after hour trying to track down something which I know in advance will probably only mean a single sentence in the completed book. When my leave is over I shall continue giving it every possible moment of my time, and I think that the momentum I am gaining now will carry me through to put in the required work after a day at the office. All being well, I hope to have the first few chapters in draft form by sometime in February.

I tend to be like a yo-yo about my feelings about the quality of the thesis: at times I feel that I am going to be able to turn out something of quality and significance. Most other times, however, I am filled with deep depression about my lack of ability to do this job as it should be done. Whatever happens, it won't suffer from any lack of trying on my part.

Much to my regret, Margie[108] leaves for Cape Town on Tuesday. I shall be travelling down on December 23, remaining there until January 15. I shall be staying with my parents in Sea Point so I shall be looking across at you ... Jenny will also be down there then and will be staying with me for a few days – which both of us are already greatly looking forward to.

All for now, my friend. I hope you are keeping well, and that your spirit remains undaunted. Margie sends you her best wishes, and so do Jill and Ernie.

God bless you,

108 Margaret Marshall, who moved to Cape Town from Johannesburg as president of the National Union of South African Students. She later emigrated to Boston, studied law and education at Harvard and Yale, and in due course served as Chief Justice of Massachusetts.

Benjamin Pogrund
to Robert S. Bilheimer,
19 December 1966 (Ba4.82)

Dear Bob,

Mr Gandar was recently in the US, as you might know. Before he left I gave him your address and urged him to make a point of seeing you. I saw that your office address was the same as that of the Society for Human Rights (correct name?), the organisation which had invited him over to receive one of their awards.[109] When Mr Gandar returned, he told me that he had told the secretary of the society that he was anxious to see you and he understood you were in the same building. The secretary immediately undertook to contact you. When Mr Gandar got there he was given a message that you were busy and would try to see him, but there was no further contact from you. Mr Gandar was disappointed at not having been able to see you. I did not know whether I should write to you about this, but I consulted Fred van Wyk who urged me to write to you as he was sure that there had been a misunderstanding somewhere down the line.

I recently wrote to the Taylors, and if you should ever see them I would be most grateful if you could ask whether my bulky letter reached them safely.

Can I again importune you on behalf of our friend? Some massive expenses are looming up during the next few months, and I hesitate to write again to Charlotte. They have been tremendously generous, as you know, and I feel ashamed of having to write continually to them. For that matter, I feel the same about writing to *you*, and only do so because I hope that you can pass on this plea to some other person of good will. The wife[110] has to go to Cape Town next month for a three week visit, and the four children will be with her. I have raised the cash for the train tickets locally, and will have to add the expenses of bedding, meals, etc en route. I have found someone to cover the cost of her hotel, but am short for the children. Then early in the New Year there is the school fees for the children, books and clothing. I feel

109 In 1966 Laurence Gandar, editor of the *Rand Daily Mail*, received the "Award for Excellence" in the field of communications from the US Society for the Family of Man. He had his passport returned to him to enable him to attend the ceremony in person.

110 Veronica.

ashamed at having to write to ask for help because this is something which we should be able to do in this country. Unfortunately, there is a limited number of people here to whom one can turn and I have milked them as hard as possible already! I have organised Xmas gifts for everyone locally so this is one small expense which has been saved. Please forgive me for again turning to you with this plea.

All quiet here. I am leaving for Cape Town on December 28 on holiday, and will be there until January 15.

In case you wish to reach me in that period, my address will be: 4 Firmount Road, Sea Point, Cape Town.

I trust that you are keeping well, and enjoying your new work. My very good wishes to you and your family for Xmas and the New Year.

Sincerely,
BENJAMIN POGRUND

Benjamin Pogrund
to Robert Sobukwe,
20 December 1966 (Ba4.84)

My dear Bob,

I was in Cape Town briefly over the past weekend, and my thoughts were much with you. I drove to Sea Point on Saturday afternoon, and from De Waal Drive looked across at the Island, wondering how you were and what you were doing. I so much wished that I could see you again. With the New Year coming you have, however, a great deal of joy to look forward to with the arrival of your entire family in Cape Town. I know that it will be a happy trip for everyone.

With the aid of Ernie and Jill and a number of other friends, I shall be sending to your wife and children this week an assortment of gifts to brighten Xmas day. I thought you would like to know this.

Since last writing to you I have posted to you another batch of study books:

[A.J.P.] Taylor: The course of German history
[Bernard] Pares: A history of Russia
[G.M.] Trevelyan: English social history, Volumes 1, 2, 3, 4.

I have been advised that [Arthur James] Whyte: *Evolution of modern Italy*, is being sent to me shortly, but that [Roy] Pascal: *Growth of modern Germany* is out of print.

Will you please let me know whether there are any other study books which you need?

Also sent off last week, via Recordia of Johannesburg, was a batch of six records, which come to you from me, Jill and Ernie and other friends. As you will see, they are a selection of Beethoven, Bach, Mozart, and Haydn. These are all records which *I* like, so I have naturally assumed that they will be to your taste also. Will you let me know whether you want more in the same strain? I hope, by the way, that your record player is still in good shape and that it gives you reasonable reproduction of all this music.

I took down with me to Cape Town some other things for you, but I was there so briefly that I was unable to deliver them to the Island ferry boat. I shall be flying down again on December 28, remaining there until January 15, and will deliver the goods then. They are:

Books:

[Morton] Thompson: Not as a stranger
[Noël] Coward: Seven stories
[Marcia] Davenport: Of Lena Geyer
[Bruce] Marshall: The month of the falling leaves
Wilson: Jazz
[Lawrence P.] Dowd: Principles of world business
[Farida] Wiley: John Burroughs' America
[John] Brooks: The seven fat years
[Herman] Melville: Short novels
[Richard Henry] Dana: Two years before the mast
[Thomas] Bulfinch: The age of fable
[Perry] Bliss: Marketing and the behavioural sciences
[Camilla] Bittle: The boy in the pool
[Howard S.] Dye, [John R.] Moore and [J. Fred] Holly: Economics
Argosy short story magazine: 8 issues.

As always, a very mixed bag, some of which at least I hope will be to your taste. I have been sending down numbers of Argosy magazines without knowing whether you really like them. I find them ideal light reading, just the thing to use as a break inbetween doing some work. Let me know, will you, whether you also enjoy them and I'll put aside the copy I get each month to send on to you.

Also waiting in Cape Town at the moment for delivery to you next week are another three records: Samuel Barber, Symphony No 1, etc; Carl Sandburg: Cowboy songs and spirituals; Douglas Moore: The devil and Daniel Webster.

Before taking the records along, I listened briefly to the first two and I can't say that they appealed all that much to me. But I thought it was worth trying them out on you in case they struck some responsive chord within you!

I have just received Jenny's end-of-year report from her nursery school, and can proudly report that, during the last three months, she gained one and a quarter inches in height and is now a whopping 44 ins. In the same time, she put on 2 lb. in weight. And if you will forgive me again for being the proud father, the report says: "On the whole Jenny presents the picture of a bright outgoing child with good intellectual potential."

I am so eager to be with her, and will be having her stay with me for five full days from December 29. I get terribly resentful at having to ask for the opportunity to be with my own daughter and these brief periods we have together are deeply happy ones for both of us – which makes parting from her at the end of these times even more dreadful for me.

Your letter of November 23 reached me safely and I thank you for it. I haven't yet heard from Miliswa, so I suppose that her shyness has overcome her. When you see her next month, you can tell her that when she returns to school next year she will have a foam rubber mattress on which to sleep, and will be able to take this away with her when she finally leaves the school.

About your reference to the book by Jacobs of Johannesburg: I think you have his origins mixed up ... there are two ways in which to pronounce the name, you know. And why "Afro-American"? While I'm on the subject of labels, do you perhaps know the origin of the name "Azania"? I first saw it quite recently in some political stuff, as apparently some characters believe that this is what Africa should be called. They gave a rather confused description of the origin of the name, going back to pre-Roman times. I dismissed it as nonsense, and was surprised recently to come across a reference to a reputable scientific research society in East Africa – in Kenya, I think it was – which actually issues a publication called "Azania" which is devoted to studies on Africa.[111]

And while I am throwing questions at you, did you ever have a chance to read the Bonhoeffer book which I sent to you some time ago?[112] If so, I would be most interested to get your views on it.

I get the London "Sunday Times" every week and it often has top-class material in its supplement. For example, they have run extracts from Schlesinger's book on Kennedy,[113] Macmillan's book[114] and Charlie Chaplin's

---

111 *Azania: Archaeological Research in Africa* was the official journal of the British Institute in *Eastern Africa.*

112 Pogrund has Dietrich Bonhoeffer's *Letters and Papers from Prison* in mind here. Sobukwe received the book, but not Pogrund's letter of 7 December 1965 where he alludes to Bonhoeffer's relevance to the apartheid situation.

113 Arthur Schlesinger's highly regarded book, *A Thousand Days: John F. Kennedy in the White House,* was published in 1965.

114 Harold Macmillan, *The Winds of Change 1914–1939* (1966).

autobiography.[115] I'll send down batches of these supplements to you in the future, and will you let me know if they get through to you all right, and if so, if they interest you? They also contain excellent book reviews.

Do you remember that old friend of yours, the one with the thick beard who always wore a long overcoat?[116] I've just had a letter from him and the poor man is pretty destitute. One of his requests to me, which I think indicates how he is living, was for a 1967 calendar. I have organised some help for him.

All for now, my friend. I hope your celebration of Xmas will be fortifying your spirit, and I pray for your welfare in the New Year.

Affectionately,

115 Charlie Chaplin, *My Autobiography* (1964).

116 A coded reference to Josias Madzunya (1909–early 1970s), an ardent African nationalist, described by Pogrund (2015: 83) as "a familiar and striking figure … he had a large black beard and wore a long black overcoat throughout the year … He had a long record as an African Nationalist. He would also acquire a reputation in due course of backing away from campaigning at the last moment."

1967

View toward the mainland from just in front of Sobukwe's fenced-off area.

Secretary for Justice,
Pretoria,
to Veronica Sobukwe,
14 January 1967 (Ba5.3)

Greetings,

RE: PERMISSION TO VISIT YOUR HUSBAND MANGALISO ROBERT SOBUKWE.

With further reference to your letter of the 28th November, 1966, I wish to inform you that the Honourable the Minister of Justice has granted permission to you and your four children to visit your husband on Robben Island five times a week during the period 9th January, 1967, to the 20th January, 1967. No provision, however, exists to the effect that you are entitled to free transport or a refund of rail fares in the event of visiting your husband.

Greetings,
SECRETARY FOR JUSTICE

Robert Sobukwe
to Benjamin Pogrund,
5 February 1967 (Ba5.11)

Dearest Benjie,

Thank you for both your letters which I received on the 3rd and 20th January respectively.

I am glad to know you are working on your thesis and I have no doubt you will produce an outstanding work. You know, of course, that I shall be happy to give whatever assistance it is in my power to give.

In my letter of the 14th September, 1966 I told you what I thought of our relationship.[1] On this occasion all I'll say is thank you very much.

First of all, please give my thanks to Ernie, Jill and their friends for the presents to the family. And then thanks ever so much to you and Margie for the enormous trouble you took to make my family comfortable. They have never had such a full two weeks. I'll be very glad if you could send me Father McBride's address so that I should thank him myself.[2] And also please thank Mrs Stott on my behalf for all she has done.

I have received all the books you have sent, both textbooks and reading matter. I have enough reading matter for a year and some! And I have all the textbooks I need, Benjie, thank you very much.

The records I have not yet received. But as I said to you some years back, this is the type of music that *sends* me!

When I receive your book packages, what I read first are the Argosy copies.[3] I enjoy them immensely. And thank you for the Hemingway books.

Thanks for news about Jenny. I am looking forward to meeting her one day. I know how you feel about the rationing of the time you may spend with

---

1 In that letter, Sobukwe thanked Pogrund for his "unfailing solicitude and … palpable love and concern", noting that what Pogrund has done for him "is much more than I would have expected even from one who had shared the same womb with me".

2 The Rev. Clive Sidney McBride was a Coloured Anglican priest in Cape Town, who ministered in working-class parishes in the city. He was a champion of the poor and oppressed.

3 *Argosy* was a short story magazine published in London.

her. Children are very sensitive and sensible, Benjie. Jenny knows how you feel about her and I think that is reward enough.

I stand corrected on the Jacobs affair.[4]

At this conference in America to which I referred, the chairman remarked, *inter alia* that "negro" is a term used of "the enslaved and enslaveable. Rocky Marciano[5] is described as an Italian American and von Braun[6] as a German American, terms indicative of geographical (or national?) origins and citizenship. Afro-American has the same signification. European nomenclature is no longer accepted as unquestionable, Benjie.

I'm afraid I do not know the origin of the term *Azania*.[7] When first I came across it in the South African Press (reporting Raboroko[8]) I thought it was an uninspired contraction of Tanzania. Furious research work is being done in West Africa and in rejecting European norms some of the historians may tend to be chauvinistic I fear. They lean heavily on Arab sources.

Yes I read Bonhoeffer's book.[9] In fact I have bought all his published works. I won't be able to comment fully on the book in this letter. It influenced the Bishop of Woolwich profoundly and his *Honest to God* has rocked the Christian Church to its foundations. You'll be shocked to learn and so will many of my friends that these authors and others of their school have freed me to face the fact that I am not a Christian and do not desire to be one.

---

4 See the letter of 23 November 1966 in this volume.

5 Heavyweight boxing champion in the 1950s.

6 Aerospace engineer and space architect who initially worked in Nazi Germany's rocket development programme, before being secretly moved to the United States to work for the US Army and later NASA.

7 According to Lodge, the PAC adopted this new name for South Africa in the mid-1960s, "a name favoured by early cartographers for part of eastern Africa and derived originally from an Arabic expression". Evelyn Waugh used it as the name of his mythical African country in his satirical novel *Black Mischief.*

8 Peter Nkutsoeu Raboroko (1915–2000) was an ANC member who identified with the Africanist faction within the organisation. He helped launch the Youth League in 1944, and subsequently became secretary for education in the PAC after its founding in 1959. He was considered the PAC's party theoretician, and was the author of the Pan Africanist Congress Manifesto. Following the Sharpeville Massacre, he took on the role of PAC representative in Accra.

9 Pogrund asked Sobukwe about this book, Bonhoeffer's *Letters and Papers from Prison*, in his letter of 20 December 1966.

I don't think there should be any objection to literary articles whatever paper they appear in. I hope so at any rate and will certainly be happy to receive them.

Thank you for helping my friend of the overcoat.[10] Two years back he asked you for some articles of clothing I remember. I have great respect for him, Benjie.

Greetings to my friends and love to the ladies,

Yours affectionately,
Bob

10 Josias Madzunya.

Robert Sobukwe
to Nell Marquard,
5 February 1967 (Bd2.1)

Dear Mrs Marquard,

First of all, thank you for the Christmas Card which I received on the 11th January, 1967. I also got the impression that on the 1st December you had sent me a Birthday Card. At any rate that is what I assume for I did not receive it.

You know, of course, that my wife and the children were here for ten days or so. They all looked fine indeed and reported that they were being wined and dined in true Cape Town fashion. I should have liked my daughter to have met you. I am sorry she didn't. They left on Saturday, 21st January. Then on Friday, 3rd February, my priest-brother paid me a visit.

I am sorry I am not a U.C.T. graduate. It would have been a pleasure to cast my vote. However, I was very pleased to note that Professors A.C. Jordan and Kunene were among the sponsors of our candidate.[11]

Incidentally, did you stop sending *The Listener* on your own, or were you told to stop? The last issue I have is of June, 1966. I had asked my wife to get that information from you but apparently she couldn't.

I realize that you must be very busy these days. I shall, therefore, keep this letter short and write again when our pulses have returned to normal. In the meantime let us give the philistines a run for their money.

With very best wishes

Yours sincerely
R.M. Sobukwe

11 Sobukwe is referring here to Nell's husband, Leo Marquard, who stood as a candidate for the position of vice-chancellor of the University of Cape Town. The post went eventually to Sir Richard Luyt. A.C. Jordan was a noted African scholar and novelist, who was Professor of African Languages at UCT. Daniel P. Kunene, later a Professor of African Languages at the University of Wisconsin, had received an MA from UCT in 1951 and a PhD in 1961 and was therefore entitled, as a member of UCT's Convocation, to vote for the new vice-chancellor.

Benjamin Pogrund
to Veronica Sobukwe,
20 February 1967 (Ba5.15)

My dear Mrs Sobukwe,

I returned from Cape Town last night – I was there for ten days – to find your letter waiting for me. I would also very much like to see you and wonder whether you could telephone me so that we could arrange to meet? The best time is to phone me first thing in the morning at my flat (44.9030).

My application to see Bob was, I am afraid, refused by the Magistrate in Cape Town. Mrs. Suzman saw him, however, and reports that he is keeping well.

I look forward to seeing you soon.

Sincerely,

Robert Sobukwe
to Nell Marquard,
22 February 1967 (Bd2.2)

Dear Mrs Marquard,

An article, in the Reader's Digest, I think it is, states that we can gauge our feelings towards people by the feeling aroused in us when we receive a letter from them. When I read the article I thought – what nonsense! I still think so. There's so much else involved. These "experts" tend to over-simplify and make us suspicious and wary of all "expert opinion", just as the quacks and charlatans have made me suspicious of all "witch-doctors"!

However, this I *can* say: I am always happy when I have to write to you: hence my inordinately long letters. But I intend to discipline myself this year.

Thank you for your letter dated 26th January. I am really glad you have met Benjie and he is all you say and more. He is so close to me that the term "friend" hardly suffices to express the relationship. In any event I have been very fortunate not in *my* choice of friends (I didn't choose) but in those who have *chosen* to be my friends. I couldn't have asked for a more sterling lot!

As you read in the press, Helen [Suzman] was here last Wednesday morning. It was the first time I saw her in the flesh.

And still the wonder grew
That such a small body
Could harbour so stout a heart!

With hearty apologies to Goldsmith's Village teacher.[12] She mentioned something about books you had sent but we were neither of us quite sure how recently that was. As my letter of the 5th February will have indicated I have not yet received the "Listener" and perhaps the books too are still held up. It is also possible, of course, that the books you sent are among the numerous books I received during my wife's visit, from numerous sources.

Thank you for the information about your birthday. I shall be grateful if you would let me know the date. I wouldn't like to miss your hundredth.

12 An adaptation of Oliver Goldsmith's tribute to the village schoolmaster in his poem "The Deserted Village".

I received a telegram this morning to the effect that my mother and my sister-in-law will be arriving at the end of THIS MONTH: no longer in April. Natives!!!

I will arrange that they come to see you, if they are staying for some decentish time. I don't know where they'll be staying. They will let you know. And will you please give Benjie this information, if you know where he is staying? I want him to meet them.

You will have read that America has resumed the bombing of North Vietnam. I think they have misread the signs and have lost a glorious opportunity to terminate the war. Johnson is acting out of character on the Vietnam issue.

Thank you for news about your garden. You make it sound like sheer poetry.

Yes, I see in the press that Mr Marquard has been doing some work on the Boer War.[13] No, you hadn't told me before; however, I read the news in your letter before I read it in the newspapers. I shall certainly be happy to receive a copy. Thank you in anticipation.

With regard to what you say about Benjie's arrangements with Stuttafords, I'll write to him soon. My immediate needs will be in the line of clothing and I think it is best that he makes the purchases himself so that he can decide on style and colour and price. I'll send him a list. The trouble is that I think he is doing more than enough while he feels he is not doing half enough.

With best wishes
Yours sincerely
RM Sobukwe

---

13 This is Leo's edition of his mother's *Letters from a Boer Parsonage* (1967).

Robert Sobukwe
to Benjamin Pogrund,
1 March 1967 (Ba5.17)

My dear Benjie,

I am not yet using the "executive-type" fountain pen you sent me. I want to get my money's worth out of this contraption that American high-pressure salesmanship has foisted on us.

Mrs Marquard wrote to me a few weeks ago and told me she had had a visit from you. She was obviously most favourably impressed (as I had expected) and spoke warmly not only of you as a person but also of our friendship.

Helen Suzman visited me here, too, as you know, and she greeted me with the words "I was with your friend, Benjie, yesterday." I was forcibly struck by the inadequacy if not the incongruity of the term. I *have* friends, of course, of whom I am very fond, and high on the list are Mrs Marquard and Prof Wellington. But I have long passed the stage of even thinking of you as a friend. I don't want to be sentimental about this. So I suggest that you and I stick to simple Bob and Benjie in our dealings with each other, in the same way as my biological brother, Charles and I stick to our nicknames.

Thank you, on Miliswa's behalf, for the mattress. She is growing into a glorious Watusi woman.

Thank you for the arrangements with Stuttafords. I was expecting word that you had fixed (or is it "clinched"?) matters with the management. I shall still, however, be obliged to ask you to do the buying of clothes and such like, as colour, texture and price are things that require an "inspection *in loco*". I am appending quite a list.

Two weeks or so after my wife had left, my eldest brother[14] dropped in on a Friday afternoon. He is an Anglican priest, as you know, and the humour of the situation is that that very morning I had written to stop all visits by priests and padres in their official capacity, that is. He is a very good man but has always had certain prejudices and biases that I do not share. He thinks I am annoyingly stubborn!

---

14 Ernest.

You will remember I said my mother and my sister-in-law would be visiting me in April. Well, they are doing it either this WEEK or next week, according to a telegram I received last week. As I had heard from Helen [Suzman] that you were around, I asked Mrs Marquard to contact you and inform you about these changed arrangements. I should very much like for you to meet. They'll be staying with friends in one of the locations but they'll let you know where they are as soon as I have met them.

Your last batch of reading books was really outstanding. I have enjoyed the plays and the Short Stories and two or three novels. Taylor's *History of Germany* & Pares' *History of Russia* (on the serious side) make delightful reading.[15] Thanks a lot.

I have just seen the card you enclosed. My thanks to Margie. As I had said to you I love her even in absentia. I subsequently saw her picture in the papers and got my wife's report. I loved what I saw and heard.

I have received the six records from Recordia. Please thank my friends for me. I can never tire of the music of these fellows, Benjie. Have you experienced this acute pain, a straining of the nerves of the heart, as Mozart piles music upon music: "Why is all lovely thought a pain?" [16] asks Walter de la Mare.[17]

I haven't received the other three records you mentioned: Barber, Sandburg and Moore. I haven't received any of your book-reviews, either, that is, *if* you've sent any.

Thank you for news about Jenny. I have heard of your frustrating experiences. Just you be true to yourself. Give her the love, all of it, you have for her. She'll grow up, Benjie, and she'll choose to be decent like her father.

I am attaching the list of my requirements. But if my sister-in-law meets you before you've received the letter, I'll give her the list to hand over to you.

Love to Margie, Jenny and all my friends.

Yours affectionately,
Bob

---

15 A.J.P. Taylor, *The Course of German History* (1945), which Sobukwe later commented on in his letter to Mrs Marquard of 5 June 1968, and Bernard Pares, *A History of Russia* (1926).

16 This line comes in fact from the play *A Night of the Trojan War*, by John Drinkwater.

17 Walter de la Mare was a British poet, novelist and short story writer.

List—

3 pairs Pyjamas, size: 42, dark preferably.

2 charcoal or black shirts: collar 16½ & casual like the "Bronzoni" you sent me

1 casual wear shirt to go with the brown trousers you sent.

2 pairs coloured or striped sheets

1 pair rough pig-skin shoes as before or rougher still (size 9½)

1 Khaki shirt and trousers (trousers 5½)

1 slop pail

Thanks

P.S. 1 balaclava cap, black or grey, for a large head (7¼ hat)

Robert Sobukwe
to Veronica Sobukwe,
12 March 1967 (Bc41)

Hullo Darling:

I received your letter on Wednesday, 8th March. Your telegram I received some time in February. Thank you for both.

I am glad to learn that the question of the children's accommodations has been settled. And I am, of course, very grateful to Mrs Mokhele and the Mfaxas[18] taking them in.

I, too, have no doubt that Dini will be happy with the Mfaxas. My fear is that they may molly-coddle him and spoil him. The same goes for the twins. So I shall be very happy if you will send me the addresses of both Mrs Mfaxa and Mrs Mokhele (or their husbands!) so that I can write to them.

A week or two after you had left Buti came to see me. He was alone. He was attending a Church conference in Cape Town and he came loaded with more cakes and sweets.

He was grossly overweight. But then so was I after two weeks of gross overeating and stuffing myself with cakes and sweets. I have put his sweets and raisins aside, and the cakes I am eating sanely – as a *luxury* and not a food. I no longer feel comfortable in a big body and, unfortunately, I put on weight very easily.

You will have read that Mrs Suzman visited me around the same time. She remarked, according to Press reports, that the lengthy solitude was beginning to affect me. Please don't interpret this to mean that I am losing my mind. I am very sane, darling. (Of course, madmen also think they are very sane!). But please don't be anxious about me.

Buti had a lot to tell. Apparently Charles was given beans by Mercy's brothers when he visited her in P.E. When he addressed them as Sibali they wanted to know for what reason he so addressed them!

A week after his departure Buti sent me a telegram to say Nenti and Mercy would be coming at the end of February and no longer in April as they had originally intended. I wrote to inform Mrs Marquard and Mrs McBride[19]

---

18 Elliot Mfaxa, a PAC leader, had been arrested in Basutoland in 1963.

19 Presumably the wife of the Rev. Clive McBride.

(a European) who have been very anxious to meet Nenti. Needless to say the natives have not yet arrived nor have they written to say why not.

On Wednesday (8th) I received a letter from Buti, too. He says the doctor has diagnosed diabetes. He is receiving treatment for that. On Thursday or the same Wednesday, I am not sure, I received a telegram from Cousie informing me that Tiyani, his youngest brother, had died. He is being buried today, Sunday.

I have looked up the prices of bicycles and the average price appears to be R34.00 (thirty-four rands). Only children's bicycles are quoted at R12.00. But I still feel that Dini should have his bicycle. I sent Nenti R25.00 (Twenty-five) for her trainfare. What I have left will just about cover my examination fees. But by June I should have almost R20.00 saved and I'll contribute that for the bicycle.

I have sent Benjie a list of my clothing requirements. So don't bother about the pyjamas and khaki outfit.

It was a pleasure having you around and you looked absolutely luscious.

Please tell Benjie the "Cape Argus" and the "Reader's Digest" have been renewed and thank him for me. He told me he sent Mili a rubber foam mattress.

Cheerio Darling,
Mangi

Benjamin Pogrund
to Robert Sobukwe,
16 March 1967 (Ba5.20)

My dear Bob,

I owe you a very humble apology for not having written before now. As you will probably have learned, I had hoped to be able to see you, and I was grievously disappointed when this fell through. I have written to the Minister of Justice to express my disappointment and also took the opportunity of raising the question of your release. But apart from all this, with life as chopped up as it has been recently, I have failed to write. Your letter of February 5 reached me on March 4. I did, in fact, write immediately, but my letter was so dismal in tone that I decided that it would be unfair to inflict it on you so I tore it up. So, as you see, you are subjected to a double censorship! Then your letter of March 1 arrived on March 13. It seems that Helen [Suzman]'s submissions about the delay in your letters has borne fruit.

Both your letters moved me very deeply, particularly your second one. There is no shame – there cannot be any – in my telling you that I cried when I read it. I feel so very close to you, Bob. I recall constantly the last times we were able to see each other, of the many hours when we ranged in our chats over every conceivable subject as though we had never not been seeing each other. I have said before, and I say again, that it is little that I do for you and your family. You deserve a lot more, and so often I berate myself for not doing more for you, and so often too I pray to G-d that I had the power to act effectively on your behalf. I feel a terrible pain within me about your situation. What more can I say than to agree with you that it should continue to be "Bob" and "Benjie"?

I saw your wife recently and can report that she is very well. She said the kids were doing fine. And I must compliment you on your fine turn of phrase in referring to Miliswa as a "Watusi woman". It is a perfect description of her willowy gracefulness. She has a beautiful face, filled with a great peace and serenity. Your boys also are youngsters of whom you can be proud, as indeed I know you are. One thing though about the children is worrying me and I have discussed it with your wife, and that is that they are not learning enough English. There are practical difficulties involved but I have in the meantime suggested that ways and means be explored of arranging special tuition for them. I hope that this will meet with your approval.

As you say, Fr. Clive McBride was great about the arrangements for the family. He would be delighted to hear from you. His address is: 31 Maryland Street, Factreton, Cape Town. He will also, incidentally, be arranging for the delivery of the slop pail requested by you.

Regarding the clothing list sent by you, it has given me a sense of triumph to have succeeded, at long, long last, in wheedling it out of you. You do not say whether you want winter weight or ordinary sheets so I shall send you the latter. But if you have found the winter sheets which I previously sent a boon please let me know and I shall have some more sent. The clothing is being attended to and should reach you before not too long. I shall try not to go too mad in the choice of colours and materials.

There are a few ideas for your greater comfort which friends have suggested and I would be glad if you would let me have your comments on them. Firstly, are you interested in any occupational therapy-type activities (sorry about the dreadful phrase, but it's the only one to convey what I mean). For example, a painting kit, or painting by numbers, or carpentry, or fret work, or tapestry work, or anything else in this line? Secondly, could you perhaps sound out the authorities about allowing a 16 mm film projector for you? We would then either try to get someone to donate one outright to you, and have say two films a weekend sent out to you from Cape Town, or else hire a projector and films for you over the weekends. I am certain that there would not be any objection to this arrangement, but I would be glad if you could make inquiries informally about it – that is, of course, if the idea appeals to you. Thirdly, what about brightening your quarters with a couple of paintings, a bedspread, small carpet, etc? I have also been wanting to ask you for some time whether you were satisfied with the plastic easy chair which you have, or whether you would prefer something more comfortable. In line with all this, could you describe what furnishings you have at present, and what more you would like to have? Well, I have provided a hefty questionnaire for you to answer, and I shall get cracking on these various items just as soon as I hear from you.

I am sorry, Bob. Several days have passed since I started writing this letter and was interrupted. It has been a hectic week, but a pretty good one on the whole.

You will have seen in the Press that there has been a rush of cases this week. Best of all, from my point of view, is the success I had which is giving me new heart. If you lose solidly over a period of nearly two years and then suddenly win, it does something for you! In fact I have been in a state best described as euphoria.[20]

Ernie and Jill were at my flat the other evening for a victory drink, and we talked a lot about you. They naturally send their warmest greetings. They are sending you a thing called "auto bridge" which apparently enables you to play bridge on your own. I don't know whether you are a bridge or card fan, but it should provide an entertaining means of exercising your wits. I'm a lousy card player. A girl friend once tried to teach me to play bridge. She explained everything carefully to me for an hour in the lesson then broke up in uproar when I asked her, in an embarrassed sort of way, if she would mind explaining to me which were the clubs and which the spades. I just can never remember the difference between them!

There have been so many books going out to you that I think I have lost track. I have an idea that I have misplaced one list of which I should have advised you, but am not too sure. In any event, this week another batch was delivered to the Island on my behalf – it was collected from friends – and the list reads:

The Chamberlain Letters
Weimar Germany and Soviet Russia 1916–1933 [by H.L. Dyck]
Poems of Miles Burrows
Before the Armada [by R.B. Wernham]
Religious thought in the 19th century [by Bernard Reardon]
From Puritanism to the Age of Reason [by Gerald R. Cragg]
The Sermon on the Mount
Sophocles the Dramatist [by A.J.A. Waldock]
The Pastoral Letters
Letters from Jack London

20 Pogrund refers here to his legal victory against Dr Percy Yutar; the Appellate Court found for him in his libel action against Yutar, Deputy Attorney-General of the Transvaal. Pogrund had lost in the lower courts, but continued the fight by taking his case to the highest court. The verdict created a legal precedent: that a prosecutor did not have the right to say whatever he liked about someone who was not a party in a case. This stemmed from Yutar's attack on Pogrund in the Gysbert van Schalkwyk trial in 1965 (see Pogrund's letter of 30 September 1965).

Death of a naturalist [by Seamus Heaney]
Poems of Louis Zukofsky
Man's place in nature [by T.H. Huxley]
Religious controversies in the 19th century
Post-Victorian Britain
Mayakovsky
Poems by Alexander Pope
The Stuart Constitution [by John P. Kenyon]
The Icon and the Axe [by James H. Billington]
The making of the English Protestant tradition [by E.G. Rupp]
Textual and literary criticism [by Fredson Bowers]
The Reichswehr and politics [by F.L. Carsten]
The heights of Macchu Picchu [by Pablo Neruda]
Art Afterpieces [by W. Kimball]

I have been at fault in not sending the "Sunday Times" literary supplements[21] but will rectify this shortly.

As you predicted, I was indeed shocked to learn about your change of feelings about being a Christian.[22] Even more so, I was taken aback at the apparent immediate cause of your change of feeling – the books which you have read. I haven't yet got around to reading "Honest to G-d", but I have always understood it to be *positively* critical. But I can understand that this sort of book would push one away from one's religion. But what effects have Bonhoeffer had in this regard? I know that, for myself, my readings of Bonhoeffer have caused me to veer in my view of him. I started off, having heard a great deal about him and having read only a little, with a tremendously high regard – I placed him on a pedestal high above other mortals. But I have come to see him as a very simple, ordinary man who stood up for basic beliefs, lived – and died – for them simply and sincerely. In a way, this is a disappointing thing about him to have to accept. One likes to see one's heroes cast in a giant mould, and from what I have read, Bonhoeffer wasn't that at all. Also, I must admit that in reading his writings, it has often presented a

21 The *London* Sunday Times, not the Johannesburg paper.

22 Given the evident extent of Sobukwe's Christian faith as on display in his letters to his wife (see particularly the letters of January and February 1964), this was indeed a surprising change.

challenge to faith – to have believed so implicitly, and to what end? And I would also admit that it does seem to me (although I might be wrong about this through lack of enough knowledge) that his opposition was not all that clear or effective. I rather tend to suspect that this aspect of him has become inflated because there were so few who did oppose, so that the role of those who did must necessarily be inflated. As I know my history of that period, it seems to me that the initial opposition was wiped out in the very early 30's, and the opposition which developed in the early 40's was of a very different character and motivated by feelings and drives which, in a way, had been responsible for bringing the evil originally into power. But I am digressing here. I would very much like to hear from you, Bob, why there has been this great change within you. I know, of course, how the ministers have failed you as people and this must have had its effect. But I know that you had accepted this, and your change has bewildered me.

Also, while I think of it, I have always wanted to ask you how you reacted to the books on Judaism. Let me hastily add that I am not seeking to offer you an alternative, but am merely interested in your response as such.

And when you say you are no longer a Christian, does this extend to a rejection too of G-d?

You will probably have seen a recent report that my passport has again been refused. As a result, and for other reasons which I have previously outlined, I intend leaving South Africa, within the quite near future. I shall probably head initially for the U.K., and will either stay there or try for university work in the U.S. I wish I could discuss this with you. There are still great conflicts within me, revolving mainly around my feelings of responsibility for bringing about change, my feelings of despair at having to leave Jenny behind, and my feelings also, as you will know, at having to leave you behind. When I recently conveyed my decision to your wife, her reaction of dismay pushed into the open all my own concealed fears and guilt. Yet it is a decision which I feel must be taken. Only one assurance can I give you, as I gave to your wife: that whatever I have been able to do for you and the family will continue unchecked. Others will do the direct work, and I shall continue to do whatever I can from wherever I am. I am not going just yet as there are still things I must do, and there are still responsibilities which I must face up to. If, and as I write the "if" is an unknown quantity, these responsibilities do not materialise, then I would hope to be away within the next couple of months.

I know that what I am writing will cause you great unhappiness, and it is in fact the reason why there has been so much delay in writing this letter to you, and why I tore up the one which I first wrote. But I felt that I wanted you to know my thoughts and my intentions in advance so that anything which I did would not come as a complete shock to you. I have, of course, about a year ago I think it was, told you of my intention of leaving, but it is now a cut and dried decision. Provided, as I say, that nothing befalls me in the way of having to face up to responsibilities. On that score, you must know that I fully accept the responsibilities and would not contemplate actually leaving until I know that I am not to be called upon to meet them.

[...]

Since starting this letter, I have ordered the clothing needed by you, and I hope that it will be to your taste. While doing the buying it struck me that I did not know whether you washed your own clothing – and ironing? – or whether it went to a laundry. Anyway, to play safe, I relied as much as possible on drip-dry articles, for pyjamas and shirts. You did not specify whether the pyjamas should be winter or summer weight so I bought you two pairs of the former and one of the latter (in a drip-dry material which will dry within a couple of hours). The sheets also you did not specify so I have bought ordinary ones. Will you please let me know whether you need winter weight sheets?

P.S. You can relax about the clothing this time: nothing really daring except a Bri-nylon cloth for a shirt which I hope you will find comfortable. But colours and materials are conservative.

This letter is developing into a serial ... It's Saturday morning already and I am still writing it. There is so much else that I want to write to you about, but I have taken so long with this letter that I think I shall end off now and write again in a few days time.

I gave your love to Jenny and she reciprocates – although I should mention this is not the word which she actually used!

Keep well, Bob.
With great affection,

Robert Sobukwe
to Nell Marquard,
22 March 1967 (Bd2.3)

Dear Mrs Marquard,

I am sorry for the false alarm. The ladies haven't arrived and I do not know whether they left their respective locations at all.

I have written to Benjie and have sent him a list of the articles I require.

Thank you for the postal order for R4.00 (Four Rands). And thanks a lot for the [G.K.] Chesterton book. You must have loved it to have kept it all this long.

And please assure Mrs. Henderson that the fruit is reaching me regularly and in good condition.

God bless you all

Yours Sincerely,
RM Sobukwe

Robert Sobukwe
to Benjamin Pogrund,
6 April 1967 (Ba5.23)

My dear Benjie,

It amuses me, the regularity with which you disregard my instructions completely and buy clothes of your own choice which, invariably, appeal more to me than my own choice had done. I say it amuses me because if you were that type of person, you could claim, as many do, that you know better than I what is good for me.

After this introduction I need not tell you that I have received all the articles I asked for and am delighted with every one of them. For the record, these are the articles I have received:

2 pairs of coloured sheets
3 (three) pairs of pyjamas
4 (four) shirts – including the khaki one
1 pair of khaki trousers
1 pair Hush Puppies and their special cleaner.

Thanks a lot.

I have also, subsequent to my letter, received the other records:

Samuel Barber: Symphony No 1, etc and
Douglas Moore: The devil and Daniel Webster

Carl Sandberg's record has been withheld and, I suppose, returned to you.

Congratulations on the outcome of your case.

Mrs Marquard has suggested that we proceed to a first-name basis. I am very happy about that because though we have never met I've grown very fond of her.

The fruit is reaching me regularly, too, and I notice that Mrs Henderson's name appears on the invoice. I have asked Mrs Marquard to thank her for me.

I wrote, early in March, to ask Mrs Marquard to inform you that my mother and my sister-in-law would be visiting me and I should like you to meet them. A subsequent letter explained that it was all a mistake and that the visit was still scheduled for April. As they say in Xhosa, "sendiyakubana ngoko" (I'll see *then*).

Miliswa's letter reached me early this week. She seems to feel that her contacts in Cape Town helped her tremendously to improve her English.

Incidentally, I did not receive the October issue of *Economica*. I wondered if you had forwarded it. Also the "past examination papers" have not reached me yet. Can you throw any light on the matter?

I hope your work is getting alone fine. Best of luck.

Finally, allow me to congratulate you on the tremendous leap you have made up the ladder of culture. I have had time to read a number of the books you sent me and, Benjie, they are undoubtedly "class". I couldn't miss it. I picked up one book after another and I read "class". I said to myself: "Benjie is being surrounded by a tremendous cultural influence". I am not being disparaging, old fellow. After all, your line is psychology, not the humanities. Thank that child for me, please. She is doing exactly what Jackie Kennedy did for her President husband!

Well, Benjie, so much for now. Love to Margie and Jenny.

Yours affectionately,
Bob.

P.S. I came across a reference to "Azania" in one of the books I've been reading. Apparently it featured in a great novel by either Aldous Huxley or some other big shot:[23] I just can't recall who. I'll find out.

I am using the engraved pen. I really am going places! Bob

---

23 Actually Evelyn Waugh, *Black Mischief.*

Robert Sobukwe
to Benjamin Pogrund,
12 April 1967 (Ba5.24)

My dear Benjie,

I enjoyed your letter immensely although your pain came through very forcibly. I may not be able to answer your letter fully in one letter of mine; in which case I shall write two letters.

First of all, with regard to your intention to leave the country: I approve wholeheartedly. The only stumbling-block I am prepared to consider are personal ties: but true greatness, Benjie, lies in being able to sever those ties in pursuit of the Holy Grail. [...]

The dismay with which my wife received your news is quite understandable. She had come to lean very heavily on you regarding you as a restless younger brother who, unless watched very carefully, could be guilty of extreme extravagance on behalf of Bob and all his. She complained rather proudly of how you had been dissatisfied with the room they had been given at the hotel and had arranged for a larger and more comfortable room.

In other words she has never felt with you that she was receiving "assistance". She has always known that the suggestion would come from you that the children needed this and that (even special tuition in English!) and Bob this and that. There's a vast difference, Benjie, between: "Please tell me what you need" and "I think you *should* have this, don't you?" And, gentleman that you are, you knew it instinctively.

My wife is not concerned about material assistance. You know her well enough to know that. She knows and I have told her that I have four brothers: two biological brothers and you and Dennis Siwisa[24] of Port Elizabeth.

You have decades of fruitful labour before you, Benjie and you must make your contribution. The intellect blossoms only in freedom.

Whether you decide on the UK or the USA, academic life or the typewriter, I should like you to regard that as preparatory work for service to Africa. In fact, once you are settled down I might seriously consider sending the children to you.

I have no anxieties, whatsoever. We shall meet.

24 Dennis Siwisa was a school friend of Sobukwe's.

What you say about the children's English is quite correct. And whatever steps you take to improve their command of the language will meet with my approval. In the circumstances, I believe, all one can hope for, in the immediate future that is, is greater fluency even if the accent remains a "separate development" accent.

Thanks for Father McBride's address. I'll write to him.

As I said in my previous letter, the clothes are just grand. In my draft list I had stated that I should like winter sheets and 2 pairs of winter pyjamas. It appears that when I transferred the list I omitted the qualifications. The previous winter sheets most certainly were a boon. Winter can be quite nasty out here.

About ideas for my greater comfort: I haven't had time to develop what are known as hobbies. I have been an active sportsman in my "free" life. (Incidentally, the kids found it difficult to believe that I won the Eastern Province Tennis Singles Championships in 1944, just about nine months after I had left a TB hospital. They don't know how remarkable their father is!)

I should suggest that we leave the "occupational therapy" activities until next year when I shall have done with my exams. It requires a great effort, as it is, to concentrate on the lectures and I am afraid that if I had something more interesting to do I might neglect my work!

The idea of a film projector we can discard altogether, Benjie. Even if the principle were to be approved – and I don't think it would be – there would still be the question of constant censorship of the films. And, I am afraid, some humiliating experiences would be unavoidable.

I should like to have a bedspread of my own, certainly. But I do not think a small carpet will be necessary. I have a felt mat here for my feet. Nor will the pictures be necessary, Benjie. You see, all these, after a time, become part of the environment. And it *is* a jail environment. And there is something in me which does not wish to forget that either.

The plastic chair is a little uncomfortable on the neck and I should be pleased to have something more comfortable.

Continued in 2nd letter.

Robert Sobukwe
to Benjamin Pogrund,
12 April 1967 (Ba5.25)

[Second letter]

I am afraid I cannot tell you what furnishings I have in my quarters. It may be classified information for all I know. However, I am quite certain that I do not require any *additions*. Replacements, perhaps.

And the first replacement will be that of my medium-wave radio. It has a chronic defect of wiring, I believe. The volume recedes and returns at will. I have had it sent in twice, at least, for just that specific trouble but after a month or so the trouble is back. In the meantime, the instrument *devours* batteries. If you think such a replacement possible please let me know and I shall inquire whether there is any objection to your purchasing the set yourself, provided, of course, that it produces only South African programmes which I think is what a medium-wave FM set does. My knowledge of physics is very limited.

Thanks, in advance, for the auto-bridge that Ernie and Jill are sending. I *am* a card fan, but my tastes are plebeian. My wife left me a packet, in January, after teaching me "Patience" – a non-proletarian game!

Thank you for the books. I received them all. Please don't bother to send the "Sunday Times" supplement. It is a "foreign" *newspaper* and foreign newspapers are forbidden, irrespective, I believe, of their contents.

Now for the main thesis. Let me assure you that my break with Christianity is fundamentally doctrinal. Even if everybody around me were to live a truly Christian life, I still would reject Christianity.

After some sober reflection, Benjie, I don't think you should be bewildered. After all, we are Christians because we were subjugated by Europeans, whose cultural religion Christianity is. If we had been subjugated by Turks we would be fanatical Mohammedans as are eighty million Africans on the continent. Similarly, if Indians had subjugated us we would be fanatical Hindus. There is nothing *inevitable*, therefore, in our being Christian.

In South Africa, hardly a quarter of our people are Christians, in spite of the fact that, as in Nigeria, it is those who professed Christianity who got the most lucrative jobs. They were the "good boys" – trustworthy, obedient and loyal. If you wish me to expatiate on this, please tell me and I'll gladly do so. But to return to the doctrinal aspect.

I agree with all you say about Bonhoeffer. In the early years of Hitler, he like many others, was impressed by the dramatic change that came over Germany. Many church leaders admired the appeal of Nazism "to the best in German youth". They pointed with approval at the way young people were being called out of the dance halls and the beer cellars into the open air. They applauded a movement that made so much of purity … They saw that young Germans were learning again to be proud of being German.

Two days after Hitler's assumption of power Bonhoeffer spoke against the "leadership principle". But his sermon was academic. He did not seek a clash with Hitler. He was pushed into it. All this information and more you will get in his book: "No Rusty Swords".[25] Bishop Stephen Neill, in assessing Bonhoeffer says: "To suffer demands courage; to suffer and to hold on, although the suffering seems meaningless, is the work of supermen". It is not at the beginning, then, that his greatness lies but at the end, as with Churchill.

Now Bonhoeffer says Christians have made of God a *deus ex machina*, a God of the gaps, to explain whatever men's reason and experiment could not. And, of course, with the increase of scientific knowledge, God's sphere has decreased. What for centuries have been described as mysteries, known to God only, man has mastered, explained and understood. Bonhoeffer says 20th Century man has come of age and God might want man to become independent of him.

Of Christianity he says it was not founded in a temple or by a priest. It was founded in a desert place, Caesarea, Philippi, on the most unreliable of men – Simon Peter. But he doesn't define "God" nor does he question the "Christ" doctrine. It is the legalistic, tradition-encrusted Christianity that he rebels against.

Bishop John Robinson in his *Honest to God* goes further.[26] He says there is no God "up there" (as in a three-storeyed universe); nor is there a God "out there" in outer space. God is not a "Daddy in the Sky", he says. OK, then who is God? "The depth of our Being", he says. He questions traditional interpretations of Christianity.

---

25 *No Rusty Swords: Letters, Lectures and Notes, 1928–1936*, from *The Collected Works of Dietrich Bonhoeffer*, volume 1, edited and introduced by E.H. Robertson and John Bowden (1965).

26 John Arthur Thomas Robinson was the Anglican Bishop of Woolwich, and a New Testament scholar. He was a lecturer at Trinity College, Cambridge, where he later served as Dean. His book *Honest to God* caused a storm of controversy when it was published in 1963.

Now I've been brought up in a home where to even think of questioning anything in the Bible is scored up as a success for Satan. I've suppressed all questioning. "Believe!" I've told myself. And when I found these theological minds asking the questions I've always wanted to ask, I applied my intelligence and found that they, too, were skirting the problem. They feared their own conclusions.

Central to the Christian doctrine is acceptance of Jesus Christ *alone* as saviour of the world. No one who rejects Christ as his *personal* saviour can be saved. Now, whatever its origins, Christianity today is the religion of Europe. So to me, an African, this statement means that only Europeans, whose religion Christianity is, and those of other nations who are the "spiritual assimilados" of the Europeans qualify for salvation. I reject that.

In the light of present-day knowledge I cannot accept the story of the ascension.

And all that the critics of Robinson have said is that he has caricatured Christianity. No one critic has refuted any point he has made. Christianity still has to say, unequivocally, in public:

(a) Is God *a* being? An *additional* being even if he is a Super-being?
(b) When we say Jesus Christ is *the* son of God, what do we mean? Mohammedans, of course, say God has no son. He is self-sufficient.
(c) Do they believe in a geographical heaven from which Christ *came* and to which he *returned*?
(d) Do they believe he *physically ascended* through the atmosphere and stratosphere against the pull of gravity?

Do I believe in God? I don't know. Robinson quotes [Paul] Tillich with approval as saying: "The name of this infinite inexhaustible ground of history is God" and that belief in God is a matter of "what you take seriously without any reservation, of what for you is *ultimate* reality".[27] How many "Gods" does such a definition permit? So much for that.

---

27 In Tillich's *The Shaking of the Foundations*, first published in 1948, he states: "The name of this infinite and inexhaustible depth and ground of all being is God. That depth is what the word God means. And if that word has not much meaning for you, translate it, and speak of the depths of your life, of the source of your being, of your ultimate concern, of what you take seriously without any reservation."

But I told you, Benjie, that the books on Judaism did not come through. Only [Martin] Buber's "*Two Types of Faith*" came in. However, I'll give you my honest opinion in a later letter.

[...]

Love to Jenny and thanks for her greetings.

Yours affectionately,
Bob.

Veronica Sobukwe
to Benjamin Pogrund,
18 April 1967 (Ba5.27)

Dear Mr. Pogrund,

I am sorry I left that note which I was supposed to hand it over to you on the table.

It was a pleasure seeing you at the clinic. I felt so proud that we had a true friend like you. Please forgive me for having doubted your friendship to Bob.

It was only after your visit at Pretoria that I realised that you really cared for each other.[28] I have never seen him so excited at seeing a person I had brought along with me.

I remember him telling me at Baragwanath Hospital that he was sorry that he couldn't come with Benjie to see the twins. We will miss you.

Good-bye,

Yours sincerely,
Veronica

P.S. Please also mention that I am surprised that after his major operation he has never been to the hospital for a routine post-operative "check up". This is very important. VS.

---

28 Veronica Sobukwe is referring to Pogrund's original visit to Robert when he was in Pretoria prison.

Robert Sobukwe
to Nell Marquard,
1 May 1967 (Bd2.4)

My dear Nell,

I'll have to make sure that my letter is coherent. I have been trying to arrange it in my mind for a couple of weeks but this and that come up demanding to be said first and I am having quite a struggle maintaining discipline over my thoughts.

First of all, regarding the salutation: I am not feeling as confident as the grammatical "possessive" might suggest. And I have traced the reason for my uneasiness back to Graaff-Reinet.

They are a lot that is very status-conscious those Graaff-Reineters. And status is determined, by and large, by the years of the calendar, so that anybody who is a mere five years older than one will remark, when addressed by name: "Jy moet 'n draai maak"![29] They would tell me "ek vat slegs kanse"[30] in addressing you by name but I shall make the draai when we meet.

Thank you indeed for suggesting that the formality come to an end:

Something there is that doesn't love a wall,
That wants it down[31]

says Robert Frost. As a generalization this is probably more poetic than "social scientific". But, poets are prophets and there is, today, an impatience with walls and curtains. The twentieth-century technological present is an age that tears down – a strip-tease age.

Incidentally, thank you for the copies of "Contrast".[32] I found the Afrikaans poems less abstruse than the English and enjoyed Rabie[33] and

29 You must call round.

30 I only take chances.

31 From Robert Frost's poem "Mending Wall", which contests the proverbial idea that "Good fences make good neighbors".

32 *Contrast* was a poetry magazine founded in 1960 under the editorship of Jack Cope.

33 Jan Sebastian Rabie was an Afrikaans poet, novelist and short story writer.

Hennie Aucamp.[34] I shall most probably ask you to send me some of the works of the "Sestigers"[35] together with an Afrikaans dictionary. But this will have to wait until next year, after I have written my exams. I want to be a "modern" man and concentrate upon *passing* my exams. The relevant *knowledge* I shall acquire later – if ever. You don't have to *know* to pass an exam.

There I go, digressing. The second point I wanted to raise concerned the chancellorship.[36] Now that it is all over I think we can speak frankly to each other.

You realize that I don't *know* Leo. I met him once – in Pretoria – and thought him a stable well-balanced gentleman. After knowing you I was more than ever convinced that he was a gentleman because I couldn't imagine you living happily – as you most obviously do – with anybody who was *not* a gentleman.

But I must admit that the Press shook me a little. The "Cape Argus" hinted, suggested, implied – not in *words* mind you: most delicately indeed – that Leo was just this bit short of being a revolutionary anarchist. Of course the Cape Argus is very "patriotic" and one can therefore smile superiorly at its views.

But the "Cape Times"? Well it didn't say anything against Leo. But there was no mistaking the profound sigh of relief that went up in the editorial column.

The only people who were obviously disappointed and chagrined were the academicians and the student body. And there, dear Nell, is the rub. At Fort Hare we used to say that "ornithological specimens of identical plumage habitually congregate in the closest proximity" which being interpreted means "Birds of a feather flock together".

Now anybody who can be badly desired by the staff and students of U.C.T. must be one of their kind. And I don't need to tell you what that "kind" is like. Absolutely beyond the pale, my dear. They should all be in jail, if you ask *me*.

---

34 Hennie Aucamp was an Afrikaans poet, short story writer and academic.

35 The Sestigers were a group of influential Afrikaans writers, also known as the Beweging van Sestig (the Movement of Sixty), who aimed at producing a literature that would both break with past literary traditions and confront the apartheid state. The group included (among others) Hennie Aucamp, André Brink, Breyten Breyetenbach, Jan Rabie, Ingrid Jonker and Adam Small.

36 Leo's candidature for the vice-chancellorship of UCT was discussed in an earlier letter with Nell Marquard.

So much for the chancellorship. I am a law-abiding native, my dear, and I want to see our universities in good hands.

My mother and my sister-in-law arrived at last. Thank you for entertaining them. They enjoyed your company as much as my wife did – despite the subsequent aberrations. And, of course, I am glad they met you. I shall have to make application to the relevant ministry for you to be allowed to visit me. As it is only my relatives who are allowed to visit me I don't know how we shall achieve that. There is no philological affinity between von Tecklenburg and Sobukwe, is there now?[37]

About my hobby. I have none at the moment, though if I were to cultivate one I should choose carpentry. But even that will have to wait until next year. I am afraid that such a hobby would make me turn my back on my lectures altogether. And it already is a burden concentrating on the minute provisions of the Poor Law of 1834 and the political theories of Jean Bodin and St Augustine!

Please don't be anxious about me. I have all I need. Incidentally, thank you very much for the cake. That is my weakness: a sweet tooth.

I won't be making any garden this year, so I won't need any seed. If I need anything I'll let you know, don't you worry.

With best wishes to you both,
Yours sincerely,
Robert

---

37 See the letter of 23 November 1966 to Nell Marquard.

Benjamin Pogrund
to Robert Sobukwe,
4 May 1967 (Ba5.34)

My dearest Bob,

Your letter of April 6 and the two of April 12, which both, or rather all, reached me a few days ago, provided most entertaining reading – and in your references to your views on Christianity, most thought-provoking reading. But I so much enjoyed the letters, and thank you for them. Your writing style is superb – and in *English* at that! – and I wonder whether you are not in fact the potential candidate for the writing of that Great South African Novel for which we are all still waiting. The teasing aside, the letters really were great. And having read that you won the Eastern Province Tennis Singles in 1944, I am as suitably impressed as were the children. I see you now in a new light, and realise how grievously I have underestimated you.

Firstly, about your material needs. The winter sheets will, I hope, be sent off on Saturday or Monday at the latest. The chair I have written to people in Cape Town about (sorry, the grammar of this sentence has got a bit cock-eyed – see how your new image as a champ tennis player causes me to offer these apologies), and I hope that a new one will soon be reaching you. I hope to be able to send a new radio to you – FM, of course – by early next week. Actually I am a bit upset about the question of the chair as some months ago I suggested to people that a new one be sent to you and I was assured that it would be done. I note and accept your reservations about the other matters about the environment. How can I phrase my reaction to reading it? You expressed it so nobly. I know that you will squirm at my use of this word, but you will just have to accept it from me as there is no other way to put it. On the radio, you did not say whether you would prefer to have a mains-operated instead of battery set. Have you been sitting under that tree outside, baking in the sun and listening to soft music? I have often chuckled at the memory of our conversation along these lines the last time we saw each other. I think a mains set would be best as it would save you the bother of batteries. What I think I will do is to ensure that an extra long lead is included with the set so that you can hear the radio outside if you wish it. If I recall correctly, you have two power points, in your bedroom and kitchen, so I hope this plan will be all right. On the bedspread, I wasn't quite sure from your letter whether I should send it or not. But I shall play safe and send it anyway, and hope that this is indeed what you want.

I plead not guilty on the question of the choice of clothing. I did my best to get exactly what you had ordered, but the outfitters I went to did not have everything exactly as you wanted, so I had to approximate as closely as I should. Anyway, I am glad that everything was to your taste. In the list you gave of what you have received you omitted to mention the balaclava. I included one – not the exact colour you wanted, I must admit, because they didn't have it – but it was included. Is there any way in which you could check whether it has gone astray? Was the invoice included with the parcel, perhaps? I shall also check with the outfitters that they did in fact send it.

I'm writing to you from work – I've been doing a lot of night work lately as night news editor, and I am able to write now as it is a slack night, after a public holiday, with little happening in the world around, except for the occasional phone calls disturbing me. A few minutes ago it passed midnight: it's now May 5 and my 34th birthday. And hell, Bob, I do feel old sometimes these days!

About "Economica": this has not been reaching me at all regularly, but as they come in I send them to you. I think I had better write direct to them and ask them to post it straight to you. Under separate cover I am also sending you the latest booklist from the Economists' Bookshop[38] in Britain. If there are any books you need or want, will you please let me know? I was surprised that the exam papers had not reached you as I ordered these a long time ago. I am checking to see what happened. Sorry about this, Bob. I hope it has not affected your studies. When are you writing, by the way? I thought you were now on your second year of study but you mention that you will be writing your finals next year … I thought you had planned to spend two years on each normal one year or have I got it all wrong?

I am glad the books are proving OK. Another batch was recently delivered for you by the same old friend of mine and I am enclosing the list which she has sent me. I have asked her to go on supplying you with books of the same quality. Also, in the next few days I shall post off another batch of Argosys. I shall also send off some of the magazine supplements of the London Sunday Times. Although foreign, they are straight literary supplements and I cannot see how there can be any possible objection to them. Some have extracts of the

38 A famous bookshop founded in 1946 in London at the heart of the LSE.

Manchester book on Kennedy[39] – I didn't worry about sending these to you regularly as I knew that you receive the Johannesburg Sunday Times which also published them. Will you let me know whether the supplements get to you?

Turning to your letter of April 12, thank you Bob for what you wrote about my going. There is still a great deal of hesitancy within me, but on balance I accept that it must be done. I most certainly regard it as "preparatory work for service to Africa", as you put it. My greatest hope is to land up in a U.S. university, where I will have the chance of broadening my knowledge of this continent through study and visits. I am too deeply emotionally involved with South Africa and with Africa as a whole to try to contemplate an existence separated from it. This is my existence. You know, nearly ten years ago, when I went to the UK for about six weeks, I had to come back in a hurry for domestic reasons. I hadn't particularly wanted to return – in London, I found a freeing of the spirit and I revelled in being there. But however much I might decry all the talk of the "mysticism" of Africa – and I do tend to scoff at it – I know that as I flew down the continent, and peered through the plane's windows at the ground far below, and touched down at Nairobi and Salisbury and then Johannesburg, I simply knew inside me that this was *my* home. Oddly enough, I found also that out of the antagonism which I had had in London came a surging desire and direction to work for what I believed in this country. And then followed the most fruitful period of my life. Now that I have written all this, I remember that I have previously spoken to you along these lines. So forgive please the reminiscent ramblings of an old man on his 34th birthday.

Anyway, what I am trying to say is that I am part of this place – this broader Africa of which you are so acutely aware, and it is in the service of that Africa that I would wish to spend my life. Speaking to any other person I would feel that this was a melodramatic statement. I know that I need not have this reservation with you.

I have, of course, a great deal of worry within me of how best to fulfill this, while maintaining a reasonable life. I am worried particularly about not becoming like so many South African expatriates of whom I have heard – pining away, frittering away their lives in useless activity (or what I regard as useless, anyway!). Sitting here now, I tend to feel that I will have to be strict

39 William Manchester, *The Death of a President: November 20 – November 25, 1963* (1967).

with myself and aim at severing my close emotional ties with this country as quickly as possible, while trying at the same time to broaden my interests northwards, equally as rapidly as possible. How this will work out I just don't know, and I might well be talking arrant nonsense and it will all prove to be vastly different, once I am out of here.

Some time ago, when I first wrote to you about M,[40] I also told you about another woman[41] with whom I had been terribly close. Well, last year, as I think I told you, I virtually sent her away, both for her own sake and because I felt things could not work out between us. That was in October last year. Since then, we have continued to write and to speak also occasionally on the phone. And we have both realised that our feelings have remained as strong as ever. In February I took the step of asking her if she would wait for me, and she agreed. When I go to the UK I shall be going to her and we intend seeing if, in the different quieter atmosphere of living there, we can resolve those differences between us. She is a married woman, Bob, with two children. We are hoping that her husband will agree to a divorce but so far he has refused. It is a tangled story which I shan't embark upon at this stage – except to give you my assurance that I was not the cause of their marriage breaking up. She was already seeking a divorce when we first met. She is a remarkable woman, highly intelligent, attractive, with extraordinary perception of people – and particularly of me! She has great courage and has demonstrated this while still in this country. She is intensely alive and vital, a woman who fills my every need. Both of us are aware of the problems we have, and we both accept that we just do not know if things will work out between us. But we also both accept that we must come together in a sane environment and see whether we still wish to be together. In the meantime, I shall be going to live with her in London and it is with her that I shall be making my initial adjustment to leaving this country, and to leaving behind my Jennikins, you, my Parents. Of course, she knows a great deal about you – and accepts you as my brother. You can be sure, Bob, that should we marry, our home will be a home too for the four children. For that matter, whatever happens to me, you know, as indeed you have shown that you know by what you wrote, that my home is their home also.

---

40 Margie Marshall.

41 Norma Kitson.

With the phone interruptions and the odd accident to attend to, it's now nearly 1.30 am and I still have lots to write about. I think I shall end off this letter and continue writing over the weekend. I shall post this off tomorrow (today, rather!).

Affectionately,

Telegram from
Benjamin Pogrund
to Robert Sobukwe,
10 May 1967 (Ba5.36)

Please advise whether I can send FM radio immediately. Fond regards Benjamin

Robert Sobukwe
to Benjamin Pogrund,
11 May 1967 (Ba5.38)

My dear Benjie,

I received your telegram this morning, but I choose to reply by letter rather than telegram. I do so because I want to make sure there is no mistake. It will have to be a medium wave Radio limited exclusively to programmes of the S.A.B.C. If that provision is met then, the prison authorities agree, you may send the Radio. Thank you IN ANTICIPATION!

Will write later.

Love to Jenny,

Yours affectionately,
Bob

Benjamin Pogrund
to Robert Sobukwe,
15 May 1967 (Ba5.40)

Dearest Bob,

In my last letter of May 4 I promised to write again within the next couple of days. I am sorry it has taken me so long. Also in that letter I said I was enclosing a list of books delivered to you, but did not do so; the list is now enclosed.

I have checked with the outfitters up here about the balaclava cap and they say it was posted with the other goods. Could you check at your end and let me know? The winter sheets were posted to you last week and I hope they have reached you safely and are to your taste: one has yellow flowers and the other, red flowers! And the bedspread, as you will see, has green as the predominant motif which I chose with the idea that this would be a good colour for brightness, to cheer you up, and yet be serviceable. I think you could either wash it or preferably have it drycleaned, if possible. Incidentally, in a previous letter I think I asked how your clothes were washed – in the communal laundry, by yourself, or what. I need to know so that I can choose the best type of material, for your clothing.

About a radio: on May 10 I sent you a telegram reading: "Please advise whether I can send FM radio immediately fond regards – Benjamin". I haven't had a reply so I wonder whether it reached you? I sent it because obviously I can buy a radio somewhat cheaper through my contacts here than you can and I can select one personally. Your radio has probably been using up batteries because it is an FM set (is it?), as these consume more power than the old medium-wave sets. So I have chosen a mains-operated set (which incidentally, are a bit difficult to come by without short-wave), and am waiting to hear from you as to whether I should send it.

I learnt today that I cannot get a passport so I am applying for an exit permit. [...] My departure date is set for June 24. I plan first to visit Israel and then to fly on June 30 to London. In view of this, I would suggest – because of the delay in letters – that you write your next letter to me at the address at the head of this letter and not to my flat as usual. Any letters sent to this new address will be forwarded to me in case they arrive after my departure. Otherwise, my London address will be:

c/o Mrs N. Kitson,[42]
2 Hurstwood Court,
Finchley Road,
London NW11.

It is, of course, my hope that nothing untoward will occur to delay my departure. I imagine you will know of it should it occur.

Out of the blue last week I received a letter from a British TV group saying they had heard I was coming and would I like to join a new type of current affairs programme being started. Most exciting this, as it sounds top-rate work. I have written telling them that I first want to complete my book and that I would be interested after that. I can see a tussle within me whether to continue in journalism or to follow my present desire to climb the ivory tower and to get away from the travails of the mortal world. I am rather attracted to the notion of myself sitting in remote isolation on that tower, surveying those below with a cold, beady eye. Come to think of it, *you* tried it and it didn't work out that way! Oh, well, one can always dream …

I shall, by the way, be in Cape Town with Jenny to say goodbye to my Parents from mid-morning on June 10 until lunch-time on June 13. […] We shall be thinking of you and will be living in Sea Point right across the bay from you. In fact, at 2.00 pm on June 10, if you happen to look across at Signal Hill and you see two people standing there – among the houses at the bottom – and waving to you, you will know that it is us!

I saw Veronica last Wednesday and was able to satisfy myself again that all is well with you and the kids. I need not again tell you, because you well know it, what a magnificent wife you have. Her quiet courage and strength is awe-inspiring. What delights me particularly is that she has come to relax whenever she is with me now and we chatter away about all kinds of things. I am seeing her again this Wednesday, so that Ernie [Wentzel] can meet her. And when the kids are home from school we are all getting together so that I can say goodbye to them and so that Jenny can meet them properly.

About your views on Christianity: I have re-read several times what you wrote, and I face the obvious difficulty of being a non-Christian. I can't

42 Norma Kitson was detained without trial for three weeks in 1964. Her husband, David, from whom she had been separated, was in Umkhonto we Sizwe High Command. He had been detained and was subsequently jailed for 20 years.

put myself in the role of defending the religion, sympathetic as I am to it, as indeed I am to any religious outlook which seeks to bring men together. I tend to be simple-minded about this, I know, and I am always terribly upset and surprised when I find a minister of the cloth lying and cheating, as has been my unhappy experience several times in my encounters through my work. So, as I say, I do not feel myself able to argue about your premises. Indeed, from what little I know, I would tend to agree with what you say.

On the more general question of the existence of G-d, you put your finger on a painful spot within me, and I suppose it must be a painful spot for most people who do not simply blindly believe. I too was brought up simply to believe but I rebelled against this in my teens. Only later, in my early 20s, I began to find my way back, and I have see-sawed ever since. I *want* to believe but I don't always do so. Now why should one *want* to believe? There is so much meaningless in existence anyway, that one desperately wants to be able to believe that there is a higher power who watches over us, who has brought us and this world into existence, and perhaps most important of all, who offers the hope of some form of existence in after-life. I must admit to feelings of sheer terror when I contemplate the end of my earthly existence without any knowledge of anything to come after. The terror grips me in my bowels, and I shake with it. Do you have such feelings? So I want to believe, to try to give some point to my being here. But this, of course, is a purely negative approach. There are those who say: "Look around you at the beauties of our world – at the flowers, the trees, the birds … could anyone but a Supreme Being have created these?" There are times, when I feel joyous in existing, that I do feel this feeling, but I must admit that it is a purely emotional reaction and has no real validity. Basically, what I have long believed is that there can be no logic in accepting a Supreme Being: one either BELIEVES or one does not. This belief goes back to my student days when, of course, we always took part in interminable discussions on the subject. And in talking to priests particularly, because I was a frequenter of the Catholic students' residence, I was always struck by the fact that logical argument could be carried only just so far – and then it was belief.

Then too there is another emotional feeling within me: my forefathers suffered untold horrors and persecution for their belief in their faith. I have a fierce pride in them and I feel that I have a duty, a responsibility, not to let go of what they died for. Even if I lack faith, surely I must be willing to concede that perhaps I am at fault, that the nobility of their belief and what they suffered for it, deserves – demands – that I carry it on. I think there is more than mere blind acceptance in this view, Bob, on the simple basis that we are because of what has gone before us, and it is our function to sift out the good from the bad (hell, don't ask me now to define *those* terms!).

And then, from a purely expedient basis, and speaking now from the standpoint almost of my psychological training, I accept religion as a positive, stabilising factor in an individual's existence, and especially in the upbringing of a child. But, as I think I have written to you previously, I certainly don't believe in blind acceptance, but the instilling of religious beliefs should be accompanied by encouragement of critical faculties so that the grown child can decide for herself what she wants. Reverting to the point I was on in the previous paragraph, as it has just come to my mind, I would be appalled if Jenny were to toss aside lightly all pride in her forefathers. And if she is aware of her forefathers, this necessarily involves too an acceptance of their religious beliefs. And obviously the same point applies to me.

I hope this has all made sense to you. At the best of times I tend to be hesitant about the whole subject, and to add to it I am writing in the early hours of the morning (note lousy typing!).

Incidentally, I did not know that the books on Judaism had been withheld, and I am upset about it. I intend taking up the matter as they should have been returned to me, or at the very least, I should have been advised of it.

To round off this discussion, I still do pray, although I am going through a bad patch at present. When I am conscious of not living the sort of life which I feel I should be living I find difficulty in praying, but I do go on trying. And in my prayers I pray for you and the family – and I hope you will not object to this!

My affectionate greetings to you.

LIST OF BOOKS

Hunter, Jim: Gerard Manley Hopkins
Cunningham, John: Restoration Drama
Devlin, Sir Patrick: Trial by jury
Rupp, E.G.: Studies in the making of the English Protestant tradition
Belloc, Hilaire: The French Revolution
Muntz, Hope: The Golden Warrior
Holdsworth, William: Some makers of English law
Betjeman, John: High and low (poems)

Sisson, C.H.: Catullus
Stevens, Holly: Letters of Wallace Stevens
Carter, C.H.: From the Renaissance to the Counter-Reformation
Weber, Brom: The letters of Hart Crane
Chardin, Teilhard de: The vision of the past
Chapple, J.A.V.: The letters of Mrs Gaskell
Hardy, Sir A.: The divine flame
Hall, Donald: The life and work of Henry Moore
Cawley, A.C.: Medieval miracle plays
Thompson, D'Arcy: On growth and form
Fraser, Peter: Joseph Chamberlain
Berry, Wendell: The Broken Ground (poems)
Larkin, Philip: The North Ship (poems)
Jarrell, Randall: The Lost World (poems)
Pater, Walter: The idea in Nature
Leach, Bernard: Kenzan and his tradition (Japanese art)
Kaplan, Justin: Mr Clemens and Mark Twain
Bush, Douglas: John Keats
Stewart, J.I.M.: Rudyard Kipling
Gilbert, Martin: The roots of appeasement
Douglas, Keith: Collected poems

Benjamin Pogrund
to Robert Sobukwe,
1 June 1967 (Ba5.47)

Dearest Bob,

I saw Veronica this week and was so glad to have news of you. She is very worried about your state of health, and I share her concern. She told me that you had had an X-ray taken in March but had not yet received the results. Can't you ask about these and let us know? Also, isn't it time that you had a complete medical check-up from head to toe? This is something which older people like you and me should attend to at least once a year (see how I pull myself down in the hope of convincing you!). But in all seriousness, you should have a check-up and not just the rather cursory one which a G.P. normally does, but the whole bang shoot with blood tests, checking of lungs, heart, etc. Can't you apply for this to be done? I am sure that the authorities would react sympathetically. Please do not neglect this, Bob. We are worried about you, and would like to know that you are well.

It is June now and you are still there. What can I say to you, my brother, except that there is a terrible pain inside me. The few difficulties which I have, and of which I make so much, are so small compared with your situation. When I do pray I pray to G-d for you, to continue to give you strength and hope for the future, and I pray also for Veronica and the children.

I cannot leave South Africa without making a last attempt to see you. I have accordingly written to the Minister asking whether I may have permission to see you before I leave – on June 13, when Jenny and I will be in Cape Town.

And speaking of Jenny, I am sharing my pleasure in her by sending you three photographs in colour which I have just had developed. Veronica has told me about your album of pictures, and I know you will like to add these. Also, a few days before I leave I shall be spending an afternoon with the children, and Jenny will be with us. I shall take some pictures and will send them to you. Another point: I have arranged for a professional photographer to take pictures of the children when they are at home and these will be sent down to you. And while I think of it, those pictures which Veronica brought to you are excellent ones of her, as I am sure you will agree, but my vanity insists that I tell you that *I* do not look like that!

Earlier today I arranged for a radio to be posted to you. I finally decided to send you a mains-operated set so you will not have to worry about batteries. As required by regulations, it is only an FM and medium-wave set and is incapable of picking up foreign stations. As I told you previously, these mains-operated sets are difficult to come by these days and I hesitated to buy this one in case of possible difficulties about spare parts. But the people from whom I bought it assured me that there should be no difficulty about this. The set carries a three months guarantee which I shall send on to you.

Your telegram inquiring about the non-arrival of pillow-cases for the sheets – the winter ones – reached me, and Veronica tells me you received my replying telegram, sent on May 25, reading: "Apologies stop pillowcases en route stop why no reply my query regarding radio regards Benjamin." (your letter of May 11 has answered the point about the radio). In sending you the pillowcase, I sent only one of each set as I was not sure how many pillows you have. I now know you have two, and will attend to this within the next couple of days. I am just waiting for the label from Veronica to go and show the people from whom I bought the goods.

Your need of an overcoat is noted and you will be receiving one soon. In view of your strictures about choice of clothing in a recent letter, I'm a bit nervous about this one!

Sorry about the delay in getting you a new chair. I have discovered that the person to whom I wrote in Cape Town about it is away, and I shall attend to it personally when I am down there at the end of next week.

I still hope to be away on June 24 and am waiting at present for an exit permit. My London address will be: 2 Hurstwood Court, Finchley Road, London NW11, England. Before I go I shall send you a supply of air letter cards, and will also telegraph you just as I go so that you can know to re-address your letters to me. A lot of butterflies in my tummy about it all …

I have been meaning to tell you that among my last writing jobs was a campaign, recently concluded, to raise money to provide bursaries to enable bright but needy African youngsters to complete their high school education. I was appalled at the numbers of children forced to leave school for lack of a paltry sum. So I ran an "adopt a child" scheme to ask the public to "adopt" a child for R20 a year – which pays half to a third of the required school fees and books. It's a small enough amount, and although so much more is needed by a child I kept it at this low figure so as to be able to bring in the ordinary middle-class person. About 1,200 people responded and we raised about R24,000 – again pitifully little in terms of total need, but it does at least mean that about 450 children can continue at school. With your own school-teaching history,[43] I know this will be of interest to you.

Some points in your recent letters about your reasons for rejecting Christianity have been worrying me. In particular, there was the one sentence: "Now, whatever its origins, Christianity today is the religion of Europe." I would have thought rather that its origins were in Europe, but that it was today no longer such. In this country, certainly yes, and I believe that Christianity is suffering (example, the rise and extraordinary growth of the African separatist churches), and if things continue in the same way, will suffer even greater inroads because of this. But surely this does not apply to the rest of the world? Even allowing for the conservatism (?) of the churches, isn't there convincing refutation of this in the existence say of an African who is R.C. Archbishop of Maseru, or in Nigeria, or a Sinhalese Bishop of the Anglican Church? While voicing these queries I must say that I do agree with the other points mentioned at the same time by you – namely, that only Christians qualify for salvation – and you will readily appreciate why I do agree with you! But while chuckling over your reference to "spiritual assimilados", I wonder whether this isn't perhaps an over-harsh label which ignores the profound and sincere acceptance of Christianity by Africans and other "non-Europeans" (used in the broad sense, of course).

Earlier today I had to condense a speech which the Rev. C.F.B. Naudé[44] – who is incidentally an admired and good friend of mine – gave in Cape Town at the university tonight. You will probably have already read the report of the speech in the Cape papers, but tomorrow I shall enclose the local version which contains about 50 per cent of what he said. I must confess to having been very greatly moved by what he said. Particularly at this time, it aroused echoes within me, and brought to life again all my conflicts about staying or

43 Sobukwe had taught history, English and geography at a secondary school in Standerton from 1950 until he took up an appointment at Wits University in 1954.

44 Beyers Naudé (1915–2004) had been a prominent minister in the Dutch Reformed Church and a member of the Afrikaner Broederbond. After the Sharpeville Massacre he began to question the biblical and theological justifications for apartheid. In 1963 he founded the Christian Institute, an ecumenical organisation that sought to promote reconciliation between black and white. He was forced to leave the Dutch Reformed Church and in the 1970s was placed under house arrest after the Christian Institute was closed down.

leaving here. To return to the original point, I would be interested in your reactions to his outlining of a pure and good Christianity. Without in any way discounting the other objections expressed by you on doctrinal grounds, what I am concerned about is that it is really Christianity as applied in this country – and not in its natural, world-wide application – which brings about rejection. On another level, I have the same fear about democracy. One can hardly blame people for rejecting the concept as a whole and wishing to turn elsewhere for a system of government after looking at the local variety. But this is another matter, and probably one best left alone.

Before I end off, one point has just occurred to me: you might wish to play the radio while sitting outside, as I understand you are fond of sitting in the sun and exchanging playful banter with those about you as to who sends you clothing.[45] I am arranging for a longer lead with the necessary plug attached to be prepared and will send this down to you shortly.

With much love and my prayers for you,

45 This rather oblique allusion is a reference to a story Sobukwe related to Pogrund about a white warder. The warder, who was sitting in a sentry box a few metres away from Sobukwe on a particularly hot day, observed the former PAC leader sitting in a chair in the shade, reading and listening to the radio, smoking. Presumably irritated by this, the warder asked him, "Hey, what's it like to wearing clothes from a Jew?" to which Sobukwe offered a most uncharitable retort best left to the reader's imagination.

Benjamin Pogrund
to the Minister of
Justice and Prisons,
P.C. Pelser,
2 June 1967 (Ba5.48)

Dear Sir,

Re: Permission to visit R.M. Sobukwe

As you may perhaps know, I have applied to the Secretary for the Interior for a permit to enable me to leave South Africa permanently. I plan to leave on June 24.

You are aware of the very close personal relationship which I have with Mr Robert M. Sobukwe, and I write to ask whether I can pay a final visit to him before I leave. You will appreciate our mutual desire to see each other, possibly for the last time for some years.

I shall be in Cape Town on June 12 and 13, and if you are willing to accede my request, I wonder whether I may visit him on June 13. I apologise for the late notice of this application and would like to suggest that, to save time, I telephone your Private Secretary on June 12 to obtain your decision.

I trust that this suggestion will meet with your approval.

Yours faithfully,
BENJAMIN POGRUND

Robert Sobukwe
to Benjamin Pogrund,
4 June 1967 (Ba5.49)

My dear Benjie,

Thank you for both your letters. Accept my belated good wishes on your birthday. I knew you were young but I did not think you were that young! You must have been twentyish when you got your Masters and still in your early twenties when you got married. Damn it man where are you hurrying to?

You will have heard from Veronica that we had a very lovely time together. She came with her youngest sister, Mrs Ribeiro of Pretoria, and Clive [McBride] accommodated both of them. He's been very wonderful: said Mass for Veronica before she went to interview the Minister [of Justice]. As usual she is being rather perverse. All these years she's been rather an indifferent Anglican and a more indifferent Christian. But now, because I abjure this faith, she's beginning to swear by it!

For the occasion I used your yellow-flowered sheets. She said she would tell you about it. They are very fine sheets indeed. Thank you for them and the pillow cases which arrived later. I am sorry I did not list the balaclava in my letter. I have been wearing it night and day in a separate development way.

The books on Judaism to which I refer are those listed in your letter of 7th December, 1965. I wrote to you, after you had sent me a copy of that letter with your letter on 28th March 1966. I listed the books that I had received as follows:

Weiss Rosmarin: Judaism Christianity: The Difference
Epstein: Judaism
Lewisohn: Selections of Jewish Short Stories
Conquest: Marxism Today
Griffiths: The Road to Freedom
Honey: Communism in North Vietnam
London: New Nations in a Divided World
McKay: Africa in World Politics
Carew: Moscow is not my Mecca
Appleton: The Student Trap

Fortunately, you had earlier sent me Epstein's Judaism. As I said in an earlier letter, if I were not an African, I would choose to be a Jew – in the ethnic not just the religious sense. With the present crisis in the Middle East I had better not state my reasons lest I encourage an incipient chauvinism!

The BBC, a year or so ago, gave Jewish scholars an opportunity to state their faith and say where it differs from Christianity. Their impact, it is said, was shattering.

Speaking of the BBC I am glad to hear they have made you so thrilling an offer. You will be working in a congenial atmosphere where your integrity will be respected. And, of course the professors will be ready to challenge your views at every turn. I don't think I can advise you here. You will enjoy academic life in the USA, I am sure. The opportunities for research are great. And the collision of ideas is fiercer than in the UK I think. Whichever you choose, you know you have my best wishes.

[…]

By the way, I have not yet received the Auto-bridge set you said Ernie and Jill were sending me, nor have I received the slop-pail that you said Clive would be sending. He has, however, bought me a charcoal grey pair of trousers which my wife took in for alterations.

Finally, Benjie, you are undoubtedly going to be quizzed about me. You knew me when I was a timid lecturer at the Wits in my early years. You knew the pressures to which I was subjected and you saw me react to them. You were, yourself, a struggling, frequently frustrated beginner on the Rand Daily Mail. I saw you react to the pressures to which you were subjected. In other words, I am not a superman and it will be your task, more than anybody else's, to keep my proportions true. On my side, too, I'll keep yours true.

A safe and pleasant journey, old man, and success attend your work.

Yours affectionately,
Bob

P.S. Thanks for your photo. You look executivish without a beard! Norma,[46] as an individual, I find most attractive. But I don't want you hurt any more. Bob.

---

46 Norma Kitson.

Robert Sobukwe
to Nell Marquard,
21 June 1967 (Bd2.5)

My dear Nell,

Just to say "thank you" for the books, your letter and your card. I have always enjoyed Thurber[47], perhaps because he laughs at himself so much. I once read that at a dinner held to honour him, he knocked his glass of wine over twice in succession and then stood up "to express his indignation at the untidy habits of the honourable member whose flimsy excuse is that he is blind." You never know whether to laugh or cry on such occasions.

Thanks for the Letters from the Parsonage. The author and her husband are very nice-looking, don't you think so?[48] None of that Victorian stiffness, hinted at slightly by Stephanus. The Dutch evoked pleasant memories. I think I'll have to take a course in High Dutch next year. I have always found those Zs irresistible. I'll comment on the contents at a later stage. At the moment I am merely enjoying the "unrevised" history.

I was amused by your reference to "meisie"[49] and rather sorry to receive your apology for the "mistake".

Now, Nell, you know as well as I do that you were being very indulgent to pretend to have heard a diphthong[50] in Mercy's pronunciation of her name. What you heard was [mɛsɪ] "messy". The phonemes /ɜ/ of "earth", /æ/ of "mat" and /ɛ/ of "met" all come out as /ɛ/ with the majority of Africans in South Africa. In Central Africa their difficulty is with diphthongs so that /eɪ/ in "cake" comes out as /ɛ/, /kɛk/ and gold comes out as /gɔld/.[51]

We don't have to apologize to each other for the amendments our people make to English. You'll remember my references to Western "syphilisation" (civilization). At Healdtown it was the accepted thing for fellows from

47 American humourist, novelist and playwright often celebrated for his wit.

48 *Letters* from a *Boer Parsonage* : *Letters* of Margaret *Marquard* during the *Boer* War, edited by Leo (Margaret's son) and published in 1967.

49 Afrikaans for "girl" or "young woman".

50 A diphthong is a sound made by the combination of two vowel sounds into a single syllable.

51 Sobukwe's evident love for, and skill in, linguistics is on display here in this rather technical digression on styles of pronunciation.

Basutoland (as it then was) to tell the girls "I laugh you" for "I love you". And then there is your Afrikaner's difficulty with the aspirates [t] and [p]. These are our "separate development" peculiarities!

You've heard that my wife and children will in future stay with me here when they come a-visiting – a bit of very welcome privacy and an occasion I look forward to very much.

My mother hasn't written yet, but I expect she'll do so soon.

Benjie is leaving the country, as you've no doubt read. He is tempted to join the staff of some university or other. I've told him there's a greater and fiercer collision of ideas in the USA than in Britain: but then, there are so much more casualties too.

I enjoyed Leo's introduction to the Parsonage letters, particularly his broad sweep over the Victorian era with Tennyson's freedom broadening from precedent to precedent.[52]

You know, I have found very often that when I read a book I invariably overlook what almost everybody else regards as important, and fasten on to some trivial nondescript fact. In Coleridge's "Ancient Mariner", for instance, I was unimpressed by the philosophy and the moral of the story. I picked these lines:

> The wild foam flew
> The furrow followed free
> We were the first that ever burst
> Into that silent sea

And I have carried those lines in my mind for over twenty years. Like Wordsworth:

> The music in any heart I bore
> Long after it was heard no more.[53]
> Don't worry: I am all right.

With best wishes.
Yours sincerely,
Robert

---

52 From Tennyson's poem "You Ask Me, Why".

53 From William Wordsworth's poem "The Solitary Reaper".

Robert Sobukwe
to Benjamin Pogrund,
28 June 1967 (Ba5.51)

My dear Benjie,

I am writing this letter on the eve of your court appearance.[54] It appears that you will be around for a quite a while, after all, as I assume that whatever the outcome the case will be taken on appeal. You know my feelings on the matter.

I wrote to you on the 5th June before I received your letter. Thank you for it and the fine shots of you and Jenny. She is a lovely little girl and I can understand your sorrow at having to leave her behind. And I think you look very fine without a beard – "executivish" is the term I used in my letter of the 5th.

You have been misled by imaginative reporters, I am afraid. Signal Hill is not visible from my quarters. And talking of imaginative reporters, when am I supposed to have made the application for an exit permit that the parliamentary reporter of the "Cape Argus" referred to when reporting the debate on my further detention? If I am not mistaken he attributes the question to Helen [Suzman]. I would have told you, of course, if I had made such an application.

Thank you for the overcoat: it is very fine indeed. When she was down here my sister-in-law had very uncomplimentary things to say about my old overcoat. It was unfashionably long she thought. I suppose I was influenced by our bearded friend from Alexandra Township.[55]

The chair, too, has arrived and it is very comfortable. But I couldn't take it to the tree outside. It belongs in a polished lounge.

You have a lot on your mind and I shouldn't like to bother you more. But I think you should know that the Radio has not arrived yet nor has the slop-pail that you said Clive [McBride] would be sending: and the exam papers, too, haven't arrived yet.

---

54 Pogrund had applied for an exit permit. The day before he was due to leave the country, two policemen served a court summons on him, thus putting an end to his hopes of leaving the country. Sobukwe is referring here to Pogrund's related court appearance.

55 Josias Madzunya.

Veronica told me about the bursaries you have arranged for deserving youngsters. I know you wouldn't expect me to thank you for that: I am proud, nonetheless.

She has also spent some time reading through your letters to me. She has become quite inquisitive.

Well Benjie, let this do for the moment. I am sorry you couldn't come to see me. It would have been quite an occasion. I can still see you stepping out of the car in 1964 when you suggested that I sit more in the sun – from which day dates my association with the tree outside!

Very best wishes old man.

Yours affectionately,
Bob

Robert Sobukwe
to Benjamin Pogrund,
18 July 1967 (Ba5.52)

My dear Benjie,

You will please overlook the fact that I am using a ball-point instead of the expensive fountain pen you sent me. I find that ball-points flatter my hand much more than a fountain pen does.

I have received the radio: a real beauty! It is cracked along one of the "legs". I am told it arrived in that condition. But the performance has not been affected in any way. And what a glorious performance it gives!

The cord was a five feet affair and I have had it lengthened by a further fifteen feet to enable me to have the radio in the kitchen where I do my studying in the evening.

I am glad you did not have the additional lead you had thought of arranging to enable me to play outside. This is a lovely set, Benjie, and I want it moved as little as possible. I am, therefore, keeping the battery-operated set for use outside. In fact, as a rule, I have the radio playing during the day only when I listen to sport commentaries. The chair and the radio belong in civilized surrounds – in a polished lounge, as I said in an earlier letter.

Thanks a lot old chap. And thanks for the books, also. You must have spent a pretty fortune on them. My shelves are bursting at the seams, so I'll have to ask that you don't send any more for the time being. When Veronica arrives we'll discuss the position and she will let you have her recommendations!

You amaze me, Benjie. Christianity originated in Europe, indeed! Don't you know that Jesus and all twelve of his disciples were Jews? In fact, except for Judas the Iscariot who came from the South, they were all Galileans. And the first thousands of converts were Jews. When Paul set out to proselytize the Gentiles the Christians were already established as one of the thousand and one sects which the disputatious Jews were throwing up. The Deep Sea Scrolls find a very strong affinity between Jesus and the Essenes.[56]

56 The Essenes were a sect of Second Temple Judaism who may have been the authors of the scrolls found in a cave near the Dead Sea in 1947.

I have been reading Stephen Neill's history of the Christian Church[57] – "red in tooth and claw",[58] bearing out Epstein's contention that Christianity, unlike Judaism,[59] has been spread by the sword and not by the pure strength of its message.

Well the Middle East War is over.[60] Already vicarious Israeli heroes are individually and severally telling us that lessons are to be drawn from the conflict. Unfortunately, the lessons are merely a rationalization of prejudices. I would have felt happier if Levi Eshkol[61] didn't have a Dayan[62] to put up with. As one correspondent has said, Dayan is no Churchill. I am afraid he is allowing the ululations of the vicarious heroes to go to his head. And yet the touch that is needed is the toning down of the humiliation under which the Arabs smart. Somebody has said a man will forgive you, after some time, for defrauding him or even taking his wife away from him, but no man will forget or forgive a humiliation. Eshkol has the personality and the ability, I think, to wash his enemies' wounds.

What are you doing for a living now? I believe at the time of your arrest you had resigned your position on the "Rand Daily Mail". I liked your replies in court.

It was very painful for me to read about Pat's death.[63] I hadn't known, you see, that he was ill. And now comes Kagan's death. He was my "personal physician", you know i.e. if I may use that pompous phrase.

Incidentally, I haven't received the Literary Supplement articles you said you were sending and the examination papers haven't arrived yet. However, there is still plenty of time.

---

57 Stephen Neill, *A History of Christian Missions* (1964).

58 From Tennyson, "In Memoriam": "Nature, red in tooth and claw".

59 We know from earlier letters that Sobukwe had received a copy of Isidore Epstein's book *Judaism* (1934) from Pogrund.

60 Sobukwe has in mind the Six-Day War between Egypt and Israel, 5–10 June 1967.

61 Levi Eshkol, Israeli politician who served as Israel's third Prime Minister between 1963 and his death in 1969. He led the Israeli government during the Six-Day War.

62 Moshe Dayan, Israeli military leader and politician, who was the Israeli Defence Minister during the Six-Day War with Egypt.

63 Patrick Duncan, a member of the PAC, had died of a blood disease in London earlier that year.

You remember I wrote you that somebody was sending me books from the U.S.A. Well I have just heard from his wife in Lusaka that AB [Ngcobo] has been arranging that. These are not the books from Lincoln University. They are a separate batch on African Prehistory.

I am waiting to hear how the party went off. By the way, in addition to the twenty nine books you sent, I received about five, including Koestler's latest: *The Act of Creation*. I was told these had been sent by Ernie. My thanks to him.

Well Benjie so much for now. Thanks for making Veronica's trip possible in May. I love and respect her more with each passing day. She is a mixture of vulnerability and toughness.

Love to Jenny. "Tell Ragesh ..."[64] Keep your head high, boy.

Yours affectionately,
Bob

---

64 See Sobukwe's letter to Pogrund of 1 June 1966.

Benjamin Pogrund
to Cultural Attaché,
British Embassy, Pretoria,
7 August 1967 (Ba5.54)

Dear Sir,

I enclose application forms, duly completed, by Mr Robert M. Sobukwe, c/o Officer Commanding, Robben Island Prison, Robben Island, via Cape Town, for Approval of Candidature for Part II of the B.Sc. Economics Examination at London University.

Also enclosed is my cheque for R26 in payment of the examination fees.

I am sending the application forms and cheque to you at the request of Mr Sobukwe.

Thanking you.

Yours faithfully,
BENJAMIN POGRUND

Robert Sobukwe
to Nell Marquard,
30 August 1967 (Bd2.6)

Dear Nell,

Thank you for your letter dated 27th July.

Before I reply to points raised in your letter, I should like to comment quite lightly on the Chinese "happening". I must confess I have been highly amused by the Chinese goings-on. I doubt if it has ever happened in the history of diplomacy that members of a foreign legation should attack the natives and their police with "bottles, sticks, bricks and dustbin lids".[65]

In these days when we have psychological "explanations" for all human behaviour it will no doubt be said that the Chinese have become frustrated and neurotic because of their sustained isolation to which American policy has subjected them. I am afraid I can't accept that view. I think the Chinese are deliberately flouting "accepted" international norms because they regard them as bourgeois. Their behaviour is on a national scale what the behaviour of the "jet set" is in the countries of Western Europe. One would have liked to compare them to the "flower people" but, unfortunately, they are very violent.

It is unfortunate, however, that those who claim to represent the proletariat should assume that the chief trait of that class is boorishness. It is

---

65 In August 1967 Chairman Mao's Cultural Revolution had reached its peak. Ostensibly "counter-revolutionary" elements were subjected to humiliating, violent and often murderous persecution. The Cultural Revolution had a somewhat bizarre effect on international diplomacy, as a June 1968 CIA intelligence report – tellingly entitled "Mao's Red Guard Diplomacy" – put it: "For several months during 1967 Communist China's diplomacy was characterized by an extraordinary degree of irrationality. In Peking, foreign embassies were violated and their personnel abused. Abroad, Chinese diplomatic personnel staged provocative demonstrations and went out of their way to insult host governments. The purpose was to bring the benefits and therapeutics of Communist China's "cultural revolution" to foreign policy and the foreign policy establishment. It was as though the Chinese, in their dealings with foreigners, were seized by a kind of madness; for a time Peking's usual non-diplomacy – or at best semi-diplomacy – gave way to outright anti-diplomacy" (CIA Intelligence report, 1968). Sobukwe is thus referring here to the Chinese "anti-diplomacy" mentioned above, particularly the seemingly unprecedented actions of Chinese diplomatic figures attacking the natives of the countries that hosted them.

very easy to mistake rudeness for honesty and forthrightness. It is said that at the conference with Germany when the treaty of Brest Litovsk was signed in 1918 Trotsky replied to the "diplomatic" speech of the German representative by observing that: "we are not friends: we haven't met here as friends. Let us not pretend that we have." That, I think, is forthright, but not rude. But when Khrushchev takes off his shoe and bangs the highly polished table at the U.N.O.[66] he was being boorish: and yet some papers saw in his behaviour the "naturalness" of the peasant.

I have always had a soft spot for Communists, though. Michael Stewart says they show an "imaginative disregard" for the truth. I should like to add that they have a poetic feel for language. Their abuse is in the grand style of Shelley's:

The herded wolves bold only to pursue
The obscene ravens clamorous o'er the dead.[67]

Incidentally, has it struck you that for over a year now the Red Guard have been abusing China's President but he is still untouched. In fact, from all reports, a civil war is raging in China between his supporters and those of Mao and yet no attempt has been made to arrest him. Well, so much for that.

Thank you for remembering Veronica's birthday. They'll be coming down in January. When she same down in May for the interview with the Minister she exhausted her unpaid leave.

D.P. Faure[68] does appear to have been a brave and courageous figure. It must be a tragic experience to be cast out of the bosom of one's church.

Unfortunately I did not know Prof Bruwer. I read about the invitations to his widow from K.K. & Dr. Banda.[69]

---

66 At a meeting of the UN General Assembly on 12 October 1960.

67 From Percy Shelley's poem "Adonais".

68 David Pieter Faure was the founding minister of the Free Protestant Church in Cape Town. He broke from the orthodoxy of the Dutch Reformed Church in the 1870s by publicly defending Darwinism. In referring to this history, Sobukwe is referring to reading material sent him by Marquard.

69 J.P. Bruwer died in March 1967 when the aircraft he was travelling in crashed under mysterious circumstances. At the time of his death Bruwer was the vice-rector of the University of Port Elizabeth and the acting chair of the Broederbond. Despite his membership in this nationalist Afrikaner organisation, Bruwer had started to speak out against apartheid for its policies of racial discrimination and had advocated closer ties

I have just finished reading two very interesting books: one is the book you sent me on Richard III. And I enjoyed it immensely. Isn't it frightening to realize that people will cling to a myth and reject ascertainable facts for generation after generation – Tonypandy![70] The other book is *Roots of Appeasement*, showing that appeasement was a policy deliberately and honourably pursued by British leaders like [David] Lloyd George, [Stanley] Baldwin and [Ramsay] MacDonald, before [Neville] Chamberlain. Even Churchill spoke strongly in favour of appeasement. What was wrong with it at Munich was that everybody knew it was ineffective. It was *acquiescence* then – not appeasement.

Oh yes, I like Thurber. And I like George Orwell also. I have read his *Story of an Animal Farm* and *1984*. They are both outstanding works. Animal Farm is a classic, I think. I read it with relish. Do you have any of [P.G.] Wodehouse's works? Malcolm Muggeridge's review in the "Sunday Times" reminded me of the pleasant hours I have spent with Wodehouse's stupid aristocrats and the matchless Jeeves.

"Ek hou van 'n man wat sy man kan staan".[71] Not much of that around is there now?

With good wishes to you both.

Yours sincerely,
Robert

P.S. I have not heard from Benjie at all. I hope he has received my letters. RM

---

with newly formed African states such as Zambia and Malawi. Sobukwe's mention of "K.K." refers to Kenneth Kaunda, first President of Zambia, and Dr Hastings Banda was the leader of Malawi at the time.

70 Perhaps a reference to the riots that broke out in this Welsh mining town in 1910–11. Winston Churchill, as Home Secretary, controversially intervened by sending in the army.

71 This is the first line of the poem "Trou" by Jan F.E. Celliers. It means "I like a man who can hold his own".

Benjamin Pogrund
to Robert Sobukwe,
31 August 1967 (Ba5.57)

My dear Bob,

My delay in writing has not been due to any lack of thinking about you; as always, you have been constantly in my thoughts – not in any mere academic way, but as part of my daily existence. I am sorry I have taken so long to write, but this has been a trying period, in which I have had to make both mental and physical adjustments of a far-reaching nature. The first you will understand. As regards the second, I had, of course, given up my flat and disposed of most of my furniture and it has taken quite a while to get myself comfortable again. Poor Norma [Kitson] has suffered most in all this, and has made heavy weather of it. Her life was being created against the expectation of my coming and now this has had to be indefinitely postponed. She and I now send tapes to each other, to supplement letters, and although this is a vastly-improved form of communications it is still not what we wanted …

Late in June, just before I was due to go, we all had a lovely afternoon together and I took some colour pictures. I am enclosing them – again with my deepest apologies for having taken so long to send them. I am enclosing three pictures for you. As you will see, the kids got on famously together. I thought that Miliswe photographed particularly beautifully. You were right: very much a Watusi maiden. The extra little boy in the pictures, by the way, is your sister-in-law's child.

I must confess also that I haven't seen Veronica for a while but we shall be getting together within the next couple of days. I have had extra prints of the pictures made for her.

The failure in the exam papers reaching you baffles me. I have written to Nana [Mahomo] several times about this. I am writing again as I am sure something has gone astray in the post. But could you please let me have the details again? I ask this because all my papers were sent off to London some time ago and I cannot refer to my records any longer.

Your letter of July 19 reached me safely, as did yours of June 28. In regard to the former, I am sorry that the radio reached you with a crack in one of the legs. The trouble is that I think it would be impossible to lay the blame at anyone's door: the shop would claim that it was sent off in perfect condition, the GPO would deny liability, etc. Anyway, as long as reception is not impaired, that is the important thing. I am glad that at long last the easy chair reached you and that it has proved comfortable. About your comment that the chair and radio belong to civilised surroundings such as a posh lounge: just a stray thought in my mind – *your* being there makes it a civilised surrounding.

Your plea that no further books be sent for the moment is noted – but I am anxious all the same that you might run out of reading matter. Shortly before your letter arrived I had sent off another carton of books by rail and I hope this has reached you safely. What happened was that I packed up all my books for shipping to London and in going through my library I put aside a mass of books which I thought might be good light reading for you. As always, some won't be to your taste, but I hope that others are giving you enjoyment. You will now know why my name is at the front of so many of the books! The literary papers were with the books.

In your letter you taxed me with having said that Christianity originated in Europe. I am talking from memory now, but I seem to recall that it was you who originally said this. No?

I am still on the paper, and in fact was given a generous increase in salary last month. The arrangement was that my resignation only took effect the moment that I was in the air. And, of course ... With one thing and another I am being kept very busy. In addition, I work on Sunday nights as night news editor, and on Fridays (when I have a day off) and again on Saturday nights I sub-edit at the Sunday Express (this is in a free-lance capacity).

I too was shocked at the report of Pat's death, as I also hadn't known that he was ill. I learned subsequently that it was as a result of that accident to his leg which he suffered in about 1952. Apparently he was given some new type of drug at the time and it wasn't known then that the drug, or rather prolonged use of it, induced cancer of the blood. I am told now that he had been ill for at least the last year or so but had shown signs recently of recovery. I wrote to Cynthia[72] to express my sympathy and I had a note from her.

I'll write again soon.

With great affection,

72 Patrick Duncan's widow.

Benjamin Pogrund
to Eulalie Stott,
31 August 1967 (Ba5.55)

My dear Eulalie,

A little while ago I had a letter from Bob advising that a new chair had reached him. I assume that you were responsible for this, and I write to express my deep appreciation.

In his letter, Bob said that the chair was extremely comfortable. He is so impressed by it that he refuses to take it outside as he maintains that it belongs to a polished lounge!

Thank you for once again giving help to Bob.

I hope you are keeping well.

Sincerely,

Benjamin Pogrund
to Robert Sobukwe,
12 September 1967 (Ba5.60)

My dearest Bob,

I saw Veronica earlier today, and am happy to be able to report that she is looking and keeping well. After conducting a strenuous cross-examination, I was satisfied that neither she nor the children lack for anything. And I can promise you that I subjected her to a host of questions!

Veronica told me that in response to a telegram from you recently she telegraphed R10 to you, which we hope was safely received. In case you are still short, I have, under separate cover, sent an additional R10 to the Officer Commanding with the request that it be put into your account. It is some time since I last sent you postage stamps and I thought that, among your other needs, you might wish to buy stamps from the post office on the Island. And if you need more cash, you will promise to let me know without delay?

I asked Veronica about your clothes position and she said that she thought that you were still all right. But will you let me know about this, Bob?

Ernie and Jill, as always, send their fond greetings. Ernie asks me to tell you that the books which you acknowledged in a recent letter (I think there was a Koestler book among them) were sent by him as a Xmas gift last year. Have they only recently reached you?

In my last letter (of August 31) I omitted to tell you about Jenny's first-ever school report. It was one which gave me a great deal of joy. It said her reading and number work were good, and on co-ordination it said: "Very good. Jennifer is artistic and creative in her work in this sphere."

The general comment was: "Jenny has made very good progress at school. She is a confident, capable and bright pupil." To which the principal added: "A very pleasing and encouraging report from a delightful little lady."

In fact, this has been my week for "nachas" (do you know the word? – it is a peculiarly Yiddishe phrase which means "joy" and is usually used to describe what parents derive from their children!). I had a verbal report yesterday from Jenny's school that, when the children have to write down their news of the day, Jenny writes more than anyone else – and when questioned by her teacher, she smilingly agreed that she wanted to be a journalist like her daddy (so the Government of 20 years hence had better watch out!). And I took her to her ballet class today and was delighted by the lovely things which the teacher told me about her – her intelligence, her independence, her charm and her good manners. So my chest is very much puffed out tonight …

How are the studies going? Are you still having difficulty in concentrating? I have, by the way, attended to your examination fees and entrance forms. But I haven't had a reply from the British Embassy – perhaps they have written direct to you? – and I had better phone them tomorrow to check that everything is in order.

There have been some hilarious stories going the rounds about the recent Israeli war. One of them tells of the Russian officer handing over a batch of new tanks to an Egyptian who asks why there are five reverse gears and no forward gears and, of course, getting the answer: "What do you need a forward gear for?" The latest variation on this is the tank with five reverse gears and one forward gear. And when questioned by an Egyptian about the need for a forward gear the Russian replies: "Well, what if you are attacked from the rear?" There is another one about Nasser[73] phoning Kosygin[74] and asking for 200 tanks and being told: "Look, if Eshkol wants tanks, let him phone me direct."

Sorry, Bob, for the display of chauvinism, but you know, whatever might happen politically now in the Middle East – whatever settlement is reached – the recent events have had a profound effect on Jewish behaviour. The 2,000 years of being quietly led to extermination are past. Today, among Jewish youth, there is almost anger – in fact, it is anger – at the six million who went without a fight to their deaths. The real original turning-point, I suppose, came with the uprising in the Warsaw ghetto (do you know the story?), and it has reached its climax in modern Israel and more particularly in the recent war.

Did I tell you that Jenny and I now go regularly to synagogue on Friday evenings? I think the main reason she goes is so that she can have a sip of the wine after the cantor has recited the blessing at the end of the service! But, in addition, I have for long been unhappy about my ignorance about my own religion, and now, with my rabbi's help, I am trying to get started on a proper study of it.

---

73 Gamal Abdel Nasser Hussein, second President of Egypt, resigned after Egypt's defeat by Israel in the Six-Day War of 1967.

74 Aleksei Nikolayevich Kosygin had been made the Soviet Premier in 1964.

Otherwise, life is very quiet, and I am afraid that this dull letter is a reflection of it.

Oh yes, one thing which I forgot: I spoke to Veronica about the possibility of you and her each having a small tape recorder and exchanging tapes every week or so. If you are interested in the idea, perhaps you could approach the authorities on the Island and find out if they would be willing to accept the idea. It would be simple to carry out as the machines are uncomplicated, and the tapes are sent through the post at little cost. Let me know about this will you?

All for now. I look forward to hearing from you soon, and as always, you are in my thoughts and in my prayers.

God bless you,

Affectionately,

Robert Sobukwe
to Benjamin Pogrund,
27 September 1967 (Ba5.62)

My dear Benjie,

It would appear that you did not receive my letter of the 5th June. In it I thanked you for the overcoat, commented on yours and Norma's relationship; recalled that I was a hesitant, timid lecturer and you a struggling, 'frequently frustrated" cub at the "Daily Mail" when we met. I remarked also that I did not wish to encourage an "incipient chauvinism". And that was before the Middle East war.

As you say, whatever the peace settlement, the war has had an immense impact on the Jewish people throughout the world. But, Benjie, you are an intellectual; and that imposes upon you the obligation not only to think but also to carry about with you an awareness of history.

You make the point which has been made frequently of late that the Jews of Europe had no excuse for allowing themselves to be led meekly to the slaughter: and that the resistance of the Warsaw Ghetto indicates the birth of a new spirit – the determination to assert Jewish manliness.

What you young fellows must remember is that the Jews that Hitler murdered were citizens of Nationalist Socialist Germany! A new Hitler with an equivalent military power could do the same thing today AND GET AWAY WITH IT!! Israel couldn't save them, nor could U.N.O. Why didn't they resist? Hardly a tenth of the population and facing the most efficient and scientific tyranny the world had ever produced!

And was the Warsaw Ghetto's resistance so unusual? It was remarkable, yes; but unusual? Jewish military strategy has always been suicidal in its recklessness, from the time of David to the Maccabees. As for resistance to the last man, woman and child you have the recent excavations at Herod's temple – I forget the name of the place – Harad or something.[75]

75 Sobukwe is evidently thinking of Masada here, the site of Herod the Great's fortified mountain-top palace, built between 37 and 31 BC and subsequently occupied by a group of Jewish rebels who opposed the Romans. When, as a result of the first Jewish-Roman War, Masada was besieged by the Roman army, 960 Jews committed suicide rather than surrender to the enemy.

Now for the point I made about peace. In the American Civil War, it is recorded that [Ulysses S.] Grant treated [Robert E.] Lee when he came to surrender, as though he were his superior officer. When he left the hall, Grant and his men saluted. Quite recently, in a boxing championship in Britain, the Scottish champion [Walter] McGowan was forced to retire because of a badly-cut eye. The defending champion, an Asian, who was defeating McGowan for the second time, went to McGowan's corner – and they say McGowan was in tears – and knelt before him. The grand gesture, Benjie!

A further illustration, Moshoeshoe I when attacked by the Zulus, inflicted a crushing defeat on them at Thaba Bosiu and, as they retreated, sent a large herd of cattle to "his brothers". The Zulus never again attacked him. He cut the English forces to ribbons in 1859 (?) while Warden, the British Commander, was in a state of bewilderment and humiliation, sued for peace![76] I am not saying Israel should be "magnanimous". If I were Nasser I would want no magnanimity from the Jews. All I am saying is that it is Eshkol and not Nasser who can afford a diplomatic rebuff, it is "adulations" that might go to Dayan's head, not "ululations". I love the sound of the latter, though!

It had been my intention in 1959 to have Egypt and the "Arab north" taxed with the direction of their loyalty.[77] Are they African or Arab? If they are Africans then the Middle East problem is not theirs except in so far as Egyptian territory is concerned. Algeria, Morocco and Tunis have no reason whatsoever to be involved. I have asked myself whether that would be my attitude regarding the Afro-Americans and the West Indians and I think I can honestly say "yes". As soon as Hitler saw himself as the guardian of Germans anywhere and everywhere he chose the path of war for he was bound to find it irksome that Germans *anywhere* should be under non-German rule.

Sorry for the lengthy sermon! Thank you for the letters and particularly for the children's photographs. They truly came out well. But you'll have to warn Veronica that unless she counts her calories she'll soon look like the female version of the Prime Minister of a neighbouring state![78]

---

76 Major Henry Warden, the British Resident of the Orange River Sovereignty, was defeated by Basotho forces at Viervoet in 1851.

77 Sobukwe has in mind the debates that occurred as part of the formation of the PAC, where the issue of who might be considered an African was of clear importance in establishing the remit of Pan Africanism.

78 A reference to Leabua Jonathan of Lesotho.

Both she and Miliswa wrote and told me about the party which they obviously enjoyed immensely. Miliswa wrote to me in English and begged that I allow her in future to write to me in English. Reading between the lines I gathered that "Ntate Benjie" was not pleased with the progress they were making in English. Times have changed, of course, and I do not offer it as an excuse, but believe me, she writes much better English than I did when I was in Standard IV. Admittedly I was much younger. I was eleven then.

It appears I will have to make it two letters once more. I still have a lot to say.

Thank you for the news about Jenny. You have every reason to be proud of her. In your photographs together she is, indeed, very much the "young lady". She has a relaxed, unaffected appearance.

With regard to books, I am afraid I have not received any books that bear your name. The twenty-nine books I acknowledged were straight from the booksellers – poetry and autobiography mostly. Continued in letter 2.

[Letter 2]
Mr. Benjamin Pogrund,

Regarding the question of clothing, Veronica has been rather remiss I fear. As I told you earlier, Clive [McBride] had sent me a grey pair of trousers. Because of my diminished "public opinion" (paunch), it required alterations particularly as regards length. I gave it to Veronica together with the khaki pair of trousers you sent and a grey pair which was to serve as a pattern. She left them with Clive she says; but I have not received them up to now and I haven't heard from Clive either. Incidentally, the slop pail hasn't arrived yet either.

Consequently, I shall need additional trousers. I intend sending you the brown pair as a model so that you may get me a similar brown and charcoal grey. The styling and material I leave to you.

The British Embassy have sent me a receipt for the exam fees: Thank you. Yes, I am still finding it difficult to concentrate; and I expect the trouble to get worse, not better. It is unavoidable in the circumstances, I think.[79]

79 Although it was not well understood at the time, a variety of cognitive impairments – such as difficulties in concentration – have now been shown to be the result of extended solitary confinement.

You seem to be having quite a busy time. I am glad, therefore, you were able to write to Mrs Duncan. Strange as it may sound, Pat was the first man, after PAC was formed, to accuse me of racialism! Came up to the Wits to tell me I was a racialist and he would fight me. I spent a whole afternoon trying to persuade him I was not a racist. He was very honest. I liked him.

Thank you for the R10.00 (Ten Rands). You see, I sent R25.00 (Twenty five Rands) to my mother in April to enable her to visit me here and paid about R18.00 (eighteen) for the newspapers "Cape Times", "Cape Argus" and "Sunday Times". So my funds were very low indeed. But I am all right now.

When Veronica comes we shall work out what quantities of washing powder, tooth paste, toothbrushes, blades etc. I use per year, so that these can be sent from outside to enable me to use my funds on edibles only.

I have been working, on and off, on some Xhosa short stories and poems and an unambitious English novelette. I read some of these to Veronica but dammit, she's puritan! I am sending you a free translation of one Xhosa poem I read out to her. She thought it was not quite "nice". I ask you! Later I'll send you a translation of one of the Xhosa stories and perhaps the first two chapters of my English work. Your comments, I need hardly say, will be appreciated. Here goes, then:–

They All Say So

I'm not going to keep quiet
I'm going to tell you what you are:
Oh you can beat me, to your heart's content.
You're very brave when it is women you face.

I've been holding my peace too long
I must speak or I'll burst.
The water in which
The midwife washed you at your birth,
Was a whore's water.

Don't promise me; hit me
Your scowl doesn't scare me this bit.
What's that? That's your mother!
Yes I say so; I say that's your mother.

I was a virgin, me, boy,
When I met you
"They all say so"?
I am not concerned
With what others say.
I ... What's that?
"My breasts had already fallen"?
I have a high bust, that's what I have.
But as for carnal knowledge of a man
That I acquired when I met you.
What is it you say? You're insulting me!
You are going to produce the woman
Who helped me procure abortions.
"It's my mother"? You say it's my mother
Who has removed my stomachs? (procured abortions)
Oh no you've gone too far today.
My father's house is intact, you know;
The roof does not leak.
What's that? "I shouldn't come back?
I shouldn't come back
Until my manners have improved?"
Sis! Look who's talking!
I beg your pardon? I don't hear:
Bah! That doesn't disturb me
You can collect all your whores
And accommodate them here;
But all this is mine
I am taking away with me.
You will lie on the bare ground
For you do not have a mat even;
O! Is that what you say!
"You're going to change us,
Trade us in like motor cars"?
I'm going to stay; just for that reason;
This gall that you have
I'm going to empty you of it!

There you are Benjie. The gall is what we would call cheek, I believe. As I say, Veronica was not impressed. This isn't typical of the poems I've written. I'll send you further samples. My weakness is I hate revising anything I have written.

I'll answer your question on religion later. But religion is part of a people's culture. With the Jews, their religion is, in fact, their history: their past, their present and their future. Divorced from your religion, you are divorced from the God of Israel.

With the very best wishes, Benjie. Love to Jenny and friends.

Affectionately,
Bob

Nana Mahomo,
105 Irving Street,
Cambridge, Mass., US,
to Benjamin Pogrund,
[1967] (Ba5.68)

Dear Ben

Please forgive my delay in answering your letter of January 27th. The truth of the matter is that the letter was redirected from London and has only now reached me.

I am completing arrangements to have a credit with the Economists' Bookshop against which we can just order any book for Bob. As soon as this arrangement has been completed you will be able to write direct to the bookshop, place the order against Bob's account and they will forward the book(s) direct to him. The credit shall be in the region of $100 in the first instance. I shall let you know when you can begin to operate this account. In the mean time I have ordered the book indicated in your letter.

I am here in the States for a period doing some work at MIT. I am still not certain how long I will be here. But you should be able to get me care the above address. I shall also notify you of any immediate changes in my future plans regarding my continued stay at MIT.

My warm regards to Bob.

I shall appreciate whatever news you can give regarding his state of health, etc.

Sincerely,
Nana [Mahomo]
Forgive the untidiness. I was trying to operate an electric typewriter!

Robert Sobukwe
to Benjamin Pogrund,
1 November 1967 (Ba5.63)

My dear Benjie,

It has struck me that in most of my letters to you I leave unanswered the questions you raise in your letters. I assure you it is not intentionally done.

First of all, as regards the exams I decided to do the course over five years instead of three. I have no difficulty in understanding the lectures. The difficulty lies in retaining the material, linking it up and systematizing it. It is primarily one of concentration then. I realize now that I could have done the course in three years and would not have been the worse for it. But to delay it would work to my disadvantage. I would get so bored I wouldn't be able to open a textbook. Mind you I have always hated exams even when I was doing exceptionally well in them.

The Examination Papers go back five years and cost 2/- a set. I do not know how I got the impression that the total cost will be £1 (one pound). However, packing and postage will have to be provided for. The papers are obtainable from:

University of London Publications Dept.,
1 Malet Street,
London, W.C. 1 and you must state *EXTERNAL* on your order.

Regarding the exchange of tapes with Zodwa[80] I would encourage the idea if it were somebody else. But she, who takes months to answer a letter, knowing that it would be weeks reaching me, would not be improved by a change in the medium of communication. The honest truth about Veronica is that she is undemonstrative by nature and upbringing. It must be hell for her to tell me that she loves me in letters she knows will be read by eyes other than mine. It is that knowledge that tempers my impatience and annoyance at her casual attitude to letters.

Clive [McBride] has sent the trousers, together with some articles of toiletry from his wife. However, I may still give the pair of trousers to Veronica

80 Veronica.

when she comes as I want to make sure I am reasonably "insured" before you leave the country. I have confidence in your tastes.

I have written to Veronica to ask her to bring one hard cheese and honey. And I wonder what typical Jewish dish you could prepare for me. It will form part of their provisions.

Incidentally, their meals for the fourteen days they'll be here will cost them R30.00 (thirty Rands) to the nearest round figure. I thought it would be best to have that sent to the O.C.[81] and have it done with. Whatever remains will be transferred to my account.

I find that I cannot translate the Xhosa stories I have here. In fact, I am sure that if I were to send you the original of the poem (free translation) I forwarded to you, Mrs Bernard Friedman[82] would render it into the most delightful English. She and I did a few Xhosa and Zulu poems together. Tell me if you want the Xhosa originals.

The English novelette has beautiful descriptive passages and I think its chief characteristic is the conveyance of smell. Its defect is that the story does not hang well together. I shall have to work longer and harder on that aspect. I am quite certain that you would love it, Benjie.

You have every reason to be proud of Jenny. As I said, she is quite unaffected – naturally gracious. But you will have to watch yourself, too, Benjie and make sure that while you are encouraging her to unfold and develop to her fullest, you do not rush her. She loves you very much and you can, therefore, lead her as far as you please. In this competitive world too many parents push and rush their children out of sheer competitiveness.

By the way, I have always wanted to ask, is Bob Connolly[83] still around? I wish you could send me his cartoons if he is still on the job. Did you say you had sent the articles from the Literary Supplement? I didn't receive them, if you did.

Finally, I am going to ask you to make arrangements for the circumcision of the boys – all three of them. At a later stage they will have to undergo, like me, the *rite de passage* of circumcision. But I shall feel happier if the surgical

---

81 Officer Commanding, Robben Island Jail.

82 Florence Louie Friedman was the wife of Dr Bernard Friedman, a Progressive Party MP. She was a noted translator of, among others, Bernard Vilakazi.

83 American born political cartoonist (1907-1981) who lived and worked in South Africa, and drew daily cartoons for the front and leader pages for the *Rand Daily Mail* for 40 years.

operation is done now while they are young, under hygienic conditions – unlike with me! You will have to override Veronica's objections. I am going to tell her I have given you those instructions.

Tell me, this one M. Pogrund who was robbed at Langa, is he any relation of yours? Love to Jenny.

Please don't send me any Christmas Card.

With best wishes.
Yours affectionately,
Bob

"D.M. Zwelonke",
statement,
[1967] (A2.618)

It was a *span* [team] of prisoners to which I was present in 1967 which was working on the sea-shore end of the Atlantic Ocean on Robben Island.[84] We were working not far from the house in which the Prof was house-arrested. It was a good moment for young members of the Pan Africanist Congress like myself. When the Prof heard the sound of our voices he came out of his room with the spade and the rake.

Immediately he appeared we simultaneously took our caps off our heads having not been told by anybody to do that. He first made signs such as clasping his hands together and we understood him to be urging us to unite, and crossed his arms on his chest and that meant to us that he would be happy if we remained united.

Matthew Mokoena[85] started saying in Xhosa:

"Xa kunje siye sikhumbule amazwi ka Horatius"

(When it is like this we remember the words of Horatius)

"Indodo ingafa kakuhle njanina"

(How can a man die better)[86]

Before Mokoena finished the stanza of that poem the Prof. responded saying in Xhosa

"Ewe"

(Yes)

It was remarkable because Xhosa wasn't the home language of Mr. Mokoena but because he came from Natalspruit in the cosmopolitan

---

84 Undated handwritten document by an unknown author, included among the Sobukwe correspondence for 1967. Pogrund (2015: 192) notes that a version of this account was published by an author writing under the pseudonym of D.M. Zwelonke in *The New African* magazine in London.

85 Matthew Mokoena, a former primary school teacher, had been chairman of a PAC branch outside Johannesburg.

86 From the poem "Horatius", written in 1842 by Thomas Babington Macaulay. These words were used by Benjamin Pogrund as the title of his 1990 biography of Sobukwe. Pogrund explains that the poem had taken on a particular symbolic value among PAC members on Robben Island, who used it in commemorations of fallen comrades.

Witwatersrand area, he didn't find it difficult to perfect his Xhosa on Robben Island. Many people from the rural areas of the Cape and some of whom were arrested working as migrant labourers in cities such as Cape Town made many Africans from Transvaal to learn Xhosa to be able to communicate with their fellow PAC [comrades] ... who were illiterate.[87]

87 For another account of PAC prisoners seeing Sobukwe on Robben Island, see Magomolo (2009: 140) who remembers that "as we marched past the cottage, about a hundred metres away ... Sobukwe would acknowledge us with his brilliant smile and the open hand salute ... Then he cheered us on ... by picking up sand and slowly pouring the sand back, from near his shoulder. This was the reinforcement of an idea. He was telling us ... that the land belonged to us and our struggle was, therefore, a legitimate one."

1968

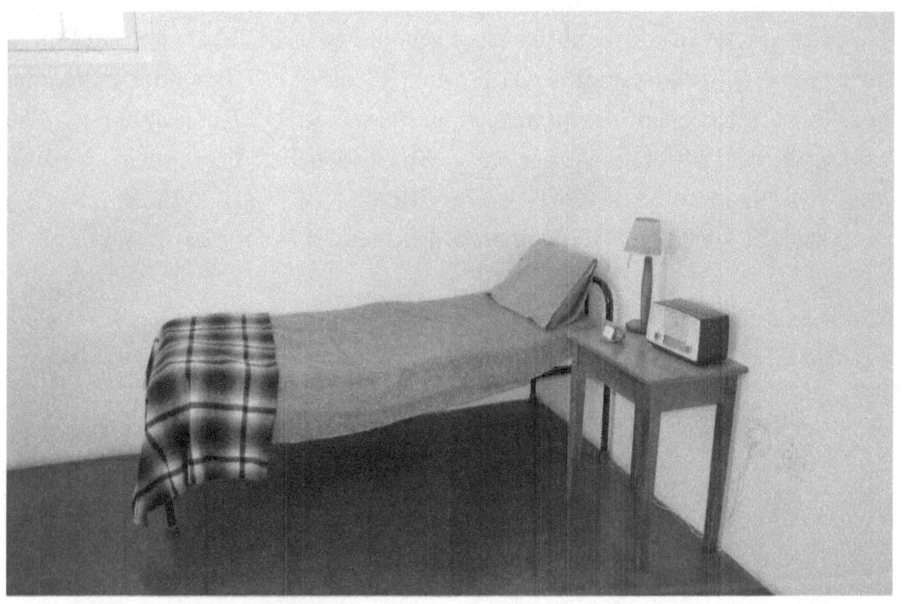

Sobukwe's bed and side table – with radio – as it appears today on Robben Island.

Veronica Sobukwe
to Benjamin Pogrund,
13 January 1968 (Ba6.1)

Dear Benjie,

I was extremely disappointed to have missed you at Cape Town station.

Bob asked me to thank you very much for the food parcel you sent him. He was in good health and happy to be surrounded by his family.

I have a pair of his trousers with me which he said should be handed over to you. I shall try to see you sometime next week.

I have received a final notice from school that I should always send them wire money. Miliswa's address: 11 St Mary's Hostel, P.O. Box 43, Leribe. The boarding fee has been increased to R56.00 a yr. School fees R8.00 a yr. The twins' address is: Mrs. E. Mokhele, P.O. Box 47, Leribe. I think their boarding fee is still the same, i.e. seventy-two rands each.

I shall be very grateful if you are able to send it as soon as you can.

Yours sincerely,
Veronica

Benjamin Pogrund
to Robert Sobukwe,
7 February 1968 (Ba6.2)

My dear Bob,

I have had a letter from Veronica telling me of your happiness in having your family with you. I am so glad that all the arrangements for the visit worked out, and that you had the opportunity of having Veronica and the children with you. Veronica and I hope to see each other within the next few days and I am looking forward then to receiving first-hand news of you. As you know, I did not see her at Cape Town station. I still do not know just what happened. I was there with Jenny, and also with Clive McBride and Eulalie Stott. We all reached there only a few minutes after the train had arrived, while the passengers were coming off the platform. But no Veronica. A bedding attendant on the train then told us that, although she had been booked, she had not been on the train. I was amazed to read in the paper the next morning that she had in fact arrived. Not knowing what to do, I did, however, deliver to the ferry boat that afternoon some of the food you had requested, and the warder there promised to put it into the fridge. I hope it reached you safely. As I recall, I sent you a polony, roll-mops, some cucumber (I think) and bread and chicken fat. I held back a cheese cake which I had bought as I couldn't be sure that it would get to you fresh.

Do you think Miliswa would like to write to me? I would love to hear from her regularly about her progress. It would also give her some exercise in writing English! I think that I will write to her and ask her to keep in touch with me, but it would be a good idea if you could also suggest it to her the next time you write to her.

About the parcel of books and magazines which I sent off to you in July last year. I wrote to the Railways and they have advised me that the carton was accepted at the Island in August, I think it was. I shall wait to see Veronica to check whether she knows whether you have it yet, otherwise I shall write to the Officer Commanding about the matter. While I think of it, late in December, at Veronica's request, I sent R30 to the Officer Commanding to cover the costs of the food for Veronica and the children during their stay with you: I hope that this was safely received and put into your account. I asked that any money left over after payment of the food should be left in your account for your use.

The recent past has been eventful for me. Norma[1] was granted a visa for five days late in December, and once she was here it was extended by a further three days. We were blissfully happy together, and were able to resolve many of the problems which had been outstanding between us. She is going ahead with a divorce, and it seems we might eventually get married when I leave here – eventually. But there is no certainty, obviously, about it because we just don't know what will happen in the future. But our present aim is marriage. I want the two of you to meet so much, Bob. I know that you would get on tremendously: her vitality, intelligence and her perception of people would appeal to you enormously, apart from her concern for people as individuals – almost an obsessional basis to her existence. One day, I hope …

Then, Jenny and I had two weeks together in Cape Town and had a superb holiday. We travelled back to Johannesburg on the Blue Train which was tremendous fun for both of us. Jenny was beside herself with joy about the train: it was a holiday all on its own for her. She did very well at school last year and now is in Grade II. All her subjects were "very good" last year. While in Cape Town we spoke constantly of Uncle Bob, and she was disappointed at not meeting Veronica and the children.

Incidentally, I was also in Cape Town for a brief visit early in December: the London Sunday Times sent me down to cover the Washkansky[2] heart transplant. While I was there on holiday the Blaiberg transplant was performed, and reluctant as I was to work on holiday, I felt it was too big to be ignored so I covered this one also. They were superb stories to report from the journalistic point of view: I have never, but never, had such cooperation from any people on a story. However much this is welcome, though, I think the Cape Town people have overdone it a bit, and at times it's become too much of a circus.

As you will have seen, my case is again postponed for three months. But at least I now report only once monthly, instead of weekly. I think, by the way, that the Cape Press reports, and I am thinking especially of the Cape Times,

---

1 Norma Kitson had emigrated to the UK on an "exit permit", which allowed her to leave the country without a passport but with immediate loss of South African citizenship.

2 Pogrund is referring here to the world's first human-to-human heart transplant performed at Groote Schuur hospital on Louis Washkansky by Dr Christian Barnard on 3 December 1967.

perhaps did not convey an altogether fair picture of the proceedings. Things are, in fact, going well and I am hopeful that the strain might end fairly soon.

Do you need any further study or reading books? Will you let me know? And I am looking to Veronica to tell me about any clothing or other needs of yours.

I haven't heard from you for some time. I do hope that you are well, and that you have not been too depressed in the aftermath of having had the family with you.

As always, Jill and Ernie send good wishes to you – and there is love for you from Jenny.

With much love,

Robert Sobukwe
to Benjamin Pogrund,
14 February 1968 (Bb8)

Dear Benjie,[3]

I've looked all over for your last letter but can't find it. I remember that Veronica read it as she read all your other letters to me. It's just possible that she put it in some other place. That's the price one has to pay for company.

Well, you no doubt have the full report by now. Thank you for everything. I was very pleasantly surprised to note that you had arranged for the circumcision of the boys so expeditiously. They were themselves very anxious to pass on that information to me.

They brought their toys along and before they left we played a little badminton, although I took the opportunity to introduce them to tennis. The car rally we didn't assemble. I didn't have any glue. But they have left their toys behind and when I have my exams behind me I'll have time to attend to such matters.

It was the first time I could talk to the children without feeling rushed and I found myself sharing your concern: they are almost completely inarticulate in English. [...] We played plenty of scrabble, though, and at least here I had the pleasure of seeing them use their heads.

Zodwa and I couldn't agree on the matter of their weight. I thought they were grossly overweight. She thought they were fine on the whole – just a little paunchy!

By the way, thank you for the paintings. They were most interesting. I have read the biography of Michelangelo and Lautrec and van Gogh. I had read bits about the others, too, Cezanne, Seurat and the others. And it was a real delight to have the work of all of them in front of me.

Ernie sent me a couple of expensive records but I haven't played them yet. And that brings me to a matter I wish to discuss with you.

---

3 Pogrund (2015) notes that this letter only reached him on 4 March – an indication that it had been held by the authorities for several weeks. Sobukwe's references to newspaper subscriptions made Pogrund aware that some previous letters (those of 23 November and 14 December 1967) had been seized.

Zodwa will have told you, perhaps (you will excuse me if I do not always refer to her as "Veronica". I call her and refer to her as Zodwa and that comes more naturally to me than Veronica which, incidentally, is what all her sisters call her!). She will have told you then, as I say, that I played a sample record to demonstrate that the Record Player is "busted". I had hoped she would take it along with her as I believe it can still be repaired, but she didn't want to carry too many things.

I have now received word that the heater, which, in my last letter to you, I told you was in for repairs, cannot be repaired. It appears a whole part of something will have to be replaced and the repairers apparently cannot get that part.

In my last letter I asked you to arrange that I get another heater. I had hoped this would be an *additional* heater, but it would appear now that it will have to be a substitute. In that letter, I had raised the question of subscriptions to the newspapers. I hope you received it – dated 23rd November, 1967.

While we are about it I think it would work out cheaper if, for such repairs, I could have either Clive or somebody else collect the article at the docks and take it to a shop of their choice and then send it back from the docks. Please let me know what you think about it.

Thanks for the cosher [*sic*] food. I'll comment on that in my next letter, when I'll also deal with the Israeli-Arab conflict. But I may as well say now that as I had had instructions I ate the bread first and found it absolutely delicious. But the fish! I finished it out of loyalty to you.

In my letter of the 14th Dec. I'd said I would prefer that Zodwa bring the heater with her rather than have it sent by post. I had hoped that this one here could be put right in a jiffy. But in the altered circumstances, I'll have to ask that the new one be sent as soon as possible.

There's a lot I should like to discuss but I'll leave it off for now. Again, thanks for everything. The reports I received concerning your skirt-world aren't particularly sublime, you know. Glad to know Bob Connolly is still around.

Love and best wishes to Jenny. Shalom.

Yours sincerely,
Bob.

I've long been wanting to inform you that "toothless bulldog" is a typically Fort Hare expression used to indicate that however brilliant the speech the means to effect it are lacking. It was used of the Native Representatives in Parliament – Mrs Ballinger[4] & Co. – they didn't command the votes! We ex-Fort Harians knew what Simbule[5] was talking about. Bob.

4 Margaret Ballinger (1894–1980) was elected to the all-white Parliament in 1938 as one of three "Native Representatives" to represent African people in the Cape Province after African voters there were removed from the common voters' roll. Politically aware people like Sobukwe scorned these MPs. The system was ended in 1960 and Ballinger lost her parliamentary seat. She was the first president of the Liberal Party when it was formed in 1953.

5 Soon after the Zambian politician and diplomat Ali Simbule was appointed as Zambia's High Commissioner in London in 1967, he gave a speech in which he called Britain a "humbled, toothless bulldog", causing outrage among the British.

Benjamin Pogrund
to Robert Sobukwe,
18 March 1968 (Ba6.6)

Dearest Bob,

I have delayed replying to your letter of February 14, which reached me on March 4, until I could have the chance of speaking to Veronica (and in my turn, forgive me for referring to her as Veronica – that's the way I met her and that's the way I know her!). This was necessary because it was only from your February 14 letter that I learned that your letters of November 23 and December 14, 1967, had not reached me. So I have had some difficulty working out what you need.

So let's deal with each point in turn, and see whether we can make rapid arrangements for you. Firstly, about the heater: I note that you say it cannot be repaired and I shall take steps to have it replaced. I see that you actually had been hoping for an additional heater, so let's see whether we can't arrange this too. I am working on the assumption that we have a few weeks in hand at least before the onset of cold weather and that we therefore have time to exchange letters on the subject. If this assumption is incorrect, can you please telegraph me immediately and I shall make emergency arrangements. Otherwise, if we have the time to debate it, tell me whether you especially want at least one fan heater (if I remember correctly, your existing heater is a fan type), or whether the bar heaters provide sufficient warmth. Depending on what you want, I shall arrange for either one fan heater and one 2-bar heater to be sent to you, or two 2-bar heaters. O.K.?

Second, about the record player. I suggest that immediately you receive this letter, you send the player to the Cape Town end of the ferry boat service and then, at the same time, telegraph Eulalie Stott (6 Bishopscourt Road, Newlands) to let her know that it is there. Meanwhile, I shall write to her to tell her about the arrangement. I am sure that she will be willing to have the player repaired and returned to you.

Thirdly, the newspaper subscriptions leave me flat-footed until I can hear from you as to what you need. I only hope that you have had enough money in your account in the meantime to maintain subscriptions and that you are still getting the papers. If necessary, I suggest that you telegraph me about this if it is an emergency situation.

Fourthly, when I saw Veronica the other day (and incidentally, she is well and spoke happily of the visit she and the children had had with you), she gave me a pair of your trousers. As requested, I shall purchase another two pairs for you, have them trimmed to the same size to fit your paunchless state and have them posted on to you. I hope to be attending to this within the next day or two.

My question, in my letter to you of February 7, about whether the money for the food was received was answered by Veronica, and I have also just received the cashed cheque from the authorities, so that's all right.

I have, by the way, today written to the Officer Commanding, to ask for his assistance in ensuring that your letters do reach me, and in cutting down the average three week delay between your writing of a letter and its posting. I have also taken up the matter of the carton of books which I sent you in July last year and which apparently has not reached you, from what I can work out. I do again suggest, Bob, that you send your letters by registered post to avoid possible mishaps in the post. And while I think of it, a few weeks ago I sent you a batch of Argosy magazines and I hope these arrived safely. And I haven't heard from you for a long, long while as to whether you need any more lighter reading matter. Will you please let me know?

Jenny was in a school play last week and played the part of Queen Esther. She was utterly delightful and somehow or other a picture of the event found its way into the Mail! I am enclosing a clipping for you. [...] Jenny [...] is as delightful and as lovely as ever. I am having her portrait done at present by a leading painter who is a good friend of mine [...].

I am in the thick of preparing to launch another major campaign for the Rand Bursary Fund. Last year we built up the fund from 60 scholars to a total of 746. This year the fund will have 1,000 scholars and is also giving 30 teacher loan bursaries to enable people with J.C. but no other qualification who are teaching to go and spend another two years studying. I have set a target of R50,000, and have set up a whole series of projects aimed at bringing in this money. The basis of the plan is to decentralise, and I have a set of project leaders who run their own shows. The trouble is that I have to supply all the material needed to get the groups going and I've been working until the early hours for weeks now to prepare the material. But it's worthwhile work. Actual budget for this year is about R22,500, but we need the extra amount for reserve to ensure that kids in the lower classes who get bursaries will be able to complete their matric. So from the tiny operation of a year ago, this has now mushroomed into an enormous project, and by this time next week, some 350 people will be actively engaged in it in one way or another.

Its *k*osher food – you wrote *c*osher. You disappoint me about the fish. Imagine a nice Jewish boy not liking rollmops! Actually, I took a bit of a chance on that bottled stuff. One day you will have to try the non-bottled variety and see if it is more to your taste. The only thing that can redeem you now is a prompt assurance from you that you did at least like the polony.

Norma is not at all well at present: poor girl, she is suffering heavily under the strain of waiting and just isn't able to stand up to it. She was in a bad way last week and I have just applied for permission to go to London for two weeks on compassionate grounds. I am waiting to hear if I succeed.

When do you write your exams? And are you able to swot properly for them?

As always, my thoughts are with you.

Affectionately,

Benjamin Pogrund to
Eulalie Stott,
26 March 1968 (Ba6.9)

My dear Eulalie,

Can I trouble you again on behalf of Bob? Two things are required: firstly, his record player is not working, and I have suggested to him that it should be sent to the docks in Cape Town to be collected for repair. Could you attend to this and let me know how much it costs? As two letters from Bob on the subject did not get to me, and his last one was much delayed by the authorities, in replying to him I have taken the liberty of telling him to telegraph you to let you know that the player will be at the docks. I hope you will not mind, but it hasn't been working for some time now.

Secondly, his fan heater which I provided in 1964 has packed up and he tells me that he has been advised that it cannot be repaired – so he has been told by people to whom it was sent for repair. Is it possible to purchase and to have delivered to him a new fan heater? He also needs a second heater, and in this case I would suggest a normal two-bar affair. If possible, is there someone in Cape Town who might foot the bill for these? I ask because funds here are very low at present. But if there isn't anyone, then please buy the heaters anyway and let me know the cost. With the sudden cold snap, I am terribly anxious about the cold he will be experiencing.

I hope you will not mind my asking for your help in these matters.

There is some hope that the Government will allow me to travel to London for two weeks, in which case I hope to fly off at the end of next week. If I hear from you before then about the costs, I shall naturally reply immediately. In any event, I don't know if you are in Cape Town at present, so could I beg you to acknowledge the receipt of this letter?

Hope you are well,

Best wishes,

Robert Sobukwe
to Nell Marquard,
27 March 1968 (Bd2.7)

My dear Nell,

I hope I don't owe you more than one letter. I allowed my correspondence to pile up during my wife's visit and I find now that I owe replies to a number of my friends.

Thank you for your letter of 26th February. I received both Wodehouse books. Thanks a lot. I enjoyed them immensely. I am sorry about the *S.A. Outlook* and *Optima*.[6] I had thought they were respectable journals. I used to read the Outlook as a student at Healdtown, over twenty years ago. It was very "Christian" then. I have never read Optima. I thought it was a "capitalist" journal of the Chamber of Mines. Thank you for Réalités.[7] I received only one copy – not two. However, I am grateful because the number that came through contained an article on Britain's attempt to enter the Common Market – a very valuable article to me.

It is an admission I am ashamed to make but do you know that I haven't read a single of Arnold Toynbee's[8] books. I have read *about* him and his works, but nothing *by* him.

You touch on a number of contemporary matters in your letter and I couldn't help thinking how, in a manner of speaking, events have overtaken your letter. There's the shake-up in Vietnam and the no-hold-barred political fight in the U.S.A. and then there's the rebellion against the establishment in Eastern Europe.[9] I cannot help feeling, though, that the American Central

---

6 *South African Outlook* was an ecumenical Christian journal first published in 1870 at the famous Presbyterian mission school of Lovedale College in the Eastern Cape. *Optima* was a glossy PR magazine produced by Anglo American Corporation.

7 This must be the US edition of the French magazine, a high-class, profusely illustrated monthly that dealt with French culture, society and politics.

8 Arnold J. Toynbee (1889–1975), British historian, philosopher of history and a leading expert in international affairs during the 1918–1950 period. He is most famous for his multi-volume *Study of History*.

9 A reference to the "Prague Spring" in Czechoslovakia in 1968 when the Communist Party under Alexander Dubček embarked on a process of liberalisation.

Intelligence Agency will be found to have had a very sticky finger in the pie with regard to Czechoslovakia and Poland. There seems to be a verligte-verkrampte[10] battle royal raging all over the world. There is no stability, either economic or political or social.

Will you please congratulate Leo for me on his election to the Presidency of the Institute?[11] I hope you enjoy your leisurely "tour" of the country.

It's been good to read about Dr Blaiberg's[12] operation and recovery, although there does seem to be a mad scramble by the scalpel-wielders to transplant everything in sight. One of them speaks seriously of transplanting teeth. Teeth! I ask you.

Do you think you could send me a 1968 calendar, please. I asked Clive McBride to send me one early this year but as I have had no word from him I can only assume that either he has not received my letter or his calendar has gone astray. Brother Albert[13] has tended to neglect his dept. Perhaps things will improve now that this new man is in.

Best wishes to both of you.

Yours sincerely,
Robert

P.S. I apologize for my categorical statement earlier that China's intransigence was not caused by her systematic violation. Her hatred for America and Russia is becoming frightening. Robert

---

10 These two terms have a particular frame of reference in South African politics of the mid-1960s: the two factions of the dominant National Party at the time. The (relatively) progressive group – the *verligtes* (enlightened ones) – were less tied to a strict or dogmatic version of apartheid than the more conservative *verkramptes* (reactionaries), who preferred to maintain a stronger Afrikaner nationalist position.

11 The South African Institute of Race Relations.

12 Dr Chris Barnard's second heart transplant recipient at Groote Schuur Hospital in Cape Town, and the third in the world. The operation was performed on 2 January 1968.

13 A reference to the arch-conservative Dr Albert Hertzog, who was replaced as Minister of Posts and Telecommunications in 1968.

Robert Sobukwe
to Benjamin Pogrund,
3 April 1968 (Bb9)

My dear Benjie,

I am always happy to receive a letter from you: probably because I can hear your voice behind the words. Thank you for yours of 18th March, then. I hope I shall have space to discuss some other matters after I have answered your queries.

First of all let me apologize for mis-spelling *kosher.* I realized this even before I had submitted the letter. But after I had attended to some other matters I could not remember what it was that I had wanted to correct. And my weakness as a writer is that I hate drafting and re-reading my material: I want it to be *spontaneous*! What fools we mortals are.

Right then: the heater. I should like at least one fan heater. Veronica – I am an obliging fellow, you see – is a compulsive window-closer and when she was here in June last year she was delighted with the fan-heater because it kept the air fresh. Will you make the cord fifteen feet long and the cord-grip a 5 amp 250 volts three-pronged one, please.

In my letter of 23rd November I had said I didn't want to make more calls on your pocket, particularly at that time of the year when heavy demands were being made on your purse. I shall have to space my "requisitions" over the year in future. So it will be one fan-heater and one 2-bar.

Thanks for writing to Mrs Stott about the Record-player. I shall send it to her towards the end of the month. If I have it now it might tempt me away from my studies. And to answer your question while I'm about it, I'll be writing in May. I don't know the date yet. I don't think I'm good at swotting any more. There's something in me that hates having to acquire knowledge for an exam! But I hope I'll be able to collect what we termed "madoda score"[14] at Fort Hare, which entitles one to travel the class frequented by the *mobus vulgus.*[15]

About the newspaper subscriptions. The "Cape Times" expires on 17th May and the "Argus" on the 8th May. I have renewed the "Sunday Times"

---

14 That is, 50 per cent.

15 Sobukwe may have the Latin phrase *mobile vulgus* in mind here, which can be translated as "the fickle crowd".

but was able to do so for a six-month period only. This subscription expires on the 8th September.

The clothes: Thanks for attending to the trousers. When I didn't hear from you I wrote to Ernie and asked him, among other things, to request you to include warm underwear in the clothes parcel you'll be sending down. I asked that they be as far removed from white as possible (no prejudice!) and that you get me trunks instead of briefs (size 38 trunks: vests 40). I should also like a shirt to go with the charcoal – the type worn above the trousers: and a pair of black shoes. It will be quite an order as you can see.

I shall have this letter registered, Benjie, but I doubt if I can do so with all my letters to you. It would drain my resources. At the moment I have exactly 1.45 cents (one Rand forty five cents) to my credit. In fact I had suggested in one of my letters that the washing powders, blades for shaving and scouring powders be sent from outside so that any allowance can be used exclusively for luxuries like cheese, peanuts and sweets etc. The quantities required for a year you can work out with Veronica. Yes I do my own washing and ironing.

I received eight copies of the Argosy and read through them in a couple of days. Enjoyed them immensely, thank you. When I have the exams behind me I'll need cartons of light matter. I'll want some Hemingways, too. I have read only his *For Whom the Bell Tolls*.

Thank you for Jenny's picture. I tend to forget that she is only six. I am looking forward to the day when I shall meet her.

I won't comment on the Bursary Fund. Thanks for the work.

Sorry about Norma. I hope she recovers and I hope you get permission to go to London to see her. At times I feel absolutely annoyed – I won't say "frustrated", I hate the term: reminds me too much of the psychologist's rats – that I can't say to you the things I should like to say. And they are so many.

So Johnson has withdrawn from the race.[16] I'm sorry about that: particularly as it is only now that he thinks of playing the role which the whole world thought he was singularly cut out for, at the time of his election. I have always had the feeling that he was acting out of character on the Vietnam issue.

With Kennedy I am rather disgusted. His behaviour smacks too much of opportunism, calculating, ruthless opportunism. I am always ready to forgive

16 The 1968 US presidential election was fought between Richard Nixon and Hubert Humphrey.

a mistake, however serious, if the intention was good. Johnson's blunders I can, therefore, understand and forgive. But I hate the statistics-watching "hero". I really wish McCarthy beats him.[17] McCarthy had the guts at least to challenge Johnson when nobody thought it could be done. I'll take up the Israeli–Arab issue later. But if you have any influence you'd better warn Dayan. He'll be seeking to talk genuine peace when Arab humiliation has rendered such a prospect impossible.

Love to Jenny.

Yours affectionately,
Bob

P.S. I haven't written to Miliswa yet. Not one of them, Veronica included, has written to say how they have fared on their journey back home. Natives!!

P.P.S. The fruit arrives regularly. Thanks to Mrs Henderson.

---

17 Eugene McCarthy (1916–2005) launched his presidential campaign in 1967, hoping to win the Democratic Party's nomination for President of the United States, after Lyndon Johnson had announced he would not stand for re-election. He proposed a swift end to the Vietnam War and a withdrawal of US troops from the region. Although he won the popular vote at the Democratic Convention, he lost to Hubert Humphrey.

Veronica Sobukwe
to Benjamin Pogrund,
4 April 1968 (Ba6.14)

My dear Benjie,

This is just a note to let you know that you have paid Miliswa's school-fees for the whole year.

Should I pay the remaining R6.80 or have you found the owing slip and paid for it?

I have not received any letter from Bob. He is writing his final examination in May.

I shall make arrangements to see you after the Easter holidays.

With best wishes,
Sincerely
Veronica

Benjamin Pogrund
to Eulalie Stott,
4 April 1968 (Ba6.15)

My dear Eulalie,

Many thanks for your letter: your willingness to help is much appreciated. The fan-type heater is as you describe it, except that the reason I think it is preferable to a bar heater is that it warms a room so much quicker. Will you let me know if you require any cash from me for the two heaters?

I wonder whether I may raise a more general point with you. As you know, my time here is limited: either we shall soon be going on trial with a jail sentence likely to follow, or else I shall be leaving the country. In either event, I am most anxious to have secure arrangements for looking after Bob's interests – and I wonder whether you would be willing to take over the supervisory work?

What is involved? Well, you will have some idea from what I have told you when I have seen you, and also from my intermittent requests to you. It's basically a matter of keeping Bob supplied with his various needs, including clothing, stamps, chair, radio, etc, and keeping in touch with his family. Financing will be O.K. as I shall ensure that there is no lack of it, and will remit money whenever necessary.

I have naturally discussed the matter with Mrs Sobukwe, and would like you to know that she would be as delighted as I would be if you were to agree to look after Bob's interests.

To be frank, I just cannot say if there are any risks involved in it. I have been doing this for quite a few years now, and certainly have not experienced any difficulties that I am aware of as a result of it. But then I have been having so many other difficulties that perhaps any arising out of this have simply been obscured! I would, however, say that I continue to correspond with the authorities on the Island about various matters and no troubles occur here either, except of course, their red tape and so on.

Will you think about it and let me know?

All good wishes to you,

Sincerely,

Benjamin Pogrund
to Robert Sobukwe,
6 April 1968 (Ba6.16)

Dearest Bob,

Knowing that you are to write your exams next month, I am terribly concerned with the fact that you have not received any back copies of exam papers which you requested months ago. I have written to Nana [Mahomo] about it several times, and I just do not know what has happened as I have never had a reply from him, and perhaps he has moved from the address which I have for him. In a letter of mine to you dated November 27, 1967, I asked you to let me have the details again of the papers you needed, but I have never received any answering letter from you on this point. Perhaps your reply was contained in one or other of the two letters from you which failed to reach me.*

Incidentally, on this issue, I told you in my letter of March 18 that I had written to the Officer Commanding about the non-arrival of letters, the delay in letters and the non-delivery of books. He has now advised me that "the matter will receive the necessary attention".

Eulalie has written to tell me that she will be glad to attend to the repair of your record player, and she awaits word from you, by telegram or letter, that it is at the docks ferry for her. Also, she is attending to the supply of two heaters for you, and I trust that by the time you read this, they will have reached you. I asked her to be good enough to arrange for a fan and a bar heater. Will you let me know if these are enough for your needs? The two new pairs of trousers, together with your old pair, should be in the post to you during the coming week, and I hope that the tailor will have made a satisfactory job of adjusting them for your girth.

I have been glancing through our correspondence over recent months, and there are a number of points which I want to raise. I want to start by attacking you: months ago I asked you to see about having a complete medical check-up, from head to foot. I am sure the authorities would cooperate in this. You ignored me! Will you please let me know about this?

I have been thinking about the question of the standard of the children's English, and wondering what we could do about it. I have today written to Miliswa's hostel teacher to ask whether she has anyone in mind who could give Miliswa – and perhaps the boys also – conversational classes. As I think you found, her grammar, etc is fine, but she badly needs practice in speaking and getting the feel of the language. I thought also that when they again visit you in June, it might be a good idea if you were to try to spend an hour or so each day getting them to read aloud and to practise speech. I know it won't add up to a great deal of time, but it would help. And regarding the boys' arithmetic, which you believe to be not too good, shouldn't they perhaps bring their school-books with them to you, and you can check over their work with them and try to give them some guidance? And if you have any other ideas of what I could do from up here, I would be glad to have them and to act on them.

In my letter of March 18, I told you that Norma had been ill and that I hoped to go to her for two weeks. I was given to understand that I would obtain a passport and I had an air booking for last night. At the start of the week, my passport application was refused. It was a heavy blow as I have been beset by anxiety about Norma. So I have had to use the telephone instead, and have probably spent about R90 in the past three weeks. She is somewhat better at present, but I fear for her. She lives under extraordinarily great strains.

Some while ago you sent me a translation of one of your poems. I appreciated Veronica's remark of "not nice"! Now, don't misunderstand me – I am no prude – I was merely looking at it through her eyes! At the time, you spoke of sending further poems in Xhosa which Mrs Friedman could translate. Well, where are they? And where is the English novelette which you promised to send?

I have niggling worries in my mind about our discussion last year about religion. I asked you one question which you have not yet answered: what about the many, many Africans – and other non-Europeans (in the non-South African use of the term) who have a profound and sincere acceptance of Christianity? What of the R.C. Archbishop of Maseru who is an African, the Sinhalese Anglican Bishop, etc? Where do they fit into the view of Christianity as a religion of Europe only? They cannot simply be dismissed as "stooges" or anything like that. These are intelligent, believing and devout men. Also, I do not have all your letters with me any longer, but there is confusion in my mind as to whether you reject Christianity as such or the entire concept of G-d. Will you elaborate? And why should you show a preference for Judaism, as you say you do?

Also, in about June last year, I sent you a Press report of a speech made by the Rev. C.F.B. Naudé. Did you receive it? – and if so, what did you think about it?

One other point: has that auto bridge set reached you yet?

After my recent correspondence with the O.C., I am hopeful that there will be a quicker turn-round of letters, which should be of great help. I hope it will be so.

Bob, May is nearly upon us. Throughout the year you are in my prayers, but never more so than at this time. I pray for your speedy release, for you, Veronica and the children to continue to have strength, to have the courage you have shown for all these long years.[18]

God bless you,
With much affection,

P.S. *As time is pressing for your exams why not write per airmail direct to London for the papers, and ask them to ship them by airmail to you? I am today sending off R10 to the O.C. to be deposited to your account.

---

18 Reflecting on this letter, Pogrund (2015: 181) comments that he was "anguished about [Sobukwe's] ... absence of hope". Sobukwe had now been on the Island for six years and "it was clear ... that he had no illusions and no hopes: he accepted that he was to be in jail indefinitely".

Benjamin Pogrund
to Sister Stephanie,
St Mary's Hostel,
Leribe, Basutoland,
6 April 1968 (Ba6.17)

Dear Sister Stephanie,

Enclosed please find my cheque for R6.85 (including exchange) for school books for Miliswa Sobukwe.

I am sorry to have taken so long to send this to you: it has been an oversight on my part.

With best wishes,
Yours sincerely,
BENJAMIN POGRUND

P.S. Both Mr Sobukwe and I are concerned about Miliswa's apparent lack of ease in speaking English, and I wonder whether you can perhaps give us some advice as to whether anything can be done about it. If it is at all possible to arrange for her to have conversational classes I would be happy to pay whatever was necessary. In fact, the same problem occurs with her brothers who are at school nearby, and I wonder whether any suitable arrangements can be made to assist all of them? I hope that you would not mind my approaching you about this.

Robert Sobukwe
to Benjamin Pogrund,
24 April 1968 (Bb10)

My dear Benjie,

You will no doubt have received my letter by now and will have, consequently, realized how true it is that "great minds think alike". Your style is becoming progressively relaxed and I am getting to enjoy your letters not only for their contents, as in the past, but also for the aesthetic arrangement of words. Keep it up.

It really appears as though you are determined to make it quite clear that you are no admirer of the "Black Power" cult. I have received the clothes – three trousers, three vests, three shirts and three hankies. As usual and as was to be expected your choice was faultless and with one or two exceptions met with my unqualified approval. I loved the trousers and thought them attractive in colour and style. I couldn't have made a better choice. However I did not fail to note that you went as far from charcoal as you could! We'll accuse you of racism if you don't look out.

You anticipated my request for vests and chose just the style I've been wanting for years. In any letter to Ernie I had made the size 40 but I think you were wise to stick to 42 which is my size after all.

A Mrs Russell of Parkhurst expressed a desire to meet Veronica. Her daughter, who is now a missionary's wife in Zululand, was a student of mine. Incidentally, her name is Jennifer. I advised her to contact you as you are the only one that can arrange a meeting. Prof Wellington, too, has been wanting to know what help he can give with regard to the annual visits. I told him you've been arranging these trips since 1963 and he should approach you for information. In any event I don't think Veronica will agree to meet him except in your company.

I replied to your letter of November 27 1967 and I gave you the details of the exam papers. In addition I asked you for an article by Douglas Jay on the Common Market[19] and a pamphlet on the British Department of Economic

19 The Labour Party politician Douglas Jay, an opponent of Britain's entry to the European Common Market, was to publish the book *After the Common Market: A Better Alternative for Britain* in 1968.

Affairs. You didn't receive the letter, obviously. It's too late to do anything about all this now, Benjie. I'll just have to prepare all round and not try to anticipate questions. I think I should be able to scrape through.

Regarding the children's English I can do no better than adopt your suggestions. I received a letter from Miliswa this afternoon. She's so careless about spelling, tenses and punctuation. [...] Thanks for writing to her teacher.

Sorry to hear that Norma's condition has not improved. I had really hoped they would permit you to go and see her: or do they fear you'll jump bail? After all you have a case pending, remember.

I have not worked on the Xhosa poems lately. I have been promising myself that once I have these exams behind me I am going to work on these poems and the novel as well as on Dutch and Swahili. I read the first chapter to Veronica and she appeared interested. I then asked her to read, as I felt that, reading the stuff myself, I might be enveloping it with my own enthusiasm which a disinterested reader might not feel. She said the writing was illegible – probably correctly – but that was the end of that venture. The story is quite simple: but I feel it could develop into something compelling if one could discuss it with knowledgeable people.

Briefly: on the question of religion. My faith in God remains unshaken, Benjie. At the moment I don't care to know what he is like and where he resides. It is enough to know that He is and that His will will triumph.

It is not Judaism that I show a preference for, Benjie. It is the uncluttered God of the Old Testament – of Moses and Joshua and Isaiah and all the prophets – that appeals so strongly to me. It is Moses I think, who says: "Blessed are you, O Israel. What people are like you whom God has chosen for His own?" With such a faith, Benjie, one could go through Dachau and Belsen with a song on one's lips. The chief contribution of Christianity has been to assure the whole world that the promises made to Israel apply to all who confess Christ as their Lord.

Intelligence has nothing to do with faith, Benjie. Just the other day I was reading how Fortescue,[20] a fifteenth-century Chief Justice boasted that "there were more men hanged in England in a year for robbery and manslaughter than there be hanged in France for such manner of crime in seven years. There is no man hanged in Scotland in seven years together for robbery. But

---

20 John Fortescue (1394–1479) was Chief Justice of the King's Bench.

the Englishman is of another courage".[21] Men accept the norms of their time, by and large. You just read what the 19th century British industrialists said of their men. And how many professors of religion supported Hitler?

Finally, what is it, Benjie, that people believe in? To most people God is a talisman: an additional spirit. In Ghana, for instance, many Christians worship their own fetishes as well. I have read the Koran through and through, and I can't see what it is that Muslims find in it to give comfort or spiritual enlightenment. And yet they worship their Allah fanatically. In the Christian religion I think that my difficulty is that Christ is hidden behind the pretensions, superstitions and arrogance of Western Europe. By himself, alone, he is as lovable as Isaiah. But the claims made on his behalf by Western theology are unscientific. I don't even mean the mystical claims. I mean the purely historical. To say he was the one and only perfect man is purely unhistorical.

> Full many a flower is born to blush unseen
> And waste its sweetness on the desert air.[22]
> He is the only one about whom the West has a record. That's the most that can be said.

The Christians of African and Asia are not stooges, Benjie, I agree. But usually we speak of them as Westernized, to indicate that we associate Christianity with the West. But these are matters best discussed in a person to person situation, not by post over vast distances.

I received the article by Rev. Beyers Naudé. I'll comment on it later. The auto-bridge set has not reached me yet. Thanks for good wishes.

My love to Jenny. Greetings to friends,

Yours affectionately,
Bob

The turtle-neck shirt is a bit mod, don't you think? You can't modernize me forcibly, you know! Thanks. That's the only article on which I have reservations. Bob.

---

21 A quotation from Fortescue's *On the Laws and Governance of England*.

22 From Thomas Gray's "Elegy Written in a Country Churchyard".

List of books posted
by Benjamin Pogrund
to Robert Sobukwe,
15 May 1968 (Ba6.28)

Snow: The new men
Maugham: The painted veil
[Evelyn] Waugh: Put out more flags
[Max] Beerbohm: Seven men
[John] Steinbeck: The pearl
[Saul] Bellow: The adventures of Augie March
[John] Le Carré: The looking-glass war
[Romain] Gary: The roots of heaven
[James] Joyce: Dubliners
[Edgar Allan] Poe: Great tales
Huxley: Those barren leaves
[F. Scott] Fitzgerald: The last tycoon
[John] Masefield: Sard Harker
[D.H.] Lawrence: Kangaroo
[Oscar] Wilde: A picture of Dorian Gray
[Jean] Cocteau: Les Enfants Terrible
[John] Steinbeck: Of mice and men
Aristophanes: The frogs
Sinclair Lewis: Cass Timberlane
[Margot] Heinemann: The adventurers
[Margaret] Drummond: Thursday's Child
Dylan Thomas: Portrait of the artist as a young dog
[George] Orwell: The road to Wigan pier
[G.B.] Shaw: The Black girl in search of God
[Thomas] Hardy: The return of the native
Ovid: Metamorphoses
[James] Michener: Hawaii

Robert Sobukwe
to Nell Marquard,
5 June 1968 (Bd2.8)

My dear Nell,

Thank you for your letter of 21st April which I received early in May – on the 6th to be precise. Thank you also for the calendars, both the maxi and the mini – and also for Realités – one copy.

I had hoped to answer your letter almost immediately: but I decided to wait until I had written my exams. These started on May 17th and ended on the 28th. I wrote eight three-hour papers, six of them in three days, morning and afternoon. Makes you wonder what is being examined. I was absolutely mentally exhausted when I wrote and I am grateful the examiners did not concentrate exclusively on the type of question that requires regurgitation. The papers were very fair and if I had been a student at Varsity I'd have thought I'd done badly if I'd failed to obtain a First Class. Under the circumstances, as I wrote to Benjie, I can hope for no more than a proletarian pass. I am glad, however, that all this is behind me.

In his book, *My Glorious Brothers,* Howard Fast makes the Maccabee say: "Go through the land, Rabbi, and see how the people live". Your letter gave me just that sort of feeling – a kind of "Rural Ride",[23] noticing how green this side of the river bank was and how barren and dry the other side. Thanks a lot.

I am glad you liked Lesotho. I am emotionally involved in that country. I do not know the Mohapeloas, though I have heard a great deal about them. But I do know Prof Stuart[24] and am grateful to you for news of him. He was the English lecturer at Fort Hare when I was there and his classes were most delightful.

In your letter you commented on the assassination of Martin Luther King. As I am writing this letter, the Radio programme is being frequently interrupted by news flashes on the condition of Robert Kennedy.[25] The first temptation is to say American society is sick. But I think the reason is the vastness of their

---

23 *Rural Rides* was written by the English political reformer and journalist William Cobbett and published in 1830.

24 Donald Stuart had been Professor of English at Fort Hare and a friend of Monica Wilson.

25 Robert Kennedy had been mortally wounded in a hotel in Los Angeles by an assassin on 5 June, and died the following day.

communications system. Not only do you read about the doings of a particular character in morning, afternoon and evening papers, but you hear his voice over the radio and see his face on television. You can't escape him. It is all right for those who approve of him; they are grateful. But those who hate him are driven to despair. They feel he is hogging the limelight. And the common man, today, is very status-conscious. He wants to share the limelight.

The advantage that Britain has is that no politician there can ever be a pop idol. There are too many of the organs of mass communication ready to cut him down to size. Or should one make an exception of Enoch Powell?[26]

You do have a way of putting things, Nell. You say Britain is the most civilized country … "and that in spite of her restricting the entry of Kenya Indians." I laughed when I read that. It's such a gentle rebuke! But aren't we being unfair to Britain. She has enormous economic difficulties. And this is not a steady immigration flow: it is a flood. And contrary to economic laws it is not moving towards an area of economic expansion. The *timing* has been bad. The workers feel very insecure with over 500,000 already unemployed. Unfortunately the immigrants happened to have a high melanin content and in our colour-sensitive world this fact was over-emphasized.

I've not been making use of the library service for a considerable time now. It is a frustrating experience. However, I have enough reading matter. I have just finished A.J.P. Taylor's work on German history[27] – a brilliant piece of analysis, heavily spiced with anti-German prejudice. I have started on Mayakovsky's poetry – a mammoth volume. No I wouldn't say I was a reader of Joseph Conrad, though I have read two or three of his works, including Something *Jim*[28] which I enjoyed. I haven't read the book you mention.

Yes the student demonstrations are very interesting.[29] They defy an easy and undemanding leftist–rightist classification, since they are equally violent and determined on either side of the iron curtain.

---

26 Enoch Powell (1912–98) was a British politician, Classical scholar and soldier most famous for his notorious "Rivers of Blood" speech, delivered on 20 April 1968. The speech, widely attacked as blatantly racist, opposed anti-discrimination legislation and voiced strong opposition to mass immigration into the United Kingdom.

27 A.J.P. Taylor, *The Course of German History* (1945).

28 Joseph Conrad, *Lord Jim* (1900).

29 A reference to the 1968 protests, a worldwide series of social conflicts characterised by popular uprisings against military and bureaucratic state control. In the United States,

It was with pride that I read of the Liberal Party's decision to disband. To have argued, in the circumstances, as liberals have tended to do throughout the years, that "half a loaf is better than no bread" would have been tragically despicable.[30]

Mercy hopes to come a-visiting again early next year. I have to give them a suitable month. I'll make it April or May. I am expecting the children this month. It will be lovely to have them around.

With best wishes to both of you.
Yours sincerely,
Robert

---

these protests were typically focused on the Vietnam War – and the struggles of the Civil Right Movement – and gave rise to revolutionary movements like the Black Panther Party. In France, in the May of that year, students joined with millions of striking workers in a movement which threatened to topple the government. In many capitalist countries, socialist movements gained momentum along with angry opposition to state repression, colonisation and authoritarian rule. In Eastern Europe, there were widespread protests against the lack of freedom of speech and the violation of civil rights by Communist bureaucratic governments.

30 The Liberal Party disbanded because of the impending passing of the Prevention of Political Interference Act in 1968, which outlawed multiracial parties. Sobukwe's reference to feeling pride at the party's decision to disband might, initially, seem somewhat puzzling. His political stance – like that of the Black Consciousness movement to follow – was to be suspicious of the influence of white liberals (see his political speeches in Karis & Gerhart, 2013). It was invariably the case, for Sobukwe, that such liberals stood in the way of a genuinely Africanist agenda. For many within the PAC, an Africanist politics – which squarely foregrounded the needs of the oppressed African majority – took clear precedence over an assimilationist liberal vision of equality. (Hence the PAC's opposition to the multiracialism of the ANC's Freedom Charter, a type of multiracialism that, as Sobukwe put it, "simply means transfer of the prejudices and bigotry that applies to in the present [apartheid] society to a new society" (Sobukwe, cited in Pheko, 1994: 57)). Also relevant here was the PAC's opposition to the Freedom Charter's declaration that the land belongs to all who live in it; Sobukwe by contrast contended that "South Africa is an integral part of the continent of Africa which historically and geographically belongs to the African people" (Pheko, 1994: 58). One can thus appreciate why Sobukwe may have been gratified to hear of the Liberal Party's decision to disband. Sobukwe, however, notes that it was "with pride" that he heard of the decision, an indication of an apparent identification with at least some of the ideals of that same Liberal Party. Pogrund (2015: 204) even argues - a point that scholars like Pheko would doubtlessly contest - that by the mid-1960s Sobukwe and fellow PAC leaders "would have been willing to accept the amalgamation of the PAC and the Liberal Party, had the situation arisen".

Robert Sobukwe
to Benjamin Pogrund,
12 June 1968 (Ba6.73)

My dear Benjie

The exams are over, thank God. I started writing on 20th May and finished on the 28th May. I wrote eight papers in all: two on Tuesday 21st, two on Friday 24th and two on Monday 27th: and then the one on Monday 20th and one on Tuesday 28th. You will notice then that they were bunched up.

However, they were very fair. On this occasion I made sure that I scrupulously obeyed instructions. On that score I have no fears whatsoever – no ink splashes and no scratch-outs. I wasn't at my best, though, so instead of a First Class Honours I shall be satisfied with a plebeian pass. One thing that struck me was the difference in approach between the University and the Correspondence Colleges. The latter are kind of cram institutions: the exam papers demanded interpretation rather than a regurgitation of the facts. I think I have passed. If I fail I authorize you to arrange a re-examination of the scripts!

I don't want to waste time and so I want to start on the next course immediately. I have to decide between a Masters in English and a basic course in Maths, Physics and Chemistry. For a Masters in Economics I shall need Maths in any case. Please advise. I should prefer to do English for the next two years or so, provided I am not required to do French as a "pre-requisite".

For three weeks or so before the exams I decided to put everything aside and concentrate on my studies. For that reason I have not yet sent the record-player to Mrs Stott nor have I written to thank her for the heaters and the chair. I'll do so soon but you may, in the meantime, do it on my behalf.

And thank you for the shoes. And if I sounded ungrateful about the beige shirt (or is it mustard?) I apologize. I have worn it since and find it very comfortable and not at all as loud as I thought at first it was. Also I have seen that it has been worn by Lord Snowdon and the late R.F.K.[31] – the latter, at any rate, could not be described as a mod – so, I apologize!

31 Lord Snowdon (Antony Armstrong-Jones) was Princess Margaret's husband; R.F.K. is, of course, Robert Kennedy.

Incidentally, I am very sorry about Kennedy's death. I know it is easy to praise a man when he is dead and no longer offers any competition. But I am going to be truthful and say I stand by all that I said about him in my letter. I did not want him dead. I wanted him to be beaten by McCarthy. Failure would have done him a lot of good.

I think it is Robert Frost who says – I am paraphrasing – when you meet the common man, note him well; for tomorrow there will be more of him than today. The papers are full of diagnoses and examinations, I know. But what does impress me forcibly is this determination by the "common man" to make and break kings: his utter rejection of the "accepted" standards. First was the rejection of status based on birth – the aristocracy. People apologize today for belonging to the "nobility". For two centuries money and education have been the determinants of status. But both have become common-place and are, consequently, rejected as determinants of status. There is nothing to take their place. What prevails is an attitude of rejection, deep dissatisfaction. Some fool is going to suggest war as a cure, and he'll be heeded: to give mankind's accumulated frustrations release.

Now that I have the time I intend to work on the novel and the Xhosa stories and poems. I shall also, at a later date, try to work out my religious problem. Someone from Three Anchor Bay, incidentally, has sent me Muhammad's biography. Many thanks to him/her.

Also I have received a stack of books. I lost my head, I am afraid, and approached them greedily. I was reading a stolid volume – *Reichswehr and Politics*[32] – when they arrived and it has demanded tremendous self-discipline to continue with it in the face of the blatant coquetry of Shaw, Somerset Maugham, Oscar Wilde, George Orwell and other luscious characters.

Did you read in the "Sunday Times" of 4th of June the article by Dayan's daughter? Very well balanced, I thought, with none of the arrogance that characterizes her father's references to Arabs. I say it once more Benjie: nobody is going to be "taught a lesson" by anybody. The days for that type of mentality are over between nations and between individuals. Our own children demand that we justify our "right" to teach them a lesson.

Am looking forward to the children's visit. I don't know yet when they'll be arriving.

---

32 F.L. Carsten, *The Reichswehr and Politics: 1918–1934* (1966).

How is Jenny faring? And what is the news from Norma? I'll remember to answer fully your question about what I thought of Dr Beyers Naudé's article.

My love to Jenny and to all friends.

Yours affectionately,
Bob

Eulalie Stott
to Benjamin Pogrund,
19 June 1968 (Ba6.30)

Dear Benjamin,

Thank you for your letter of 15th May and all the information contained therein.

I have paid for and sent the Cape Argus and Cape Times for a further year and arranged for a fan heater, a single bar heater and a folding chair to be sent with the adapters etc., required.

Will you tell me (as soon as you know) what your definite future plans are, namely, whether you will be going overseas or to less pleasant places and if so for how long.

I am not anxious to receive money from overseas or anywhere else unless I know exactly from whom it comes and clearly there are some sources from which I would be very reluctant to accept any funds. If you should unfortunately have to go to gaol I would much prefer to have overseas money handled by a lawyer friend or by Social Services or sent direct to Mrs. Sobukwe. As I have explained I am often away and I would not want my absence to result in inconvenience to Mrs. Sobukwe or anyone else.

I understand your desire to avoid Mr. Sobukwe feeling more "institutionalised" than is necessary and in the circumstances I shall be glad to attend to any of his personal needs but I honestly am filled with gloom at the prospect of having to raise anything like large sums of money.

To sum up therefore; if you go overseas I would like you to send money direct to Mrs. Sobukwe for her needs. I would be willing to accept money from you and to give my personal attention to seeing that Mr. Sobukwe's requests for clothes, furniture, etc., are cared for. If funds are low I shall endeavour to provide what is needed from my own resources.

I would undertake to keep any money that you sent to me for use by the Sobukwes in a separate account and I would pay out by cheque or Bank Drafts.

This morning I received a telegram to say that the Record Player was at the Docks awaiting repair and have arranged for this to be attended to.

I hope that you are keeping well and that things will go well for you.

Yours sincerely,
Eulalie

Benjamin Pogrund
to Robert Sobukwe,
25 June 1968 (Ba6.32)

Dearest Bob,

Looking at your last two letters, I am horrified at the time which has passed since I received them: your letter of April 3 which came on April 25, and your letter of April 24 which came on May 13. Do please forgive me, Bob. I just do not know how the time has passed like this. In these past few weeks, I have felt especially grieved about you, and I have made pleas for you, Veronica and the children in my prayers. I pray that you will all continue to have the strength and belief which you have had to battle to maintain for so wretchedly long a time. You know the extent of our closeness, and I need not say more. God bless you, my brother.

By the time you are reading this, I shall have made another of my public appearances.[33] It isn't quite an applauding public, but then the appearances are against my own desires! There is so much that I wish I could talk to you about. To have a brother relatively so late in life (note my sensitivity about my age), and then not to be able to talk to him freely and to share ideas and to obtain his guidance on matters on which I so badly need guidance and wise counsel …

Norma has applied to return here. It is the only hope for her, because she simply cannot go on existing in London. The children, too, show worrying signs of insecurity. She is waiting to hear now whether it will be allowed. Her divorce was heard in Pretoria last week, and will be final on July 31.

I have some lovely pictures of Jenny and am enclosing two for you. As always, we speak consistently of Uncle Bob, and you are assured of a place in her heart. She is seven on July 8 and I have promised her a budgie for her birthday.

There are several other enclosures with this letter and I had better explain them: there is a picture taken a couple of weeks ago of Ernie and me. We were at an academic function at Wits, and took great delight in dressing up. Jill was disgusted with us and screamed that we were nothing but children! But I suspect that she was cross because Ernie hadn't got her *her* academic dress. Anyway, I got a Mail photographer to take our picture, and here it is. Ernie asks me to tell you that he doesn't really look as rotund as the picture shows.

---

33 In court.

That man worries me because he is over-weight, and it isn't healthy for him. I keep on making nasty remarks about his girth in the hope of shaming him into keeping to a strict diet, but I don't have much success.

There is also a picture of a painting which I recently bought. It is by Bill Ainslie:[34] I already own a number of his works. This particular painting is intended as a gift for Norma. I am sorry that it is in black and white as the colouring is superb: chiefly oranges and browns with white in the top right hand side. But I hope it will give you an idea of what it looks like. Also enclosed is a picture of a bronze sculpting which I obtained from the foundry only last week. It's by Dumile,[35] an outstanding African artist who has just left to go and study in London. The picture is not a very good one, and does not catch the essence of the piece – an extraordinary blend, in the mother, of protectiveness, arrogance, defiance, primeval strength and all kinds of other things. But again, I hope it will give you some idea of what it looks like. I don't think I have mentioned it before, but for the past couple of years I have been doing a fair amount of buying of art works and I have quite a nice little collection. Certainly, I love all that I have bought. Most of the stuff is with Norma in London, as I shipped it over to her last year when I was due to go. She has it in her flat, but she has so many financial problems that I have told her to go ahead and try to sell the pieces if she has to. It's sad, but it cannot be helped.

And to round it off, I am enclosing the text of an article which I recently wrote.[36] It appeared in Mail, but in much summarised form, so I am sending you the full text. In view of our discussions about Israel, it will, I know, be of especial interest to you. I was impressed by this man – Shimon Peres [37] – and thoroughly enjoyed meeting him and writing him up. It's one of the few pieces

---

34 William "Bill" Ainslie (1934–89) was a South African artist, teacher and activist.

35 Zwelidumile Geelboi Mgxaji Mslaba "Dumile" Feni (1942–91) was a South African artist whose drawings, paintings and sculptures often depicted various aspects of the struggle against apartheid.

36 "Assessing Israel's Hopes of Peace", *Rand Daily Mail*, 9 May 1968. The article was based on an interview with Peres, who was then visiting South Africa.

37 Shimon Peres (1923–2016) was an Israeli politician and the ninth President of Israel (2007–14). In addition, he twice served as the Prime Minister of Israel. He received the 1994 Nobel Peace Prize, along with then acting Israeli Prime Minister, Yitzhak Rabin and the Palestinian Liberation Organization's Yasser Arafat, for his role in the Oslo Accords signed after peace talks between Israel and the Palestinian leadership.

of writing that I have done for some time. At the same time, and I think this comes out in the article – it was meant to – I was unhappy about the extent to which his cold logic took him in regard to the terrible problem of the Arab refugees. I felt at times that I was talking to an alien being, that this was not the sort of Jew to whom I was accustomed and in whom I believe.

Perhaps this is the metamorphosis in the modern Jew to which I referred in previous letters. Perhaps it is due to the fact that Peres and his countrymen must be like this simply to survive. But I cannot ever accept that, even in the fight for survival, there can be no room for compassion. And even apart from this aspect, I agree with you fully that Israel must show compassion if only for reasons of expediency, if it is ever to live in peace with the Arabs. I might tell you that, because of you, I committed a bit of a blue with Peres. When I first met him I was a bit vague as to exactly who he was. As we were walking along to sit down, I quoted to him your last letter, which I had received very shortly before, in which you said that if I had any influence with Dayan, I should get him to display compassion towards the Arabs. I was a bit surprised at the coolness with which Peres responded. Only later, during the interview, did I understand why – when I learned he was secretary-general of the party to which Dayan belongs and they are close friends!

I spoke to Veronica earlier today and she is well. She plans to be with you in August and I shall be seeing her soon to assist with train, etc. arrangements. The children are up here at the moment and I am hoping that it will be possible for me to see them.

In a letter dated June 19 Eulalie Stott told me that she had just that day had a telegram from you advising that your record player was at the docks. She was going to attend to it immediately. She also renewed your subscriptions to the Cape Times and Cape Argus and I hope there was no break in the delivery to you. She also sent across a fan heater, a bar heater with adaptors and a folding chair, all of which I hope have reached you safely and are as you wanted.

Exams are over now ... how did they go? Will you let me have the results as soon as you get them? And will you let me know as soon as possible your book needs for your third year of study?

I haven't even started to reply to your two letters, but I shall write again in the next few days.

With much love

Benjamin Pogrund
to Eulalie Stott,
25 June 1968 (Ba6.31)

Dear Eulalie,

Thank you for your letter of June 19. And thank you for the good things you have done for Bob. Were you all right for money for the various items?

If any money is sent to you from overseas I promise that you will know who the donor is. I can add the assurance that you need not worry about the respectability of any donors: both for Bob's sake and for my own protection. I am always at pains to ensure that the donors are above board.

The arrangement you suggest – that money be sent direct by me when I am overseas to Mrs Sobukwe for her needs, and to you for Bob's personal needs, is fine. I am grateful to you for this arrangement.

I think you need not fear too much about having to raise any large amounts of money yourself. I am confident of being able to provide what is needed, even though I tend to run short now and again.

Mrs Sobukwe will be visiting the Island in August. I shall attend to her train-fare, food on the Island and any other necessary expenses. I shall, of course, ask her to make a point of contacting you when she is there, and will try to let you have, in advance, her arrival date.

All good wishes,

Sincerely,

Robert Sobukwe
to Benjamin Pogrund,
26 June 1968 (Ba6.33)

My dear Benjie,

Once more I find that I have so much to say but so little space in which to say it! However, there is a lot of unimaginative, "stock-exchange" matters that I want to discuss with you and I shall start with those. Incidentally I wrote the exams with your pen.

I don't know when your case is coming up but I presume you still intend to leave the country. It is in that connection that I want to raise the "stock-exchange" matter. You wrote to me last year, suggesting that I make use of your account with Stuttafords for my needs. The disadvantage with such an arrangement, as I see it, is that I may decide to make my purchases at a time when you would like to reduce your account.

But I have an account with Markhams in Johannesburg which Veronica is using right now. I was wondering if you could help her have that account extended to the Cape Town branch. The advantages of such an arrangement are that

(a) I can make use of it without inconveniencing you. My purchases, in any case, will be occasional.
(b) The Joh'burg branch caters for men only while the Cape Town branch caters for both sexes. Veronica could, therefore, when she is down here, make use of it for herself and her daughter.

The second point concerns my cash. I want to suggest that you make regular payments into my account: anything from R5 (Five Rands) to R10 (Ten Rands) a month. I had a savings account with the Braamfontein branch of Barclays. I didn't close it completely. We could arrange then that I make all my payments by cheque and as soon as the new deposit arrives at the bank they would automatically transfer whatever balance I have on the open account to the savings account. In this way you will be able to check my finances any time you please and my money won't be idle but will earn interest. I'll make application to the proper authorities for the arrangement to be approved (i.e. as far as paying by cheque is concerned). I foresee no difficulties. So much then for the "stock-exchange" matters.

I received a letter from a Mrs/Miss (she didn't say!) M.L. Tracey of Flat 2 (two), 28 Dene Road (twenty-eight), Guildford, Surrey, who says she and others would like to know what things they could send. I answered her letter. But I think she would be glad to hear from you and you could tell her what you think she could send. I thought they could relieve you of the warm pyjamas, underwear etc. Or perhaps you could assign part of the "stock-exchange" arrangement to her. Her circumstances are humble, I believe. She was a nurse in Pondoland from 1923 to 1955.

Now about my "Communist" inclinations. I think you know the Hon. member for Heilbron well enough by now to take whatever he says with a ladle of salt.[38] All I wish to say is at no time was I alone with him. Whatever I said to him was heard by five other members of Parliament and by the Commissioner of Prisons who accompanied them. And not one of the others – me included – heard the "Confession of Faith" alluded to by the Hon. member for Heilbron. In any case books on Marxism and Leninism are banned. And if they can't get into the country, how, except in a James Bond film, can they get into Robben Island? It is you who sent me the books that examine Communism and you know that they are all, WITHOUT EXCEPTION, anti-Communist books on Communism. Sorry to waste your time: but I resent the implied slur on the efficiency of the Security Branch!

I am writing today to London University for the syllabus for M.A. English.

---

38 Gabriel Francois van Lingen ("Sampie") Froneman (1909–81) acted as deputy chairman of the Bantu Affairs Commission in the Nationalist government in the 1960s. Not only had Froneman recently declared to Parliament that Sobukwe was a Communist, he maintained moreover that Sobukwe had himself informed him of this fact. Pheko (1994: 120) quotes Froneman as stating before Parliament that "He [Sobukwe] is a Communist. He admitted that to me personally", to which Helen Suzman retorted: "I do not believe that for one moment and I challenge the Hon. Member from Heilbron to prove when Sobukwe ever admitted that he was a communist." Froneman had also claimed to see books on Communism and Marxism on Sobukwe's bookshelf on Robben Island and to have ascertained that Communism was Sobukwe's ideology. Pogrund (2015: 283) comments on this as an "improbability", before noting a further reported slice of conversation that may have occurred. After Froneman allegedly asked Sobukwe if he would ever change his views, "Sobukwe allegedly replied: 'Not until the day of resurrection.'"

Mind you I wanted to study Nederlands and brush up my Linguistics. But these are for pleasure and will not provide sufficient incentive to keep me wholly and completely occupied. I feel the same about my novel and short stories. I don't want my mind to get accustomed to prolonged relaxation lest it become slothful!

I think I told you I am reading Mayakovsky's[39] poems. In his "A Cloud in Trousers" occur these stupendous lines:

Wherever pain is – there am I:
On every single tear that's shed
I myself have crucified.

How these boys write!

Did Ernie receive my letter? I said in it that though we'd not met I had heard of him in my student days. It was Tobias and Brenner (?) I had in mind.[40] I think I heard of Ernie only when I came to the Wits. Sorry for ageing him.

Could you send me more stamps, please: 2½c and 5c as well as air mail forms (overseas). Thanks. Love to Jenny. Will write again.

Yours affectionately,
Bob

39 Vladimir Mayakovsky (1893–1930) was a Russian poet, playwright, artist and actor who was active in the Soviet era. While his work lent patriotic support to the Communist Party and Lenin in particular, his subsequent relationship with the Soviet state was often highly conflictual. He committed suicide in 1930 at the age of 36.

40 Phillip Tobias, later known as a palaeontologist and anatomist, studied medicine at Wits in the late 1940s and was appointed to a lectureship in the Department of Anatomy in the Wits Medical School in 1951. Sydney Brenner studied medicine at Wits in the late 1940s, qualifying in 1951. He then went on to study, teach and research at Cambridge where he made important contributions to the field of molecular biology. He won a Nobel Prize for Physiology in 2002.

Robert Sobukwe
to Nell Marquard,
26 June 1968 (Bd2.9)

My dear Nell,

Thank you for both your card of the 1st June *1868* and your letter of 8th June, a century later. I have been long on this island, haven't I?

Yes, I received the January copy of Realités. Thank you very much. I'll be glad to have any copies you can spare as well as copies of the "New Yorker", if you still receive the journal. Thank you also for the R2.00.

Thank you for your words of encouragement. When you have time please read Jeremiah 45. It was Dietrich Bonhoeffer's favourite passage.[41] I got it from him and have made it mine. Incidentally, he was hanged by the Nazis just two months before their collapse.

Yes, Stellenbosch is becoming troublesome. If you remember they invited Kennedy to address them.[42] In fairness I must admit that Pretoria University invited me, too, in 1959. Only I refused because my audience would have been all-white! And the late Dr Xuma[43] was warmly applauded at Potchefstroom University. But Stellenbosch is the more relaxed of the Afrikaans universities.

It is a pity about Z.K. Matthews.[44] As you say, he was a fine man. While I was a student at Fort Hare I came to know him quite well. He was too tolerant and broad-minded for many of us nationalists and we quarrelled with him frequently and fiercely. But he never lost his pride.

I hope you have not been alarmed by what "Sampie" Froneman[45] said about me in Parliament. His approach to truth is that of a *poet* – not of a

---

41 "The Lord saith thus: Behold, that which I have built will I break down, and that which I have planted I will pluck up, even this whole land. And seekest thou great things for thyself? Seek them not: for, behold, I will bring evil upon all flesh, saith the Lord: but thy life will I give unto thee for a prey in all places whither thou goest."

42 Robert Kennedy spoke at the University of Stellenbosch on 7 June 1966, having been invited by students at one of the residences.

43 Alfred Bathini Xuma (1893–1962), typically referred to by his initials – as AB Xuma – was a medical doctor who served as president-general of the ANC from 1940 to 1949.

44 Z.K. Matthews died on 11 May 1968.

45 A reference to the allegation that he, Sobukwe, was a Communist.

scientist. It seems to be an affliction of most of those associated with the BAD department.[46] Dr de Wet Nel,[47] the former BAD minister had it to an alarming degree. Blaar Coetzee[48] is also heavily infected. All the more honour, I think, to the Minister of Justice, for resisting the temptation to make the sure but cheap appeal.

I am sorry to trouble you but do you think you could get me a pair of warm pyjamas, size 40 (forty) in a dark colour? If you could throw in a handkerchief or two I'll be much obliged.

In closing, may I quote a few lines from Mayakovsky. I know they'll thrill you.

I,
laughed at by tribal contemporaries,
like a lanky
joke obscene,
see coming over time's mountain-peaks,
one whom nobody sees.
...
And I amongst you – am (his) prophet:
wherever pain is – there am I:
on every single tear that's shed
I myself have crucified.
...
And when
he arrives,
by rebellions accompanied,
and you go to greet your saviour with hosannas
I will
tear out my soul for you,
to make it big
stamp on it!

46 The Department of Bantu Administration and Development.

47 Dr M.C. de Wet Nel was Minister of Bantu Administration and Development, and of Bantu Education, in the National Party government between 1958 and 1966.

48 Blaar Coetzee acted as Deputy Minister of Bantu and Education in the mid-1960s.

and hand it to you, bloodstained as a banner.[49]

And you say I should consider writing my personal reminiscences, Nell! I should have liked to say "I won't do it!" But I can't very well say that to you so I'll temporize and say "I'll think about it."

You know, when I read about Kennedy's death and the messages from great men which came in from all sides it struck me that a certain Jewish agitator was hanged outside Jerusalem and a mere handful mourned his death – among them a one-time tart. But today, the "great" send messages of condolence, in the name of that Jewish Rabbi! Oh well, Nell, enough for now. We have a saying in Xhosa, used for purposes of condolence. It is a little stoic: ukuhlanga lungehlanga – lala ngenxeba: (Daar het nie gebeur wat nie al gebeur het nie: slaap op jou wond).[50]

Thank you for writing to Veronica.

With best wishes to you and Leo. God bless you.

Yours sincerely,
Robert

P.S. I am well: am only plagued by a cold in the head. But have had it for over a decade now. It knows neither summer nor winter. Robert.

---

49 As in many instances, Sobuwke's rendering differs slightly from available published versions. These lines are largely drawn from Mayakovsky's (1915) poem "Cloud in Pants", also often referred to as "Cloud in Trousers". The poem, considered to be Mayakovsky's first major poem, was initially entitled "The 13th Apostle", but was then renamed as a precaution in an attempt to evade censorship. Written from the point of view of a rejected lover, the poem depicts the subjects of love, art, revolution and religion, all of which would have been of interest to Sobukwe.

50 My colleague Sipho Mbuqe, a clinical psychologist and native Xhosa speaker, helped me explore the associations of this aphorism. In his view, to say "There has not occurred what has not occurred before" means: What has occurred (usually to you and your family) is not what has never occurred before (to humanity). It is tantamount to saying that what you are experiencing is a common human experience; it is a part of the human condition. Importantly, continues Mbuqe, the tone of the aphorism does not convey a sense of dismissing or minimising the loss the other person is going through; it works instead to tie them and their loss to the rest of humanity. As Mbuqe puts it: "In some sense you are not alone, but you are alone as you bear the wound at this point, yet you have to soldier on. Usually when you have a wound or deep cut you would not lie on it … However, this calls you to go against natural inclinations. In doing so, you open the path to healing, however painful it might be" (Sipho Mbuqe, personal communication, 11 September 2018).

Benjamin Pogrund
to Robert Sobukwe,
14 July 1968 (Ba6.34)

My dear Bob,

I received your letter of June 12 only a few days ago, and am taking the first opportunity to reply.

I want to see you proceeding to your next course of studies as quickly as possible, but there is something puzzling me: I thought you were doing a three-year Bachelor of Economics degree through the University of London, and that these were your second year exams. Yet it seems that you have completed the degree examinations? Were you allowed a year off because of your Fort Hare B.A. or what?

I hope that the results will be better than you anticipate, and that you will, in fact, emerge with a first class. I am looking forward anxiously for news of your results. Your authority to me to request a re-marking in case of failure is noted – but I have more than enough belief in you not even to accept this as a possibility.

About the next course: I strongly recommend English for a Master's degree. I think that it would provide opportunities for freshening your mind, through contact with the world's literature (even if it is only English literature, that still presents a tremendous range!), to an extent that mathematics and physics can never do. I definitely think that English would provide a vast amount of both pleasure and profit, and would be a means of maintaining your spirit. The other subjects are too dry and dull – for you certainly, I believe. I do not understand why you should not wish to do English if it means that you must first do French. I think it an excellent idea to study French: it will be useful in the future perhaps, and in turn will also open up a vast range of new reading to you. There need be no great problem about studying it, as I will ensure that you receive a teaching course on gramophone records.

Whatever you decide, will you let me know as soon as possible what your book requirements are, so that I can get them organised? It might perhaps be a good idea, when you write to the university concerned, to send an additional copy of the syllabus and the list of books needed direct to me. Then when you get your list you can also write to me letting me know your particular preferences. But it will enable me to get a flying start in obtaining at least the basic books.

Mrs Stott told me, as I think I said in my last letter, that she had had your request about the record-player. I hope it has been safely returned to you and is working well.

The batch of books you received were probably the ones I sent a while ago. I am sorry that I omitted to let you have a list of them, but am enclosing this now. I plan to send you more shortly. I think that I must again write to the Officer Commanding about the very big batch I sent you in July/August last year, which apparently have still not reached you.

I am writing to you from the office, and it is just on 2 a.m. I am flying off to Durban in the morning until Thursday with Jenny, who grows more adorable by the day. I need a break badly, but in the evenings down there, when Jenny is asleep, I hope to do some quiet writing. I am always completely relaxed when I am away with her, and I am looking forward to these few days of peace. There are a lot of personal problems at the moment, Bob, but I hope they will be resolved by next week, and I shall then write to you about them. It was Jenny's 7th birthday last Monday, by the way, and I gave her a budgie as a present. What excitement! What a light in her eyes, and how incessantly she talks about how her budgie "tweets" to her. The budgie's name is "Laila", which is Hebrew for "evening". There's a lovely Hebrew lullaby I know of this name, and I often sing it to Jenny, so she was happy to accept the suggestion for naming her pet. Her school results: again a string of "A's", which again have delighted me.

I wrote to Veronica recently, but we have not yet had a meeting. I shall rush a message to her as soon as I return from Durban as I know that she plans to visit you next month. I am sorry, deeply sorry, that the children's visit apparently fell through.

With deep affection,

Veronica Sobukwe
to Benjamin Pogrund,
20 July 1968 (Ba6.36)

My dear Benjie,

Thank you for writing to me on my birthday.

Also, thank you for the money you sent us early in July. The children left for school on the 12th July.

It is very difficult to contact you by phone. I shall try to telephone you next week. If I fail please phone me or leave the message to any-one on the phone. I can see you any-time after 4 pm during the week.

I shall be very grateful if you could assist me with the train-fare. I shall be leaving for Cape Town on the 17th August.

Sincerely,
Veronica

Robert Sobukwe
to Benjamin Pogrund,
24 July 1968 (Bb13)

My dear Benjie,

Before all else thank you for Jenny's photographs. I was tempted to write directly to her and tell her she is developing into a regular Rose of Sharon and that we shall have to consider entering her for the Miss Universe contests. But then she has shown prowess as an actress as well and we shall have to decide whether the stage should be her career. Please tell her all this from me. She is really sweet, Benjie. Congrats.

Thank you also for the "academicians".[51] Your fellows look quite donnish. So this is Ernie? He looks quite amiable. I agree with you, though, he should shed a few pounds.

Please tell him also that now that the record-player is back I have been able to play the records he sent me, as well as your lot. What a feast: what a feast, Benjie. Thank you fellows.

I have had some further trouble with the record-player, with the turn-table grinding and some records scraping against the arm. I sent a telegram to this effect to Eulalie. But it has been suggested to me here that the trouble might lie with the records: they may be out of alignment. I find myself persuaded as it is not all the records that give this trouble: and the turn-table sometimes performs smoothly the whole day. I shall hold back then and see how things develop. Unfortunately, the records which are the culprits are, among others: Mozart Concerto no 1 in G major and no 21 in C major, Haydn Symphony no 100 & no 102: as you can see, absolute class! These two, at least, I'll give to Veronica to take back with her so that you guys may doctor them if you can. I received all the articles mentioned by you as coming from Eulalie. Incidentally, I am taking the liberty of calling her by her first name because you do so!

The picture by [Bill] Ainslie looks good. Unfortunately as far as "fine arts" go I am like the English described by the late Sir Malcolm Sargent.[52] He

51 A reference to the photograph sent by Pogrund in his letter of 25 June 1968, of Ernie Wentzel and Pogrund himself in academic dress.

52 Sir Malcolm Sargent (1895–1967) a British composer, conductor and organist.

said the English love music. They don't understand it: but they find the noise pleasant. Same with me. I am moved by music and pictures without being able to analyse them – more so with pictures.

The sculpture, too, even in the photograph breathes a primitive power and force. Thanks for them all, young fellow.

I am sorry about Norma. I hope she recovers completely and soon.

Briefly about the observations of Shimon Peres. Firstly, have you read the works of C.P. Snow? They are brilliant. And yet I always read them reluctantly. He is pitiless. His characters stand before you naked and vulnerable. And my chief weakness – and strength – is that I never enjoy looking on the nakedness of another. I am tempted to cover them. Secondly, in *The Rivals*, a play by Sheridan, Sir Anthony gives his son, Captain Absolute, a tongue-lashing. He in turn lambasts his page who complains to himself that it is unfair for superiors to work off their frustrations on their subordinates. Just then the "boy" comes in and makes some cheeky observation. The page kicks him down the stairs telling him the while to remember his place. This was in the 18th Century, I think. But you can see how well the dramatist knew human nature.

C.P. Snow and Peres have this in common that they claim to be realists. But such a creature does not exist. Life would be impossible for the realist. We all of us live because we hope for better things to come. When, under the reign of Nicholas I, Vissarion Belinsky[53] said: "Our lot puts the cowl on us. We must suffer, that life may be easier for our grandchildren. We must renounce all happiness, because destiny is cruel to its instruments"; and when Robespierre [54] on the occasion of the Austrian invasion, addressed himself to posterity, they were being extremely optimistic: "tomorrow will be better."

The only "realists" I have known are victors who are preening themselves and those who climb on the bandwagon.

Throughout his speech Peres says: "We told them …". Just imagine [King] Hussein [of Jordan][55] in Peres's place, with the roles reversed, saying "We told you Jews …" and taste it in your mouth.

---

53 Vissarion Belinsky was a nineteenth-century Russian literary critic.

54 Maximilien François Marie Isidore de Robespierre (1758–94) was a French lawyer and politician, one of the best known historical figures associated with the French Revolution and the subsequent Reign of Terror.

55 King Hussein bin Talal reigned as king of Jordan from 1952 until his death in February 1999.

In any case his analysis is superficial, I think. Hussein does not want peace: he wants his land back. He realises that he is not militarily strong enough to take it back: so he will consider a peace settlement which will restore it to him. But he will be waiting for his opportunity. Israel is asking him to choose between them and the Arabs – his people.

As for Nasser, his popularity arises from the fact that he is committed to war with Israel. And far from the intelligentsia holding him back, they are pushing him forward. It is the intelligentsia who feel humiliation most – not the masses. I'll answer Peres point by point later, Benjie. So long for now.

Yours affectionately,
Bob

Benjamin Pogrund
to M.L. Tracey, Flat 2,
28 Dene Road,
Guildford, Surrey,
14 August 1968 (Ba6.42)

Dear Miss Tracey,

Bob Sobukwe has written to me from Robben Island to tell me he had received a most kind letter from you. He said he had replied, but asked me to write to you in regard to your offer of help, made on behalf of yourself and friends. He and I are very close friends of many years' standing, and I handle most of the practical arrangements for his welfare and for that of his family.

If you are able to get together books it would be greatly appreciated. He has catholic tastes, so you send as wide a variety as you please. But books on political subjects should not be sent. You can send the books to him by sea mail addressed to: Mr Robert M. Sobukwe, c/o Officer Commanding, Robben Island Gaol, Robben Island, via Cape Town. It would be helpful, if it is not too inconvenient for you, to send me a list of whatever books you send, so that I can ensure that they are delivered to him. The books need not necessarily be new ones, and they can be paperbacks. He is a voracious reader, so books are constantly needed.

I do not know how much money you and your friends might have available, but if any is, it could be put to good use for Mr Sobukwe. Until now, we have met his clothing requirements by his sending me lists of what he needs and I make the purchases and post them off to him. We are at present going into the question of him having his own banking account, into which regular amounts would be paid each month, of about £5 at a time. He could then order clothing from a firm of outfitters in Cape Town and settle by cheque. I hope I am not being presumptuous in asking about this: I am writing this letter to you "blind", so do please forgive me if I go too far.

If you have any other suggestions, I would be most happy to hear about them.

Your interest in Mr Sobukwe is much appreciated, I assure you.

With the best wishes,

Yours sincerely,
BENJAMIN POGRUND

Benjamin Pogrund
to Robert Sobukwe,
14 August 1968 (Ba6.39)

Dearest Bob,

By the time this reaches you, Veronica will either still be with you or will recently have left. I hope that it will be a happy visit for both of you. I hope, too, that it will have been possible for her to buy some kosher foods on her way through Cape Town. I wrote to Mrs Stott, who will probably meet Veronica on her arrival, and suggested buying some polonies, etc. But no roll mops! I saw Veronica recently, as she will have told you, and have also spoken to her several times on the phone lately.

As requested, I am enclosing 2½c stamps (30) and overseas air letter cards (20). As you probably know you need an extra 5c of stamps on the air letter cards for the USA if you should be writing to anyone there. I am also today sending R90 to the Officer Commanding to be deposited to your personal account. Last week I sent R15 to him for the costs of Veronica's meals on the Island, and asked that any balance left from this be credited to your account.

There were a number of items you raised in your letter of June 26, and I want to deal with these. The Markhams account arrangement sounds fine, and should prove most convenient for you. If the authorities agree, I think it also a good idea to have your own bank account and cheque book. Let me know about this as soon as possible. I will start with initial payments of R5 a month into the account, and hope to be able to increase this quite substantially within a while. But I am not too clear about how you will run both a savings account and an open account. If it is a savings account I don't think you will be able to draw cheques on it. Unless I am mistaken, you will have to stick to an open account if you want to use a cheque book. I suggest that, if the authorities agree, you write immediately to the manager of Barclays Bank in Braamfontein to give him the necessary instructions, and let me have a copy of this letter. In this letter you could also raise this point about a savings/open account. As soon as I receive your letter to him, I will phone him to discuss it. Perhaps it would also be best to have the account transferred to a Cape Town branch?

I have written today to Miss (?) Tracey, and will let you know what she says when I hear from her.

I am glad that you have decided to do an M.A. in English, for the reasons I set out in my letter of July 14. Please let me have your syllabus and list of books as soon as possible so that I can get all this fixed up for you. And I am still anxiously awaiting the news of your exam results.

My deepest apologies, Bob. I've just again looked at your letter and I see that you also want 5c stamps. I am enclosing these also (20). Will the quantities of stamps enclosed carry you through for a while? Because of postal delays, I hope that you are letting me know well in advance about your stamp needs.

Yes, Ernie [Wentzel] did receive your letter and was most glad to hear from you. He has been reluctant to write because it will take up one of the letters you are allowed to receive, but, as always, he and Jill send their warm good wishes to you.

You don't mention the record player in your letter. Has it got back to you safely and is it working properly now? And would you like some more records? And if so, what kind?

The lines from Mayakovsky moved me deeply. They have been haunting me ever since your letter arrived. Not a very healthy reaction, I suppose! Yet they represent, I think, the basic reason why I want to leave: having to stand by and see what happens, and yet be able to do so little about it, fills me with a [illegible] it is anguish in itself. Being helpless [illegible] creates a level of pain and frustration within me which I often feel will destroy me, leaving either an empty shell or a hard, cynical being – or both, for that matter. How much worse, my dear friend, it must be for you, and yet you continue to stand erect. It is the reason why so many of my actions are dictated by the thought of how you would wish me to behave.

While on this theme, did I send you a copy of "The Last of the Just"?[56] It deals with it in brilliant terms, and I regard it as one of the greatest books I have ever read. I would be surprised if I have not already sent you a copy. Please let me know.

I owe you profuse apologies for sending you all-white underwear, instead of the coloured ones you requested. This was a pure oversight on my part.

56 *The Last of the Just,* a post-war novel by Andre Schwarz-Bart was published (in French) in 1959. Winner of the Prix Goncourt, the novel is widely regarded as one of the most profound fictional depictions of the Holocaust. It traces the history – and anti-Semitic persecution – of the fictional Levy family across eight centuries.

Anyway, I console myself with the thought that the white ones will at least look colourful on you.

I have noted, by the way, that your "Sunday Times" subscription expires on September 8. I shall ensure that it is renewed.

As I indicated in my last letter, I have been beset by personal troubles lately. Basically trouble in regard to Norma. She is not at all well, but has now been given permission to return here. It will be a break she desperately needs because otherwise she will go to pieces. She will probably be returning next month and then we shall see what happens between us.

Within the next few days I shall send you more copies of "Argosy" and will also send some Hemingway as requested.

Another point which comes to mind: Veronica phoned me early on Monday. I was still three quarters asleep after being on late night duty as news editor. I *think* I asked her to work out with you the amounts of washing powder, blades, etc which you needed for six to 12 months. In case I omitted to do this, will you do the calculations and let me know so that I can send these things to you?

And another point: while we are still getting the Markhams set-up arranged, if you need anything, will you make use of the facilities arranged for you with Stuttafords in Cape Town?

We have ended the bursary fund campaign for this year: R40,000, which is most pleasing.

With much love,

Robert Sobukwe
to Nell Marquard,
7 August 1968 (Bd2.11)

My dear Nell,

Thank you very much for the pyjamas and the handkerchiefs as well as for Realités and your note of 14th July. You did well to disregard the specifications. I asked for a size 40 because I wanted to ascertain whether that wasn't perhaps the size that would fit me best now. I am finding that my normal sizes – even with shoes! – are too big for me now but I fear to take a lesser size lest it be too small. I am, in fact, in a position where I do not know my correct size.

But, as I say, you did well to disregard my specifications with regard to both size and colour. I prefer dark colours as a matter of constitution, I believe, as well as for the utilitarian reason that they don't show dirt as easily as the lighter do. But your pair is very snug which is all that matters. The hankies are most welcome – thanks.

I hope you received my letter of the 5th June in which I commented on the dissolution of the Liberal Party as well as on your remarks on Britain. I would not like you to think I did not answer your letter of 6th May. I did.

What an eventful year this has been! But what I find very interesting is man's intense dissatisfaction not only with his social order – be it Capitalist or Communist – but also with himself. Perhaps as important as the assassinations of King and Kennedy have been the rebellions in Czechoslovakia[57] and the clerical rebellion against the Pope's encyclical.[58] Laski had predicted, however, that Capitalism which emphasizes political democracy would be compelled to concede economic democracy as well, and that Communism which emphasizes economic democracy would be constrained to move in the direction of political democracy. But I know of

57 Sobukwe is referring to the "Prague Spring" of 1968, a period marked by popular uprisings against the Communist state of Czechoslovakia, which ended when Soviet troops were sent to quell the unrest.

58 A reference to the revolt against Pope Paul VI's encyclical *Humanae Vitae: On the Regulation of Birth*, a document reaffirming the Catholic Church's rejection of forms of artificial contraception. This encyclical, published in July 1968, met with open dissent in the church.

no writer who had predicted that the Catholic clergy (Roman) would one day tell their Pope that he was an old fuddy-duddy. My goodness me, what is the world coming to!

There is the farther observation that both Communism and Roman Catholicism claim to be the last word in material and spiritual development, respectively. Beyond them there is no salvation. At the moment the rebels are criticizing merely the *interpretation* by authority. Soon they will challenge the *basis* of that authority. Of course, Marsiglio of Padua (a priest) had said as early as the 14th century that the Bishop of Rome was no more than the Bishop of Rome with no greater spiritual claim than the least priest.[59]

Then there are the great moral problems surrounding scientific research. I have been asking myself whether this clinical detachment of science, this emotionless observation and control, do not subtly convert us into monsters whose radius of human feeling is being more and more reduced. The articles in the Cape Times on "sub-humans", shook me, I tell you. And, of course, I have just been reading C.P. Snow's *The New Men*. Can anybody tell me what kind of a man Snow is in actual life? I remember reading that during the war, after they had listened to a broadcast by Churchill, he had said to his companion: "we must never allow ourselves to forget our gratitude to this man" or words to that effect. So he isn't without profound feelings. But his writings!

If you do write to Prof. Stuart please give him my kindest regards and inform him that if I am successful in my B.Econ. exams I intend to proceed to an M.A. in English.

How's the garden behaving?

Best wishes to both of you.

Yours affectionately,
Robert

59 Marsiglio of Padua, also known as Marsilius of Padua (c.1275–c.1342), was an Italian scholar and political figure who attempted to refute claims that the Pope possessed a "plenitude of power" in affairs of church and state.

Benjamin Pogrund
to Veronica Sobukwe,
15 August 1968 (Ba6.43)

My dear Veronica,

I am rushing this letter out to you to catch you before you leave for Cape Town.

I have sent Bob a quantity of stamps (2½c and 5c and overseas air letter cards) which he asked for. But in case he is very short of stamps, and my letter is delayed, I thought it might be a good idea if you took some stamps with you to give to him. Will you also please tell him that I have just sent R20 to the Officer Commanding to be deposited to Bob's personal account? As arranged, I also sent R15 to pay for your meals on the Island.

I have written to Mrs Stott, but have not yet received a reply. If she is in Cape Town at present I am sure that she will be at the station on Sunday to meet you. I only hope that she is not out of town at present.

My best wishes for a happy trip and a happy stay with Bob. You carry with you my love to him.

One other point: Bob has suggested that his annual needs for washing powder, blades, etc be worked out so that we can send a whole lot down to him. Will you work out with him the amounts he needs and let me know when you return?

Sincerely,

Eulalie Stott
to Benjamin Pogrund,
21 August 1968 (Ba6.46)

Dear Benjamin,

Thank you for your letter of 14th August. I met Mrs. Sobukwe and delivered her safely to the docks. It was nice to see her again, looking so well. I shall see about renewing the Sunday Times subscription – don't worry about the money.

Sincerely,
Eulalie Stott

Margaret Tracey,
St Patrick's,
49 Cholmeley Park,
London N6,
to Benjamin Pogrund,
1 September 1968 (Ba6.49)

Dear Mr. Pogrund

Thank you very much for your letter. I am sorry for the delay in answering. I was so very glad to hear that you are able to help your friend & his family. I am trying to collect some books for him and shall be sending some out this week, I hope, & will send the names to you. If at any time you could hear from him of any special books that he wanted, I would try to get them 2nd hand in London, as this is a good city for getting books.

I am enclosing a cheque for him for R10 which is all I can manage at a time, I'm afraid. I haven't any friends who I can ask to help at present, and I have many other claims and commitments. But I shall hope to send another small cheque at Christmas time.

I am looking forward to the visit of an African friend this weekend – Mrs. Sarah Jane Molefe who trained with us at Holy Cross, Pondoland about 15 years ago. She is high up on the staff at Baragwanath [Hospital] but is coming over for a course. I wonder if you know her?

I shall be writing again later on.

With all good wishes,

Yours sincerely,
Margaret Tracey

Robert Sobukwe
to Benjamin Pogrund,
4 September 1968 (Ba6.50)

My dear Benjie,

Veronica was still around when your letter of the 14th August arrived, providing us with a further opportunity to discuss you. She'll probably report to you on that and on the fact that she brought me none of the kosher items you had advised her to get.

Thank you for the stamps and air-letter cards as well as the R20.00 (Twenty Rands).

I am glad you approved of the Markhams arrangements though I learn that the Cape Town branch, too, caters only for men and their sons.

About the cheque-book and the savings account, it is a system with which banks are familiar. What it amounts to really is that I draw on my current account on a purely monthly basis. When a deposit is made into my current account, at the end of the month, whatever balance I had from the month then coming to an end is transferred to my savings account. If at any time I want to make a purchase that will involve an amount above the monthly current balance I shall either make a deposit and finish off payment in the month following or will make the requisite withdrawal from my savings account.

At the moment my Savings Book is with Veronica. It could remain with her and she can take it to the bank monthly for the entries to be made. While you are around it could be kept by you so that you would know exactly what the position was at any moment. I don't think it would be necessary either to transfer the account to Cape Town or for me to write specially to the manager of the Braamfontein branch. If I have made myself clear do you think you could see the manager at Braamfontein and make the arrangements with him? I'll await your answer. If you still want *me* to write to him, I'll be happy to oblige.

About my studies, I wrote asking for the M.A. syllabus under the impression that like us here they would regard B.A. Hons. as the first but integral part of the Masters. These Londoners sent me the M.A. syllabus with the information that as I had no degree of the London University I could not be admitted to M.A. and they were sorry but "there can be no exception made". So I have to write once more to ask them to send me the B.A. Hons. syllabus. And once more I am going to harness you, Benjie. Will you then please write to:

University of London Publications Dept,
1 Malet Street,
London, W.C. 1.

and ask for Oversea Regulations and Syllabuses for the B.A. Hons in English. Prices are: 3/- (three shillings) including postage, surface mail; six shillings by second class air mail. Ordinary surface mail will do. The BSc Econ. results will be available towards the end of the month. I'll let you know by telegram as soon as they arrive.

Thanks for writing to Miss (?) Tracey. I haven't heard from her yet. I haven't heard from Prof Wellington for some time now: I hope he is well. Nell Marquard writes steadily: quite impatient her letters often are!

The Record Player is fine. And I have enough records for the present, thanks.

I am delighted to know that Mayakovsky's lines moved you. I knew they would. Also, I have read *The Last of the Just*. It was among the first batch of books you sent me in 1963. If you've read it you will understand why Dayan antagonizes me. One has to be careful, at all times, not to allow the Press and other publicity media to create an image of one to which one finds oneself compelled to conform. It happens so often and so easily. Herod addresses a public meeting and the people shout: It is a God that speaks. He doesn't correct them and God strikes him down. As soon as you appropriate to yourself the glory that belongs to God, He strikes you down. Once you say my arm, my wealth, my wisdom have brought me this, you already belong to the scrap heap of history. Blessed are the meek (?).

I shall soon be sending you the rough copies of my Xhosa stories and poems and my incomplete English novel. I am writing under a pseudonym and should like an unbiased literary opinion on them. Will write later, Benjie. Thanks for everything.

Affectionately,
Bob

Mrs Stott sent me a hot plate and pots. Can't find her address. But will wire her as soon as I have. Bob

Veronica Sobukwe
to Benjamin Pogrund,
12 September 1968 (Ba6.52)

My dear Benjie,

I am sorry that I have delayed in sending Bob's list to you.

He asked me to bring his old sports-jacket to you so that you could buy him a new one – if possible.

I have just come across these jacket measurements. If I am not mistaken, I think you handed them over to me.

With best wishes,
Sincerely,
Veronica

Margaret Tracey
to Benjamin Pogrund,
17 September 1968 (Ba6.54)

Dear Mr. Pogrund,

You asked me to send you a list of the names of the books I have recently sent to Bob Sobukwe. I was careful to follow out your instructions & sent them to the exact address you gave me. They didn't seem to be a very exciting lot but I hope they will keep him interested.

2 paper backs on science – A new Biology & Science of the Modern World
An illustrated book on the successful Mt. Everest expedition
A book on Albert Schweitzer & his work
The Story of St. Paul's Life & Letters
A paperback of Eight great Tragedies, Shakespeare's & others

I do hope these will at least be interesting & worth reading.

I don't know if he would like any of the English classical novels, like Dickens, or if he would like any religious books like Paterson Smyth's Life of Christ, or Thomas a Kempis' famous Imitation of Christ. One can get almost *any* sort of book in London & I *would* like to know what he really likes.

I had Mrs. Molefe (Sarah Jane Gumenke) stay with me for a weekend a few days ago. She trained with us at Holy Cross, Pondoland & I much enjoyed seeing her again. I think she knows you.

All good wishes,
Yours sincerely,
Margaret Tracey

Telegram from
Robert Sobukwe
to Benjamin Pogrund,
26 September 1968 (Ba6.56)

Just made respectable ranks stop Third Class Honours stop received sports coat fabulous stop convey results to Veronica. Bob

Officer Commanding,
Robben Island,
to Benjamin Pogrund,
1 October 1968 (Ba6.59)

Geagte Mnr. Pogrund,

Een boek "Allied intervention in Russia" gaan hiermee terug aangesien die boek nie aan Robert Sobukwe oorhandig mag word nie.[60]

Die uwe,
BEVELVOERENDE OFFISIER

60 In English: A book, "Allied intervention in Russia" is being returned to you as this book cannot be given to Robert Sobukwe.

Robert Sobukwe
to Benjamin Pogrund,
2 October 1968 (Ba6.61)

My dear Benjie,

Thank you for the sport coat. It is fabulous, as I said in my telegram. It fits perfectly, although I do not know how I feel about the length of the cuffs. I always wear my jackets long in the arms, covering the shirt cuffs. I know that it is not fashionable so to do, but I have always done so – "traditional way" etc, etc. But for a fashionable man about town the length in all directions is perfect. Thanks a lot.

I am sending you enclosed herewith, the Pass List. I hope you're not too disappointed with the results. I have already applied for registration for the B.A. (Hons) English.

I am having some difficulty with the plot of the English novel. But I'll soon be sending you, before the end of this month, what I have done so far in both Xhosa and English.

Enough for the present. Love to Jenny.

Affectionately,
Bob

P.S. Thank you for the books. They're so interesting they are interfering with my writing. Bob

PPS. I am reading Irving Wallace's *The Man*: stupendous! I should please like you to get Veronica a copy: I'd like her to read it. Bob

Robert Sobukwe
to Nell Marquard,
16 October 1968 (Bd2.12)

My dear Nell,

Thank you for your letters of 27th July and 12th September. I am sorry I didn't answer the July letter earlier. I can't understand what happened unless I was waiting for the children's visit. Please accept my apologies.

As you now know, Veronica came instead and we had a joyful time together – alone for a while. She brought me the malt you had recommended and some gargling stuff which I have found very useful. She told me also of your letter to her and the birthday present. Thank you a lot.

It is just possible that you will have heard by now that I have been successful in my BSc. Econ. exams: I obtained a Third Class Honours. I have written to register for the B.A. Hons. (English). You'll be able to help me there. I hope I am mistaken and they do not require Latin as a prerequisite. French I may endure, but Latin I can't take at all.

Thank you for your comments on the U.S.A. and Japan. As you observe, it is remarkable how greatness and pettiness, refinement and barbarism graze contentedly on the same pasture. I have always been an ardent supporter of the ecumenical movement. Of late I have gone a step farther: I should like to see an Inter-Religion movement designed to bring together the worshippers of God – be they Jews, Christians or Muslims.

I had the pleasure of meeting Lord Walston[61] when he was out here. I enjoyed the few minutes we had together. He left me a copy of the address he delivered at the Wits. I thought it was very fine.

The verse in Jeremiah 45 [verse 5] that you refer to is translated thus:

"I will let you escape with your own life, wherever you must go" (Moffatt version).

---

61 Lord Henry David George Walston was the chairman of the British Institute of Race Relations. He had recently delivered a lecture in Johannesburg at the University of the Witwatersrand. After rebuking Vorster over his government's treatment of Mandela and Sobukwe, the Prime Minister offered him the opportunity to visit Robben Island. Pogrund (2015: 293) tells us that after the visit Walston reported that Sobukwe "appeared devoid of hope, and resigned to staying on Robben Island indefinitely".

"Your life will I give to you as a (snatched up) prize of war wherever you go." (Amplified Old Testament).

Thank you for the message from Prof Stuart. It was a pleasure to attend his classes and I am grateful that he was able to serve in Lesotho as well.

When Veronica was out here she picked up Snow's *The Masters* and enjoyed the opening chapters immensely. She took the book away with her and I am really eager to know what she thought of it.

And how did you enjoy your brief absence from mature Cape Town? And how is Leo's health standing up to the strain of his numerous offices?

Thank you for John Buchan's[62] book: and I hope I thanked you for the Sydney Smith biography by Bullett.[63] I get the *Reader's Digest* regularly, Nell, thanks. Benjie pays the annual subscription for that.

My mother tells me you wrote to her. Thanks. Like you, I feel it would be an occasion for celebration if we could meet: not to discuss but just to talk or keep silent as the mood takes us. I am becoming quite sentimental about you and that gives me hope that I am not an incorrigible racist.

Alles van die beste.[64]

Yours affectionately,
Robert

---

62 John Buchan (1875–1940) was a Scottish novelist, historian and politician who served as the Governor General of Canada. He was a prolific author – best known for his adventure fiction, most notably *The Thirty Nine Steps.* It is unclear which of his many books Marquard sent to Sobukwe.

63 *Sydney Smith: A Biography and a Selection* by Gerald Bullett was originally published in 1951.

64 All the best.

Veronica Sobukwe
to Benjamin Pogrund,
4 November 1968 (Ba6.62)

Dear Benjie,

I don't know whether it is possible for me to meet you at your office this week so that we could discuss our trip to Cape Town in December.

I am aware that you are busy these days with your case.

I am sorry that I have failed to save for my train-fare even this year.

I shall be extremely grateful if you could, once again, help us with the fares before the end of this month.

Sincerely,
Veronica Sobukwe

Robert Sobukwe
to Nell Marquard,
27 November 1968 (Bd2.13)

My dear Nell,

Thank you for your letter of 20th October. You wrote it, I notice, before you had received mine informing you of my success.

I received Wodehouse's *Ice in the Bedroom* and devoured it almost immediately. The *Longest Day* and *Homes Sweet Homes* I received too. But I have not received Faulkner's *Intruder in the Dust.*

Like you I have not been impressed by the little of Faulkner's that I have read so far, in spite of the reputation he enjoys. I have thought that it was because my tastes were plebeian, perhaps. He tries too hard, as you say.

Thanks for looking up Mercy in P.E.[65] She was thrilled, I am sure and will have much to tell me when and if she comes in April.

Yes, I have heard about Naomi Mitchison and her "adopted" tribe.[66] We have such few eccentrics these days that one is always glad to learn that the species has not altogether died out.

I am not anxious about Benjie. Whatever the outcome, the experience cannot but benefit him. And I know that he, himself, is morally and spiritually prepared.

How is Leo? I read a bit of the speech he made in Joh'burg. You've known him a long time. Do you think he is mellowing or getting wilder by the day?

Well Nell, God bless and keep you both. We'll see you in the New Year.

Yours affectionately,
Robert

P.S. Speaking of "eccentrics" (in the good sense) do you know Gladys Lee?[67] I should love to meet her.

---

65 Port Elizabeth.

66 Naomi Mary Margaret Mitchison (1897–1999) was a Scottish novelist, poet and activist. A committed socialist and feminist, she was politically active for many years. She acted as spokeswoman for the island communities of Scotland, and became an adviser to the Bakgatla chiefdom of Botswana.

67 Gladys Lee was a doughty solo campaigner in Cape Town, who was often seen in town with a placard protesting against government policies and actions.

Benjamin Pogrund
to Robert Sobukwe,
18 December 1968 (Ba6.64)

My dearest Bob,

It is with a sense of horror at myself that I realise how much time has elapsed since last I wrote to you. The time has just slipped by, day after day, week after week. But you will know that, however long the time that has passed, you have not been out of my thoughts and prayers, and there has too been no neglect of your interests. On one score though I was remiss – I failed to send you a telegram on your birthday earlier this month. Please forgive me for this, Bob, and accept my belated good wishes.

I saw Veronica recently and again found her well. We made arrangements about her coming trip to the Island, and I shall be at the station in Cape Town when she arrives and will deliver her and the children to the ferry boat. Within the next few days I shall be sending to her a set of gifts for everyone for Christmas, which I collected from a number of friends. By the time you get this letter, I hope too that you will have received the dictionary which Ernie and I have sent you. I am sure that you will be as excited about it as we have been – it is American published, and superbly printed and presented. We had a look at a range of dictionaries before choosing this one, and are satisfied that there is nothing better available. From both of us, affectionate good wishes, for much happy delving into it.

As Veronica told you when she last visited you, I had insisted that she buy a new dress specially for the visit, and she told me that you were well pleased with it. I have tried to persuade her to buy a mini-skirt for the next visit but have encountered a deal of resistance from her. In fact, I am certain that she will not obey me!

I am glad that the batch of books reached you safely. Only one was returned to me by the authorities.[68] I shall see soon to sending more to you. I hope that all the toilet articles also arrived safely. One point I must mention – you asked for Gillette blades, but I sent you Feather instead. They are not only far cheaper, but I have found them to be much better also. The

68 *Allied Intervention in Russia*, returned by the prison authorities on 1 October 1968.

first shave is sometimes not too good, but thereafter they give a better shave than Gillette and last longer. How's that for a "plug" for Feather? I stuck to your list as closely as possible, but in one or two cases diverged from it, either because what you wanted was not exactly available, or I thought I would get you a better product. Did you get the after-shave lotion which I sent you? These were intended as a special gift. I note, from your letter of October 30, that you were sent only one each of the Meltonia creams and I will remedy this defect. And while I think of it, I have renewed your "Reader's Digest" subscription. Will you let me know in good time when the subscriptions to the "Cape Times" and "Cape Argus" and "Sunday Times" are due to expire so that I can attend to them?

The manuscripts you referred to in your letter of October 30 have not yet arrived. I look forward eagerly to receiving them.

About your studies: I am again ashamed of myself for not having sent a telegram to congratulate you on your exam success. I thought it a great effort. Quite the Yiddishe kop[69] you have! You passed, and that is the important thing. I am, however, a bit worried about your next course. I am enclosing the syllabus of London University and as you will see, to undertake graduate studies in English, or even History, you need certain languages. I don't quite know what to advise about this. If you have any thoughts, it would be as well to send them to me by telegram as soon as you receive this letter so that I can attend to the next stage without any further delay.

About your letter of September 18: I noted what you said and had earlier received your telegram, about not running a bank account for you. I take it that you will have your Post Office account on Robben Island. Do you want me to send cash to you, to be paid into this account by you, or how should we work it? In the meantime, and even later, please do not forget that you must let me know about any clothing needs of yours – and you still have the Stuttafords facilities open to you. I recently sent the clothing requested by you, but have still not been able to raise a set of GI pyjamas. One outfitter told me that he knew what they were but did not have them and did not know anyone else who did; others I have approached have never even heard of such a thing so I don't know what next to do about them. I understand that they are pyjamas fitting snugly at the ankles and wrists. Is that right?

---

69 Literally "Jewish head", i.e. having the ability for Jewish scholarship, a smart person.

From your letter of October 2 I see that I have still failed to get Veronica a copy of "The Man" by Irving Wallace. I will attend to this. It is a most readable book, isn't it? I too was fascinated by it.

Jenny is in Cape Town at present with her mother, and I shall be flying down there on December 28, and she will come to stay with me at my Parents from December 30. We leave for Johannesburg on January 13 together by train – a special treat for her –and for me, for that matter. She has outdone herself at school this year, and came first. They do not officially place them but the teacher is a friend of mine and told me about it. I am not allowed to tell Jenny how well she did! But I could at least give her a beautiful children's dictionary to show her how pleased I was about her progress.

I am so appalled at my delay in writing that I shall end this letter now so as to get it off quickly. I shall write again during the next few days.

My best wishes to you for Christmas, and if not for Christmas then certainly for Chanukah (or Hanukah)—that's the first word you can look up in the dictionary – and for the New Year. May you, Veronica and the children be blessed during the year ahead.

With much affection,

Benjamin Pogrund
to Veronica Sobukwe,
23 December 1968 (Ba6.67)

My dear Veronica,

I enclosed a copy of a letter I have today sent to the Officer Commanding, Robben Island, Gaol.

I hope that the Christmas presents reached you safely and that they are suitable for the children.

As arranged I will meet you at Cape Town Station at 7.30 a.m. on January 7.

All the best wishes for the new year.

Benjamin Pogrund
to Robert Sobukwe,
27 December 1968 (Ba6.68)

Dearest Bob,

When I wrote last week I said that I would write again within a matter of days, and this time I am determined to keep my promise. Tomorrow morning early I fly to Cape Town, and on Monday I collect Jenny from her mother – they are there already – and we shall spend two weeks together. In case that sentence does not read properly, that is, Jenny and me! You will know that our thoughts will be especially of you during the coming fortnight: when we drive across the top of the hill from the city to Sea Point each day, on our way to my Parents' home, we will be looking out across the bay towards you.

Last week, I sent you a batch of reading books – I think there were eight altogether – and today posted another lot of six books. As always, they are a mixed bag and I hope that at least some will give you enjoyment. They are sent with the good wishes of the donor.

And just this week I heard from Charlotte Taylor after a long period of silence. She has come through a bad time – her marriage broke up after 25 years – but she seems to be on her feet again. She is as generous as ever. She sent me a note for you and I am glad to be able to enclose it with this letter. Its warmth and concern reflects her spirit.

While I think of it: I have sent R30 to the Officer Commanding to cover the cost of meals for Veronica and the children while they are with you next month. I have also asked him to let me know whether it is, in fact, necessary to send money like this for the meals. On the subject of money: as soon as I receive your reply to my last letter, as to how payments should be made to you, I shall start sending R10 a month. Will that be enough or would you like more?

As you have probably gathered, the past few months have been a source of some strain. It has all gone far, far better than expected and we are very cheerful. Winning is another matter, but that is not the important thing.[70]

70 The Prisons Act trial, with Pogrund and Laurence Gandar as the accused, finally began in November 1968. As Pogrund (2015: 297) tells it: "Gandar made an opening statement in which he repudiated utterly the charge that he and I had knowingly published false

But it has left me feeling terribly tired and drained. This has not been helped by the troubles with Norma. [...] There was a big bust up between us, then she flew out here and stayed for nine days, and then went back to the U.K., where she now intends remaining. [...]

Otherwise, I am working very hard, both because of the events of recent months and because I have started to write again. I now do a fortnightly feature called, "Talking it Over" in which I interview ministers of religion – two or three at a time – on a range of subjects, including immortality, Sunday observance, Christmas, the moment of death and spiritualism. Some of the articles are quite good; others are lousy. It depends on the calibre of the people, of course, and also on how tired I am! I don't set out to give answers to anything, but only to set out contrasting views of different denominations on interesting issues, with the purpose of encouraging people to do some thinking about the issues. The denominations, all mixed up, include DRC,[71] Hebrew, Anglican, Apostolic Faith, Methodist, etc. Would you like me to send you some of the articles? And any issues you would like to see debated? I'll do some specially for you and send them on to you.

I have also resumed being the sole South African correspondent for the London "Sunday Times", and this, together with the bouts of news editing which I do at the Mail, keeps me very busy indeed. But I prefer it that way. I also did a long article on the Press recently which I must try to send you.

By the time you get this, I hope to have seen Veronica and the children as I have arranged to meet them in Cape Town at the unearthly hour of 7.30 am on January 7, to take them to the ferry boat. I hope the kids will have liked the presents which friends gave for Christmas.

For this coming year, my brother, my prayers for your continued strength.

With much love,

---

information about jails. It was an essential part of the tradition and philosophy of the *Rand Daily Mail*, he said, to safeguard the interests of the less privileged and more vulnerable elements of society ... By 11 December, when the case was adjourned for Christmas, the State had already called ninety-seven witnesses. Truth was largely absent. It was an eerie experience to sit in a courtroom day after day and to realize that we were the centre-piece of a public show trial."

71 Dutch Reformed Church.

1969

The four beds used by Sobukwe's children when visiting him on Robben Island.

Robert Sobukwe
to Benjamin Pogrund,
8 January 1969 (Ba7.1)

Dearest Benjie,

Thank you for your letter of 18th December. All I am thankful for is to learn that you are all right. You have been through a great deal, Benjie and it shows an extremely high degree of consideration on your part to have thought of my interests. Thank you.

As you know, Veronica and the children are here and we are very happy to be together. I have seen the toys you got them, Benjie, and they are very fine toys indeed. Thanks a lot. And thank you too for Miliswa's watch. I can't thank you enough for all you are doing but I can assure you that I appreciate it more because it is done by you.

I have not yet received the dictionary you and Ernie sent: so I can't comment on it. But I *can* thank you, as I now do, for sending it.

Thank you for renewing the "Reader's Digest" subscription. The "Cape Times" and "Cape Argus" subscriptions expire in May while the "Sunday Times" will continue to be delivered until the 9th September. I am not sure whether I shall ask you to renew subscriptions for the latter. It has become quite barren.

About my studies. The syllabus arrived and I noted the requirements. As I told you, I had applied for registration but have not yet received confirmation. I suspect that the snag is my lack of a classical language. I, therefore, intend to write to Senate House and find out whether I can do the required language at the same time as I am doing the degree or whether I must have the language before I can study for the degree.

After much thought I have decided to attempt Arabic, in spite of the emotions such a choice might arouse! The reason is, really, that it is an African language in which a great deal of early African history has been written. I hope you will have no Yiddish objections.

Yes, I'll have my Post Office account here and you can send the money direct to the Post Office. Thanks, once more, for the Stuttaford facilities. As I informed you in my letter, I have ordered some articles from Stuttafords, on your account, but haven't heard from them yet.

The clothing you refer to, Benjie, is that the sports jacket? I note that you say you sent these "recently". After Veronica's August visit, the Sport Coat is the only item of clothing I received from you. The G.I. pyjamas are just what you describe.

Thanks for news of Jenny. I'll write more later. I want this off.

Affectionately,
Bob.

Officer Commanding,
Robben Island,
to Benjamin Pogrund,
10 January 1969 (Ba7.2)

Dear Sir,

1. I acknowledge the receipt of your letter dated 23 December 1968.
2. I have to inform you that Mrs. Sobukwe and children have to pay for their meals during their visit to Robben Island.

OFFICER COMMANDING

Benjamin Pogrund
to Officer Commanding,
Robben Island,
15 January 1969 (Ba7.3)

Dear Sir,

I understand from Mr Robert M. Sobukwe that an amount of R12 is required for the food for his wife and children in addition to the R30 which I sent to you last month. I accordingly enclose my cheque for R12.

Yours faithfully,
BENJAMIN POGRUND

Dini Sobukwe,
Leribe, Lesotho,
to Benjamin Pogrund,
28 January 1969 (Ba7.5)

Dear uncle Benjie,

I am sorry to write this letter to you so late, but the fact is I have kept my promise.

We arrived here in Lesotho on the 25th January 1969. I am doing well at school hoping to pass my Standard 6 which is Standard 8 in Lesotho. I am at Leribe already and it is quite a dull place, not as enjoyable as Maseru. Please uncle Benjie let me know when the books come. I am very lonely, and I need reading very much.

I hope to write to you twice a month but the reason is I have no money for stamps, but I will try by all means to write to you, we are all doing well at school.

And please uncle Benjie find me a pen-friend. I have been looking for one but without success. Please, I need a pen-friend very much.

Your son,
Dini

Veronica Sobukwe
to Benjamin Pogrund,
28 January 1969 (Ba7.4)

Dear Benjie,

You'll excuse me for writing with this type of paper, my writing pad left with the kids.

We spent a lovely holiday with Bob on the island. He looks fine although he has lost weight as far as I am concerned.

He has asked me to give you his trousers so that they should be altered please. He also asked me to pass his warmest greetings to you and to thank you & Mr. Wentzel very much for your wonderful Christmas gift. It arrived, together with the books, during our visit. He was really overjoyed when he received them, especially the dictionary.

I shall very much [like] to see you on Friday 30th at 4.45 p.m. I'm going on night duty next month.

I have just arrived from Lesotho. I told Sister Stephanie and Mrs E. Mokhele that the boarding fees for the children will be following very soon.

Sr. Stephanie is very nice. I was meeting her for the very first time.

Goodbye,
Veronica

Benjamin Pogrund
to Japie Basson, MP,
House of Assembly,
2 February 1969 (Ba7.8)

Dear Japie,[1]

As arranged, I am writing to ask for your kind help on behalf of the Sobukwe family.

The Government allows them to visit Mr Sobukwe on Robben Island twice a year, for a fortnight at a time. In practice, Mrs Sobukwe goes down for a fortnight on her own in mid-year, and she and her four children go together in January.

Despite an approach to the Minister of Justice, they have to pay their own train fares. When Mr Sobukwe was first detained on the Island in 1963 it was understood that the Government would provide his family with rail warrants to enable them to visit him, but this has been refused. I say "understood" because there is some confusion as to just what was promised at the time.

It is only since 1967 that the family has actually been allowed to live on the Island. They apparently are provided with food from the warders' mess – and must pay for it. The cost for their last visit was R42. It is about R10 when Mrs Sobukwe goes on her own. It's a negligible amount for the Government, and it does seem mingy to charge for the food.

Any help which you can give will be much appreciated.

Sincerely,
BENJAMIN POGRUND

1 Japie Basson (1918–2012) was a maverick South African politician who was expelled from the National Party by Dr Hendrik Verwoerd and then joined the opposition United Party and, later, the Progressive Federal Party. He was the MP for Bez Valley for many years.

Robert Sobukwe
to Benjamin Pogrund,
5 February 1969 (Bb17)

My dearest Benjie,

Thank you for your letter of 27th December written partly, as you admit, to religiously keep your promise to write soon made in your letter of 18th December. It is always a pleasure to hear from you even if you write merely to tell me that no rain has fallen in Joh'burg for months.

And thank you a lot for Mrs Taylor's letter. It is the more poignant because of what you have told me about her.[2] What can one say, Benjie, on such occasions? Is it good to attempt to bandage every wound? Aren't some wounds a private concern: what they term *umvandedwa* in Xhosa ("That which I feel alone"); the type which we nurse like some secret disease?

Thank you for the books: they'll keep me fully occupied. As you know I have no urgent studies this year and I have learnt to appreciate Lord Walston's references to a "purposeless" freedom.[3] I am, however, studying Nederlands – a year's course – with the Maxwell Instituut of Utrecht. Theo Kloppenberg[4] about whom I told you in 1963 – he's Dutch – has arranged for me to take the course. He is now back in Holland; was banned in Durban.

When I wrote to you I had not yet received the dictionary. I have now. It and the American Judaism Reader. Thank you immensely for both. Without sounding like Oliver Twist, may I ask you for more books by Jewish authors

2 Charlotte Taylor's marriage of 25 years had recently ended.

3 Henry Walston was Under-Secretary of State for Foreign Affairs in the Labour government of Harold Wilson from 1964 to 1967. In 1968 he undertook a lecture tour of South Africa, held a private meeting with Prime Minister B.J. Vorster and visited Nelson Mandela on Robben Island.

4 Theodore Johannes Kloppenberg had been involved in various anti-apartheid organisations and activities in Durban in the early 1960s with people like Eleanor Kasrils and Phyllis Naidoo. He was banned in April 1967 under the Suppression of Communism Act and left for the Netherlands after his banning expired in 1968.

– particularly Malamud,[5] Golden[6] and others. Only don't send me anything by Leon Uris.[7] I have become allergic to him.

You will have met Veronica by now and will have learnt why we required the extra twelve rands. It was a pleasure having them here, Benjie, and I thank you sincerely for all you are doing.

One point I couldn't understand in your letter, though. You say you have written to the O.C. to ask if it is "necessary to send money like this for meals". Do you mean is it necessary for Veronica and the Kids to pay for their meals or do you mean the account could be sent to you after the visit? If it is the necessity for paying that you are questioning then you must direct your question to the Minister of Justice. That is one of the stipulations he made. And I am glad he did, Benjie. I feel happier knowing that Veronica and the children pay for their meals. And so does she: ask her.

I have written to the O.C. requesting permission to open a Savings Account at the local Post Office. Ten Rands a month will be quite sufficient. As I said in my last letter, you could send that straight to the post office.

It relieved me to note that your attitude to your case was quite relaxed. I had written to assure Nell Marquard that the Jew boy who's been through his *bris mila*[8] and *Bar Mitzvah* shouldn't mind a year at Pretoria Central – at least not now!

[...]

It is good to know you are writing again. Certainly, most certainly I'll be glad to get your articles on "Talking it Over".[9] I should like you to pin these fellows down on their conception of heaven. Is it a geographical locality? If not what is it? If not, where was Christ from then? Where did he return to? Pin them down to concrete, unambiguous categorical statements! I'll look

5 Bernard Malamud was a Jewish-American author, who won the Pulitzer Prize for fiction in 1967 for his novel *The Fixer* (1966).

6 Harry Golden was a Jewish-American editor, journalist and humourist. He often addressed the absurdity of racial segregation in works like *Only in America* (1958).

7 Leon Uris was a Jewish-American author best known for his novel *Exodus* (1958).

8 The *bris mila*, also known as the *brit milah*, is the Jewish religious male circumcision ritual performed on the eighth day of the infant's life.

9 "Talking It Over" was a series of panel discussions that Pogrund arranged and wrote for the *Rand Daily Mail* featuring the contributions of a range of religious ministers.

forward to that. Let them reconcile the historical Jewish Jesus with the eternal Christ in unmythical language. It's time they did.

Incidentally, I have been hearing from Arthur Blaxall,[10] of late, and he has sent me some very interesting and enlightened publications of the World Congress of Faiths.

My mother and my sister-in-law should be visiting me some time in April if all goes well. It's something to look forward to.

About the purchases at Stuttafords that I wrote you of, I have received no word up to now. I shall make inquiries and will be pleased if you do the same. Also I asked Eulalie Stott to get me an electric iron, slop pail and a bath. I gave the list to Veronica. I also gave her some old trousers of mine I wanted you to have altered as you'd done with the new ones.

I'll write again. For the present, Benjie, best wishes. And love to Jenny.

Affectionately, Bob.

Did you say you sent me some Hemingway books? Sorry I didn't receive them. Could you try again?

---

10 An Anglican priest (1891–1970) who became known for his work among the blind and deaf in South Africa. In 1963 he had been charged with various offences under the Suppression of Communism Act, was given a suspended sentence, and then went into exile in Britain.

Veronica Sobukwe
to Benjamin Pogrund,
14 February 1969 (Ba7.10)

My dear Benjie,

I have just received a letter from Bob in which he informed me that his finger is completely healed. A new finger is appearing.

I applied for the children (boys) in a multi-racial school in Swaziland.

They have replied and enclosed the application forms together with the prospectus. A lot of money is involved but I think they do give some financial help to those who cannot afford the full fees.

Don't you think we will get good and quick results from this school?

They say entry is by means of a test which should be written at school. They also stress the fact that they will have to repeat their standards because most probably their present school has a lower general academic level than their school.

When can I see you so that we could discuss this matter?

With best wishes,
Sincerely,
Veronica

P.S. Please choose any day (for the appointment) except on a Monday.

Benjamin Pogrund
to Dini Sobukwe,
18 February 1969 (Ba7.11)

To Dini,

It was so nice of you to write to me, and I was very pleased to hear from you.

I have written to friends of mine in England, the United States and Israel, and have asked them to arrange for penfriends for you. I hope that you will soon hear from some people of your age in these countries. Will you let me know if you hear from penfriends?

I have posted three parcels of books to you. I had to get them together in a hurry and I am not sure if they will be books that you will like. Will you write to me and tell me which books you liked, which were too difficult and which were too easy? Then I shall know what to send you. And you won't forget to give Miliswa these books also? And what about the twins? I know that their English is not too good so I am not sure if I should try to send books to them. Will you let me know?

I am enclosing a postal order for 50c so that you can buy stamps. You must take the postal order to a post office and they will give you money for it with which you can buy stamps. If penfriends write to you, you should ask the post office for air-letter cards. They cost 5c each, and are much cheaper to send overseas than ordinary letters. If you write to England and Israel, you can use these 5c air-letters. But if you write to the United States you must put on an *extra* 5c stamp because the postage there is 10c.

I also want to send you and the twins some pocket money so that you can buy sweets, stamps and anything else that you might need. But I am not sure how much to send you. Will you write and tell me what you think? And should I send the money to you, for you to keep and to give to the twins, or should I send it to Mrs Mokhele? You don't have to worry about Miliswa, as I am making separate arrangements about her.

I hope I shall hear from you soon,

With a lot of love to you and the twins,

Robert Sobukwe
to Nell Marquard,
19 February 1969 (Bd2.15)

My dear Nell,

There is so much I have to thank you for. But first, please let me tell you that on Sunday I met John Betjeman[11] in "High and Low" and I felt that I had not read poetry before then. What sound, what rhythm, what motion!

What chance has any inland lung
Against this multi-water noise?[12]

That's the ocean he is writing about. And then, somewhere, he observes that:

It's strange that those we miss the most
Are those we take for granted.[13]

I suppose Wordsworth and company must have made the same impact on a society bored with lovely little rhymes and rhythms about drawing-room society. We too have had to contend with so much obfuscation, obscurantism and obscuration in poetry that we began to wonder whether we had any intelligence at all. And lo and behold, Betjeman shows us that we are not such nitwits after all.

Well, Nell, I had to tell you that.

Well now, my last letter to you was written on the 21st November, last year and I hope I thanked you and Leo for the birthday wishes and the Five Rands. Thank you also for the calendar which I received at the beginning of the year. It is a lovely thing. One feels reluctant to get rid of the pictures.

Veronica and the children were here once more. She's beginning to feel the strain, I suppose. She was quite snappish! The children are growing up

---

11 John Betjeman was an English poet, journalist and broadcaster. He was the Poet Laureate of the United Kingdom between 1972 and 1984.

12 Sobukwe here is citing Betjeman's poem "Winter Seascape".

13 These are the two closing lines of Betjeman's poem "The Hon. Sec.".

fast and require this and that. Benjie met them at the station and took the children to Table Mountain.

As for books and journals now what have I? You will remember that I didn't receive the Faulkner book. But Realités, and Discovering Art[14] and the Sunday Times Magazine article; these I received. Thank you.

I had so hoped to send you good wishes on your birthday, but Veronica and the children were arriving on the seventh and I believe that in the excitement I forgot to send your card. But I did not forget the day and I blessed you in my heart.

Whether Mercy and my mother will come I April is still uncertain: their hosts of last year have moved to pastures new – Fort Beaufort to be precise. I am writing to hear from Mercy what their plans are.

My plans for studying for the Honours degree in English are running into trouble. I am supposed to have done a classical language – Latin or Greek – or Arabic, Hebrew, Hindi and similar tongues. Unfortunately I haven't done any. I have decided to do Arabic and will have to acquaint myself with the Ibn Il Saffiq and clowns of the same sort.

Well, Nell, so much for now. Keep well.

Best wishes to you and Leo.

Yours affectionately,
Robert

14 *Discovering Art: The Illustrated Story of Art through the Ages* was a full-colour periodical series issued quarterly in soft covers between 1964 and 1966, which purchasers could collect and eventually store in ring-back binders.

Dini Sobukwe
to Benjamin Pogrund,
20 February 1969 (Ba7.15)

Dear UNCLE Benjie,

I thank you very much in sending those books I asked for and the 50c you gave to me for buying stamps and all the necessary equipment.

Most of the books were to my standard, although I found some of them quite interesting especially the one about Robin Hood and the PILGRIM'S PROGRESS and the others. My hobbies in books depend mostly on classics such as those of Julius CAESAR, OLIVER TWIST, THE RIVALS and so on. I think all that loneliness I used to have will soon disappear.

Please uncle Benjie do not forget to seeking pen friends for me. I would prefer ones from Israel and America and of course every available one will be welcomed. I have grown interested in writing letters.

Your son,
Dini

P.S. Greeting to Jenny

Benjamin Pogrund
to Robert Sobukwe,
4 March 1969 (Ba7.19)

My dearest Bob,

Your letter of February 5 came today. Because of the inordinate delay in it getting to me I am hastening to reply.

No, I have not sent any Hemingways yet but I am attending to it this week. In fact, I shall be sending down quite a batch of books for your pleasure, and will also be sending a batch to Miliswa and Dini. Various friends up here have been generous in making this possible. In my next letter I shall let you have a list of the books which will have been sent to you.

About Stuttafords: your letter has taken so long to get to me that I hope that the order you placed has by now been executed. But in case it has not, I have tonight written to the Manager, Stuttafords, Adderley Street, Cape Town, reminding him of the arrangement whereby you can purchase whatever you want on my account. If you have not yet received what you ordered, I suggest you write immediately direct to the Manager.

About the trousers: they are at the tailor at present, and will be in the post to you before the end of this week. I am a bit worried about them because you gave contradictory instructions! You first said to alter them to the pattern of the brown trousers, I think your note said, and then at the end you said that the brown ones should also be altered. Anyway, the tailor and I looked at the brown trousers, I gave a description of what you look like, and we examined your body measurements which you sent me some time ago. So the measurements will be an amalgam of all these. You had better start praying!

While on the subject of clothing, do you need anything which I can send from here? Especially with winter coming? I note your requests sent to Eulalie. I am sure that she has attended to them, but I shall write to her in case there was any misunderstanding. And again while I think of it, I had planned to enrol you in a book and a record club, but I have now received their prospectus and I don't think it would be advantageous. I am thinking of trying to get someone overseas to take out membership in a top-class book club and will see about this. As for records, I hope to be able to send you a few within the next few days.

You wrote so beautifully about Charlotte [Taylor]. The "umvandedwa" phrase sums up so much so poignantly, and I agree with it. But still, however necessary the aloneness might sometimes have to be, the love and concern of those close to us, whose love and concern we know is genuine, can go a far way to assuaging the hurt and aloneness, even though it cannot rid us of it entirely. I hope that you have been able to write to her: I know that it is something which she would deeply appreciate and welcome.

I retreat hastily on the question of my letter about the cost of the food. I wrote it because I thought it was a mingy action to charge these rands for the food, after the generous action of allowing Veronica and the children to visit you. I have in any event since had a letter from the O.C. advising that the money must be paid. I can easily send the cash in advance, as is the present arrangement. If it is convenient to send me an account afterwards, that would also do. It does not make any difference from my point of view. All that I am worried about is that sometimes I get late notice that I should send money down for the meals, so on balance, if an account can be sent afterwards it would probably be better.

This has been an exciting few days. I suddenly got the idea of not allowing this to be a wasted year. And I thought to myself: If that brother of mine on the Island can do it, so can I. So I have just this morning registered for a B.A. Hons. degree in African Studies at Wits. It's a bit crazy, I suppose, doing an Hons. when I am supposed to be working on a Ph.D., but as my research papers are in London and cannot be touched at present, it is not entirely mad. I expect that the next couple of months will be a bit of a sweat, but as the big event in my life at present is due to end in about May, possibly June, with judgment a couple of months later, it will be easier in the second part of the year.[15] I am doing four courses: two in African government; social change in Africa; and education in Africa. I shall have to do an enormous amount of reading, just to catch up in these fields, but I am looking forward to it. It should be a useful antidote to the tedium of the days. And, of course, the primary idea is also to broaden my academic base in preparation for going to lecture elsewhere. As

15 Pogrund is referring to the trial that he and his editor Laurence Gandar underwent as a result of the Rand Daily Mail's exposé of prison abuses in 1965. The succession of prosecutions of Pogrund's informants culminated in his and Gandar's trial from November 1968 to July 1969 in the Supreme Court, Johannesburg.

you know, I have for long wanted also to extend my interest and knowledge northwards and this is the chance to do it.

As indicated, the days are tedious and dreary except for the occasional high spot. But I keep well. I have your spirit to sustain and guide me. That, and my own belief in what I have done, ensures that I go on.

I shall get the religious articles together and will send them in my next letter. Hope my letter of February 23, with the enclosed pictures and cheque, has arrived safely.

Affectionately,

Robert Sobukwe
to Nell Marquard,
6 March 1969 (Bd2.16)

My dear Nell,

You were at your Oxford best when you wrote your letter of 18th February which I received this morning. And I refer not only to the smoothly flowing language.

> the vale profound
> Is overflowing with the sound,[16]

but also to the calmness that pervaded the whole letter. It was a soothing letter. Thank you very much for it.

When I wrote to you on the 20th February I had not yet received your letter of January. That is why I made no reference to it in my reply. And I hadn't received the books either.

I have subsequently received both the letter and the books. *All* the books, Nell. Thank you. I have enough reading matter now to last me till your return.

I am delighted to learn that you and Leo will be going overseas. And by ship at that. I pray that you have a "white road", as they say in Sotho (They haven't met the Black Power advocates yet!). It is indeed refreshing to think that there are such friends.

Yes, Nell, I received the New Yorker and would certainly like to continue getting it. Incidentally, I pounced on the [P.G.] Wodehouses and devoured them. I felt disgusted afterwards. Intellectual greed is just as bad as the physical, don't you think so? One must control one's appetite.

As you will have seen in my letter of February, I have not yet started on my Honours course and it does not seem likely that I will start before August or so. But I am grateful for the offer of books and would prefer that you act as agent.

The drought has been severe, there's no doubt about that. And the Karoo can be very pathetic when drought-stricken.

---

16 From William Wordsworth's poem "The Solitary Reaper".

So you attended the Summer-School?[17] You've expressed your fears too late my dear. It already *is* the done thing to attend these lectures. But I am intrigued by your statement that the problems and sentiments of Greek Tragedy are modern. I have always felt that we Africans can appreciate Greek drama much more than we do Shakespeare, for instance, because the taboos and rituals are so like ours:

"The growing years lay heavy on his head", I read in Murray's translation of *Oedipus*, and it could have been an African speaking.[18]

Oh it's no use complaining about the amounts spent on armaments and lunar exploration, Nell. A study of economics will show you that over sixty per cent of what is termed production is unnecessary and, in the long run, harmful. The sole aim appears to be to create jobs. It's not cynical, I suppose, to say: "the poor ye have with you always."[19]

Well Nell I really wish you a lovely time over there. We'll miss you quite a lot. I note that you say Leo is looking forward to a quiet pint at the pub. Please remember Barbara Castle's breathalyser.[20] She's quite a kill-sport I'm told.

My good wishes go with you both.

By the way, please inform Mrs Stott that I received the alarm clock. And thank her for me.

Yours affectionately,
Robert

---

17 An annual series of lectures, open to the public, held in January at the University of Cape Town.

18 Gilbert Murray's highly regarded translation of the play *Oedipus: King of Thebes* by Sophocles is still in print.

19 Matthew 26: 11.

20 Barbara Castle was a long-serving Labour MP and a vocal opponent of apartheid. As Minister of Transport (1965–8), she introduced the breathalyser as a means of combating drinking and driving.

Robert Sobukwe
to Benjamin Pogrund,
27 March 1969 (Ba7.24)

My dearest Benjie,

Thank you for your letter of 4th March which I received on the 19th; and the trousers which were all well done indeed.

My mother and my sister-in-law have been visiting me this week. Their trip was made possible by Eulalie and friends. They have been staying at the Tafelberg Hotel. They leave tomorrow afternoon. Today is their last visit.

From the enclosed receipt you will realize that we have been to Stuttafords. I sent my sister-in-law there. Her tastes are expensive – as are mine and she has run up a formidable debt.

I wonder if I can share the debt with you? I was going to suggest that instead of sending me the Ten Rands you intended for April and May, you hold those back as my contribution to the payment of the debt. The stuff she got is first class, Benjie, there's no doubt about that. I shall be happy and proud to wear it.

I don't think I'll need anything else this year in the way of clothing. I have all I want.

About the children: I am glad you are sending them books to read. The toys were first class and have drawn them out of themselves.

But instead of sending them money to spend I should be glad if you could encourage them to start saving – either by means of a piggy-bank or Savings Accounts which they will themselves control. Miliswa and Dini, particularly, should be told that they are saving towards their University education.

By the way, I learnt from my sister-in-law that Eulalie has sent the articles I requested. You'll thank her for me.

Thank you for *your* comments on Charlotte [Taylor]. I shall write to her soon. And what you say about the genuine concern and love of friends is, of course, too true.

About the food for Veronica and the kids I think we'd better stick to the present arrangement whereby you send the money beforehand. Until further notice, make it fifteen Rands (R15.00) when Veronica is alone and R45.00 (Forty-five) when the whole family comes a-visiting. I suppose when Miliswa and Dini have passed the "children's" age – is it *sixteen*? – you'll have to adjust accordingly. At present, two children count as one adult.

It is very exciting news indeed that you have started on the B.A. Hons. yourself. You are, in fact, ahead of me because ever since I wrote asking to register for the course, *I* have had no reply from the Senate of London University. It appears I shall have to make a fresh application. And that means I won't start on the course until late in the year.

I shall write again later. But so far, this has been really a blessed year for me, with unexpected pleasures following closely on one another.

Leo and Nellie Marquard are going overseas for about six months. Unknown friends have made this possible.

Well Benjie, best wishes.

Yours affectionately,
Bob

P.S. Veronica intends to buy some land. Could you discuss the matter with her and advise? I approve the *site* she has decided on. But I should prefer emphasis on *seclusion*: no property development schemes!

P.P.S. Have written to Charlotte – Registered. Bob.

Robert Sobukwe
to Veronica Sobukwe,
16 April 1969 (Bc44)

Hullo Darling!

Some time ago I wrote to you, but, of course, did not expect a reply. I hope you received the letter, though, because it had good news from Mrs Mokhele. Since then, I have heard from Mili as well – a very lovely letter!

Nenti and Mercy have been here. They spent about a week. Mercy is still as big as she was last year and Nenti looks just the same.

I asked Mercy to get me some stuff on Benjie's account – the same items as I discussed with you. She chose very expensive items and built up an account of R46.00, forty-six rands. I have written to Benjie to suggest that at least R20.00 (twenty rands) could come from me – from the amount Mrs Taylor sends.

Incidentally, Benjie has written me a very fine letter, too. He wants to know what more he can do for the children. I have sent him my suggestions.

Yesterday I wrote to Ernie Wentzel on a rather serious matter, affecting my health. I have also written to the Minister of Justice on the same.[21] I may require you to come down some time soon, for a week or so. If it becomes necessary I shall send you a telegram, but I should like you, meanwhile, to find out whether you can get a week's leave at short notice. Better still, discuss this matter with Benjie.

That will be all for now, darling. I shall write more later.

Love to the children.

Your loving husband,
Mangi

---

21 Mention of such an uncharacteristic gesture – Sobukwe had always firmly rejected the prospect of making any appeals to the Minister of Justice – would have been a cause of alarm for Veronica. Veronica only received the letter on 2 May, after it had been held up by the authorities for almost two weeks, panicked, and called Pogrund, who immediately set about finding out about Sobukwe's condition. The health issue was a serious one, and it led to the sudden announcement by Justice Minister Pelser, on midnight of 24 April, that Sobukwe was to be released. Sobukwe received a letter informing him, that it was not intended to detain him beyond 30 June, but to release him, in Pelser's words, "at the earliest possible date subject to such restrictions as are deemed necessary for the safety of the State" (cited in Pogrund, 2015: 300).

Benjamin Pogrund
to Dini Sobukwe,
20 April 1969 (Ba7.27)

My dear Dini,

I am sorry that I have taken so long to reply to your letter which I was very glad to receive. As you know, I am in this trial about prison conditions, and the trial has been taking up all my time lately.

I have written to friends of mine overseas about getting penfriends for you. By now I hope that you will have heard from some of them. Will you let me know when you do hear from them? Later you will also be receiving books from overseas.

Last week I posted to you another batch of books which I hope you will find interesting. I also sent, in a separate parcel, a set of girls' annuals for Miliswa. Will you please give these to her? I have noted that you wrote about the sort of books you prefer: I have ordered a set of classics for you and these will be posted to you soon. Please let me now when all these books reach you and whether you like them. I have also sent you, by registered post, a set of two books dealing with people in other countries. Will you let me know whether you and Miliswa like these? If you do, I shall arrange for you to receive a different one dealing with different countries every month.

I am enclosing postal orders to the value of R2.50. Of this, R1.50 is for you, and 50c each for Dedani and Dalindyebo. Will you please see that they get it? In a letter I received from your Father this week, he said he is very anxious for all of you to start saving money. Can you buy money boxes in Leribe for yourself and the twins? If you can, please buy some small ones and whenever you can, put a few cents away for the future. If you cannot buy such things there, let me know and I shall send them to you.

I told Jenny that you had sent your greetings: she gave a big smile and asked me to send you her regards.

I hope that you and the other children are well. Please give them my love. Will you ask Miliswa to write to me.

Benjamin Pogrund
to Robert Sobukwe,
20 April 1969 (Ba7.29)

Dearest Bob,

I was so pleased, on Friday, to receive your letter of March 27 and to see that your spirit remains high. I am glad that the trousers were received safely and that you are all right. Was a white shirt perhaps enclosed also? If so, it is one of mine which I gave to the tailor for alteration. If you can, you can send it back to me. But if it fits you well, then by all means keep it.

You were obviously very happy of the visit about your mother and sister-in-law[22]and this was reflected in the tone of your letter. The expensive tastes of your sister-in-law in clothing do not matter as long as she bought you what you like. Don't worry about the Stuttafords account: I shall settle it direct from here. I recently had a letter from Stuttafords in Cape Town saying that they could not find any record of an order placed by you. They assured me, however, that they would give immediate effect to any order which you might place. If you want anything, Bob, please write to the Mail Order Department at Stuttafords. The reference number on the letter was LOD3/.

You haven't said that the system of sending cheques in your name is unsatisfactory, so I shall do it again in the same way. With much pleasure I enclose my cheque for R30, for April, May and June. Sorry that the amount for April is reaching you so late. But at least May and June will be early!

I am seeing Veronica this week to talk about the children. I shall also then discuss with her the question of the plot of land which you mentioned. Dini wrote to me a while ago to tell me that while he had enjoyed the books I had sent him, he had found most of them too easy. It seems I had under-estimated his ability in reading English, and I am very pleased that he has a higher standard than I thought. I have sent him another batch, and will also soon be sending him a set of classics which he specially requested: Oliver Twist, Julius Caesar and The Rivals are the ones he specified. I have also, in a letter earlier today, told him what his Father requires of him in the way of savings! If he cannot buy money-boxes there for himself and the twins, I'll send them by post. I have written to Sister Stephanie at St. Mary's Hostel in the same vein

22 Nenti and Mercy.

about Miliswa. The Sister, by the way, is always the essence of kindness and help when I write to her.

About the books I promised to send to you, Bob: my apologies, but they haven't gone off yet. The cash for them, or most of it, was given by a friend, Mrs Irene Menell,[23] with her very good wishes. But she wanted certain books chosen especially, and I want to choose some, and you have stated your preferences, and Jill and Ernie have theirs, so it has taken some time to knit it all together – as well as arranging to buy them wholesale so we can buy even more. Anyway, they will be reaching you soon so you have something to look forward to. If you have the energy and the inclination, can you assist me in regard to the books? Can you perhaps send me a list of all the books you have so that I can ensure that I do not duplicate? Am I asking a great deal? If it's too difficult, don't bother about it, but it would be a help.

Enclosed is a letter for you from Jenny. All her own work, except for asking me to spell Easter for her and Monday. She has again done well at school: an A plus average at the end of the first quarter, with her teacher again giving me glowing reports about her. On Friday evening I introduced her to serious opera by taking her to see the film of "La Traviata". She sat spellbound, so her life has been broadened yet a bit more. Coming out of this cinema, walking hand in hand up the street, we passed a beggar sitting on the pavement. Jenny asked me for some money to give him and she went across and handed it to him. Then we walked on. After a few paces she said to me, terribly thoughtfully, "That's a good way to make money, hey." So you see that some of her father's cynicism is rubbing off on her.

I am worried that you haven't yet started on your varsity studies. What about enrolling with the University of South Africa? Apart from the saving of time, the entrance qualifications for an Honours degree will probably not be as rigorous as those of London. If you are interested, perhaps you could telegraph me immediately and I would arrange to have the prospectus posted to you immediately. My own studies are limping along: it requires a great deal of reading. I am more concerned about the studies than about anything else that is happening to me at the moment, which I suppose is a

23 Irene Menell was the wife of the wealthy Johannesburg businessman Clive Menell, deputy chairman of Anglovaal. She was a close friend of Helen Suzman and was the manager of Suzman's Houghton constituency for many years. She was involved in many good causes, especially the education of black children.

good thing in itself! I don't know if you were able to read the recent reports in your local newspapers, but if you were, then you would have seen that things have gone extremely well, once one accepts that the result is virtually pre-ordained.[24]

Much love to you,

24 Pogrund was still involved in legal matters. The trial on prison conditions continued, and Pogrund evidently had little hope that he and Laurence Gandar had any chance of winning.

Benjamin Pogrund
to Sister Stephanie,
St Mary's Hostel,
Leribe,
20 April 1969 (Ba7.28)

Dear Sister Stephanie,

Please forgive my delay in replying to your letter of February 28. I am glad to fall in with your suggestion regarding pocket money for Miliswa Sobukwe, and have pleasure in enclosing my cheque for R5. If more money is required, will you please be good enough to let me know?

I am arranging with friends of mine overseas for young people to write to Miliswa. I thought that it could be of help to her in improving her English, while it would also serve to broaden her outlook. I hope that she will be receiving letters from young people in the United States, England and Israel. Could her pocket money please be used to enable her to purchase air letters?

I am also now sending her brother Dini supplies of books to read and have asked him to share these with Miliswa.

Thank you once again for your kind help,

Sincerely,
BENJAMIN POGRUND

P.S. In a letter I had this week from Mr Sobukwe he said that he was anxious to encourage the children to save money. Perhaps Miliswa could buy a small money box and learn to put aside a few cents whenever she can.

Benjamin Pogrund
to Robert Sobukwe,
27 April 1969 (Ba7.32)

My dearest brother,

There is little I can say, or need to say, at this stage.[25] Just that I share your happiness, and the happiness of Veronica and the children. And that in saying a prayer of thanks, I have prayed also for your future. There is a life stretching ahead of you: may it be as useful and purposeful as so much of your life has been up to now. More, may you be given the opportunity to lead a full and rich life, and to contribute from those great talents which are uniquely yours. Again, I need not say it and you will know it, but you have only to tell me if there is anything I can do.

I have not yet seen Veronica since the news came out. We spent a short time together on Tuesday, and knowing that the issue of your future would soon be arising, and not knowing then what good news was soon to follow, I felt extremely depressed in speaking to her. I did not know what words of comfort I could offer her. In any event, I have sent Veronica a note – a series of circumstances prevented my seeing her on Thursday night – and I hope to speak to her on the phone tomorrow. Incidentally, I sent you a congratulatory telegram on Friday and I hope it reached you safely.

In the meantime, I shall not go ahead with sending you the batch of books I mentioned in my last letter. Instead, I shall be sending a separate small batch to you tomorrow, just to tide you over. These are: 7 issues of Argosy, Hell Box by John O'Hara, Man in the Middle by Fast, The Groves of Academe by Mary McCarthy, Who's afraid of Virginia Woolf by Edward Albee, and The Letters

---

25 Although Pogrund had by now obviously heard of Sobukwe's release, neither he nor Veronica had received the disturbing news of Sobukwe's health problems as announced by Sobukwe in his (delayed) letter to Veronica dated 16 April (above). As Pogrund (2015) recollects, there was a pervading sense of apprehension following the announcement of Sobukwe's release: how restrictive would Sobukwe's subsequent restrictions be; where would the government relocate him to; what had prompted such a sudden decision on the part of the government, after years of recalcitrance?

of Vincent van Gogh.[26] If you require further reading, will you telegram me immediately and I'll rush books to you?

You must have a formidable range of goods in your bungalow at present: books, clothing, radio, heaters, etc. I hope that the authorities will be assisting you in shipping them off to your home. As the shipping of the furniture and goods of warders is constantly being attended to, it should not present any problems.

While I think of it: if you need suitcases, can you order them from Stuttafords, and have them charged to me; alternatively, you can telegraph Eulalie who I am sure will be glad to attend to it.

I hope, I hope, that we shall soon be seeing each other again.

With much affection,

---

26 John O'Hara, *Hellbox* (1947); Howard Fast, *Man in the Middle* (1963); Mary McCarthy, *The Groves of Academe* (1952); Edward Albee, *Who's Afraid of Virginia Woolf?* (1962).

Benjamin Pogrund
to Helen Suzman,
MP, House of Assembly,
27 April 1969 (Ba7.31)

My dear Helen,

It's great news that Bob Sobukwe is to be freed. Now one must wait and see what restrictions they are going to place on him. I am fearful about these.

In the meantime, it strikes me that, over the years, Bob has accumulated a formidable mass of goods on the Island: books, clothing, bedding, heaters, easy chairs, radio, radiogram, etc., all of which is his own property. I was wondering whether it might be possible for you to make a quiet approach to the Minister to ask him if the authorities will ensure that all these things are packed up and shipped home for Bob. It would be a decent gesture if the State would bear the costs. The furniture and goods of warders transferred to and from the Island are regularly shipped so there must be a definite arrangement in existence about this sort of thing.

As always, I hope you will not mind my approaching you.

Hope you are well.

With warm good wishes,
BENJAMIN POGRUND

Telegram from
Benjamin Pogrund
to Robert Sobukwe,
29 April 1969 (Ba7.33)

Have spoken to Veronica & Eulalie. Please telegraph Eulalie regarding requirements suitcases and boxes for packing. Fond regards, Benjamin

Helen Suzman
to Benjamin Pogrund,
1 May 1969 (Ba7.36)

Dear Benjy,

Great news indeed. I only hope the restrictions imposed are not going to be too crippling.

I will certainly make a quiet approach to the Min. about Mr. S.'s goods and chattels. I think they probably will agree to bearing the cost of transport.

Kindest regards & holding both thumbs re the judgment.

Helen

Telegram from
Benjamin Pogrund
to Robert Sobukwe,
3 May 1969 (Ba7.37)

Deeply concerned your letter April 16 to Veronica Stop Can you provide further details Question Please advise whether you want Veronica to travel to island.[27]

Fondest regards,
Benjamin

27 The details of Sobukwe's ill health – the effects of an apparent psychological breakdown – would only become evident in the weeks to follow. The effects of long-term and sustained solitary confinement – today considered by experts as a means of psychological torture – had, after six years, taken their toll. One result of being cut off from social contact and being subject to constant surveillance and vilification was that Sobukwe formed the idea that the Security Branch was using a machine against him, a machine which influenced various of his bodily functions (see Sobukwe's letter to the Minister of Justice of 22 May 1969).

Benjamin Pogrund
to Robert Sobukwe
[no address given],
4 May 1969 (Ba7.43)

Dearest Bob,

I was so glad to get your letter of Monday, even though it only arrived on Thursday and I collected it on Friday. Making it express and registered seemed to have delayed it! So I am sending this letter by ordinary post to see how long it takes to reach you. Incidentally, forgive this typewriter: I am at the office – I sub-edit for the Express on Saturdays – and the machine is not so hot.

I saw Veronica yesterday evening and we had a long chat. She will be seeing you this coming weekend, and I have asked her to please tell you to phone me. Isn't there perhaps a public phone box in the area which could be used? As I said in my last letter, you can simply ring the exchange and put through a reverse charge call to me, which means you won't have to bother about having small change available.

What a relief to be able to write in comparative freedom, without having to worry whether this word or that word can cause difficulties for you. And the letter delay from your end wasn't a mere two weeks. I found that your letters invariably took three to four weeks to reach me.

This has been a tough week at the trial, with a flood of abuse flung at [Laurence] Gandar and me and our attorney. Had it been justified and related to facts one could not and would not mind. But it has all been entirely unrelated either to actual events or to our evidence, so I have found it sick-making. To add to it, it was at an extraordinarily low intellectual level. The deceitfulness of the argument was something astonishing in itself: for example, slamming me for having been untruthful in my evidence by referring to the evidence of another witness who contradicted me. But the reference to the other witness was confined to his evidence in chief, whereas even a cursory glance at his cross-examination shows that he was clearly concealing information, probably because he was frightened! When the State reaches this low level of morality it leaves me feeling ill and extremely depressed. I suppose that it's silly for me to be surprised at this stage, but that's me!

Anyway, the worst is over and this week the Defence will be arguing, and that should be something worth reading. Are you getting the Mail at present?

Is it easily available? I have made inquiries here and it is uncertain whether the Mail and the Star are actually delivered to homes in your township. If they are, please let me know and I can arrange subscriptions from here. Otherwise, do you want to get the papers daily by buying them in the area? I am not sure about the Star, but I think the Mail is on sale there on the morning of publication. Otherwise, let me know and I shall have to arrange for the papers to be sent from here, which would mean their reaching you a day or so late.

The trial will, I hope, end now on June 3 or 4, and I propose to fly to Cape Town, to see my Parents, on Sunday, June 8, and then to Kimberley on Wednesday, June 11, remaining there until the Friday night. But if this is too late, and you want me to try and get down a few days earlier, let me know and I'll do my best.

I hope you will keep your promise to write often. Tell me how you are feeling, and how you are adjusting to being off the Island. I am anxious to know.

Much affection,

Telegram from
Robert Sobukwe
to Benjamin Pogrund,
14 May 1969 (Ba7.38)

Address is six Naledi Street Galashawe Kimberley Stop Would like meeting soon. Bob

Benjamin Pogrund
to Robert Sobukwe,
15 May 1969 (Ba7.39)

Dearest Bob,

Welcome, welcome. It's not quite home, but it's a big step anyway! I was so pleased to get your telegram: it came yesterday but I didn't go to the office and only got it today. I want to see you too, and want to travel to Kimberley just as soon as possible. I thought of flying down today, just for the day, but then decided that your house arrest order probably applied to public holidays so it wouldn't have been any use. The big problem at the moment, Bob, is the wretched trial because it means I cannot get away during the week. Am I right in assuming that the house arrest applies also from lunch-time on Saturdays?[28] That would make the weekends a bit of a wash-out also – unless you especially want me to come down just for a Saturday morning. Otherwise, what I propose to do is come down for a couple of days immediately the trial adjourns, which should be in about two weeks from now.

Can you telephone me in the meantime? Perhaps you could use a public phone somewhere and put through a reverse charge call to me? (Johannesburg 44.9030). The best time to reach me, if you can manage it, is before 9 a.m. I don't mind how much before that time you ring.

---

28 The restrictions placed on Sobukwe following his release from Robben Island were severe. He was far from a free man – he remained under house arrest. His banning orders prohibited him, for the next five years, from leaving the municipal district of Kimberley. Between 6 pm and 6 am he had to remain inside the Naledi Street house, and he was not permitted visits other than by a doctor or a very limited number of close family members. He was not permitted to write – or in any way prepare – anything for publication, or to assist others in plans to publish any material. He was banned from giving any educational instruction – with the obvious exception of his own children. No communication was allowed with any other banned person, or with any members of outlawed organisations, such as the ANC and the PAC. He could not enter the premises of any university, school or newspaper, and he was likewise barred from entering any hostel or premises where he could meet with black workers. His relocation to Kimberley also meant that he was placed in a geographically remote town, far removed from family and friends, distant also from any major city.

I haven't spoken to Veronica yet. I phoned the clinic and left a message but I don't know if she received it. I'll try again tomorrow.

I saw Jenny this morning and she told me with sparkling eyes that she had seen in the newspaper that you had been released. She is eager to meet you, and I hope to be able to bring this about before not too long [...].

I wrote to you on April 27 and sent a telegram when the news came through about your release: I hope you received these. I also sent a batch of books at that time to tide you over, and I hope these arrived. Also, I was darned worried because of your letter of April 16 – we were all terrified on your account, fearing the worst! – and on May 3 I sent you another telegram. Ernie received your letter of April 15 only on Monday this week and immediately telegraphed the Officer Commanding.

What do I do? Do I welcome you back to freedom? That would be silly! But what I can do is to wish you well out of what you were in!

I hope that we will soon be speaking on the phone and then seeing each other. And what do you need? You must tell me – and while I think of it, you must not hesitate to put through a reverse charge call whenever you can and want to. I will be all the happier for it.

Robert Sobukwe,
6 Naledi Street,
Galeshewe, Kimberley,
to Benjamin Pogrund,
19 May 1969 (Ba7.42)

My dear Benjie,

I promised to write to you as often as possible. I have not yet been able to phone you as I am not yet familiar with the terrain – the position of public telephones etc. In fact I still know a limited part of town. My legs are not strong enough yet to cover the distances I should like to cover.

In your last letter to me on Robben Island you wondered whether the tailor had enclosed your white shirt among the trousers. He did not. Let him explain.

I wrote to Eulalie to ask her to cancel delivery of the Cape papers as I had left the Island. But they have been very decent: forwarding the papers to Kimberley via the S.A.P.[29], who have co-operated by having them delivered.

Your case appears to be quite a marathon. Unfortunately, the other papers do not carry as full a report as does the R.D.M.[30] I am very interested in it, naturally, and would like to follow the summing up by the prosecution and defending counsel as closely as possible. Fortunately, though, Jhbg papers are obtainable here the same day.

There is a matter on which I should like your help. A niece of mine, my brother's daughter, is doing matric this year. She had a fall (was pregnant) two years ago while doing J.C. and I persuaded her to continue her studies, promising to see to it that she went to Fort Hare. You know my position, financially. Do you think you could rake up a bursary for her for next year? I know that your hands are full and I would not like to add to your burden, but you're the only one I can appeal to.

In spite of what the "Post" says, the house is still unfurnished and no curtains hang on the windows. Veronica will be getting the latter in Joh'burg, as I told you.

---

29 South African Police.

30 *Rand Daily Mail.*

Veronica has been offered a post at the local Isolation hospital. I wired her yesterday, as they wanted her to start on the 1st June. I told them, though, that that would be impossible as she feels obliged to serve a full month's notice with the Jhbg City Council and also wants to have enough time to do her packing.

Best wishes, old chap. Love to Jenny.

Yours affectionately,
Bob.

P.S. Veronica tells me you want to buy me a Dressing Gown. I'll get that myself. But could you, instead, get me a wrist-watch? I'll need one when I start work. Thanks. Bob.

Robert Sobukwe
to Benjamin Pogrund,
19 May 1969 (Ba7.40)

My dear Benjie,

Your welcome and welcoming letter arrived this morning and Veronica and I read with joy. She arrived on Thursday afternoon, brought over by Dr Ribeiro, her brother-in-law from Pretoria, and is returning to Joh'burg tonight. She hopes to see you on Wednesday, if her health permits. She has a very severe cold at the moment.

As I said in my telegram I am, of course, very anxious to meet you. There is so much we have to say to each other: and I also need your advice on a number of matters.

My banning order confines me to my house between 6 p.m. and 6 a.m. every day, Saturdays and Public Holidays *INCLUDED*. So we can have a full day any day you choose to come. You will, of course, not be allowed into the location, but we can meet anywhere in town – in fact, anywhere in the Kimberley district.

Thank you for news about Jenny. I look forward to meeting her. Unfortunately, we won't be able to be all three together at one time as that constitutes a gathering in terms of the act.

I have no telephone here and I haven't found my way around yet. But as soon as I find my *land-legs* I shall phone you. In the meantime I shall write often, if only to convince myself that my letters can reach you before fourteen days!

Your letter of 27th April I haven't received yet nor have the books reached me yet. But your telegram of congratulations I received with delight. Eulalie and the Marquards also sent me congratulatory telegrams. Your letter telegram of May I haven't received either. I am glad Ernie received my letter. If you can come over then he need not come until the two of us have met. I was not hysterical when I wrote the letter. The little that Veronica will be able to tell you will show that I had cause to write the letter. And I am still of the same mind.

The immediate problems, of course, concern employment and the furnishing of the house. Veronica will be coming over to join me as soon as the Joh'burg municipality can release her. She'll be shopping for curtains, out there. We do not know yet whether to purchase the rest of the furniture here or out there. We will continue to use our old Dining Room Suite, but the rest we will have to buy.

There is no screaming hurry and we can discuss these matters and others when we meet.

Your piece, on the *Paradox* was brought me by Veronica and I enjoyed it, Benjie, immensely.[31] The facts are correct, except for the part where you write about the *unwillingness* of the Methodist clergy to visit me on the Island. Perhaps it would have been kinder to say they were *unable*, to start with, and then that I later *stopped* the visits. It is *Christianity* per se, as I have told you before now, that I cannot accept. And I don't think I'll ever accept it, even if I attend services regularly.

My mother-in-law was here yesterday, together with one of my sisters-in-law. We had a lovely afternoon together.

Unfortunately I keep thinking I am in Pretoria and that I am, therefore, within driving distance of Joh'burg.

Quite a few people have already tried to make me feel welcome, and I am grateful. I am quite certain things will work out well. God has been good to me, Benjie, to leave his promises unfulfilled. I have no anxiety on that score.

Well, Sir, that's all for today. I wish you success in the case facing you and peace and joy in the days ahead.

Love to Jenny.

Yours affectionately,
Bob

P.S. I haven't received the later batch of books. I am writing to Robben Island to ask them to forward all my mail.

Do you think you could arrange for the Joh'burg Dailies to be delivered here? The Sunday Times subscription expires in September: so what you need see about now are the R.D.M. and The Star.

Shalom. Bob.

---

31 Pogrund's article discussed the role of South African churches in supporting – or resisting – apartheid (see Pogrund, 2015: 160).

Robert Sobukwe
to the Minister of
Justice, P.C. Pelser,
22 May 1969 (Ba7.41)

Sir,

It was reported in the newspapers that you expressed the wish that I would be able to lead a normal life, in so far as that was consonant with the safety of the state. From the little contact I've had with you, I did not find it difficult to believe that you sincerely meant what you had been reported as saying. However, it would appear that I am not yet to be allowed to lead a normal life.

You would recall, Sir, that while on Robben Island I wrote to you to complain about persistent harassment and systematic torture to which I was being subjected.[32] At the time, I blamed an unknown group of organized warders. I subsequently established that it was the Security Police who were responsible.

Because of this torture I had gone on a fast which I had intended to see through to the end, but when I received your letter I called it off because, first of all I did not want to embarrass you. I did not want you to feel that I was exerting pressure on you to release me before you were ready. Secondly, I hoped that when I had been released I would be free from practices which one associates only with the worst of prisons in the worst of countries. But there was no abatement of this torture, then, until I left R.I. [Robben Island] and it has continued here up to this moment that I am writing to you.

---

32 While Sobukwe's letter to the Minister of Justice in mid-April 1969 hasn't survived, Pogrund (2015) helpfully reconstructs the sequence of events that led to Sobukwe's release. The mid-April letter clearly rattled authorities – who were concerned how any claims of deteriorating health or torture regarding Sobukwe would be received internationally. Subsequent psychiatric evaluations conducted on the Island revealed that Sobukwe was in many respects still himself – his personality structure, affective responses and his perception of reality seemed all largely intact. The appearance of the delusionary belief – understandable given the prolonged period of isolation and surveillance – that his body was being influenced by gadgets devised by government authorities would have concerned psychiatrists. The government thus moved as quickly as possible to release Sobukwe, anxious that they would be accused of torturing Sobukwe or of causing a psychological breakdown.

I complained to the Prison Authorities and to the S. [Security] Police officer on R.I., Major Kotze, and even to Brigadier Aucamp.[33] All assumed the attitude that my complaints were impossible. Psychiatrists were called in. Unfortunately their report was not made available to me.

On the day of my release I was brought to Kbly[34] by car by Major Kotze & Sgt Coetzee who, in the course of the journey, made no secret of the fact that they were responsible for the torture I complained of. They carried it out blatantly, only taking care that I did not catch sight of the gadgets they employed.

As I am not an engineering scientist, I am unable to explain the principle on which these gadgets operate. But I am acutely & unpleasantly aware of their effects which are, *inter alia*:

(1) Dry Heat & Dry Cold or warm air or cold air are directed to any part of the body with pin-point accuracy. Cold air has been directed on my fingers, between the shoulders and to the upper arm.

With clock-work regularity air has been directed up my anus at varying vibrations, causing flatulence & pressure on my bladder.

This air can also be manipulated as a massage, causing intense sexual urges, urinal frequencies and unsettling of the bowels.

(2) There is pressure involved. The intensity of this pressure can be regulated so that it can be a weight pressing down tangibly on one, causing nightmares. I have felt it pressing down on me on R.I. when I tried to get up.

(3) It can cause cramps on the hands & feet. When one is bending down it can be applied to the back causing intense back-ache.

When applied to the head, depending on the intensity of the vibrations, it can cause drowsiness, complete lack of concentration or headaches.

(4) It can prevent, completely, if those who operate it so choose, the passing of urine or emptying of the bowels.

---

33 While historical information on the notorious Brigadier Aucamp of the Prisons Department is hard to come by, we know that he was characterised as a particularly hateful figure who was invested with disproportionate authority, authority enough, Buntman (2003) tells us, to seemingly bypass the Minister of Justice in the matter of certain decisions. Buntman (2003: 196) cites former Robben Island prisoner S'thembele Khala, who claimed that Aucamp was for political prisoners what "Mengele, the Nazi, was for the Jews".

34 Kimberley.

Since my arrival in Kby I have not known normal bodily functions. It has been a struggle to relieve myself & to pass water – with one or two exceptions.

(5) Directed to the nostrils it causes irritation of the nasal membrane, inducing head colds.

On the very first day, May 14th, of my arrival here I complained to Capt. Smit[35] who, too, assumed an unbelieving attitude, but promised to convey my complaint to higher authority.

I have not exhausted the list of refinements these gadgets are capable of, but this is a fair sample.

Knowing myself to be absolutely normal & mentally healthy I cannot pretend to believe that I have delusions. These things are happening: they are being deliberately done, in my house and in the street. But I cannot yet say how.

I am now writing to appeal to you to have them cease, for I cannot see what purpose they are intended to achieve save that of giving perverted satisfaction to those responsible. It cannot be imagined that pumping air up my anus etc. can make me change my views. As for my respecting the conditions of my ban, it is my own conscience & integrity that will arbitrate.[36]

---

35 A member of the Security Police in Kimberley.

36 Sobukwe's complaints here need to be viewed in the context of his nine years of incarceration, which included his vilification by the government, constant surveillance of all of his communications with the outside world, and prolonged solitary confinement and social deprivation. There is a growing literature on the deleterious effects of both solitary confinement and social deprivation. In a literature review overviewing empirical studies on the effects of solitary confinement, Brownlee (2012) noted the following effects: acute psychological and physical deterioration, despondency and depression, the feeling that one's self is disintegrating, various cognitive effects (forgetting of memories, difficulties in concentrating), hallucinations, panic attacks and, in some cases, lapsing into a semi-catatonic state or instances of self-mutilation. Brownlee (2012: 220) goes on to add: "scientific studies … indicate that acute loneliness, understood as perceived social isolation, generates the same threat response as pain, thirst, hunger or fear; it sets off a chain of anxiety-inducing physiological reactions known as the 'fight or flight' response. Chronic loneliness is associated with obesity, the progression of Alzheimer's disease, increased vascular resistance, elevated blood pressure, diminished immunity, a reduction in independent living, alcoholism, depression, suicidal ideation and behaviour, and mortality in older adults." John Schlapobersky, a psychotherapist who himself underwent imprisonment, solitary confinement and torture at the hands of the South African security police, helped Benjamin Pogrund understand how Sobukwe reacted: "He knew the authorities were destroying him and his mind developed the metaphor of a machine. The machine

Hoping that this letter will receive your favourable & prompt attention.
I remain, Sir,

Yours respectfully,
RMS

---

was Robben Island. It was the apartheid system. The thought was an accurate description of what was happening to him. It was an apposite image which captured the ubiquitous, pernicious quality of the system which was bearing down on him" (Schlapobersky, cited in Pogrund, 2015: 303).

Benjamin Pogrund
to Helen Suzman,
28 May 1969 (Ba7.44)

I am afraid that that personal assurance you received about Bob Sobukwe was not an honest one, and there is cause for anxiety about his condition. I am going to see him as soon as the wretched trial is over, and will be travelling first to Cape Town. All being well, I hope to be there on Sunday, June 8, and will be leaving for Kimberley on the morning of Wednesday, June 11. Can I come in to see you on the Monday?

It would be best not to do anything about the matter until I have had a chance to explain it to you. The same might perhaps apply in case there are any other matters which you might be intending to raise about him.

Any chance of asking Harry Oppenheimer[37] if he would give Bob a reasonable job with De Beers in Kimberley? I hate the thought of him having to work for any Bantu Affairs outfit, and perhaps De Beers, if so inclined, could offer him a post which would allow him to retain his self-respect. Despite his condition, he is, of course, able to work.

The trial, incredibly, is nearing an end. We had garbage flung at us by Liebenberg[38] last week, but we are now enjoying ourselves immensely: Sydney[39] is thundering away, and is quite magnificent.

All good wishes,

Sincerely,
BENJAMIN POGRUND

37 South African businessman and industrialist, chairman of De Beers Consolidated Mines and of Anglo American Corporation, and one-time member of Parliament for the opposition United Party.

38 A senior state prosecutor.

39 Sydney Kentridge is a South African-born lawyer who was a key figure in the struggle against apartheid, representing significant historical figures such as Nelson Mandela and Chief Albert Luthuli. In 1978 Kentridge took on the inquest into Steve Biko's death and played a crucial role in exposing the brutal circumstances of under which Biko died. He represented Pogrund and Gandar in the newspaper prisons trial (1968–9). He emigrated to Britain, was made a Queen's Counsel and was later knighted. He was awarded South Africa's highest honour, the Order of the Baobab, in 2008.

Veronica Sobukwe
to Benjamin Pogrund,
29 May 1969 (Ba7.45)

Dear Benjie,

I am sorry to worry you.

I have just received a telegram from Bob in which he has asked me to bring him one hundred rands.

He wants it urgently.

I really have no money with me.

I might be able to refund you when I get my pension-fund benefits.

I am leaving for Kimberley on the 30th May – Friday – after 11.00 p.m. But I do not want news-paper men to know.

Good-bye,

Yours sincerely,
Veronica

Helen Suzman
to Benjamin Pogrund,
30 May 1969 (Ba7.46)

My dear Benjy,

Thanks for your letter.

Sorry to hear that R.S. does not appear to be as well as I was given to believe – I trust nothing serious.

I had already written a private letter to H.O.[40] suggesting a possible job. I have also asked someone with considerable influence to see if a job can be found for Mrs. S. at a municipal clinic. Funnily enough, Mrs. Stott, a City Councillor here who has apparently interested herself in the case for a long time, was rather horrified when I said I had tried to arrange for a job with de Beers, because she felt sure he wouldn't want to have anything to do with a mining outfit. Just goes to show! Anyway, I think he is old enough to make up his own mind on these matters of principle, and I think it would be a good idea to have some choice.

I have been reading Sydney's closing address and to me it seems quite unanswerable – brilliant. I hold thumbs like mad.

Kindest regards,
Helen

40 Harry Oppenheimer.

Robert Sobukwe
to Benjamin Pogrund,
30 May 1969 (Ba7.47)

My dearest Benjie,

Your ordinary mail letter reached me today. It was given to me by our burly postman as I was on my way to town. I read it while waiting for the bus which arrived some half an hour later. As you say, four days is better than a fortnight or three weeks!

I am always relieved when I hear you have met Veronica, and this time is no exception. I found, when I met my mother-in-law and sister-in-law last week or so that "Benjie" was a name frequently mentioned and I was amazed to learn they hadn't met you. They'd heard from Veronica about you. My mother-in-law thinks you're a wonderful chap – and she is Zulu to the core!

A second letter of mine is on the way to you. It is registered; habits die long. It'll take me some time to believe that a letter of mine will travel "incognito" to wheresoever and to whomsoever I send it.

Yes, the prosecution had a field day: a real "stryddag".[41] But my attitude has always been, Benjie, that what matters is what my friends think of me. It bothers me not a damn what my enemies think of me or say of me. They would not be normal if they showered me with compliments!

But Kentridge is handling the summing-up in a masterly fashion – pinning them down to the LAW – after all you are appearing in a law-court; not in the House of Assembly!

The Mail and the Star are available here and I have been buying them daily. It will not be necessary, therefore, for you to take out a subscription for me.

It is good to know you'll be having a break and going down to see your parents. June 11th will suit me fine. I'll expect you then. I spoke to Capt. du Plessis of the Security division here, asking that you be permitted to come and see the house – in their company – to assess my furniture needs. He foresaw no difficulties. So I hope everything will turn out well.

41 Day of battle.

Veronica sent me a telegram saying she'll be coming over this weekend. I've been trying to clean up in order to make "a favourable impression". Incidentally, she smiles more often now and to me has never looked lovelier!

I have had no word yet from London University and I am wondering when I'll be able to start on my course. This evening a local attorney – Mr Nzimande[42] – a friend of long standing, sounded me on the possibility of my serving articles under him and preparing for the Attorneys Admission. We'll discuss this when you come. I am not sure that law appeals to me. I am a teacher, Benjie. I love the classroom and to see the look of comprehension on the faces of children.

Have you read that Eulalie has been proposed for the position of Chairman of the Langa Advisory Board? She appears to be going places City-Council-wise.

Nell and Leo Marquard are still overseas; but they sent me a telegram – WE REJOICE – when they learnt the news.

My people from Graaff-Reinet have not yet come here. Transport will be the difficulty for my mother as she'll have to wait until my brother who is a priest and has a car can get his leave. But my sister-in-law in P.E. has said she'll be coming in July; and she is the one who has accompanied my mother on both her visits to the Island. So she'll probably bring her along this time, too.

I am sending this letter by the most ordinary post for purposes of comparison! Love to Jenny.

With best wishes,
Bob.

P.S. I've been out of circulation a long time and I am not familiar with the operation of your telephone service. Wouldn't it be a TRUNK call to Joh'burg? As soon as I am able I'll phone you, be sure. Bob

42 Sobukwe did go on to serve his articles under H.Z.M. Nzimande.

Address on Behalf of the Graduating Class at Fort Hare College Delivered at the "Completers' Social" by Mr. Sobukwe, October 21, 1949

Prof. Dent, Ladies and Gentlemen, I intend to follow in my opening remarks the conventional pattern. And for that reason, I will give a very brief review of our doings within the College this year. We saw at the beginning of the year the implementation of the Student's Constitution, whereby all members of the S.R.C (Students' Representative Council) were elected by secret ballot at a mass-meeting of the students and whereby also certain powers were delegated to the Council. Of that arrangement the worst I can say is that it seems to be working well. We witnessed also at the beginning of the year the promotion of Prof. Dent to the position of Principal of the S.A.N.C. (South African Native College). He was succeeding a man who was highly esteemed, Dr. Kerr. But I do not think we lament the change, for we are concerned not with the personalities, but with policies, and there has been no change in this respect. Moreover, however much we may disagree with Prof. Dent on certain issues, we cannot say that he has ever refused students a chance to state their case. And I believe it is due to this fact that there has been no trouble in the College this year. After all, even the minor demonstration we had last term was not a reaction against the administration of the college. The stimulus came from outside.

But that does not mean that all is well in the College. I had occasion last year and also at the beginning of this year to comment on some features of our structure of which I do not approve. It has always been my feeling that if the intention of the trustees of this College is to make it an African College or University, as I have been informed it is, then the Department of African Studies must be more highly and more rapidly developed. Fort Hare must become the centre of African Studies to which the students in African Studies should come from all over Africa. We should also have a department of Economics and Sociology. A nation, to be a nation, needs specialists in these things.

Again I would like to know exactly what the College understands by "Trusteeship". I understand by "Trusteeship" the preparation of the African ward for eventual management and leadership of the College. But nothing in the policy of the College points in this direction. After the College has been in existence for thirty years the ratio of European to African staff is four to one. And we are told that in ten years' time we might become an independent university. Are we to understand by that an African University predominantly guided by European thought and strongly influenced by European staff?

I said last year that Fort Hare must be to the African what Stellenbosch is to the Afrikaner. It must be the barometer of African thought. It is interesting to note that the theory of "Apartheid" which is today the dominating ideology of the State was worked out at Stellenbosch by Eiselen and his colleagues. That same Eiselen is Secretary for Native Affairs. But the important thing is that Stellenbosch is not only the expression of Afrikaner thought and feeling but it is also the embodiment of their aspiration. So also must Fort Hare express and lead African thought. The College has remained mute on matters deeply affecting the Africans, because, we learn, it feared to annoy the Nationalists' Government. What the College fails to realise is that rightly or wrongly the Nationalists believe that the Fort Hare staff is predominantly U.P. [United Party]. So that whether we remain mute or not the government will continue to be hostile towards us. So much for the college.

Sons and daughters of Africa, harbingers of the new world order. What can I say to you? As you see, for the first time since the practice was started, we do not have the nurses with us this momentous night—Completers' Social. And the reason? The battle is on. To me the struggle at the Hospital is more than a question of discipline in inverted commas. It is a struggle between Africa and Europe, between a twentieth century desire for self-realization and a feudal conception of authority. I know, of course, that because I express these sentiments, I will be accused of indecency and will be branded an agitator. That was the reaction to my speech last year. People do not like to see the even tenor of their lives disturbed. They do not like to be made to feel guilty. They do not like to be told that what they have always believed was right is wrong. And above all, they resent encroachment on what they regard as their special province. But I make no apologies. It is meet that we speak the truth before we die.

I said last year that our whole life in South Africa is politics and that contention was severely criticized. But the truth of that statement has been proved in the course of this year. From the pulpit in the C.U. [Christian Union hall] we have heard responsible preachers deplore the deterioration of race-relations in this country and suggest co-operation as a solution. Dr. Bruce Gardner and Rev. Mokitimi are but two of a large number. Professor Macmillan and a number of speakers in our Wednesday assembly, have condemned this "naughty spirit of Nationalism and non-cooperation" and have told us of the wonderful things that have been done for us, forgetting, of course, that what they say has been done for the Africans the Africans have achieved for themselves in spite of the South African Government. The point I am trying to make is that was politics, whether we loved it or not. So that we can no longer pretend that there is a proper place and a proper occasion for politics. During the war it was clearly demonstrated that in South Africa at least, politics does not stop this side of the grave. A number of African soldiers were buried in the same trench as European soldiers. A few days afterwards word came from the high command that the bodies of the Africans should be removed and buried in another trench. "Apartheid" must be maintained even on the road to eternity.

The trouble at the Hospital then, I say, should be viewed as part of a broad struggle and not as an isolated incident. I said last year that we should not fear victimization. I still say so today. We must fight for freedom – for the right to call our souls our own. And we must pay the price.

The nurses have paid the price. I am truly grieved that the careers of so many women should have been ruined in this fashion. But the price of freedom is blood, toil, and tears. This consolation I have, however, that Africa never forgets. And these martyrs of freedom, these young and budding women will be remembered and honoured when Africa comes into her own.

A word to those who are remaining behind. You have seen by now what education means to us: the identification of ourselves with the masses. Education to us means service to Africa. In whatever branch of learning you are, you are there for Africa. You have a mission; we all have a mission. A nation to build we have, a God to glorify, a contribution clear to make towards the blessing of mankind. We must be the embodiment of our people's aspirations. And all we are required to do is to show the light and the masses will find the way. Watch our movements keenly and if you see any signs of "broadmindedness" or "reasonableness" in us, or if you hear us talk of practical experience as a modifier of man's views, denounce us as traitors to Africa.

We will watch you too. We have been reminded time and again that fellows who, while at the College, were radicals, as soon as they got outside became the spineless stooges and screeching megaphones of "White Herrenvolkism" or else became disgruntled and disillusioned objects of pity. My contention is those fellows never were radicals. They were anti-White. And as Marcus Garvey says: "You cannot grow beyond your thoughts. If your thoughts are those of a slave, you will remain a slave. If your thoughts go skin-deep, your mental development will remain skin-deep." Moreover, a doctrine of hate can never take people anywhere. It is too exacting. It warps the mind. That is why we preach the doctrine of love, love for Africa. We can never do enough for Africa, nor can we love her enough. The more we do for her, the more we wish to do. And I am sure that I am speaking for the whole of young Africa when I say that we are prepared to work with any man who is fighting for liberation of Africa WITHIN OUR LIFE-TIME.

To the completers among whom I number myself, my exaltation is: REMEMBER AFRICA! I thought last year that the position was bad. I realise it is worse this year. This is a difficult period to analyse. It is a confused period. Such as only a Mqhayi, or Bereng, or Dickens could describe. We are witnessing today the disintegration of old empires, and the integration of new communities. We are seeing today the germination of the seeds of decay inherent in Capitalism; we discern the first shoots of the tree of Socialism. In married life we see a reversal to what the Missionaries condemned when they first got here – polygamy. But this time it is not the African who is the culprit, and the third party is not a second wife, but a mistress. We are witnesses today of cold and calculated brutality and bestiality, the desperate attempts of a dying generation to stay in power. We see also a new spirit of determination, a quiet confidence, the determination of a people to be free whatever the cost. We are seeing within our own day the second rape of Africa; a determined effort by imperialist powers to dig their claws still deeper into the flesh of the squirming victim. But this time the imperialism we see is not the naked brutal mercantile imperialism of the 17th and 18th centuries. It is a more subtle one – financial and economic imperialism under the guise of a tempting slogan, "the development of backward areas and peoples." At the same time we see the rise of uncompromising "Nationalism" in India, Malaya, Indonesia, Burma, and Africa! The old order is changing ushering in a new order. The great revolution has started and Africa is the field of operation. Allow me at this juncture to quote a few lines from the Methodist Hymn-book:

Once to every man and Nation
Comes the moment to decide,
In the strife of truth with falsehood
For the good or evil side...

Then to side with truth is noble
When we share her wretched crust,
Ere her cause bring fame and profit
And 'tis prosperous to be just.

Then it is the brave man chooses
While the coward stands aside,
Til' the multitude make virtue
Of the faith they had denied.

The cowards are still standing aside and the brave have made their choice. We have made our choice. And we have chosen African Nationalism because of its deep human significance; because of its inevitability and necessity to world progress. World civilization will not be complete until the African has made his full contribution. And even as the dying so-called Roman civilization received new life from the barbarians, so also will the decaying so-called western civilization find a new and purer life from Africa.

I wish to make it clear again that we are anti-nobody. We are pro-Africa. We breathe, we dream, we live Africa; because Africa and humanity are inseparable. It is only by doing the same that the minorities in this land, the European, Coloured and Indian, can secure mental and spiritual freedom. On the liberation of the African depends the liberation of the whole world. The future of the world lies with the oppressed and the Africans are the most oppressed people on earth. Not only in the continent of Africa but also in America and the West Indies. We have been accused of blood-thirstiness because we preach "non-collaboration" I wish to state here tonight that that is the only course open to us. History has taught us that a group in power has never voluntarily relinquished its position. It has always been forced to do so. And we do not expect miracles to happen in Africa. It is necessary for human progress that Africa be fully developed and only the African can do so.

We want to build a new Africa, and only we can build it. The opponents of African Nationalism, therefore, are hampering the progress and development not only of Africa, but of the whole world. Talks of co-operation are not new to us. Every time our people have shown signs of uniting against oppression, their "friends" have come along and broken that unity. In the very earliest days it was the Missionary (we owe the bitter feelings between the Fingoes and Xhosas to the Christian ideals of the Reverend Shaw). Between 1900 and 1946 it has been the professional Liberal. Today it is again the Missionary who fulfills this role. After maintaining an unbroken and monastic silence for years while Smuts was starving the people out of the Reserves, the Missionaries suddenly discover, when the Africans unite, that the Africans have not had a fair deal. In the same stride, so to speak, they form a "Union-wide Association of Heads of Native Institutions" for the purpose of regimenting the thoughts of students. A Missionary Hospital closes even though the people are dying in its neighborhood, and there is a dearth of nurses throughout the country. I am afraid these gentlemen are dealing with a new generation which cannot be bamboozled. "What you are thunders so loudly that what you say cannot be heard."

Let me plead with you, lovers of my Africa, to carry with you into the world the vision of a new Africa, an Africa re-born, an Africa rejuvenated, an Africa re-created, young AFRICA. We are the first glimmers of a new dawn. And if we are persecuted for our views, we should remember, as the African saying goes, that it is darkest before dawn, and that the dying beast kicks most violently when it is giving up the ghost, so-to-speak. The fellows who clamped Nehru into jail are today his servants. And we have it from the Bible that those who crucified Christ will appear before him on the judgment day. We are what we are because the God of Africa made us so. We dare not compromise, nor dare we use moderate language in the course of our freedom. As Zik [Nigeria's Nnamdi Azikiwe] says:

"Tell a man whose house is on fire to give a moderate alarm; tell a man moderately to rescue his wife from the arms of a ravisher; tell a mother to extricate gradually her babe from the fire into which it has fallen; but do not ask me to use moderation in a cause like the present."

These things shall be, says the Psalmist: Africa will be free. The wheel of progress revolves relentlessly. And all the nations of the world take their turn at the field-glass of human destiny. Africa will not retreat! Africa will not compromise! Africa will not relent! Africa will not equivocate! And she will be heard! REMEMBER AFRICA!

References

Bolnick, J. (1991). Potlako Leballo: The Man Who Hurried to Meet His Destiny. *Journal of Modern African Studies*, 29 (3), 413-442.

Brownlee, K. (2012). Social Deprivation and Criminal Justice. In F. Tanguay-Renaud and J. Stribopoulos (eds.), *Rethinking Criminal Law Theory: New Canadian Perspectives in the Philosophy of Domestic, Transnational, and International Criminal Law*. Portland, OR: Oxford University Press.

Brownlee, K. (2013). The Human Right against Social Deprivation. *Philosophical Quarterly*, 63: 251, 199-222.

Buntman, F.L. (2003). *Robben Island and Prisoner Resistance to Apartheid*. Cambridge : Cambridge University Press.

Cacioppo, J.T. and Patrick, W. (2008), *Loneliness: Human Nature and the Need for Social Connection*. New York: W.W. Norton & Company.

C.I.A. Intelligence Report (1968). 'Mao's Red Guard Diplomacy: 1967'. RSS no: 0029/68. 21 June. Available at: https://www.cia.gov/library/readingroom/docs/polo-21.pdf

Dlamini, M. (1984). *Robben Island Hell-Hole: Reminiscences of a Political Prisoner*. Nottingham: Spokesman.

Fry, P. (2010). Siyamfenguza: The Creation of the Fingo-ness in South Africa's Eastern Cape, 1800–1835. *Journal of South African Studies*, 36 (1), 25-40.

Gawande, A. (2009). Hellhole: The United States holds tens of thousands of inmates in long-term solitary confinement. Is this torture? *New Yorker*, 30 March 2009.

Gerhart, G.M. (1978). *Black Power in South Africa: The Evolution of an Ideology*. Berkeley, CA: University of California Press.

Gerhart, G.M. and Sobukwe, R.M. (2016). Gail Gerhart interviews Robert Mangaliso Sobukwe (1970). *Psychology in Society*, 50, 53-85.

Haney, C. (2003). Mental Health Issues in Long-Term Solitary and "Supermax" Confinement. *Crime and Delinquency*, 49: 124-156.

Karis, T.G. and Gerhart, G.M. (eds.). (2013). *From Protest to Challenge: A Documentary History of African Politics in South Africa, 1882–1990, Volume 3: Challenge and Violence, 1953–1964.* Johannesburg: Jacana.

Kondlo, K. (2009). *In the Twilight of the Revolution: The Pan Africanist Congress of Azania (South Africa) 1959–1994.* Basel: Basler Afrika Bibliographien.

Lodge, T. (1991). A Liberal of a Different Colour. *Transformation*, 16, 76-88.

Magomolo, G. (2009). *Robben Island to Wall Street.* Pretoria: University of South Africa Press.

Mandela, N. (1994). *Long Walk to Freedom: The autobiography of Nelson Mandela.* Macdonald Purnell.

Marquard, N. (1986). Robert Sobukwe: A Personal Note. *Reality*, 10 (3), p. 8.

Mostert, N. (1992). *Frontiers: The Epic of South Africa's Creation and the Tragedy of the Xhosa People.* New York: Knopf.

Nkrumah, K. (1961). *I Speak of Freedom: A Statement of African Ideology.* London: Heinemann.

Pheko, M. (1994). *The Land Is Ours: The Political Legacy of Mangaliso Sobukwe.* Johannesburg: Tokoloho.

Pinckney Hill, L. (1921). *The Wings of Oppression.* Boston, MA: The Stratford Company.

Pogrund, B. (1990). *Robert Sobukwe: How Can Man Die Better.* Johannesburg: Jonathan Ball.

Soske, J. (2015). The Impossible Concept: Settler Liberalism, Pan-Africanism, and the Language of Non-Racialism. *African Historical Review*, 47 (2), 1-36.

Tillich, P. (2012). *The Shaking of the Foundations.* Eugene, OR: Wipf and Stock.

Index

Page numbers in *italics* refer to photographs.